Gautam Desiraju believes that if a true sense of “Indian-ness” is inculcated in young minds, professionalism and positive competitiveness, both sadly lacking today, will become a reality. *Bhārat:India 2.0* attempts to highlight this with reference to what the author believes is the core issue in India, an unsuitable system of governance that does not optimally dovetail modernity and economic growth with our civilisation, diversity and Dharma. This system of governance, laid out in the Constitution of India, is therefore the subject of this book, specifically how it should be modified to suit the present times.

PRAISE FOR THE BOOK

The fundamental premise of this book is that a governance model will work only if it enables optimal expression of the rich diversity of our nation. This diversity has to be more firmly incorporated into our governance structures. This can be done through smaller state sizes. In concrete terms, the author suggests a demarcation of India into seventy-five states with evenly balanced populations: this can be done on the basis of geographical, historical, linguistic, religious and cultural factors as appropriate in each context, but at the heart of such an exercise is the goal of administrative convenience.

Bharat: India 2.0 is a welcome addition to this illustrious genre and introduces a genuinely new and honest idea with all its ramifications in a manner that can be read and understood widely. Desiraju is a highly accomplished Indian scientist, based at the Indian Institute of Science, Bengaluru. In addition to playing a strong role in building up Indian science, he has also written several articles on policy-making, science and education.

Abhishek Banerjee and Kaneenika Sinha
India Today

Gautam Desiraju, argues that Bhārat will form the basis of the India of the future, India 2.0, and that our aspirational ideas will be feckless without realizing a civilizational state. Overall, Desiraju must be commended for attempting what may seem an impossibly daunting task of taking the complex polity, society, and diversity of India and come up with a model that would serve robustly over the next 75 years. In a way, perhaps, his immense experience in dealing with complexity in his research work enabled him to find a workable solution to the problems facing India today through 'cold, dispassionate analysis, model building and evaluation.' As he clearly states, the way forward is not by increments that we are used to but by a revolution, the Bhāratiya Revolution. Even if Bhārat as the basis for the future of India is the main theme, Desiraju intersperses the book with unusual facets of history, and his own trenchant views on several issues such as how 'Rutgers has no locus standi to dismantle anything in this country' and the amusing rationale behind the demarcation of Delhi make for a compelling reading. Bhārat: India 2.0, in that sense, is a book that takes the current themes of galvanizing decolonisation and exploring new ideas of India towards a more pragmatic pedestal, a book that should not only be read by us all, but also, and especially, by politicians and policymakers.

Bhavesh Kansara
Sunday Guardian

The book is a scientist's look at the evolution of the modern Indian state and the ancient Bharatiya nation. Healing the dangerous festering divide between the anciently vibrant civilisational organism that is the nation 'Bharat' and the formidable state machine that is 'India' is a task that needs Bhāgirathas. Eminent scientist Dr Gautam Radhakrishna Desiraju has taken it upon himself, this sacred work of Bhāgiratha. Bhārat: India 2.0 is an important medicine for healing and harmonising the wound caused by Nehruvians and politicians with vested interests between the civilisational nation and the administrative state.

The book contains what is, perhaps, the most eloquent appreciation of Hindutva ever written after the crisp thesis of Veer Savarkar: The author says, 'Hindutva is the single Sanskrit word that attempts to capture the instinctive nature of Bhāratiya nationalism that Savarkar tried to define analytically and Ambedkar to articulate emotionally. Hindutva is nothing less or nothing more than feeling like a Hindu. Hindutva is a philosophy that can guide Bhārat in this civilizational battle, a battle which she inherited through the misguided policies of our successive governments.'

Aravindan Neelakandan
Swarajya

Bharat: India 2.0 is a brilliant vision for the nation by one of India's most prominent scientists.

Sree Iyer
PGurus

This book is a detailed journey from the proceedings of the Constituent Assembly to the formulation of the Indian Constitution of 1950 followed up by a number of amendments. What has been the impact of all of this and what are the solutions that one can apply to get over these inherent problems are all discussed.

A fantastic book and what I like about this book is it is a continuing discussion to a topic that has been raised by many people and I will take names from all parts of the spectrum in Indian discourse, so whether you have read Shashi Tharoor, whether you have read the book written by Harsh Madhusudhan Gupta and Rajeev Mantri, whether you have written read the work of J. Sai Deepak, this book is a great addition to that that larger discourse about the nature of the Indian rashtra, what should be the Indian rajya, what should be the way forward, so you know Dr. Desiraju, thanks a lot for writing this book and thanks a lot for coming on the podcast it's been an absolute pleasure speaking with you.

Kushal Mehra
Cārvaka

A highly acclaimed scientist stepping out of his familiar territory and taking the effort to write a book on Bharat is itself quite intriguing. It is not a 'professional' writer, camouflaging his biases and prejudices in cleverly chosen words and phrases. But the book has come out of years of tapas – feeling the pain of being a Bhāratiya, struggling to understand 'what has gone wrong' with a civilization so great?

It is refreshing and makes one think about the ideas and propositions Professor Desiraju makes e,g. the idea of envisioning the future of Bharat as a civilisational state rather than merely a modern Nation State; the critique of our constitution and the need to review it; the difference between a more natural and organic complex system and a complicated system and how the idea of treating Bhārat as a civilisational state is in alignment with the way a complex system works. A must read.

Pawan Gupta
Samwad

BHARAT : INDIA 2.0

BHĀRAT : INDIA 2.0

GAUTAM R. DESIRAJU

Published by
Renu Kaul Verma
Vitasta Publishing Pvt Ltd
2/15, Ansari Road, Daryaganj
New Delhi-110 002
info@vitastapublishing.com

ISBN 978-93-90961-15-3

First Edition 2022
Fourth Reprint 2025

MRP ₹ 750

Edited by Dhanlaxmi Ayyer, Abhishek Rana, Mansi Bisht
Cover and layout by Somesh Kumar Mishra
Printed by Vikas Computer and Printers

For Madhav and Govind

And all the young people of India 2.0

India did not start the fight but
Bhārat will finish it

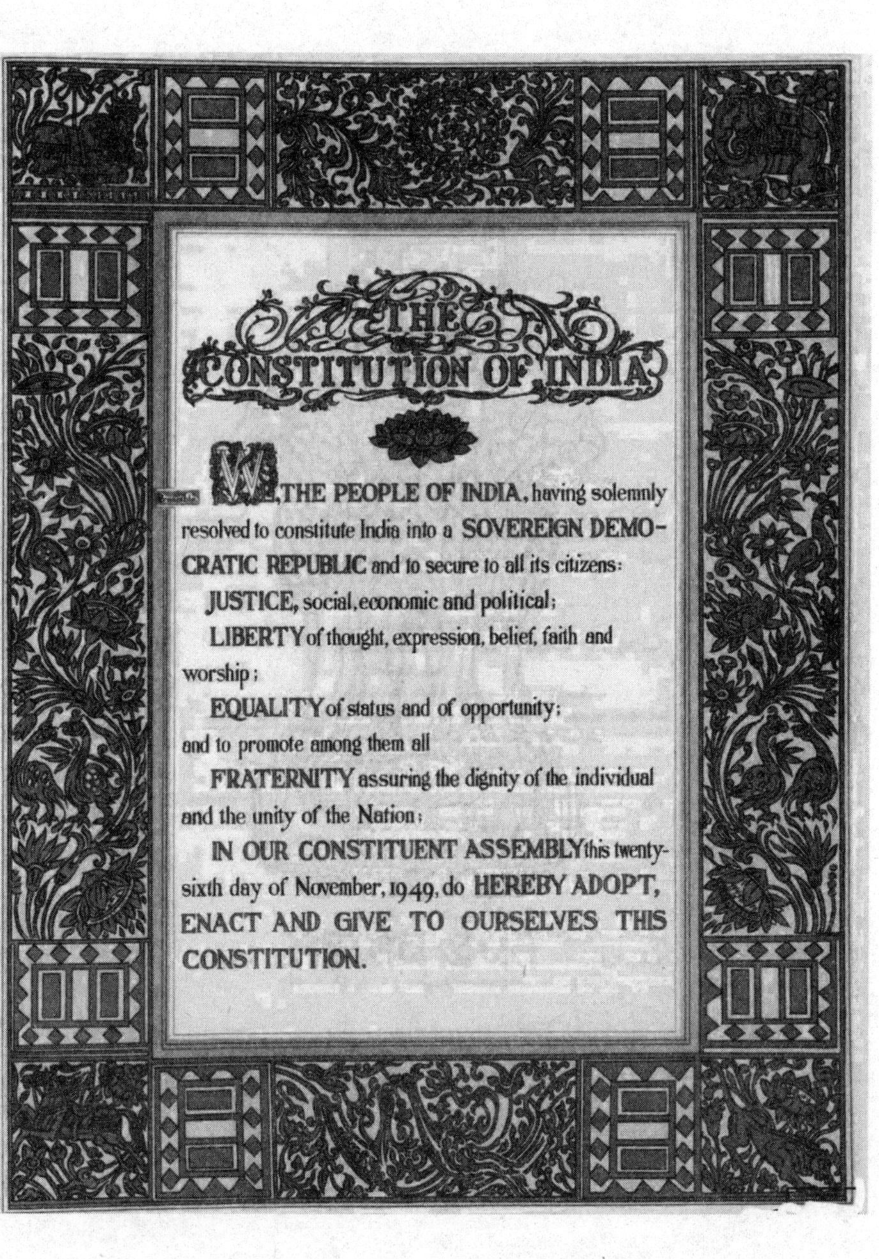

THE CONSTITUTION OF INDIA

WE, THE PEOPLE OF INDIA, having solemnly resolved to constitute India into a SOVEREIGN DEMOCRATIC REPUBLIC and to secure to all its citizens:

JUSTICE, social, economic and political;

LIBERTY of thought, expression, belief, faith and worship;

EQUALITY of status and of opportunity;

and to promote among them all

FRATERNITY assuring the dignity of the individual and the unity of the Nation;

IN OUR CONSTITUENT ASSEMBLY this twenty-sixth day of November, 1949, do HEREBY ADOPT, ENACT AND GIVE TO OURSELVES THIS CONSTITUTION.

CONTENTS

PREFACE

The writing of this book on Bhārat has given me an opportunity to reflect and recollect matters that many might have thought about in recent times. To this concerned citizen, at least one who is no expert in constitutional matters, the actions of our legislators appeared to be politically biased beyond reasonable limit (legislators must be political to some extent!). The actions of our judges seem whimsical and interventionist, whilst the executive, especially its bureaucracy, appear distant and aloof. A genuine lack of knowledge led me to believe that my reactions might simply be incorrect or impulsive, arising from information overload in the social media. However, a desire to learn more about a topic, very distant from my home turf of structural chemistry, arose from my instincts as a researcher, in particular the sure knowledge that a researcher in any given topic is by definition a researcher in any other topic provided they do sufficient reading. I use the word 'sufficient' with care. Extensive reading often leads to scholarship which need not always be research. Research produces a model which is freely open to criticism. Unlike the world of science, to which I have been habituated, and where the referee reports are seen before publication, a book receives its referee reports after publication and this is a risk all writers of books cheerfully take.

The pandemic afforded me, being virtually confined at home like so many others for eighteen or so months, adequate opportunity to read many documents, articles, blogs, videos and commentaries ranging from the trivial to the grave. Gradually, some patterns seemed to be emerging from the fog of contradictory information. As a working scientist, I became convinced that so many incongruities, distortions and aberrations in our body politic could not possibly have emerged from different independent causes. I began to search for a few primary causes of these maladies that I felt were affecting our country. Through a process of thought that relied on inductive logic, political neutrality, use of reliable data, acknowledgement of history and sympathy for all right thinking people who have tried to fashion a model of governance for us since 1946 when the Constituent Assembly was set up, I identified the Constitution itself as containing nucleation points for future faults and dislocations. My main conclusion was that this document was not sympathetic enough to the civilisational nature of Bhārat, that is India.

Chapter 1 gives the pre-independence background to the drafting of the Constitution.

Chapter 2 briefly describes the important debates in the Constituent Assembly and the usage of the Constitution in the seventy two years since it was adopted.

Chapter 3 talks about countries, nations and civilisations, in particular the age-old Bhāratiya tradition.

Rather than stop at this point, and put down my conclusions, many of which have been arrived at by others, I decided to go further and attempted to link our civilisational nature with our overwhelmingly rich diversity. Moving still further, I have tried to show that diversity is best expressed when each citizen feels unique and different, and through that process *or because of it* still feels part of an integral whole. The precise agent that I felt was the enabler of such true diversity was the size of a state in the Union of India. The need to divide large states for reasons of administrative convenience has been well recognised for sixty years. However, the thesis that the smaller a state, the truer is the depiction of diversity *at a national level* is a novel one: this book should be judged on this idea. I have accordingly proposed a model of seventy five states of roughly equal population of two crores each and have attempted to justify the demarcation of state boundaries using geography, history, culture, circumstance, language, and religion wherever appropriate. I urge the reader to avoid the jugular assumption that more states will fragment the country. This may be true in other countries but it is not true in a civilisational state. I suggest that it is only in India that more states will not fragment the country, but rather that they would strengthen it. Our civilisation is a powerful glue. If the basis for the identification of new boundaries for seventy five states is logical rather than political, such smaller states will remain stable and, beyond all these considerations, it is always true that a smaller state will be administered more efficiently. This is elaborated in Chapter 4.

A brief conclusion to the work in Chapter 5 provides a summing-up of key ideas of complexity and emergence in the context of India and Bhārat.

A few technical clarifications are in order but they are well known features of grammar and style in the English language. The reader should carefully note the use of small and capital letters, for example 'state' and 'State' mean entirely different things. 'State' is used when there is no qualifying adjective and refers to a seat of sovereignty. However, 'state' is used with reference to the twenty eight states of the Indian Union. Since both 'State' and 'state' are used often throughout the book the reader is alerted to the difference in these usages. In the same way 'Church' and 'church' need to be distinguished. Similarly, 'West' and 'west' are different. The former refers to a civilisational region while the latter is a direction. Similarly 'north eastern' is a direction while 'north-eastern' refers to a region. Italics are used at the first occurrence of a non-English word. Subsequent usages may be italicised or not depending on the context. As for conventions, I use the term 'INC' to describe that political organisation prior to Independence and 'Congress' after Independence. Abbreviations are used if the subsequent occurrences occur in the immediate proximity of the first usage. The term 'U.S.A.' is used to describe the country while 'US' is used in an adjectival sense. Political parties are mostly referred to by their abbreviations without a full name being explicitly mentioned at the first occurrence. Place names are based on the time factor. If something was called Poona, Calcutta or Madras at the time referred to in the discussion, it is called that. Alternatively it is called Pune, Kolkata or Chennai if the discussion pertains to a later time. No honorifics are used anywhere in book unless they are in quotes. All numbers are given in crores and lakhs and not millions. The word 'Constitution' is nearly always capitalised while numbers are mostly written in full (seventy five rather than 75).

The referencing in this book has been done in a way that it does not impede free flow whilst reading. Reference numbers do not appear in the text. There are no footnotes too. Several facts are so well known that they do not need specific references. There are others, which are so specific and precise that a simple search of the internet will confirm them immediately. Facts and figures that are more difficult to obtain are given as links in Appendix 2. Where the link does not give an obvious clue as to the topic it covers, a one line description is given to help the reader. Additionally, this appendix provides a list of books, book chapters and articles that I found useful before and during writing. There are some links given here that do not find any obvious connection in the book. Especially while writing Chapter 3, I found it useful to read about religions other than Sanātana Dharma and some of these links are given, while little if anything is mentioned in the book about them. Appendix 2 therefore is a reference list and also a general bibliography for general reading on related topics. One could even read this appendix on its own and decide to proceed on one's own quest into very fascinating territory. Indeed this was one my purposes in writing this book. We need more lay persons to obtain information by themselves and to form their own opinions logically rather than obtain it second hand from the media and social media. In any case, logic is preferred to emotion in these matters.

One of the challenges I faced during writing was that one's treatment of events need to be different if they occurred at a time that could be called 'historical' rather than a time that would be termed 'current affairs'. My subjective cut-off was the Emergency which young people today have not directly experienced and to which they cannot relate. I was 23 at that time, a student in the U.S.A. and deeply affected by it. My permanent (and jobless, fortunately not for long!) return to my country during the awkward time of the short Janata Party government enabled me to watch the burlesque of Indian politics from the 1980s onward. I felt that nothing could be or need be this complicated. It is what the Americans would call a Rube Goldberg contraption. Why was it so? Why were our politicians behaving the way they were? I am sure many have felt like me. I know I am not alone. So, when I started writing this book in August 2021 I had to be sure that I avoided all references to politics, political figures and political parties after say, 1990. The book would have lacked objectivity, and this was abhorrent to me as a scientist. Even so, I am still tempted to quote Voltaire who said presciently, that he "who writes the history of his own time must expect to be attacked for everything he has said, and everything he has not said, but these little drawbacks should not discourage a man who loves truth and liberty, expects nothing, fears nothing, asks nothing and limits his ambition to the cultivation of letters". So, the reader who is expecting a racy treatment of current politics and political figures might be disappointed. None of them are mentioned. This book is an analysis of a topic that is as austere as the Indian Constitution, and a logical treatment of the matter of diversity optimisation through the identification of the optimum number of small states, not as small as they stand now (twenty eight) and not as large as has been proposed by others (seven hundred and fifty). However, at the same time, I hope the book is not evaluated as a serious book for scholars—it is not. I have written it for people in the age group 20-40 who are curious and concerned. As a teacher and researcher, I have interacted mostly with people in this age group all my working life and so this was perhaps an inevitable choice.

I need to thank Siby Thomas, the creator of an older version of the map that appears as Figure 4 in Chapter 4. Several incisive comments from him about the basis of dissection in his model and in our revised scheme, which is presented here after his concurrence, are gratefully acknowledged. He has been kind with his time and has provided many insights about diversity in India. Ramanand Pandey provided encouragement and helped in the organisation of the references with some preliminary assistance by Aakarshan and Aalankrita Singh. He suggested right at the beginning that I approach Tejasi Panjiar who did all the data collection and fact checking. Her extremely rapid and cogent responses to my many questions on seemingly obscure topics have contributed in no small measure to the completion of this project in exactly three months. I am a strong believer in conveying an idea briefly and quickly——if something does not meet these twin criteria, there is probably no reason to even try to communicate it, more so in this era of information overload and extremely short attention spans. My son, Govind Desiraju contributed throughout these months with his critical reading of intermediate drafts, practically on demand, sometimes just a paragraph or two, and suggesting checks and balances in my treatment of topics. I also thank him for fine-tuning the crucial Figure 4 which is a map of Bhārat showing our seventy five new states and for suggesting that I demarcate the eight zones in which I place these states as a device to further highlight the true diversity lines of this vast land. I do feel that the zones in Figure 4 are the macro-level diversity lines in Bhārat. They are of fundamental importance and should be respected. We are indeed a diverse lot and need not be ashamed of our diversity.

The scientist in me viewed this entire exercise as an experiment in writing a general non-fiction book. Two steps had to be completed, in time, to make it successful: writing it and getting it published. I cannot begin to acknowledge the debt I owe to my wife Krishna in the first part of this project. In her typical prudent manner she asked me to consider carefully whether I should or not be even writing a book in an area that was not my domain expertise. Should discretion have been the better part of valour? Her comments challenged me to try my hand even as I counted on her to keep me grounded throughout this exercise with her dispassionate, empathetic criticism and objective thinking. She provided me, as she has many times over in the past, with the confidence to tread a new path. Thank you Krishna and I hope you will like the book!

Getting the manuscript published by a mainstream publisher was the second part of the experiment. I approached Dimple Kaul who I knew has a penchant for spotting and mentoring new talent. Her support and constructive inputs went a long way to make the manuscript submission ready. She reached out to Renu Kaul Verma of Vitasta Publishing who heard her pitch and took no time to green light the project. And that is how my book about Bhārat Māta came to fruition through their collaboration and support. I am grateful to both Dimple and Renu and the team at Vitasta who indulged me throughout the publishing cycle. Through their timely assistance, *Bhārat:India 2.0* is in your hands, dear reader, just in time for the 75th anniversary of our independence, a date that we all hold dear.

In this venture, I have been ably assisted by Mrinal Mishra (University of Zürich) and the writing began after six or so months of lively intense discussion between us on a host of matters pertaining to the current political and social climate in India. His contribution is far greater than can be conveyed in a preface acknowledgement. We were in constant touch throughout the writing process and he was generous with his time in commenting, re-reading, re-writing some parts, and also writing major sections in Chapter 3. I could not have finished this project in three months without his assistance. This book is written sometimes in the first person singular and elsewhere in the first person plural. This is spontaneous and completely natural, not a case of sloppy writing. Our scriptures provide a wonderful depiction of the concept of 'voice' as a vehicle of communication. The first voice *parā* is the voice that feels, the place where the idea originates. The second, *pashyanti* is the voice that sees and the idea appears somewhere, the third *madhyama* is the voice that thinks and conceptualises it into something real and finally *vaikhari* is the voice that communicates and exteriorises. I may confidently say that we experienced parā and pashyanti of this book together while I journeyed further and alone into madhyama and vaikhari. As the African proverb says, one travels far when one travels together and fast when one travels alone. So thank you Mrinal, once again.

Distinguishing thought from instinct, fact from opinion, logic from irrationality, *shruti* from *smriti,* country from nation, nation from civilisation and India from Bhārat has been a continuing challenge for me while writing this book. It is hoped that the reader will find enough in this work to further examine these matters.

May we awaken to ensure that our longest extant civilisation continues forever.

Gautam R. Desiraju
Bengaluru

CHAPTER ONE

PROLOGUE

INDIA ON 15 AUGUST 1947

> *...a moment comes, which comes but rarely in history, when we step out from the old to the new, when an age ends, and when the soul of a nation, long suppressed, finds utterance...*
>
> ***—Jawaharlal Nehru***

NEW Delhi 1947 ranks with Sarajevo 1914, Petrograd 1917, Gleiwitz 1939, Hiroshima 1945 and Berlin 1989; the few events of the 20th century that have had the greatest subsequent political impact on history. The granting of independence to India seventy five years ago saw the largest empire the world has ever seen spread across a quarter of the land mass of the planet parting voluntarily, or perhaps as a response to historic necessities, with its most precious possession, the jewel in its crown, leaving its fates in the hands of not one but two independent entities. This dramatic step was to lead, in a cascade reaction, to Britain shedding other bits and pieces of its colonial empire within fifteen years and getting reduced in a century from being the most powerful nation in the world to a cold, drizzly island off the Atlantic coast of Europe of somewhat lesser importance. For indeed, Britain was extremely powerful in 1918; if it had managed to somehow hold on for another century to its Indian territories at the very fulcrum of Asia—a domain that extended from Malakand to Mandalay and from Kanyakumari to Karakoram—and comprising an area that was 39 per cent greater than that of today's India, it would have had geostrategic control over an entire hemisphere today. However, it could be considered fanciful to speculate on what might have been.

If India awoke on 15 August 1947 it means there always was an India before that day. It was merely asleep or more accurately had almost been put to sleep. A political state, or rather two, were born that midnight and yet this date is but just another eyelid's blink in the timeline of a nation and more importantly, a civilisation that had been extant for 5000 years—one that remains wide awake till the present day. How does this political state that we now call the Republic of India dovetail with this ancient land that has withstood and outlasted many such states in its long and hoary history? India has tried almost every sort of governance system be it monarchy, autocracy, democracy, republicanism and even, as some say, anarchy in its long existence. Does this new republic formally launched in 1950 find echo and resonance from the soul of the nation? It is this question that this book seeks to answer. Every country in the modern world has a Constitution, a document that outlines aspirations, sketches priorities, emphasises rights and duties, and provides overall guidance for effective day to day governance. A nation wherein the Constitution is in tune with the spirit of its people, and captures this spirit, becomes strong and self-reliant. A country where there is a mismatch remains metastable even if its Constitution is entirely intelligible in intent and logical in its structure.

The Indian Independence Act (1947) and the adoption of the subsequent Draft Constitution of India (1948) led us to declare ourselves a Democratic Republic on 26 January 1950. The origin of these events may be traced back to the Government of India Act (1858) when the British Crown took over the administration of India directly rather than operate indirectly through the East India Company. The latter had modified itself from a trading company into an administrative authority after its 1757 victory in the Battle of Plassey, after which it seriously got into the business of tax collection in Bengal and soon thereafter in Bombay and Madras. The Act of 1858 followed from events in 1857 that the British refer to as the Indian Sepoy Mutiny and what we in India call the First War of Independence, a term coined by Vinayak Damodar Savarkar in 1909. All these happenings are only too well known to the educated public and have been commented upon by serious scholars as well. To provide a detailed record here is not the intent of this book; instead I shall rather regard them in the context of how they influenced the discourse between Indians and Britishers during the period of direct rule by the British Government, insofar as that discourse shaped the drafting of our 1950 Constitution. These nearly ninety years are a tumultuous roller coaster ride in the constitutional history of our country because they define a period when there was hardly any meaningful dialogue between the two groups involved. The series of documents that emerged from either side during this period more resembles two sets of monologues running on parallel and non-intersecting tracks. One group was trying to cede as little real participation as possible to the other in the matter of their own governance while the other was making increasingly strident demands for a greater role in such governance. As one side yielded somewhat gradually and reluctantly the other side became more tenacious and determined.

India is an incredibly diverse nation. Perhaps no other political state in the world today encompasses such variety. The clichéd oxymoron 'unity in diversity' might possibly be replaced by the term 'unity and diversity' in that these two attributes almost appear to be running on parallel and non-intersecting tracks. We are diverse in the matter of ethnicity, religion, language, habits, diet, dress, climate, and not least important, social class. Any nation that has such a large area and population will be diverse. Any attempt to diminish this diversity artificially and homogenise the country, from top down, is doomed to failure. Such an operation also cannot be carried out in an open democracy such as ours. The former U.S.S.R. tried it and failed. This was one of the reasons for its break-up. Yugoslavia and Czechoslovakia are illustrations where such artificial homogeneity was imposed by the Western powers after World War 1. Both lasted just around 75 years. China is trying to do so today but it is not a democracy. One could consider whether our distinctive religion, Sanātana Dharma, has been so structured, with its accent on *purushārtha,* the acknowledgement of different objects of human pursuit, to accommodate this diversity. This feature of our people must have been apparent to our ancients since the earliest days of organised and civilised life on this subcontinent.

The question of interest is how these diverse peoples were able, that too under colonial subjugation of an extreme sort, to provide coherent arguments to their colonisers about their ability to govern themselves for this is how one could regard the various putative Constitutions that were put forward by Indians in the period 1896-1947. In hindsight, these 'Constitutions' are even more remarkable because they were drafted in the rubric and shadows of the Constitutions of the European nation-states. The concept of a nation-state had gained ground widely in the 19th century and will be discussed in Chapter 3. It is based on defining a country as one in which ethnic, linguistic, and cultural boundaries practically coincide with the political boundaries. The State becomes equivalent or indeed identical to the nation, and hence the name. The idea of a nation-state is somewhat artificial for a civilisation that readily accepts diversity in all its manifestations. Possibly, the British would only consider an Indian drafted Constitution or statement of intent if it were worded in the phraseology of the nation-state as understood by them and reflecting their philosophy. However, this morphing of attitudes had a possibly unintended consequence in that when independence finally came the framers of our Constitution were for the most part inured into thinking along the lines of this homogeneous European nation-state model with its limited diversity, so much so that our constitution had little room or place for our civilisational identity, which is welcoming of diversity. It is another question as to whether we, as individuals, are still too accepting of diversity for our own good for this brings with it the risk of attack from forces within and without that would deny us our most crucial attribute, namely this defining identity.

The nation-state conditioning and singularity that the British might have imposed on us, in as much as they even conferred the name 'India' upon us, a race that revels in diversity, is probably the most reasonable explanation as to why we 'Indians' came together as one unit to fight for our freedom, an aspect of which was the drafting of the various 'Constitutions' in the 90-year interregnum between the First War of Independence and Independence itself. This is not to say that an underlying civilisational commonality was not present: indeed, it might have been the factor that bound all these proponents of self-rule together while they merely expressed their thoughts externally in the medium most likely to be understood and therefore even considered by the British.

The origins and usage of the word 'India' are also of relevance. The word is almost surely derived from Sindhu, the river, from whence it was adopted by the Greeks, who came as far as that river, and as evidenced by their coinage of the word 'indigo' as something that came from India. It is reported to occur in old English quite early but entered modern English only in the early 17th century when the English traders first came to the country. The words 'Hindustan' and 'Hindu', the latter simply meaning anyone who comes from Hindustan, are undoubtedly of Persian origin and derived from Sindhu. These terms were probably in usage as far back as 700 BCE. The name 'Hindustan' is still used in Urdu while the term 'Hindustani' is used for a Hindi-Urdu hybrid language, which has largely fallen into disuse. 'Hindi', the language itself, is yet another species within the same etymological genus.

Tremendously older and with a completely distinct provenance is *Bhāratavarsha* or *Bhārata* is a term in the Rig Veda and dates back as such to 3000 BCE, conservatively speaking. The expression *Jambudvipé Bhāratavarshé Bharatakhandé* is still used regularly in our invocations in rituals and encapsulates our civilisational identity. This description refers to the landmass Bhāratavarsha, in the island of Jambu trees and is the territory ruled by Emperor Bharata. Alternatively, *Jambudvipa* could even be the most convergent of the *dvipas* beginning with the *Pushkaradvipa* which literally represents the infinity of the universe. There is surely a geographical connection here: Bhārat is the country that lies north of the ocean and south of the Himalayas. It is where the children of Bharata reside. This description owes to the Vishnu Purāna which is younger than the Rig Veda. According to Sadhguru Jaggi Vasudev, the word 'Hindu' need not imply a religious context. A person is a Hindu if he or she lives in the land that lies between the Himalayas and the Indian Ocean. According to Savarkar, a Hindu is anyone who is born in the motherland and loves his country irrespective of his religion. Religion alone does not define our nationhood: nationhood in our context is a complex conglomerate of religion, culture, tradition, geography, history, circumstance and intuition that leads to a particular way of thinking that is very characteristic of Indians and Indians alone. One is an Indian if one thinks like an Indian.

It is significant that Article 1 of our Constitution begins with the phrase "India, that is Bhārat, shall be a Union of States". Do these names mean the same? If yes, I would not be writing this book. If not, why not? Would subsequent events and our present state of mind have been any different if the phrase had been instead, "Bhārat, that is India, shall be a Union of States"? Some might argue that this amounts to semantic quibbling in what is, in the end, a non-Indic language. However, these are indeed weighty matters and will be considered in greater detail in Chapters 3 and 5.

Other factors also contributed to the coming together of Indians as a single group in our fight for freedom. After 1858, there was growing interest among Indians in learning about their colonial masters and this was certainly heightened by the appearance of English language-based education. While Macaulay's intentions were entirely ignoble, his rather successful experiments in brainwashing the Indian educated classes towards an Anglophile mindset thereby ensuring the destruction of Indic thought in the country achieved a perhaps unintended result: with a knowledge of English, Indians were able to compete with the Britishers, even if to a limited extent, in academic activities like law, science, engineering and medicine. The three presidency universities had been set up and even if all they did was produce clerks for the British, English surely became a passport to a better life in the form of better-paid jobs, and shall we say regrettably, in the matter of getting social respect and standing. Acharya Prafulla Chandra Ray, Swami Vivekananda and Mahendra Lal Sircar all came from well-off families who felt that their scions should be educated in English for improved upward mobility of the family. Bengal was at the centre of this Anglophile drift, if one might call it that: the activities of Keshab Chunder Sen, Michael Madhusudhan Dutt and others, who were influenced by Raja Rammohun Roy, surely increased the overall consciousness of the educated sections of society, if nothing else. All this played a definite role in giving Indians the confidence to confront the Britisher on the playing field of the latter's choice. And yet, or maybe reflecting this greater confidence, Sircar, a leading allopathic medical practitioner, switched to homoeopathy and in resistance to the clerk-producing Calcutta University started the Indian Association for the Cultivation of Science, a purely research organisation that flourishes to the present day. Sircar's efforts did not go in vain. Within 25 years, IACS produced the only Nobel Prize winning Indian scientist who has worked entirely in India, Chandrasekhara Venkata Raman. In general, the three presidency universities did not encourage research, the true measure of educational progress and IACS was the forerunner of other research-based universities like Allahabad, Punjab (in Lahore), Jadavpur, Mysore, Delhi, and Andhra. The most notable in this latter category is undoubtedly the world-famous Indian Institute of Science, IISc, in Bangalore that was set up in 1908 with three entirely different kinds of inputs from a formidable trio of Jamsetji Nusserwanji Tata, the Dowager Maharani of Mysore Kempananjammani, and Vivekananda: Tata gave the money, the Maharani gave the land while Vivekananda gave the idea.

If Bengal was at the forefront of the intellectual revolution that brought out the nationalistic fervour in Indians, Bombay at the other end of the country led the industrial revolution. A country only becomes strong if both these arms of development are well in place. One is the spirit and the other the substance underlying a people's confidence. The Bangalore institute was one of the last major projects undertaken by Tata, a visionary, philanthropist, and India's first industrialist. He founded the

Tata Group of companies, and the city of Jamshedpur, the headquarters of the Tata Iron and Steel Company in 1908. Tata and his group grew in stature through the textile mills industry and diversified into what is now a huge world-wide conglomerate. The textile mills industry itself, in Bombay and Ahmedabad, subjected to constant competition from Manchester, was closely connected with the freedom movement as evidenced by the name of one of the first enterprises, Swadeshi Mills, set up in 1887. Scores of these textile mills sprouted in central Bombay in a locality called Girangaon, literally the village of mills. At their peak there were more than 100 of them, 130 mills by one count, the majority of which were cotton mills. In 1897, Ardeshir Godrej and his brother Pirojsha set up here the company that bears his name. It has grown from locks and cupboards to soaps, agrochemicals, real estate and finally today to the Mars mission. Ghanshyamdas Birla laid the foundation of his huge industrial empire by establishing a company that traded in jute in 1911. The industrial prowess of a country could be measured in those days by the size of its sulphuric acid industry. In this context, the Dharamsi Morarji Chemical Company set up in Bombay in 1919 was India's first producer of this bulk chemical. A decade prior to this in 1907 India's first big pharmaceutical company Alembic Chemical Works Company was founded in Baroda. All these developments that led directly to an influx of wealth into India occurred at a time of maximum political activity. Bengal was partitioned by Viceroy Curzon in 1905 but under the pressure of popular sentiment his decision was repealed in just six years. It was a time of ferment and resistance. It is indeed remarkable that the country progressed this much, both economically and intellectually, during the period 1880-1920, the high noon of empire, when the unfair and unjust colonial dispensation appeared to be stretching out forever.

Any freedom struggle that attempts to succeed through dialogue, discussion, disputation, and dissension as opposed to freedom obtained through an armed struggle, needs a political organisation. The Indian National Congress, INC, was founded by Allan Octavian Hume in 1885 as a forum for civil and political discourse among educated Indians towards obtaining a greater degree of self-governance. As discussed above, the INC grew and survived in its initial days during a time when the British were at the zenith of their power in India only because the British displayed a patronising attitude towards the aspirational English-speaking class of Indians who constituted its membership. Some prominent early members included Dadabhai Naoroji, Surendranath Banerjea, Badruddin Tyabji, W.C.Bonnerjee, S. Ramaswami Mudaliar, S. Subramanya Iyer and Romesh Chunder Dutt. Hume himself was patronising to some degree and his words here convey an impression that he believed that Indians were not up to the task of behaving as the British might have liked. He said, "Every nation secures precisely as good a government as it merits. If you, the picked men, the most highly educated of the nation, cannot, scorning personal ease and selfish objects, make a resolute struggle to secure greater freedom for yourselves and your country, a more impartial administration, a larger share in the management of your own affairs, then we, your friends, are wrong and our adversaries right, then are Lord Ripon's noble aspirations for your good fruitless and visionary, then, at present at any rate all hopes of progress are at an end, and India truly neither desires nor deserves any better Government than she enjoys."

With the growing resurgence of a national spirit, the INC was bound to change its approach and between 1885 and 1905 it passed a number or resolutions asking for civil rights and new administrative and economic policies. Although worded in a subservient language the intent was clear: there were increasing demands for a much higher degree of self-rule and the INC was transforming from a kept showpiece of the British to a nationalistic political party. It wanted the right to organise processions, protests, and similar meetings. It wanted the appointment of Indians in the government services as opposed to merely clerical posts. It protested against discriminatory laws. In the context of this book, it asked for a greater say for Indians in the legislative assemblies and to have elected Indian representatives in them. It also complained bitterly about the economic policies of the government that had impoverished the country. It goes without saying that this was the period when the INC was able to channelise the protests for freedom into an organic whole. The British, however, paid scant regard to these demands. They felt that the best thing that had happened to India was that they had come there and 'developed' that 'primitive' country. In fact, they imposed heavy taxes and the colonial economy in which raw materials were exported from India while finished goods were imported back into the country is estimated to have gained for them a staggering sum of $45 trillion (time corrected) in the period 1765-1938. This is eleven times the annual GDP of the U.K. today. When the British came to India, the country's share in the global GDP was 23 per cent. When they left it was an abysmal 4 per cent. Numbers do not lie and matters were coming to a head.

Despite all this, it appears that the occidental mind had still not fully appreciated that the Indian sentiment was turning. As late as 1911, a certain American evangelist based in Ahmednagar, Robert Allan Hume (no relation to A. O. Hume), opined that if any kind of national spirit was developing in what he termed a fragmented land in which no ruler could truly be called "indigenous", where there were "one hundred and fifty various languages and dialects", it was only because of the ever-beneficent British and their beautiful language! He tried to highlight the differences between Hindus and Muslims, imputing that the latter were a much more homogeneous group of 62 million people, all speaking the same language Urdu but scattered all over the country. He accused the INC of being a largely Hindu outfit and subtly conveyed the opinion that this was a country divided by religion. Such sentiments were being subtly and later systematically encouraged by the British in their usual strategy of divide-and-rule. R. A. Hume scoffed at the INC, which he said had failed even its minimum objective of influencing public opinion in Britain. He even tried to highlight differences within the INC between the so-called moderates and extremists, a schism that was indeed developing. The concluding words in his paper in a journal called interestingly The Journal of Race Development (Vol. 1, No. 3, January 1911, pages 367-371) are so revealing of the colonisers' mentality that it bears repeating here: "Because the British paramountcy is to be assumed and maintained no Indian National Congress can become anything like the British Parliament or American Congress, since under the present circumstances *there never can be one political party which can turn another party out of power and assume responsibility for administration.* It is for the leaders of the Indian National Congress to show whether their institution can more and more become a true and wise National Institution". Never say never again!

The above does not purport to be a comprehensive history of the INC in its initial years. I consider only those aspects in its early development that relate to constitution writing in the relevant period, roughly 1890-1920. A similar description is also warranted for the political party that till 1947 generally asserted what it felt were the legitimate interests of Muslims in India. While the INC did not ever seriously claim to stand for the rights of the Hindus this was not true for the All-India

Muslim League, which was launched in Dhaka in 1906 by Aga Khan III and others, and which unabashedly displayed its sectarian character at a time when concerns were first expressed as to whether Muslims would be able to live comfortably in a country where they would account for just 25 per cent of the overall population. That such a sentiment was even extant, namely that Muslims and Hindus would not be able to live together, needs further scrutiny. It was a time when the British were clearly an imperial power of the highest order. There was no sign of them leaving India anytime soon. This means that the Muslims were already becoming uneasy about living among Hindus, even under a British colonial dispensation at its zenith.

Muslims had lived with Hindus in India for at least 600 years by then. What was specific to the time around the turn of the century that prompted these feelings of insecurity among the Muslims? Generally, they had constituted the ruling classes since the time of the Mughals and even after that empire weakened, they were in positions of influence and patronage. This situation changed after 1858 when Hindus took to studies in the English language making them qualified not just for petty government positions but also eligible to enter more lucrative professions like law and medicine. Muslims probably felt dispossessed and disenfranchised. Suddenly, they might not have felt like stakeholders in India anymore. Their subdued state of mind would explain the great influence on the community of Syed Ahmed Khan who spoke about Muslim modernism. Ahmed Khan was a strong advocate of English language-based study, especially in the scientific subjects, as he was convinced that only through science could a nation prosper. He founded the Aligarh Muslim University originally called the Muhammadan Anglo-Oriental College in Aligarh in 1877 for the furtherance of his aims. AMU flourishes till the present day but it was also the hotbed of intellectual discussions pertaining to the role and fate of Muslims in India during a critical period in the 1920s and later. The change in attitude of Ahmed Khan in the late 1880s probably had a big influence on the Muslim community: till then he had felt that Muslims and Hindus were of the same nation but he made a dramatic about-turn, what scientists would call a first order phase transition, when he expressed the opposite view in strident tones that Muslims and Hindus were two nations. Whether or not they could live together was not explicitly mentioned but the implication was all too clear. This was the beginning of the two-nation theory of Mohammed Ali Jinnah that led ultimately to the creation of Pakistan. This was the first time that nationhood had been expressed in terms of religion in the subcontinent. Can religion define nationhood? Probably not, in the modern world of liberal democracies barring possibly Israel, but in its case one must consider the tragic history and the fact that Jews today account for just 0.2 per cent of the population of the world.

Against this background, one may consider a score or so documents written between 1895 and 1947 by the British government on the one hand and on the other by Indians, acting both as individuals and as members of political parties, pertaining to a Constitution. These documents attempted to sketch working arrangements for possible governance structures for India. These are the forerunners of the 1950 Constitution of the fully independent country that was born in 1947. In general, these documents from both the British and the Indian sides reflect the immediate political developments of the day. They are almost knee-jerk reactions in some cases. The patchwork quilt of documents that was available to the Constituent Assembly in 1948 give a constitutional timeline of the events of the preceding 50 years. Especially after 1935, that is after the Government of India Act 1935, one discerns a different tenor in these documents, from deferential to noncompliant, and the speed with which changes in them began to appear. Most educated Indians had realised by then that the British were finally yielding and that a day might yet come when their country would be independent. What was still unknown then was the time frame and the degree of independence that would be granted. As an aside, would anyone gazing at the new capital Delhi in 1931, constructed expansively and methodically over more than a decade to convey the physical reality and psychological messaging of imperial Britain, have anticipated even remotely that this omnipresence would be history in just sixteen short years? And no one could have predicted then that the country would be divided based on religion.

The Constitution of India Bill (1895) of unknown authorship also called the Swaraj Constitution or Home Rule Constitution might have been inspired by Bal Gangadhar Tilak and Annie Besant, known extremists within the INC. It should not be confused with another document that appeared under the same name in 1927 and authored by S. Srinivasa Iyengar and which is discussed later. The 1895 document has been described as the first non-official Constitution that was drafted in India. The term *swarāj* needs some attention. The term *swa* or *sva* refers to the self, what is one's own, and the connection with words like *swami* and *savarna* are obvious. In the Indian independence context, *swa* was given at least two distinct interpretations: Tilak and Dayanand Saraswati gave it the meaning 'of one's own' in the sense that when coupled with *rāj*, which unambiguously means 'rule', *swaraj* meant a people ruling themselves, in other words independence of some sort in physical and material terms. Mohandas Karamchand Gandhi gave the term a far wider meaning and implication: according to him, *swa* has an introspective and inner meaning that refers to answering to oneself. This is a much more personal interpretation and ultimately refers to one who is a master of oneself. Gandhi's many writings on Swaraj illustrate this idea exhaustively and he took the Vedic meaning of the word; far from being a kind of physical, temporal idea, he considered it as self-rule in the sense of self-restraint. He said, "Self-government means, continuous effort to be independent of government control, whether it is foreign government or whether it is national. Swaraj government will be a sorry affair if people look up to it for the regulation of every detail of life". These are prophetic words indeed. Government should not and should never be a *maa baap* institution providing cradle-to-grave security for everyone in all things. I shall consider this more philosophical meaning of 'swaraj' in Chapter 3.

In the context of political events at the time, the Swaraj Constitution of 1895 clearly takes the meaning of Swaraj to be home rule, in other words independence of some kind to manage one's own affairs. The ultimate aim, which was then almost fanciful, was dominion status of the type accorded to Canada, Australia, New Zealand, and South Africa. It is a sophisticated document for its times with 113 articles. Its most important feature is that it speaks of rights of citizens to free speech, property, privacy, and equality before the law. These are ideas that were mirrored many years later in the Fundamental Rights of our 1950 Constitution. The concept of privacy not only in terms of one's dwelling place but also with respect to personal information is a basic concern in any democracy. The western democracies place a very high premium on individual privacy especially in these days where most data are stored electronically and could become available to unauthorised parties. Again, as an aside, the statement "all citizens of India are required to bear arms, to maintain and defend the Empire against its internal and external enemies" has shades of the U.S. Constitution's second amendment! One notes the word 'required' here.

The 1895 document touched upon structures of government and separation of powers. There are four centres of authority; the sovereign and the legislative, executive and judiciary branches. Curiously, the executive and judiciary are subordinate to the legislature. This might have been influenced by the unwritten Constitution of Britain where Parliament is higher than the executive and the judiciary. There is a clear acknowledgment of the federal nature of India because legislative and other authority is divided between the Centre and the provinces. The provinces included the Princely States of Hyderabad and Rajputana. In a very progressive step, state education was declared free and primary education compulsory. One may reflect upon this statement, which dates as far back as 1895, in 2022 when the National Education Policy (2020) is slowly limbering up towards accepting that imaginative education in the earliest years of schooling is a must in a modern country. It has taken us this long to even acknowledge that primary school education in India is in shambles today. Thinking something, saying it, and doing something about it are entirely different things. The history of India post-independence is a sad story about how we have missed the bus on so many occasions because we have indulged ourselves in the hypocrisy, nay fantasy, that once one thinks of something and at the most says it aloud, it is as good as having done it.

There is a provision for a bicameral legislature at the Centre and a unicameral one in the provinces. Undoubtedly the drafters of the 1895 Constitution were influenced by Britain and the U.S.A. Indeed, democratic republics in the world today do have the bicameral system; the differences arise in the scope and ambit of the powers of the two houses. In the

Swaraj Constitution both houses have elected and nominated members and bills needed to be passed three times over in each house before they became law. The nominations were either *ex officio* or based on the professions, law, medicine, academics, and commerce (nothing for sports people or film stars). Intriguingly, the lifetime of nominated members in the upper house was for life while it was just three years in the lower house. The question of nominated members is a vexing one and will be taken up further in Chapter 2. Many other subtle aspects of the recommendations here need a more careful study in today's context, for example unicameral versus bicameral, elected versus nominated, and the nature of the federal structure which is the one single issue that has bedevilled the Indian Constitution ever since. Federalism, or the lack of it in modern India, is the main theme of this book and I shall revert to the topic throughout.

The Indian Councils Act (1909) more popularly known as the Morley-Minto reforms were a turning point not in constitution writing but rather in the future of India as a single country with the geographical boundaries then prevalent. With a distant memory of fig leaf reforms introduced by Ripon in 1872 pertaining to local self-government, Minto the then Viceroy and Morley the then Secretary of State for India introduced this Act in the British Parliament. It gave a certain measure, or more accurately an imaginary sense, of Indian representation in the legislative councils in Calcutta, Bombay and Madras. These so-called reforms by no means signified real representation for Indians in legislative matters. The formal act is skeletal consisting of just eight articles and two schedules that detail the composition of the councils but what was devastating were the rules and regulations that provided the operational details: while franchise was limited to males with certain educational qualifications and property ownership, the bombshell, at least for the INC, was the introduction of separate electorates for Muslims. This move was a clear announcement by the British as to their real intentions and it is even said that the AIML was founded in 1906 with some understanding from Minto to the Muslims about the matter of these separate electorates.

The question of separate electorates for Muslims and later for the Scheduled Caste communities continued to influence the nature of the freedom movement itself, and it became an issue even before real franchise was given to Indians. It continues to confront the post-1947 Indian political scenario, at least as it pertains to the SCs, right down to the present day in the form of reservations for educational opportunities and jobs, and in the form of electoral constituencies where only members of this community may be put up as candidates. It continues to be a stumbling block today, needing constant judicial and legislative tinkering. Not unexpectedly, it strongly influences the moves and manoeuvres of today's political parties. Reservations have led to reaction from groups who feel disadvantaged but have not been provided such benefits; several non-SC communities have indeed fought for and successfully obtained such reservations, most notably after the Mandal agitation in the early 1990s. A reservation ceases to be one anymore if it applies to 69 per cent of the population, which is true in one state of the Indian Union today. In the end, neither the communities that have been favoured with these reservations nor the communities that have been denied them seem to be fully happy. The former still feel a social stigma despite constitutional protection while the latter feel delegitimised, even unwanted and have taken to migration to countries where they feel a fairer deal awaits them. Related aspects are taken up for consideration throughout this book. For a decade or so after the 1909 Act, however, this matter was relevant mostly as it applied to Muslims. After that, the question of separate electorates for SCs came up.

The matter of separate electorates for Muslims is counter intuitive. As practised in pre-independence India, a separate electorate meant that some constituencies were reserved only for Muslim candidates but *voting for such reserved constituencies was also only restricted to Muslims.* The voting was proposed to take place with a system of electoral colleges, and cumulative voting where the number of constituencies would be fixed religion-wise "in accordance with its proportion to the whole population". To balance the numbers, they could be supplemented by nomination. These constituencies (electoral colleges) would then "later on elect to the Legislature of the province representatives for the two communities in like proportion". Today, one could fairly term this as number-fixing. Assuming reasonably that the Muslims felt threatened and insecure the provision of such enclaves could only enhance the ghetto mentality in the minority community. Members elected from these enclaves would hardly have had a chance to successfully promote meaningful legislation because they are, by definition, always in a minority in the legislature. As backlash polarisation develops among Hindus, the probability of a Muslim getting elected in a general constituency becomes vanishingly small (with the risk that those Muslims elected from there being termed sell-outs). Instead of Hindus and Muslims coming together, as they were before the British came to India, the effect of these separate electorates would be only to widen the chasm between the two communities.

These electorates also run counter to logic. They assume that the concerns of Muslims are limited to their identity as Muslims and not to secular concerns such as education, communication, travel and health, both physical and economic. Are not such concerns independent of religion? Should not both communities have been voting for representatives who would be legislating on such matters? Further, separate electorates are merely another way of saying proportional representation and it is difficult to reconcile this with a first-past-the post system as far as declaring a winner in the general constituencies. Who or what is being represented in the end? The only logical conclusion one might draw, or shall one term it *reductio ad absurdum,* is that the system of religion-based separate electorates will only work if all the people in a country belong to the same religion, in which case the entire exercise is unnecessary. Indeed, this is what prevails today in one of the two parts of divided India, the one that is inhabited by the descendants of those who wanted separate electorates a century back.

The 1909 Act was a masterful example of British subterfuge and intrigue designed to consolidate their divide-and-rule policy. They relied on their experience in 1883 in Cyprus when after taking the island over from the Ottomans they introduced separate electorates in such a manner that no legislation proposed by the Greeks could pass muster with opposition from the Muslims and nominated members. They simply proceeded from a pilot plant in Cyprus to a full-fledged manufacturing facility in India with the Morley-Minto reforms. The provisions of the Act were suitably camouflaged by cosmetic down weighting of Muslim representation in the Muslim majority provinces Bengal and Punjab (in Bengal and Punjab their representation was reduced to 50 per cent and 40 per cent from 56 per cent and 55 per cent respectively) and conversely a marginal up-weighting in provinces where they were in a minority. Separate electorates can only lead to demands of a similar nature on a larger scale and this is exactly what happened, especially in Punjab in 1946. In the end, the polarisation becomes extreme, and the only natural outcome is a physical partition on a geographical basis. Many problems in modern day Pakistan have arisen from these communal electorates in pre-Partition India. There is a tendency to look at all issues as Muslim issues. This can only lead to regression, which it has. There are parallels albeit at a smaller level in post-Independence India with its 20 crores strong Muslim minority, and one should take adequate warning from history of a century ago in this context. Some issues have a way of reappearing if corrective action is not taken. Apart from all of this, the Morley-Minto reforms failed to appreciate the ever-growing sentiment among the peoples of India for some measure of self-determination in their affairs. In failing to devolve more powers and authority to municipalities and districts, in not providing financial freedom to the provinces, and in Indians being still debarred from administrative posts, they were fated to fail. They were just a sop.

During the period 1858-1947, the British introduced constitutional changes in India only when they were compelled to. Their 1909 'reforms' applied the divide-and-rule policy to two situations. Not only did they polarise Hindus and Muslims, but they also increased the divergences between the moderate and extremist wings of the INC. The revolutionary movement towards independence was in full swing at the time. Names like Aurobindo Ghosh, Khudiram Bose, Madan Lal Dhingra, and Savarkar himself still resonate in our imagination today. Bhikaji Cama, from an affluent Bombay Parsi background, had hoisted the first flag of independent India in Germany in 1907, interestingly with the encouragement of notables like Munchersha Godrej, the brother of Ardeshir and Pirojsha. He had been banned from living in India. The British needed to quieten the impact of these extremist activities. The Liberal Party was in power in Britain at the time and it suited them to introduce these reforms in the name of a more understanding attitude towards Indians. The reforms were adequate enough for liberals such as Gopala Krishna Gokhale, Rash Behari Ghosh and others. With the separate electorate plank that pleased the IUML immensely, the cocktail was complete. A clumsy compromise effort between the IUML and INC called the Congress-League Scheme (1916) or more familiarly the Lucknow Pact tried to incorporate the separate electorates within the INC demand for home rule. However, all this was overshadowed by the outbreak of World War I in 1914 an event of far-reaching consequences and one that saw the end of four large European empires: Habsburg, Hohenzollern, Ottoman and Romanov. The fifth, the British Empire, was ostensibly the winner but this war, which probably outranks World War II in its long-term consequences, effectively neutered it and that too in just thirty years—with India's independence.

We have mentioned that the nature of the administrative and legislative reforms introduced by the British in the colonial period closely reflected their mind-set. World War I is a big turning point in world history because it abruptly ended a system of governance, namely monarchy, which had held sway in Europe, the most important continent in the world at that time, for nearly a millennium. The European nation-states were mostly monarchies in the 19th century. There was a sudden switchover to democracy in many parts of the continent in a welter of small countries created by the victorious allies in Versailles. This was bound to influence Indian intelligentsia for how could Britain continue to justify a colonial monarchy in India, with the people enjoying no democratic rights, if she chose to confer this form of government to so many new European states *de novo*? The war was fought, according to the Allied statesmen, to help small weak countries against big strong empires. India had put aside its struggle for freedom during those years and had contributed handsomely to the war effort with men and materials. Should not the British

Empire have reciprocated and made substantial moves towards self-representation for Indians? This justifiable sentiment indeed brought Hindus and Muslims together, giving the British further cause for anxiety, since they were assiduously cultivating the myth that the two communities were two nations with antagonistic interests. In a country that is quite diverse in character and where the Princely States, which enjoyed popular support among their subjects, had a special role to play, a system of governance that is highly centralised, with power concentrated in the hands of a small number of foreigners responsible only to the British Parliament, would not have sold well. The Lucknow Pact, however laboured in construction, brought Hindus and Muslims together politically and was indeed one of the reasons for the British to consider putting up a new set of (what they tried to convince Indians were) serious attempts at constitutional reform.

Several other factors show that the British were indeed nervous in the period roughly between the years 1915-1919 about the way they were handling India. India was too lucrative a business proposition for them to surrender easily. Yet, it was too large, difficult and complicated for them to handle efficiently. They had also realised their missteps with regard to the Morley-Minto reforms. The British are utterly empirical in their outlook with no eternal principles, but only eternal interests. It is not for nothing that Britain is described as a nation of shopkeepers. When they adopt any particular line of action it is never voluntary but only a reaction to the events of the time. Morley-Minto was given to us when the discontent had grown to a critical level. Possibly because of their discomfiture they included in these reforms communal electorates that were intended to divide. In playing divide-and-rule they had let the genie of communalism out of the bottle risking civil war but without securing sufficient long-term gains for themselves. Soon, it appeared that the INC and AIML were coming together with the emergence of younger, more educated Muslims who were able to think nationalistically. The extremist group within the INC were becoming dominant. Tilak in Bombay, Besant in Madras, Lajpat Rai in Punjab, and Bipin Chandra Pal in Bengal were powerful orators and writers and had a heady influence on the people at large. The Champaran rebellion, which saw Gandhi's entry into the rough and tumble of Indian politics, must have surely confounded our colonial masters. Other world events were also of concern to the British with respect to their Indian policies. A major development had occurred in China in 1912 when the last emperor Pu Yi was forced to abdicate following Sun Yat-sen's republican revolution. It was the end of empire everywhere. China was too close to India for comfort and these changes in a big neighbouring country were bound to affect the British. The blunders they committed in the buffer state of Tibet at that time continue to plague both India and China in terms of their border disputes down to the present day. The collapse of Tsarist Russia in 1917 led the British to a great fear that Kaiser's Germany, which had forced a humiliating agreement on the new communist regime, was all set to enter India through central Asia. This led them in turn to compromise in the other buffer state in the region, Afghanistan, where they managed to extricate themselves after an indecisive war. The collapse of the Ottomans during the War and the consequent appearance of many unstable countries in West Asia, again created by them could only have added to their general discomfort.

The Government of India Act (1919), or the 1919 Indian Councils Act, followed from the proposed Montagu-Chelmsford reforms also referred to as the Montford reforms. These were being discussed widely from 1917 onwards. One notes that these reforms were mooted by the British even when they were fighting a war. The most important aspect of these reforms was the introduction of a dual system of governance, or dyarchy, where the Government of India, now in Delhi the new capital, and the provincial governments, acted as independent centres of authority. There was further dyarchy within the provinces with a division of powers between the elected (Indian) representatives and the nominated (mostly British) ones. As a safety measure the authority of the Secretary of State for India was shared by that office and a new one, called the High Commissioner for India in the U.K., which was set up to act as the representative of the Viceroy in London. Assigning multiple points of failure is a classic technique when managing a complex problem. Dyarchy is another example of this methodology. The British had been able to manage India efficiently only because their authority emanated from a very small apex power centre. This was true both in the company and Raj eras. They would almost surely have loathed adopting dyarchy leading one to conclude that they were compelled to do so. India, which was treated by the British as a simple system was manifesting itself as a complex system—which it always was!

Operationally, the 1919 Act saw the introduction of a bicameral system at the Government of India level. The two houses were called the Central Legislative Assembly and the Council of State. These are the forerunners of our Lok Sabha and Rajya Sabha. The former had separate electorates for Muslims and other smaller special interest groups. However, the eligibility as a voter depended on satisfying income and educational criteria. In all of India, with its 300 million odd inhabitants, there were only 9, 09, 874 eligible voters for the Central Assembly in 1920 and a mere 17, 343 for the Council of State—some representation! The federal nature of the new set-up was seen in the division of subjects for legislation and administration between the Government of India and the provinces. However, the authority of Indians was diluted further with the sub-division of provincial subjects into reserved and transferred categories. The former, which included the more important subjects, could be legislated and administered only by the provincial governor and his nominated council. The latter, which the British considered less important, included subjects like local self-government, public works, roads, bridges, sanitation, and industrial research were the only ones which could be legislated upon and administered by elected ministers, Indians obviously, but again selected by the Governor. The ministers had considerably less influence and clout than the members of the council. The division of subjects into the Union list, the State list and the Concurrent list is required in any federal system to avoid confusion and overlap. However, in both pre- and post-independent India these divisions and demarcations have led to ceaseless worries and ambiguities about residuary subjects at both the central and state level. The topic is an important one and will be taken up in some detail in Chapter 2.

The nature of these reforms, namely giving with one hand and taking away with the other, typifies British actions in India: too little too late. The Montford reforms were widely criticised. There was not even a hint of dominion status, something that all Indians would have hoped to see. The wording gave full scope to the British to do exactly as they wanted. The INC rejected the reforms immediately. Besant termed them "unworthy of England to offer and India to accept". Bhimrao Ambedkar, who by then was emerging as the leader of the SC community, called it the "British Constitution of India". It is ironical that our present Constitution continues to labour under a similar epithet in 2022, at least in the opinion of some.

Even the liberals had their misgivings. A letter written by

a group of Bombay notables headed by Dinsha Wacha, to the government was largely commending of the proposals but ends with the real message of the letter: they were disappointed and upset. Their most serious reservation was that the Government of India would continue to be responsible only to the British Parliament. In their words, "this we think is wrong in principle and is bound to lead to rigidity and unprogressiveness…". They felt that the Government of India should be at least partly responsible to Indian legislative bodies, like what had been envisaged for the provincial governments in the reforms. They were thoroughly dissatisfied with the financial aspects and wished for Indian legislators to have a greater say in taxation policies for items like salt, customs, personal income, railways, posts, and telegraphs. They also had very strong reservations about the Council of State, or second chamber, and termed the institution "peculiarly British" and unsuited to India. The matter of the Upper House in our Parliament today has been discussed sporadically: I believe it is not just a peculiarity but rather an anachronism that needs thorough review and reform if not outright removal. I shall take up this matter in more detail in Chapters 2 and 4.

We shall allow the extremists to have the last word. In a prescient tone, Lajpat Rai said in his book *Young India* in 1912: "The Indians are a chivalrous people; they will not disturb England as long as she is engaged with Germany. The struggle after the war, might however, be even more bitter and sustained." The British had a way of either preceding or following up on their reforms with a coercive action. In early 1919, they enacted the notorious Rowlatt Act that continued wartime martial law regulations in peacetime. The widespread protests that followed all over the country and the actions of the repressive governor of Punjab, Michael O'Dwyer led directly to the Jallianwala Bagh massacre. Not unexpectedly there was an upswing in violent activity directed towards home rule. The Hindustan Republican Association was founded in 1923 as a secret revolutionary youth front and made its presence felt in early 1925 with the publication and dissemination of a manifesto, The Revolutionary, in the form of a 4-page written Constitution. It was written by Ram Prasad Bismil, one of its leaders, but under a pseudonym. The document expressed the ideology, plans and vision of the HRA and alluded to foreign rule, the independence movement, and the future of India. It was basically a call to the Indian people to rise up in arms and shake off the British colonisers.

As opposed to the incremental approach that relied on reasoning and argument adopted by the writers of the Indian Constitution till that point, the HRA document called for a radical approach and its Constitution bears little resemblance to previous efforts in this direction. It stated for example: "The immediate object of the revolutionary party in the domain of politics is to establish a federal Republic of United States of India by an organised and armed revolution." In short, it rejected the constitutional means adopted by the main political parties of the time. The document shocked and scandalised the Britishers, who viewed it as seditious. The HRA leaders Jogesh Chandra Chatterjee and Sachindra Nath Sanyal who were distributing the pamphlet were arrested in Calcutta but by then the message of the HRA had spread as far away as Punjab where there was an upsurge of revolutionary activity resulting finally in the hanging of Bhagat Singh, Sukhdev Thapar and Shivaram Rajguru in 1931. These drastic approaches towards independence had their own significance and relevance. For a start, the INC while not acknowledging HRA openly was offering tacit support as they sensed that the HRA's revolutionary activities were bound to affect the British and compel them to accede to some of the constitutional demands that the INC was making. Another reason why the HRA is of some interest in the context of the present book is that it represents one of the few attempts in pre-independence to draft a Constitution outside of the western mindset. The M. N. Roy Constitution of 1944 and the so-called Gandhian Constitution of 1946 also attempted to break such new ground, although they did not advocate armed rebellion like the HRA. These approaches need to be taken seriously if one entertains the question as to whether our 1950 Constitution is appropriate for us Indians in its core structuring, especially regarding federal issues.

The 1920s, a time of relative peace in the world, saw a steely determination build up in India and three constitutional documents from the Indian side, in 1925, 1927 and 1928 are notable. These were followed by a lukewarm statement from Viceroy Irwin, in 1929. The recommendations of an ill-advised committee sent from Britain in 1928 certainly influenced the last of these documents, the so-called Nehru report. One notes the rapidity with which these documents followed one another. They may be profitably considered together because they cover common ground and represent the views of a wide section of political personages and well-known citizens across India. They are consistent in their demand for dominion status, which was a kind of minimum platform in their view. All of them envisaged a bicameral legislature. They all pleaded for a federal dispensation, which was becoming a bone of contention with the British. There are individual features too some of which interestingly find a place in our 1950 Constitution. All three 1920s Constitutions seem to have influenced the Government of India Act (1935) the penultimate constitutional move made by the British in their long stay here.

The Commonwealth of India Bill (National Convention India 1925) was inspired by Annie Besant and outlines her vision for an independent India. She was the moving spirit behind this document. At the outset, she had expressed the view to the British that India would never accept a Constitution framed in Westminster. Towards this end, she formed what would become known as the 'National Convention' around a core group of her friends like Tej Bahadur Sapru, who became chairman of this group, C. P. Ramaswami Aiyar, P. S. Sivaswami Aiyar, V. S. Srinivasa Sastri, PurshottamdasThakurdas, Hari Singh Gour and others. Finally, the Convention had as members an impressive list of 256 legislators, ex-legislators and eminent citizens, including Gandhi, Bipin Chandra Pal and Sarojini Naidu. The Bill had 127 Articles and was comprehensive in that it considered almost all themes that one would expect in a Constitution. Most significantly there is a section on fundamental rights which reminds one of the 1895 Swaraj Constitution. These included the right to elementary education, freedom of expression, non-discrimination, and very progressively, gender equality. The concept of fundamental rights was getting firmly implanted in the minds of framers of the Indian Constitution by then. It is one of the main pillars of our Constitution today. In this respect, Besant's 1925 document is of great importance. For example, the demanded rights extended the notion of privacy from one's home (expressed in the 1895 document) to personal liberty and security for one's property apart from one's home.

Gender equality is a matter that needs more discussion. The last of the seven rights in the 1925 Constitution reads simply, "There shall be no disqualification or disability on the basis of sex." One should appreciate that this reiteration of gender equality, a goal that is still not fully realised in the world today, was proposed way back in Besant's 1925 document and that too before full suffrage for women was a reality in Britain. Women were able to vote in some countries, for example in New Zealand as far back as 1893, but they could not stand as candidates. The 1925 Constitution affirms that full adult franchise should be a reality for both men and women. Its delinking of eligibility as a voter from a woman's marital status was also a remarkable step. In short, this Constitution went a long way in protecting and promoting the rights of Indian women. Put another way, Indian women were thinking constitutionally.

The original idea was to get this bill passed by the British Parliament, and indeed it was introduced there by George Lansbury of the Labour Party in 1925. However, the defeat of that party in the elections put paid to any further progress in this direction. However, it had a big influence on the 1928 Nehru report which has many sections that are taken directly from it almost verbatim. Using a good idea belonging to someone else is not always plagiarism especially when there is plenty of public discussion on the matter. In turn, the 1928 document had a corresponding influence on our 1950 Constitution. These cascades of reactions are interesting. Did our 1950 Constitution benefit from the earlier efforts or is it a cut-and-paste effort assembled in haste? Was the whole more than the sum of its parts? This question has been discussed in recent years whenever the question comes up as to whether our Constitution suits the basic character and temperament of the Indian people. Do we need British laws for India?

Using the template of the Besant Constitution, and its variant that was introduced in the British Parliament, the All India Congress Committee in its 1927 session called upon the working committee to formulate a 'Swaraj Constitution' (the same name as the 1895 document) in consultation with elected members of the central and provincial legislatures. It was realised that there was no immediate chance of any agreement with the British, but it was hoped that the presence of another reinforcing document would strengthen the Indian case. Full national independence meant, at that point in time, dominion status. A pragmatic decision was taken to draft any future Constitution on the model of the Western democracies. Whether or not this was a correct decision remains to be seen to this day but in any case this was the route that was chosen. S. Srinivasa Iyengar, a well-known constitutional lawyer from Madras and the president of the 1926 session of the INC in Guwahati drafted the document along the lines of what he called a federal democracy. He was also the president of what was called the 'Independence for India League', a body that was formed in 1928 with Nehru and Bose as secretaries. Incidentally, Iyengar was the mentor of K. Kamaraj, the renowned chief minister of Tamil Nadu from 1954-1962.

The most prominent feature of Iyengar's 1927 Swaraj Constitution is that it affirms the essential federal character of the Indian polity. It was felt that the British had persisted with their unitary model for so long only because it reinforced their own steel-frame. I have referred to this in my discussion of dyarchy in the Montagu-Chelmsford reforms. The use of the term 'steel frame' by Iyengar is interesting. Vallabhbhai Patel used it two decades later to describe the Indian Civil Service the forerunner of today's Indian Administrative Service. He argued that a steel-frame in the executive branch was essential. Today, one can ask whether we need a frame. If so, how steel-like should the frame be? Should it be completely rigid? Or should it be a frame with elastic struts, flexible but still retaining its topological structure? Perhaps we need a committed bureaucracy but with the commitment to the people rather than to politicians. The IAS is discussed further in Chapters 2 and 4.

Iyengar argued for a strong federal structure. A central makeup with weak federal limbs he maintained would carry the risk that "any dominant caucus, communal, political or dynastic, ruling the Central Government of a Swaraj India will be able to disturb the equipoise more easily in a unitary system than in a federal system and might bring about the impairment or destruction of Swaraj as the history of medieval governments in India illustrates". These are wise words indeed. Post-independence India has been afflicted with direct or proxy dynastic rule at the centre for 50 of its 75 years of existence. The modicum of federal structure, even in our strongly unitary Constitution, might have been the only saving grace that has prevented India from degenerating into a crude family dictatorship.

In another comment justifying a federal dispensation in a democracy, Iyengar argues that in such a structure communities, whether religious or otherwise, must give up their political identities. Democracy is the rule of the majority, and it cannot be held to ransom by the tyranny of the minority. Federalism decreases the dominance of any one community in the national persona. His words on minority appeasement are so apposite that I quote them in full: "Let us realise that a too anxious attempt at protection of minorities against majorities only serves to defeat its own purpose and either retards or prevents that fusion and merger of communities into a secular and homogeneous nation which shall be scrupulous alike in the safeguarding of the freedom of conscience and of religion and in keeping the civic and political activities of a nation free from the serious disturbances due to the intrusion of sectarian zeal or religious antagonism. It should not matter to us, therefore, which community, religious or other, is or will be in a majority and in which province". The premise here is that all communities give up their political identity. In the context of modern India, federalism is the ideal answer to bigotry, if and only if all communities, be they be based on religion, caste, or class, surrender their political identity. This is the direction in which a new Constitution, say if one were to be drafted today, should impel us to move. It might appear to some that the idea of a community giving up its political identity is altruistic and unrealistic in today's India. It might almost appear like Gandhi's stateless society. I attempt to show, however, in Chapter 4 that this is not as far-fetched an idea as it appears if the federal structure is suitably modified.

The 1927 document argues against separate electorates and nominations for the professions, be they academic, legal, medical, or otherwise. Such profession-based nominations are rarely seen in any liberal democracy, being largely restricted to some former British colonies. The comments on the SC community are especially noteworthy and are carefully worded. Iyengar states with certainty that untouchability in India must go whether the country achieved independence or not. According to him, the removal of this scourge should not be depending on freedom and a Constitution. He argued that so long as the state treats the SCs as a separate community their sense of isolation and despair would be bound to increase. Accordingly, he asked for reservation of seats in the legislative bodies for SCs but with a common electorate. He felt that a separate electorate would only magnify their difficulties unnecessarily. This formula was indeed the basis for the Poona Pact struck by Gandhi and Ambedkar in 1930. This arrangement continues till the present day as a necessary stepping-stone before full social integration of the SC community into the body politic is achieved, which is still in the making. Curiously the 1927 document favoured linguistic states. As a temporary solution in bringing people together it might have been satisfactory in post-Independence India but in the long run language divides the union even as it purportedly unifies a state. There are examples today in India where the same language is spoken in different states and where many languages are spoken in a single state. We should evolve into a system where language does not become a political marker of one's identity and therefore a tool in the hands of unscrupulous politicians. Even a language, not in common use, Sanskrit, has become a political issue. On the question of a bicameral legislature, Iyengar was in favour of having one at the central level but opposed the same at the provincial ranks. I believe that any issue on which there is so much discussion continuing is one where all presented solutions are tentative and insufficient. We should seriously think about this matter in the context of today's Rajya Sabha.

The setting up of the Simon Commission in late 1927 by the British government to review the working of the Montagu-Chelmsford reforms caused wide resentment in the country because it contained not a single Indian member. Motilal Nehru requested Lansbury of the Labour Party to ask it to withdraw its members from the Commission, but to no avail. The British mockingly asked Indians to prove that they could draw up a constitution themselves despite the various efforts to that end till that time. The leaders of the INC and AIML responded to the challenge and the result was the Nehru Report (1928) so named because the chair of the drafting committee was Motilal Nehru. Other members included Ali Imam, Sapru, Bose and Besant. Jawaharlal Nehru was appointed committee secretary. One notes the common members in the drafting committees of all the 1920 Constitutions, documents that appeared in rapid succession to one another. It is hardly surprising then that the contents of the Nehru report emphasised dominion status, a federal structure for India, and a bicameral legislature. Above all, the report was considered an honest attempt to address head-on the problem of communalism. All this was attempted in 22 chapters and 87 articles. Once again one sees importance being given to fundamental rights: the right to free expression and opinion, equality before the law, free elementary education, right to bear arms, freedom of conscience, freedom to follow any profession, and free propagation of religion. On the communal issue, the Nehru report proposed reservation for Muslims in legislatures but these were restricted to Muslim minority constituencies which therefore included the central legislature. There was no mention of separate electorates for Muslims, and this did not find favour with the AIML members. There was further disagreement about whether the residuary powers should go to the Centre or to the provinces. The INC clearly liked the former option and the AIML the latter. These roadblocks led the AIML to reject the Nehru report. The subsequent Lahore declaration by the INC saw the final parting of ways of these two major political parties leading ultimately to Partition itself.

Notably, the Calcutta Congress in late 1928 considered the Nehru Report and decided to accept dominion status as formulated in the report but only if granted immediately; otherwise, the country was to revert to the ideal of complete independence as adopted by the Madras Congress a year before. A year's time was given to the British. In late 1929 the Viceroy made a vague statement, the so-called Irwin Declaration. This simply stated in five lines: "In view of the doubts which have been expressed both in Great Britain and in India regarding the interpretation to be placed on the intentions of the British government in enacting the statute of 1919, I am authorised on behalf of his Majesty's Government to state clearly that in their judgement it is implicit in the Declaration of 1917 that the natural issue of India's constitutional progress as there contemplated is the attainment of Dominion status." Even a lay reader of this declaration will make out that no timeline for such status is given. The wording is so ambiguous with waffling phrases like 'natural issue', 'constitutional progress as there contemplated' and 'attainment of dominion status' that the declaration actually meant nothing. And so were the 1930s heralded with respect to India's constitutional history.

Constitutionally speaking, the early 1930s are characterised by the appearance of four political developments that occurred in quick succession, resulting in the identification of certain issues that could not be ignored or discarded thenceforth. These are the Purna Swaraj Declaration (1930), the Gandhi-Irwin Pact (1930), the Karachi Resolution (1930) and the Poona Pact (1932). These developments are not recorded as constitutional documents but they were rather declarations, agreements, and compromises among the main players in the game: Gandhi, Irwin, Nehru, and Ambedkar. There was a downplaying of the communal angle perhaps reflecting that both the INC and AIML had realised by then that they would be travelling on increasingly diverging roads in the future. What did come to the forefront were questions of equity for the depressed classes and the definition of India as a socialist state. These issues were mirrored in the 1950 Constitution and characterise the nature of the Indian republic today. Both these issues have economic ramifications which are discussed in Chapter 4. All these four developments in 1930-1932 had a big influence on the Government of India Act (1935) enacted by the British.

The Nehru report was based on India getting dominion status and there was general support in the country for this. It was felt that now it only remained for this to be formalised. However, a backlash against even the mild Irwin Declaration developed in Britain and under pressure, Irwin called Gandhi, Jinnah, Nehru and Sapru to tell them that he was reneging and there would be no prospect of dominion status anytime soon. This created considerable irritation, even anger, and it was felt that the British could not be trusted. In this mood, the INC passed a resolution on 19 December 1929 in Lahore called the

Purna Swaraj Declaration. This was made fully public on 26 January 1930. The latter date is of utmost significance to us as it was originally called 'Independence Day' but is now called 'Republic Day' because it is on this day in 1950 that India finally declared itself a sovereign democratic republic and its Constitution came into effect.

If Swaraj means self-rule, Purna Swaraj means complete self-rule or complete independence from Britain with no association at all with the British crown. The Lahore declaration is a short 750-word document without a legal structure. It spoke from the heart. The strategy to obtain independence had seemingly changed. The document simply stated that "The British Government in India has not only deprived the Indian people of their freedom but has based itself on the exploitation of the masses, and has ruined India economically, politically, culturally, and spiritually." Therefore, it became the incontestable right of Indians to have complete independence. The four aspects of ruination by the British were elaborated. India had been pauperised, its people deprived of their self-respect, her talent muffled, and the education system fully destroyed. There are many echoes in the Lahore Declaration that hark back to Vivekananda, especially the paragraphs pertaining to education and culture. Let us note what he said in 1897: "A few hundred, modernised, half-educated and denationalised men are all that there is to show of modern English India—nothing else" or as he said also in the same year, "Take your universities. What have they done during the fifty years [of their existence till then]? They have not produced one original man". Vivekananda's stirring words raise an uncomfortable question: many of the prominent men drafting the Constitution were educated in the English system of education. Were they original men? Or did the ghost of Britain pervade in all our constitutional efforts?

These years witnessed rapid political developments. Gandhi launched the Salt Satyagraha in March 1930 and a civil disobedience campaign that caught the popular imagination everywhere. He and other prominent leaders were arrested. Irwin was worried and realised that the salt campaign was not just meant as a public relations exercise. He knew that he could not avoid meeting Gandhi and such a meeting was arranged and took place in March 1931 after Gandhi's release from prison. These meetings resulted in the Gandhi-Irwin Pact (1930) which emerged after intense negotiations. Each side got a little and lost a little. The Viceroy probably got more in substance, but Gandhi won in terms of a rise in his public image because all his demands in connection with the Salt Satyagraha were granted, namely liberty for local people to manufacture and sell salt and in the lifting of police cases against the *satyagrahis*. The public were also allowed to campaign publicly for Purna Swaraj, hoist flags and so on. Irwin secured Gandhi's willingness to attend the Second Round Table Conference later that year thereby assuring his credibility with the British government. Above all, Gandhi was able to talk and negotiate with the Viceroy on an equal footing, a development that drew criticism and derision from Winston Churchill with his 'half-naked fakir' remark. There is some question whether Gandhi was persuaded to compromise in his discussions with Irwin because of pressure from the industrialist lobby who by then were worried about the effects of the civil disobedience campaign on their financial health. The tussle between morality and pragmatism is an eternal one and as long as there is a creative tension between these opposing pulls, all is not lost.

By March 1931 the Pact was handed over to the INC for ratification at its Karachi session. Jawaharlal Nehru, perhaps considering the Purna Swaraj declaration of January 1930, was initially opposed to it as he felt it was taking a step back.

Scholars have argued whether the outcome of this session, known as the Karachi Resolution (1931) was a result of a compromise between Gandhi and Nehru. Gandhi wished to have the AICC endorse the Pact. In return, Nehru wished to have encoded in future policies of the INC a commitment to socialism. Specifically, this included protection for industrial workers and agricultural labour, the abolishing of child labour, and free primary education. In any event, the introduction of this commitment to socialism in the resolution had a profound effect in drawing up Part 4 of the Indian Constitution namely the Directive Principles of State Policy. A socialistic pattern of society has become a *sine qua non* for Indian policy makers ever since. Nehru's policies were an amalgam of liberalism, socialism and Gandhism. One notes that there is some overlap between these three -isms. His commitment to socialism of the mild Fabian type followed from his initial admiration of communism as practised in the then Soviet Union. The reasoning was straightforward: colonial rule followed from a repressive form of capitalism where the British became richer and the Indians poorer. In the words of Karl Marx himself writing as far back as 1853, "The devastating effects of English industry, when contemplated with regard to India, a country as vast as Europe, and containing 150 millions of acres, are palpable and confounding. However we, must not forget that they are only the organic results of the whole system of production as it is now constituted. That production rests on the supreme rule of capital. The centralisation of capital is essential to the existence of capital as an independent power. The destructive influence of that centralisation upon the markets of the world does but reveals, in the most gigantic dimensions, the inherent organic laws of political economy now at work in every civilised town."

Any socialist would argue therefore that a fight against a coloniser should be based on a socialistic program which would ensure that the poor would not be exploited. This background is important if one wishes to understand the present-day criticism of Nehru and indeed the entire Nehruvian 'Idea of India' which was based on world economics, politics, and culture of the Western world in the 1930s. The idea follows from Western liberal trends of that time when it was unfashionable to believe in anything that was particularly old or traditional. Modish scepticism and armchair socialism were in vogue. The Anglophile mindset was firmly rooted among some Indian elites—they felt that independence would come easier if one behaved as British as possible and denied one's Indianness at least in its outward manifestations—and Nehru was avowedly of the elite. This pseudo-Anglicisation possibly continues right down to the present day and has much to do with so-called urban liberals (the more extreme ones caricaturised in contemporary woke times as urban Naxals) denying their civilisational roots. It is said that Nehru was English by education, Muslim by culture, and Hindu by accident of birth. Whether Nehru said this about himself or if it originated from one of his critics is far from clear, but it is a vivid description!

The world of 2022 looks at socialism in an entirely different way. Perhaps it is good in theory but not so in practice. What looked like a brave new world became a dingy, dismal descent into a dungeon of despair. The Soviet Union is gone as are its satellites. China is socialist in name only. Some parody of political socialism probably continues in Cuba, North Korea and Kerala. Marxism as a creed is meant for textbooks and TV debates, the latter possibly only in India. Equality for the people today means equality of opportunity to demonstrate what they can achieve and be judged fairly. Socialism based only on economics may take care of the matter in its earliest stages—in a society that is abjectly poor as India indeed was in 1950. A more aspirational society like India of 2022 needs socialism of opportunity, one's chance to rise if one competence so demonstrates. By simplifying and confining lack of opportunity to basic income levels and caste, we remain mired in the past and might just have thrown the baby out with the bath water. We became fixated with this Nehruvian idea of India at least till 1991 when we had a forcible wake-up call but the mindset remains. Even today, people say they voted for someone because they thought he would bring down the prices of everything. This obsession with the price of onions and petrol and gas cylinders has cost us dearly.

On 17 August 1932, the Ramsay Macdonald government in Britain announced the Communal Award which harkened to Morley-Minto. This award gave both Muslims and the SCs separate electorates in the central and provincial legislatures. Gandhi was stricken and he said that giving these separate electorates specifically to the SCs the British were enshrining untouchability in the Constitution. He embarked on a fast unto death. He was able to convey to the public a subtle message that it was caste Hindus who could break these barriers and not any government. Political leaders understood that the best chance to get Gandhi to end his fast was to broker an agreement between Gandhi and Ambedkar. After initial reluctance Ambedkar relented and agreed to negotiate with Gandhi. The result was the Poona Pact (1932). This is a very short document written a quasi-legal style. It contains nine points, most of which refer to technical specifications for representation. The critical portions refer to the fact that separate electorates would be dropped but there would be a system of joint electorates with reserved seats. In other words, only SCs would be candidates in the reserved seats but the electorate would be general. Accordingly, a collegial system and cumulative voting are unnecessary. Significantly, the pact reserved 148 seats for the SCs as opposed to the 70 given to them in the Communal Award. Ambedkar was still not too happy but he agreed to the Pact, nonetheless. This is a key moment in India's constitutional history. From now on, there would be no Constitution where the interests of the SC community could be ignored.

The Government of India Act (1935) was the most significant piece of legislation from the British side during the 1930s pertaining to the future of India. It is written in a legal style, organised around eleven parts and ten schedules with each part divided into chapters. It is said to be one of the longest pieces of legislation passed by the British Parliament. The supremacy of that Parliament was maintained. Enumeration of the subjects at the central and provincial level was undertaken with 59 items kept in the 'Federal List', 54 in the 'Provincial List' and 36 items in a new list called the 'Concurrent List'. This is the first appearance of this latter term, one that causes ambiguity to the present day. Health and education fell squarely in the provincial list, the precursor of today's 'State List'. Dyarchy was abolished in the provinces but restored at the centre with reserved and transferred subjects. A proposed 'All India Federation' would consist of 'eleven Governors' Provinces, six Chief Commissioners' Provinces and those Indian States as would agree to join the Federation. This last aspect was not really fulfilled till 1939 and with the outbreak of World War II, the idea of a federation simply passed into history.

A peculiar feature of the 1935 Act that has implications down till the present is the nature of formation of the 'federation'. Generally, a federation comes into being when individual states come together, giving up their sovereignty, to form a larger union in which the autonomy of the states' is retained in several ways. This is the model prevalent in the U.S.A., Germany, and Canada. In India, the British wanted to retain overall control and so the unitary British India was split into autonomous provinces and then joined together with such

Princely States as might choose to join the federation. The word 'federation' is derived from the Latin *foedus* meaning treaty or agreement. In a federation, states come together voluntarily in order to better their economic prospects or security from foreign invasion. The situation in India was entirely different. The provinces were never separate political entities. This precedent obviously could be invoked again in 1947 and India was defined in our 1950 Constitution as a 'Union of States' and not a 'Federation of States'. The difference is profound as will be explained in Chapter 2.

The 1935 Act proved its worth at the provincial level because it allowed for popularly elected legislatures with the franchise increased to 14 per cent from the hitherto 3 per cent. There were separate electorates for Muslims and Sikhs but not for SCs. After elections in 1937, the INC formed popularly elected ministries in six provinces and these generally proved their worth in terms of efficiency. They brought in basic reforms and an improvement in living standards with respect to health, sanitation, and primary education, especially in the villages. Interestingly, the Muslim vote was divided and the AIML could not get a majority in any of the four Muslim majority provinces Bengal, Punjab, Sind, and the North-West Frontier Province (today's Khyber Pakhtunkhwa). The Unionist party, with Hindus in it, formed the ministry in Punjab.

An interesting side-line in the functioning of the provincial ministries especially where the INC was in power was a natural inclination on the part of elected ministers to develop their social programs for the common people even if it were to convince them that INC was for the poor, and to convey to the British that Indians were capable of governing themselves in a democratic set-up. This inclination even changed to over-enthusiasm and there was some anxiety in the central leadership that these party-men were losing sight of the main aim of the INC which was to secure independence for India. Nehru expressed himself more or less directly to the provincial ministries along these lines. This led to the development of the 'High Command' culture in the INC with an oligarchy issuing all important policy decisions. This high command culture was easy to establish in a country where, to start with, the states did not have autonomy or sovereignty. This culture has now spread to all major political parties in India and defeats the purpose of true federalism, both at the Centre with respect to the States, and in the States with respect to their legislators.

A final aspect of interest in the 1935 document in the present context of this book is that many if not most of the sections that have to do with administrative operations have been adopted by our 1950 Constitution. The often-heard criticism that ours is a cut-and-paste Constitution was also heard in the Constitutional debates. Ambedkar argued that the portions that were borrowed (mostly from the 1935 Act) generally had to do with operational procedures in the executive branch of the government, and that the basic structure and fundamental rights were uniquely ours.

Today the problem might not lie in the core features of our Constitution but with the fact that our bureaucracy might not be able to deliver the policies of the elected representatives to the people in an optimal manner. Are the 1935 provisions suited more to a colonial power overseeing the natives? Should not these procedures and systems be more appropriate to a self-governing people who would appreciate a bureaucracy that is truly a servant of the people, and is a facilitator and an assister rather than a controller and supervisor? The question becomes important because of the wide range of discretionary powers given to India's bureaucrats today. I take this matter up again in Chapter 2. In summary, the 1935 Act played a key role in the drafting of our 1950 Constitution. It might have made

Partition a foregone conclusion, but equally valid is the fact that it made Independence inevitable.

The period 1935 to 1944 was relatively quiet with respect to Constitution drafting in India. Politically speaking, too much was happening within the country and outside of it. Within India, the various provincial governments were getting used to the idea of participating in representative government while the INC leadership was focussed on getting freedom whether dominion status or Purna Swaraj. Discussions on Partition were going on in full swing within the Muslim community, with the United Provinces leading in this respect and the INC defending the idea of an undivided India; the 1937 provincial elections there were hotly contested. Separate electorates continued to seize the popular imagination not only among Muslims but also SCs. The ominous outbreak of World War II in 1939 brought international issues to the fore within the country. The decision of Viceroy Linlithgow to declare India as a belligerent on the side of Britain, without consulting Indian leaders was as clear an indication as any that the British did not consider us worthy of self-rule any time soon. Matters came to a head and in 1942 the Quit India movement was launched. It was only in 1944 when it was becoming clearer that the Allies were "closing the ring" that constitutional questions and independence were addressed again. Gandhi had been released from jail on 6 May 1944.

Several developments with regard to a new Constitution for India occurred in the period 1944-1946. The first of these was M. N. Roy's 1944 document *A Constitution of Free India: A Draft*. This little-known effort is notable because it represents one of the two attempts of the time (the other being the Gandhian Constitution of 1946) that started on a clean slate, in not following the post-1895 documents in a linear, incremental fashion. Since little is known about Roy in today's times, it is interesting to note that he was a philosopher, a strong votary of applying scientific tests to Hindu religious matters and an advocate of Marxism till about 1930. He became critical about the latter after observing the totalitarian nature of Stalin's regime in the U.S.S.R. and yet there is a strong underlying communist shadow in his Constitution. Still, it bears study today because of its novel ideas. Although his effort was largely ignored at the time, his document offers an alternative vision for India and should be considered if there is any new project that might be undertaken to frame a new Constitution for our country.

Roy drafted his document as the founding person of a political party known as the Radical Democratic Party which had a short-lived existence between 1939 and 1948. He felt that the major Indian political parties need not be acting as intermediaries between the people and their colonisers. He felt that there was a political imbroglio and stalemate because these parties were quarrelling not about what should be in the Constitution but rather how it should be enacted. Implicitly he felt that issues like representation for Muslims and SCs would get resolved automatically if the Constitution were to be drafted without being influenced too strongly by the baggage of the previous 50 years. He also felt his Constitution would hasten the British departure from India.

Roy's draft is based on radical decentralisation and direct democracy. It is grounded in what he called 'People's Committees' whose members are elected directly by citizens. Since the number of members envisaged for these Soviets was one fiftieth of the total number of voters in the locality, this would amount to an unwieldy number of 1500-2000 members in each committee if such a system was practised today. His committees had wide powers in local, provincial, and even federal governance, including recall of elected representatives and the right to ask for popular referendums. One continuing problem in India's democracy today is that the people who have voted for an MP or an MLA have absolutely no control over that person (in a technical sense) for a full five years. It is up to the elected representative to have their ear to the ground or not. What is their stand if the inputs they receive from those who elected them are at variance with the political stand they are asked to take by the leadership of their party? An important and probably useful idea in Roy's draft is the separation of legislative and executive authority at the central level. This conjoining has been described as a peculiarity in the Westminster model and will be discussed further in Chapters 2 and 4. It is not clear to the present authors whether combining these functions is a good idea in any democracy. Is too much power concentrated in the hands of too few?

The Roy document is structured around thirteen chapters of which seven deal with a 'Federal Union' composed of provinces that provide members for an elected 'Federal Assembly' and a selected 'Council of State'. There is an obvious flaw here in that the provinces, whether they are from British India or from the Princely States, have a right to join the federation or not. This right was given to these provincial units although they did not have any sort of real autonomy or sovereign existence till that point. This topic has been discussed earlier in the summary of the 1935 Act and it rationalises why modern India was defined as Union of States rather than a federation. The communist influence shows itself in the collective ownership of land, collective farms, and state control of industry. There are other anomalies such as proportional representation and separate electorates for minorities of all varieties. A noteworthy aspect, however, are the very limited powers of the 'Council of State', in other words the Upper House. Members of this body were to be nominated but only to play an advisory role. They had no legislative authority. The nearest analogue to modern India is the Planning Commission or its latest avatar, the Niti Aayog. There is a curious parallel to the U.S.A. here in that the number of members from each province to the Upper House is equal. Another intended or otherwise point of comparison is that the country is referred to everywhere as 'The United States of India' which it really is not because and as explained earlier, sovereign states did not come together to form a true federation. The entire document is a populist and radical departure from previous exercises in constitution making and this might explain why it quickly became of academic interest only. It was probably too 'out-of-the box' for India of 1944.

Other developments in the 1944-1947 period that pertain to the SC community may be profitably discussed together because they were all largely the handiwork of Ambedkar who by now, had become a formidable political figure and the acknowledged leader of that community. The Working Committee of the All India Scheduled Castes Federation passed, in September 1944, twelve resolutions "outlining the safeguards for the Untouchables in the new Constitution". These resolutions appear as Appendix XI is a book authored by Ambedkar in 1945 titled 'What the Congress and Gandhi have done to the Untouchables'. This book is a trenchant critique of Gandhi and the INC. Ambedkar was harsh and bitter about what he felt was Gandhi's patronising attitude towards the SC community. In particular he resented the appellation 'Harijan' that Gandhi gave them. He started with a quotation from Thucydides which says, "It may be in your interest to be our masters, but how can it be ours to be your slaves?" This is an apt summary of a discursive account that runs into more than 500 pages that contain criticisms of many leaders from Dadabhai Naoroji, through Annie Besant to Gandhi himself. The kind-hearted have attempted to whitewash the book by claiming that Ambedkar and Gandhi were but two sides of the same coin and that both were interested in the amelioration of the pathetic condition of the SCs. It was only that the former wanted to work through the legal protection in a Constitution while the latter wanted a moral cleansing of the higher caste communities. We have had 75 years of legal protection for the SC community. It should be clear to all, judging simply from the amount of public discourse even today, that this community still feels excluded to a great extent although there have been a few social advances. Who was right, Ambedkar or Gandhi? Or were both wrong? Is there a third way? Can social problems be addressed legally? Can a Constitution compel anyone to think in a particular manner? This is a worldwide problem and the issues with Blacks, Native Americans and Hispanics in the U.S.A., Azeris in Armenia, Aborigines in Australia, Yezidis in Iraq and Turkey, Tibetans in China, Irish in Britain or Maoris in New Zealand are not very different. Indeed it is the same in any country with a disadvantaged minority.

A short booklet called 'States and Minorities' also authored by Ambedkar appeared in March 1947, that is a few months before Independence and contained the text of a "Constitution of the United States of India". The twelve resolutions of 1944 are rewritten in legal language in the form of a Constitution. Apart from the name proposed for the new country there are two other features here that are vaguely reminiscent of the US constitution. The preamble begins, "We the people of the territories of British India distributed into administrative units called Provinces and Centrally Administered Areas and of the territories of the Indian States with a view *to form a more perfect union* of these territories...". This resembles the preamble of the U.S. which begins, "We the People of the United States, in Order *to form a more perfect Union*...". The other feature of similarity defines nationality, like in the U.S., solely on the basis of birth in the country and through naturalisation. This booklet highlights issues pertaining to the protection of minorities, remedies against invasion of fundamental rights and safeguards for the SCs. The provisions are draconian. Practically no protective measure can be withdrawn or recalled. Ambedkar wanted these provisions to be a part of the fundamental rights in a Constitution so that they could not be easily reversed later by legislation. The document was written on the eve of Independence was a certainty (late 1946) and when it was known that a Constituent Assembly was to be entrusted with the task of framing a future Constitution for the independent country. Partition appeared likely at that time, but by no means certain, and the booklet assumes that India would not be partitioned. The document suffers from the same defect as the demand for separate electorates in that it looks at all aspects of the new nation only through the prism of the SC community. This increased the possibility that it would not be taken fully seriously by the other communities.

The 1944 resolutions, Ambedkar's 1945 book and 1947 booklet lead one to the conclusion that in the view of the SC community no Constitution would be acceptable to them unless it had their consent, and secondly that it would need to recognise them as a distinct element in the polity. The intent was clear: by pushing the idea of separate identity to its most extreme limit, they were merely emulating the AIML in the way it was pushing its Pakistan demand. This is a standard negotiating technique—by placing oneself at an extreme position, one hopes that the compromise equilibrium will settle somewhere near the place where one actually wants to be. Jinnah encouraged them in this lead-up to Partition alleging that SCs were not Hindus, but this was something that even Ambedkar would not accept. To summarise, the twelve resolutions included proportional representation, separate electorates for central and provincial legislatures, reservations in the central and state executives, local governments and in the public services. Intriguingly, the SCs wanted a constitutional provision for separate settlements: they were to be transported from their current dwellings to exclusive settlements. Independent India is indeed fortunate that this particular demand was not conceded. While many of the demands did not clear the gauntlet in the Constituent Assembly, our Constitution nevertheless contains many measures to ensure and protect the SC community nearly in perpetuity. These are discussed in Chapters 2 and 4.

There is an interesting twist to Ambedkar's changes in stance on separate electorates during various periods in time. When they were first mooted by the AIML and during the Simon Commission days in the late 1920s he criticised them severely based on the logical premise that ghettoisation of SCs would condemn them to permanent minority status. Later, he swung around in support of such electorates but then compromised with Gandhi in the 1932 Poona Pact in which the seats were reserved but not the electorate. Much later he said that he had been practically blackmailed into the Pact because he had been given the impression that Gandhi's life was hanging in the balance with his hunger strike. In the 1944 resolutions he hardened his stance again and demanded separate electorates. It is believed these changes in position were both tactical and strategic. However, after the generally poor showing by SCs in the separate electorates in the 1946 elections many of Ambedkar's demands on separate electorates lost momentum. After nearly a century, one should only consider the actions of these larger-than-life personalities with a certain consideration. Their times were momentous. Ordinary men and women were doing extraordinary things. It was not clear how the British, skilled in statecraft and politics of the most subtle and devious varieties, would react in any particular circumstance. Above all, Purna Swaraj was the undoubted aim of all these towering personalities. Today, one need neither look upon Gandhi and Ambedkar as gods nor regard the Constitution that they and others inspired and drafted as a holy book. It was what any group of well-read and intelligent men and women, mostly lawyers, thought was best for the India *of that time*. Our duty today is to think about what is best for an India that is 75 years older, and hopefully wiser. One should respect the past but not worship it. Worshipping the past has become endemic in India and mostly it is an excuse to not think seriously enough about the future.

The Gandhian Constitution of Free India (1946) was written by Shriman Narayan Agarwal, an economist who was a believer in Gandhi's ideas. Judging from the introspective preface that Gandhi wrote for this document it appears that he had more than a casual interest in the matter. Rather, he seems to have been closely following its progress while it was being written. He probably approved of almost everything there in terms of broad philosophy and methodology although he might not have liked to be held responsible for each and every word in the document. The thesis is simple and instinctive: India has a rich and ancient tradition and it was an advanced civilisation for thousands of years. It had experimented with many forms of government. It was a laboratory for trying out new constitutional ideas. There were local centres of authority, states, kingdoms, and empires in its long history. All of these were based on grassroots democracy which tapered upwards with greater authority given to the rulers, who in the end were under the umbrella of *dharma* which is the moral compass and its balance with *artha,* the realpolitik of the world. Agarwal felt that only a purely indigenous constitution that drew in inspiration from Indian culture and civilisation would work for us in the long run. There was no need according to him for us to have an inferiority complex vis-à-vis Westerners and to attempt to blindly copy their governance structures and institutions.

The 60-page document is divided into twenty two chapters that included duties along with rights and delineated basic principles of a highly decentralised form of governance. It is notable in that it advocates the setting up of village panchayats as core units. These ascend through panchayats for taluks, districts, states and ultimately the centre, with the leader of the top panchayat essentially acting as the CEO of the country. Gandhi's ultimate idea was for the end of the state as such and with the global ascendancy of morality, political states as we know them today would cease to exist. All this is, of course, utopian in the extreme, which is why the Gandhian Constitution was not seriously considered in the drafting of the Constitution of Independent India. However, certain features like the panchayats do find a mention in our Directive Principles. Village panchayats were given wide powers that included judicial ones too. The conjoining of duties with rights was a very important part of Gandhi's philosophy. The document states bluntly that rights are contingent on the performance of duties. We Indians are all too eager to talk about our rights and freedoms today. We claim we are a democracy. Anything can be said in the name of free speech and freedom of expression. None of these rights are really ours in an absolute sense. They are consequent and flow from all of us performing our duties as conscientious citizens.

Any system of governance that is decentralised as the ideal Gandhian state will perforce end up with a weak centre. Is it possible that such systems, which were indeed in vogue in ancient and medieval India, rendered the country more prone to attacks from invaders from the outside? Dharma devoid of artha becomes ineffective. One needs artha to maintain dharma. The essence of geopolitical power today is a strong military and a stronger economy coupled with a large land area and long coastline. Military and economic strength can only follow from an accumulation of power at the central or federal level. How does one reconcile this with the moralistic theme of Gandhi's Rama Rajya and village-based panchayat system, knowing as we do that India's age-old civilisation is still strongly anchored to these roots? Given India's diversity which can even lead to centrifugal distortions, if unchecked, how does one balance a strong Centre with a variety of prosperous and confident States? This is the biggest question facing our Constitution today.

There were several constitutional developments in rapid succession between late 1945 and early 1947 with the imminent likelihood of Independence. What led the British to conclude that they would need to leave India in some way or another, and that too, quickly, is a matter of conjecture: it almost certainly was not exclusively a result of the freedom struggle spearheaded by the INC although this might have been a contributing cause. In the background of great power fatigue, it is more likely that their decision was the culmination of several events that occurred within a relatively short period of time. World War II had left the British economically crippled. The INA mutiny and the Red Fort trials brought a sense of urgency home to the British and the spectre of Bose hung heavy over the political spectrum. The demand for Pakistan carried with it an implied threat of violence if this were not granted. It might simply have been a case of imperial overstretch. India had plainly become an economic liability. In any case, they decided to leave and this was greatly facilitated by the assumption of power of Attlee's Labour Party government in Britain in mid-1945. What was not known was whether this decision would translate into dominion status or Purna Swaraj, and secondly whether or not India would be divided on the basis of religion.

The constitutional developments in 1945-1947 are best taken up together. The Sapru Committee Report (December 1945), Benegal Narsing Rau's Outline of a New Constitution (January 1946), and the Cabinet Mission Plan (May 1946) were all premised on the fact that India would not be partitioned. Therefore, they are largely of academic interest today, but they do contain ideas that might become useful in the future. The Sapru report was the handiwork of a non-political committee of thirty members that was constituted because of the widespread feeling that independence was being delayed because of the intractable nature of the differences between the INC and the AIML. There might have been some fear of a civil war even. The report rejected the demand for Pakistan and asked for the setting up of a constitution-drafting body that would have an *equal* representation of Muslims and caste Hindus. One notes that the Muslims, who constituted 24 per cent of the population of undivided India (Hindus were 69 per cent) had been given a sizable up-weightage in such a scheme. Much of the document pertained to minority rights. The question of universal rights was considered but nothing specific was spelled out. Whether these rights should be divided into justiciable and non-justiciable ones, was also considered in the deliberations. The AIML was hostile to this report because it did not support the creation of Pakistan. The INC in turn largely ignored it.

Shortly thereafter B. N. Rau's outline of a new Constitution appeared. Rau was on the staff of the Governor General's secretariat when the report was prepared, and one might reasonably surmise that his outline was a test balloon floated by the British to avoid partition. The impending provincial elections to be fought on the basis of communal electorates might have been a catalyst in the drafting of this short document of nineteen pages. The main recommendation was that India be defined as a 'Commonwealth' consisting of three units: Hindustan Federation; Pakistan Federation; Indian States and Tribal Areas. The commonwealth would come together for the limited purposes of defence, external affairs, communications, and customs or in other words it defined the political boundaries of the Indian state. Most of the subsequent provisions naturally dealt with federalism. The idea of the Indian sub-continent being defined as a federation has been raised sporadically after independence by idealistic persons, but it is unclear if this is feasible or even desirable. The European Community today approximates to Rau's concept of a federation, but it is limited to the absence of passport controls and customs inspection at the national borders; the borders still remain sacrosanct. The EU Parliament in Brussels operates independent of the legislatures of its member states. Relations between India and Pakistan post-Independence have been so troubled and acrimonious that no reasonable person would think about a federation as long as the latter retains its present geographical boundaries. However, with increasing and better communications systems today, and with Asian economies generally improving, an informal border with Bangladesh need not be ruled out in the future.

Rau's report had a substantial influence on the Cabinet Mission Plan (1946) also known as the Cripps Mission Plan, leading one to believe that it originated from the British. As mentioned above, the Labour Party had won the election in Britain in May 1945 and that September the new government of Attlee declared its intent to grant independence to India and with that in mind began the process of creating a Constituent Assembly that would frame the Constitution of the new country. The Cabinet Mission was sent to India to facilitate this process. They met with the principals in Simla. The meeting was not a success. It is reported that Jinnah said that the dreams of Hindus might turn into nightmares for the

Muslims of India if the INC was allowed to have its way and that the Muslims must have their own group deciding their own Constitution. Patel is said to have countered that they were in Simla to discuss the fate of a united India and not to break it into pieces. Given these intransigent positions, the British came up with a set of compromise proposals which they hoped would avoid Partition if accepted by the two adversaries. The 9-page document was organised around twenty four points that were based on a federal structure of British India and the Princely States. Each of the provinces and states would be units that came together to form the federation. This was fine as far as it seemed so and the INC and the AIML might have come around, who knows, but then the Commission came up with the cherry on the icing: a further grouping was proposed. Provinces and Princely states would be free to form sub-groups within themselves having legislatures and executives with substantial autonomy. The concern grew within the INC that this further sub-grouping would be only on a religious basis and would surely lead to two 'countries' within one. The AIML was, however, adamant on groupings and there was a complete breakdown. Jinnah took matters into his hands with Direct Action Day, a brutal call to street violence, on 16 August 1946 and the die was cast. In summary, the Cripps Mission was the final half-hearted attempt by the British to avoid Partition, but it was too late. The damage done by them in the past, starting with Morley-Minto, then with Montford and finally the 1935 Act, had come home to roost. Did they actually want Partition in order that an independent India not to become too strong? Did they realise that the new Pakistan areas would be of enormous geostrategic value in the imminent Cold War and that a client state in the form of Pakistan would be a better option for them than a powerful and independent undivided India? A necessary outcome of the Cripps Mission was the formation of an interim government for India with Nehru as the (selected not elected) Prime Minister and Patel (elected by the CWC as Prime Minister but not selected by Gandhi) as the Home Minister. Pre-independence, the Cripps Plan was mentioned in the Constituent Assembly debates but these mentions were largely critical. The whole Cripps exercise simply illustrates a larger truth that it is just not in human nature to surrender power easily.

Rau's 'Notes on Fundamental Rights' appeared in September 1946 and it was very important during the drafting of the Constitution. A Bill of Rights or some equivalent is essential in the Constitution of any democratic country. As mentioned earlier, rights may be in the justiciable and non-justiciable categories. In the former, specific action is required by the state to enforce its implementation, for example the right to not be arrested unless it is according to the due process of law. The latter category is more of a wish list of ideal situations for example, the state endeavouring to ensure for its citizens the right to maintenance in old age and during sickness. Rights in the former category are largely found in the Fundamental Rights of our Constitution while the latter generally figure in the Directive Principles. The manner in which these rights are handled in several world constitutions are different. The way in which they have been incorporated into our Constitution, including the possibility of judicial review of a constitutional provision, is a subtle matter and is discussed briefly in Chapter 2. It is, however, largely beyond the scope of this book and has been discussed extensively elsewhere. Notably, any provisions/rights regarding SCs, other backward communities, languages and minorities have become sensitive and emotional issues today. They are also highly politicised and polarised. They need careful study. That certain aspects may lie beyond the domain of what could be changed in the future is a matter of concern. The only thing that is endless is time itself, and not countries and their constitutions which are human creations. Too many in India feel we have outgrown these reservations.

A curious interlude in this account is the appearance in March 1947 of what is known as the Manipur State Constitution. Independence had been announced, and Mountbatten had just arrived in India. By early April, he realised that Partition had become a foregone conclusion and the matter of the Princely States suddenly came to a head. These states were informed that they would need to accede to either India or Pakistan after independence and that the question of their independent sovereignty did not arise. Many indeed signed the instruments of accession and the overwhelmingly large majority of States within the landmass comprising post-1947 India acceded to India because of the efforts of Patel and V. P. Menon. All this is well-known. What is not so well-known is that the Princely State of Manipur in the far northeast of the country, with a population of just over 5 lakh inhabitants, wished to remain independent. The Maharaja, Bodhchandra Singh considering the democratic aspirations of his people got a Constitution drafted and adopted by May 1947. Manipur would become a Constitutional Monarchy like Britain. The details of the document are unimportant. After Independence, there was increasing pressure on the Maharaja to sign the accession instrument and join India. He did this and the Manipur Constitution completed its short life in 1949.

The final step in our long and tortuous journey from 1858 was taken with the Indian Independence Act (1947) which obtained royal assent in July of that year. 14/15 August was fixed as the date on which the British government would hand over all responsibility to two new dominions India and Pakistan. The overwhelmingly Muslim majority provinces of Sind, N.W.F.P. and Baluchistan would go to Pakistan in their entirety, the last with some hiccups, for Baluchistan stayed independent for nearly a year after 1947. The provinces of Bengal and Punjab, as created in the 1935 Government of India Act would cease to exist and would be partitioned on the basis of majority populations, mostly district wise. The fate of a few eastern border enclaves was to be determined by referendum. Pakistan was to consist of western and eastern halves. The new countries would be completely independent of Britain and of each other. The Princely States would have to accede to one of the two dominions based on the principles of geographical contiguity, majority populations and the wishes of the ruler. The 22-page Act was written in a legal style and organised around twenty sections and three schedules. As a dominion, India still had a link to the British crown. To remove this link which would trace the country's independence to the Indian Independence Act (1947) the final draft of our Constitution was not put up for approval to the British Parliament as this above act was itself repealed through Article 395, the very last in our Constitution that states: "The Indian Independence Act, 1947, and the Government of India Act, 1935, together with all enactments amending or supplementing the latter Act, but not including the Abolition of Privy Council Jurisdiction Act, 1949, are hereby repealed." Thus all constitutional links with Britain were severed on 24 January 1950.

It is sobering to read Patel's own account of the passage of the Indian Independence Act (1947) by the British Parliament in his speech to our Constituent Assembly on 10 October 1949:

> *I give you this inner history which nobody knows. I agreed to Partition as a last resort when we had reached a stage when we could have lost all. We had five or six members in the Government, the Muslim League members. They had already established themselves as members who had come to partition the country. At that stage*

we agreed to Partition; we decided that Partition could be agreed upon on the terms that the Punjab should be partitioned—they wanted the whole of it—that Bengal should be partitioned—they wanted Calcutta and the whole of it. Mr. Jinnah did not want a truncated Pakistan, but he had to swallow it. We said that these two provinces should be partitioned. I made a further condition that in two months' time power should be transferred and an Act should be passed by Parliament in that time if it was guaranteed that the British Government would not interfere with the question of the Indian States. We said, "we will deal with that question; leave it to us; you take no sides. Let paramountcy be dead; you do not directly or indirectly try to revive it in any manner. You do not interfere. We shall settle our problem. The Princes are ours and we shall deal with them." On those conditions we agreed to Partition and on those conditions the Bill in Parliament was passed in two months, agreed to by all the three parties. Show me any instance in the history of the British Parliament when such a Bill was passed in two months. But this was done. It gave birth to this Parliament.

And so, with this patchwork of Indian and British documents spread over fifty years, with the growing shadow and ultimate shock of Partition, and with only their good sense and basic honesty to guide them did our Constitution makers and drafters begin their weighty assignment.

CHAPTER TWO

INDIA 1.0

THE REPUBLIC ON 26 JANUARY 1950 AND THEREAFTER

However good a Constitution may be, if those who are implementing it are not good, it will prove to be bad. However bad a Constitution may be, if those implementing it are good, it will prove to be good.
—B R Ambedkar

THE Constituent Assembly, set up following the Cripps Mission, held its first meeting on 9 December 1946 when independence was imminent, hopefully to be a reality by 1948. While there was a foreboding about Partition, what was not clear was the form and shape it would take especially with respect to Punjab and Bengal, possibly even Assam. The stand of the Princely States was also unclear.

Till then the freedom struggle was predominantly limited to the provinces of British India and the status of the Princely States after Independence had not been seriously considered. The Assembly discussions between December 1946 and August 1947 reflected these ambiguities. They were different from the debates after that time when all the above unknowns had crystallised and the details of Independence had become abundantly clear. The pre-Independence discussions were additionally influenced by the advancement of the date of Independence to August 1947 by the viceroy Mountbatten who assumed charge in February 1947.

Accordingly, this chapter is set out in three sections.

The first has to do with the formalities of organisation of the Constituent Assembly, which was the sovereign body of India till 26 January 1950, and its pre-Independence discussions which were perforce of a general nature because of the unknown factors mentioned above. Yet, even these general discussions were relevant to framing broad guidelines. The second section has to do with the debates in the post-Independence phase, that is, between 20 August 1947 and 25 January 1950. These debates, which included three readings of a Draft Constitution, were of an altogether different nature with the Assembly having to complete a specific job within a self-imposed timeline. This stage involved in-depth discussions in the second half of 1947 followed by a parsing, clause by clause, in 1949, of the Draft Constitution prepared in 1948 by a small committee headed by Ambedkar. The last step was the adoption of the document in late 1949 by the Assembly.

The third section has to do with the functioning of the Constitution and the three limbs of the State defined by it, the legislative, executive and judiciary, after 26 January 1950 till the present time. This period has witnessed amplification of problems identified but not completely resolved in the debates, and the attempts of successive governments to give expression to these concerns usually through amendments which tried to address real and perceived deficiencies in the original document. In some cases these amendments were in the nature of ad hoc fixes. In others, they regrettably had the effect of changing the very intent and ethos of the original document. In yet, other cases, long standing concerns have still not been addressed satisfactorily leading to basic questions as to whether our Constitution is in itself fully adequate to guide the governance of a large and complex entity like India. A Constitution should signify vision rather than mission, intent rather than content and method, which are properly taken up by the laws of the land. It should be relatively time independent and not need many amendments even in a fast-paced country like the India of 2022. How good has our 1950 Constitution been in these respects?

We shall break this chronological sequence of happenings and events by first recounting the sessions of the Constituent Assembly on 14 and 15 August 1947. While a date is only a marker in the passage of time, the brief sessions held on the midnight of freedom have more than a symbolic and emotional meaning.

There were four speakers in the midnight session and the contribution of each is noteworthy for different reasons. These four short speeches still reverberate especially in the context of present-day inadequacies in our governance and compel us to introspect. The speakers were, in order, Rajendra Prasad the president of the Constituent Assembly, Nehru the prime minister who moved the resolution, Chaudhari Khaliquzzaman the seconder and Sarvepalli Radhakrishnan the supporting speaker. It is usually Nehru's 'tryst with destiny' speech during this midnight session which is remembered. The three other speeches need to find a mention in our textbooks for they are as significant as Nehru's. Clearly, everyone rose to the solemnity of the occasion.

The first point to note is the prominent appearance of God in two of the speeches. Prasad made several direct references to the divine in his short address. The speech itself began with "humble thanks to the Almighty Power that shapes the destinies of men and nations". He went on to the fact that Gandhi represented the "undying spirit in our culture and make-up which has kept India alive". It is important to notice the strong civilisational undertones in this statement. Specifically, he said that Gandhi's weapon was his "faith in God" to which Indians should prove true and which they should not, in their moment of triumph "give up or minimise the value of" and further that Gandhi's was a weapon which had also "proved its efficacy". I shall revert later in Chapter 3 to the idea that Gandhi was primarily a devout and deeply religious Hindu who took his religion into the political sphere. More poignantly, Prasad referred to Partition in terms of the divine for he said that "the country which was meant by God and Nature to be one, stands divided today". These comments are all extremely significant for here is a direct reference to the fact that nationhood in India has a strong geographical basis and that to even think of two nations within one geographical entity that has been called Bhāratavarsha since time immemorial is nothing short of sacrilege.

Radhakrishnan reiterated Prasad's last point in his impromptu address when he stated that "the body politic may be divided but the body historic lives on", a comment that was greeted with cheers. He, like Prasad, referred to God directly when he said, that "in this great time of our history we should bear ourselves humbly before God". The civilisational aspect was also introduced when he attempted to define what a civilisation represented. He said, "Civilisation is a thing of the spirit, it is not something external, solid and mechanical. It is the dream in the people's hearts. It is the inward aspiration of the people's souls. It is the imaginative interpretation of the human life and the perception of the mystery of human existence. That is what civilisation actually stands for. We should bear in mind these great ideals which have been transmitted to us across the ages."

Nehru and Khaliquzzaman did not refer to God, directly or indirectly, in their speeches. At most, Nehru acknowledged that India was an ancient country. This is about all he was willing to concede and this at least should be borne in mind by those of his acolytes who claim today that India did not exist before 1947 and that the Constitution is their holy book.

Pakistan might have begun in 1947 but not India.

According to Khaliquzzaman, the events of that night were a culmination of the efforts of the previous 100 years. He did not go further back than that.

Partition indeed provided the sombre backdrop to Independence and all four speakers in the midnight session referred to it prominently. Some modern commentators have even said that 15 August 1947 should not be celebrated as Independence Day but rather as the day when India was divided and, as such, hardly worthy of celebration. Possibly keeping in mind such sentiments, which are commonplace enough today, the present government announced recently that 14 August shall in future be observed as Partition Horrors Remembrance Day, a step seemingly in the right direction.

Horrors, injustices and mass genocides do take place and have always taken place in the past. This is in the very nature of history. It is estimated that at least 50 million Native American Indians were wiped out over 500 years by white people in what is present day U.S.A. and Canada. More recent are the mass killings and pogroms in the Ottoman Empire, Czarist Russia, Armenia, Nazi occupied Europe and Soviet Russia in World War II, in Kampuchea, Rwanda and, closer home, in East Pakistan in 1971. The ability of today's Indians, who belong to a generation that neither initiated nor participated in the terrible happenings accompanying Partition, to cope with these traumas can only come about by a full chronicling of the events in question. This would be prerequisite for accepting and admitting they were wrong, that they should never be repeated. Above all, attempts to whitewash the killings and mass migrations by secular central governments through bland, sanitised textbooks afflicted with selective amnesia and by Bollywood in their stereotyped portrayals of Muslims specifically and also minorities in general would surely provoke a strong counter reaction now, even if they did not previously. Our invidious history textbooks are strongly Delhi centric: all of us are taught about Khiljis, Lodhis, Bahmanis and Moghuls, very little about Ahoms, Chalukyas, Cheras, Cholas, Marathas, Pandyas and Satavahanas, all mighty dynasties many of which lasted much longer than the Mughals. The word *Hindustan* is mentioned as being of Persian provenance but the word *Bhārat* is not mentioned as being of Vedic provenance.

Both Germany and Japan committed indescribable horrors in World War II but while the former did not shy away from a complete public discussion including teaching children at the high school level about the atrocities of the Holocaust, the latter did not undertake such soul-searching with regard to its treatment of Chinese, Koreans and Allied prisoners-of-war. This denial has cost the Japanese people dearly in terms of its effect on the mental make-up of its future generations and has clouded that country's relationship with China. In contrast, the repressive treatment by the U.S.A. of its small Japanese-American community in California during World War II was acknowledged albeit and reparations made after 40 years. South Africa began, at Nelson Mandela's initiative, a series of truth-and-reconciliation committees, immediately after the dismantling of apartheid in that country. This kind of open admission of past sins is extremely important because reconciliation can come only after the truth is admitted. Conservatively, it is estimated that around a million people were killed during Partition, mainly in Punjab. We cannot get away from these bald facts especially in other parts of India which were largely unaffected and more Muslims remained than migrated. The specious argument that Partition Horrors Remembrance Day is unnecessary (while the truth and reconciliation committees in South Africa were) because the participants are no longer alive is as trivial as the original sin was grave. Whitewashing the horrors of Partition has done absolutely no justice to the people of India. There is a strange argument going around today that remembering Partition is somehow antagonistic to the development of a modern, progressive country. Nothing could be further from the truth. In the German concentration camp memorials and in Hitler's birthplace there are large signs that say "Nie Wieder" which means "Never Again". It is important for the future health of India that the horrors of Partition are specifically marked and remembered. Human memory is notoriously short and while many may forget, the ones who were directly affected cannot, even after several generations.

Let us return to the midnight session. Nehru's sober words that we were not redeeming the Lahore pledge, our "tryst with destiny", in any "full measure" but rather only "very substantially" is enough evidence that he was distraught by Partition. Radhakrishnan expressed the same anguish but there was a distinct sense of introspection and self-criticism in his comments, perhaps a latent truth-and-reconciliation, for he asked Indians whether they were not in themselves responsible for Partition. He openly acknowledged the intent of those in Britain who sought to divide India. His words are so potent and at the same time so poignantly tragic that I feel compelled to reproduce this extract in full. Significantly, it is not specific to Hindus or Muslims. It applies to all Indians:

> *You, Mr. President, referred to the sadness in our hearts, to the sorrow which also clouds our rejoicings. May I say that we are in an essential sense responsible for it also though not entirely. From 1600, Englishmen have come to this country-priests and nuns, merchants and adventurers, diplomats and statesmen, missionaries and idealists. They bought and sold, marched and fought, plotted and profited, helped and healed. The greatest among them wished to modernise the country, to raise its intellectual and moral*

standards, its political status. They wished to regenerate the whole people. But the small among them worked with sinister objective. They tried to increase the disunion in the country, made the country poorer, weaker and more disunited. They also have had their chance now. The freedom we are attaining is the fulfilment of this dual tendency among British administrators. While India is attaining freedom, she is attaining it in a manner which does not produce joy in the hearts of people or a radiant smile on their faces. Some of those who were charged with the responsibility for the administration of this country, tried to accentuate communal consciousness and bring about the present result which is a logical outcome of the policies adopted by the lesser minds of Britain. But I would never blame them. Were we not victims, ready victims, so to say, of the separatist tendencies foisted on us? Should we not now correct our national faults of character, our domestic despotism, our intolerance which has assumed the different forms of obscurantism, of narrow-mindedness, of superstitious bigotry? Others were able to play on our weakness because we had them. I would like therefore to take this opportunity to call for self-examination, for a searching of hearts. We have gained but we have not gained in the manner we wished to gain and if we have, not done so, the responsibility is our own. And when this pledge says that we have to serve our country, we can best serve our country by removing these fundamental defects which have prevented us from gaining the objective of a free and united India.

While he was talking about the two new countries, Radhakrishnan might well have been speaking about Hindus and Muslims in the India of 2022 when he said that, "Political divisions, physical partitions, are external but the psychological divisions are deeper. The cultural cleavages are the more dangerous. We should not allow them to grow. What we should do is to preserve those cultural ties, those spiritual bonds which knit our peoples together into one organic whole." Unfortunately, the cultural cleavages between Hindus and Muslims have widened and deepened but these chasms have been created not by the people but by domestic politicians and aggressive and proselytising foreign-based organisations. We have still not realised that we are a people that are capable of being divided easily, the so called Jaichand syndrome. In this context, only a return to our cultural and spiritual moorings can save us as a united and economically strong India.

Nehru's well-known and short speech struck all the high notes and is marked by idealism and hope. He attempted to define the nature of India without using the words 'spirit' or 'spiritual' and in the view of this author, fell short of a meaningful enough definition of nationhood when he concluded that "At the dawn of history India started on her unending quest, and trackless centuries are filled with her striving and the grandeur of her successes and, her failures. Through good and ill fortune alike she has never lost sight of that quest or forgotten the ideals which gave her strength." With any degree of objectivity after 75 years, after these events have crossed over from politics and current affairs into history, one might ask what exactly do Nehru's words mean? Does a young Indian born after say 2000 relate to these sentiments? Does he or she even understand them? How does a failure become grand? What exactly is the quest? Why does this quest never seem to end? What are the ideals to which young Indians should aspire towards? Nehru correctly maintained that with freedom came responsibility. However, in his very next sentence he said that the responsibility "rests upon this Assembly, a sovereign body representing the sovereign people of India." This emphasis is, in my view, sadly misdirected and it has led to a widely held view that the people have all the rights while the government has all the responsibilities, in other words the *maa baap* culture.

Nehru draws the people into the exercise up to the stage where he makes an "appeal to join us with faith and confidence in this great adventure" with "us" being the Constituent Assembly. He reinforces all this in that his words are directed "to the people of India, whose representatives we are". In the extreme, these words might even be taken as patronising. Being a citizen of an independent democracy carries with it a solemn responsibility and one that cannot be abrogated to elected representatives. The strength of say the US democracy is its extremely concise Constitution which has hardly been amended over 250 years and has inculcated in its citizens a strong sense of individual and collective responsibility. Responsibilities do not follow from rights. Rights follow from responsibilities that are honoured by the people. This is the real lesson that our leaders, be they politicians, bureaucrats, judges, academics, industrialists or sports people, indeed anyone to whom the common man or woman looks up, should be conveying, not basking in self-satisfaction that they are the intermediaries between the people and their destinies.

Khaliquzzaman, the seconder of Nehru's resolution, was an interesting personality in that he was a prominent member of the AIML and an important figure in the freedom struggle. He came from the socially privileged sections of Lucknow and was well known in the United Provinces. He admitted freely that he had played a major role in the creation of Pakistan. He was sanguine enough about the status and position of Muslims in independent India and yet not bigoted about Hindus as some other leaders in the AIML. Unlike them he opted to stay on in India. He was a confidant of Jinnah who saw in him a champion of Muslim interests in post-Partition India. With Partition becoming a reality, it is clear that the Constituent Assembly wanted a Muslim speaker in the 14 August session and as an AIML member Khaliquzzaman might have been preferred to say someone like Azad from the INC. His speech is marked by a certain pragmatism as to how Muslims who opted to remain in India ought to conduct themselves. Most important were his words that "We know that great responsibility rests on this Assembly and that is of framing a Constitution, which would be acceptable *not only to the minorities* but also to all the people of the country, to the poor and to the common man and through which we may serve the people of India." By acknowledging this Khaliquzzaman, a Muslim, was affirming the fundamental reality of independent India namely that it was not going to be a country meant predominantly for the minority community. These words are in sharp contrast to what Manmohan Singh as a Sikh Prime Minister famously (even comically) said many years later in 2006 that, "Muslims must have first claim on resources"!

Khaliquzzaman's life took a bizarre twist shortly thereafter. Events in Punjab and Bengal came to his doorstep and even affected members of his immediate family one of whom, a distinguished lawyer, was threatened with his life. His family started crumbling with some opting to stay on and some migrating to Pakistan. This was not uncommon in wealthier Muslim families of north India. He developed a conviction that Partition, for which he had fought ardently, was going to be positively injurious to Indian Muslims and a disaster in the longer term for the Muslims in Pakistan. All these internal contradictions caused him to move to Pakistan by late 1947. He was given titular positions there but politically marginalised and never really got over Partition. He died in 1973 a sad and broken man.

Radhakrishnan's interesting speech touched on many unexpected points. For a start, it was by far the longest speech in the midnight session for the reason that as the last speaker he was instructed to speak till exactly 30 seconds before midnight when the members were to take the pledge affirming their loyalty to the new country. It was also an impromptu speech for like Khaliquzzaman he was only told that he would be speaking after he entered the Assembly. Under these conditions, which would have made most seasoned speakers quake, he carried his speech off with aplomb. For a start he praised the British for leaving India with a modicum of grace and without armed warfare and complimented their government for shepherding the Independence Act. About the formalities themselves he said that "the transition is being effected with the least bitterness, with utterly no kind of hatred at all. The very fact that we are appointing Lord Mountbatten as the Governor-General of India, shows the spirit of understanding and friendliness in which this whole transition is being effected." Indeed, the decision to appoint Mountbatten the last Viceroy of imperial India as the first Governor-General of independent India, the first decision of the Constituent Assembly of independent India on the morning of 15 August 1947, shows the remarkable sagacity and maturity of a people who had lived in servitude and serfdom for at least 150 years. However, Radhakrishnan saved his punch lines till the end when he said that:

> *Our opportunities are great but let me warn you that when power outstrips ability, we will fall on evil days. We should develop competence and ability which would help us to utilise the opportunities which are now open to us. From tomorrow morning from midnight today we cannot throw the blame on the Britisher. We have to assume the responsibility ourselves for what we do.*

Both points are significant, regrettably so in hindsight. Power has outstripped ability everywhere in modern India because of shoddy systems, dishonest implementation of policies, personal greed, corruption, dereliction of duty and a general lack of connection between inputs and outputs, effort and reward, merit and recognition and a total failure to look forward and move with the times. The second point about not blaming the coloniser for our woes was reinforced continuously by others in the Assembly debates. Ambedkar said for example on 26 November 1949 when the final draft Constitution was being accepted that "by Independence, we have lost the excuse of blaming the British for anything going wrong. If hereafter things go wrong, we will have nobody to blame but ourselves." In general, all our great leaders from that time seem to have been only too aware of our tendency to blame others for any uncomfortable situation that we find ourselves. At a trivial level, we are very fond of saying that something is not our job. How many times has one heard someone in an office saying that the concerned person is not at his or her desk or is on leave? At a national level we blame Britishers, Americans, Chinese, Hindus, Muslims, Brahmins, Babur, Aurangzeb, the caste system, in fact just about anyone or anything for everything we perceive as wrong today. The question is what are we as stakeholders of this ancient land doing about it? White Americans do not blame slave-owners of the 18th and 19th century for the problems they face today in their inability to integrate Blacks fully into their country. They are continuously trying to do something about it. The Germans do not blame the Nazis, in other words their parents and grandparents, for the loss of their eastern provinces after World War II. They have accepted officially and psychologically that East Prussia, Pomerania and Silesia will not be a part of Germany in the future and have moved on. Finding a scapegoat is the easiest way of avoiding constructive action.

With this backdrop, the members took the pledge that affirmed their intent to dedicate themselves "in all humility to the service of India and her people to the end that this ancient land attains her rightful place in the world". There was no attempt to deny the fact that we are an ancient land. In hindsight, this appears to be a consolation for us Indians.

A. Pre-independence Assembly Debates

For the sake of the record, we note that the Constituent Assembly held its first session on 9 December 1946 with Sachidananda Sinha as *pro tem* President. J. B. Kripalani conducted Sinha to the chair and after invoking divine blessings, inducted him into his post. In his two-day tenure, Sinha commented about the Swiss, French, American, Canadian and South African constitutions as role models. Indeed, he hinted that we needed to look at constitutions other than the British in framing our own. On 11 December, Prasad was unanimously elected President of the Assembly and continued in that role till 26 January 1950 when he assumed office as the first President of the Republic of India. He made an outstanding President of the Constitutional Assembly, speaking little, allowing everyone to speak but making firm rulings with an occasional touch of humour. Chairing a committee of 15 members for a few hours takes its toll on many of us. Imagine chairing a committee of 300 opinionated members over 165 days spread out across a period of three years!

In the pre-Independence Assembly there were 389 members of which 292 were representatives of the provinces, 93 represented the Princely States and four were from the Chief Commissioner provinces of Delhi, Ajmer-Merwara, Coorg and British Baluchistan. The members were elected by the provincial assemblies. There were 208 members representing the INC and 73 the AIML of whom just 28 participated in the Assembly debates. The others demanded a separate Constituent Assembly for Muslims and abstained from the sessions. After Independence, the membership was reduced to 299 with the departure of members to Pakistan and there were some additions from the Princely States. There were 15 women who contributed to 2 per cent of the debates. These included G. Durgabai, Sarojini Naidu, Annie Mascarene, Renuka Ray and Begum Aizaz Rasool. The elections were remarkably free of regionalism. For example, Ambedkar was elected from Bengal and served in that capacity till Independence when his constituency became a part of East Pakistan and he then moved to Bombay. Sarojini Naidu was elected from Bihar, N. Madhava Rao from Orissa and Radhakrishnan from the United Provinces.

From the varied and diverse membership, several categories of speakers may be identified and they contributed to different facets of the matter of the Constitution. A large number of political leaders figure prominently, many of them with a legal background. High profile national leaders like Ambedkar, Nehru, and Patel moved the major resolutions. Ambedkar did most of the heavy lifting for Nehru who, however, participated vigorously in the sessions where he was present. Patel contributed substantially to the matter of the Princely States and the role of the bureaucracy in particular and the executive wing in general. He also played the role of a disciplinarian when the discussions went off tangent or when members persisted with unreasonable viewpoints. He was capable of tough talk. Defending higher salaries and privileges for Indian Civil Service officers appointed by the British during the Raj vis-à-vis the newly appointed Indian Administrative Service officers he said, "As I told you, this agreement and these guarantees were circulated to the provinces and to individual members of the Service. Their agreement has been taken and signed by the provinces. They have agreed—both of them. Can you go behind these things? Have morals no place in the new Parliament? Is that how we are going to begin our new freedom? I have seen people who express their opinion about this Service [the ICS] as they used to talk in old fashion when 50 or 60 per cent were British element who dominated the Service and our members of the Service had hardly any freedom to express their opinion and they were not independent. We have difficult times ahead. We are talking here under security kept in very difficult circumstances. These people are the instruments. Remove them and I see nothing but a picture of chaos all over the country. I have difficulty because we have paucity of men." He said that the IAS officers needed to learn from their ICS seniors. Defending the right to property he stoutly maintained that "no property movable or immovable of any person or corporation including any interest in any commercial or industrial undertaking shall be taken or acquired for public use unless the law provides for the payment of compensation for the property taken or acquired and specifies the principles on which and the manner in which the compensation is to be determined". Sadly, some of these provisions were diluted in the early amendments themselves.

Other political figures who continued to play prominent roles in national and state level politics, sometimes till well into the 1970s, figured in the membership of the Constituent Assembly. Some representative names are T. T. Krishnamachari, K. Kamaraj, M. A. Muthiah Chettiar, T. Prakasam, N. G. Ranga, N. Sanjeeva Reddi, P. Subbarayan, B. G. Kher, M. R. Masani, S. Nijalingappa, S. K. Patil, Syama Prasad Mookerjee, Mahavir Tyagi, A. Dharam Dass, Feroz Gandhi, G. B. Pant, H. N. Kunzru, Shibbal Lal Saxena, Sucheta Kripalani, Rafi Ahmad Kidwai, K. Hanumanthaiah, Hukam Singh, Jagjivan Ram, Binodanand Jha, Rajkumari Amrit Kaur, Gopinath Bardoloi, Bishwanath Das, LokanathMisra, C. M. Poonacha, Sheikh Abdullah, Jaisukhlal Hathi, and Jivraj Mehta. This list includes politicians with widely varying political viewpoints. Prominent public citizens included legal experts such as Alladi Krishnaswami Iyer, K. M. Munshi, Naziruddin Ahmad and M. Ananthasayanam Ayyangar, former Diwans of Princely States like N. Gopalaswami Iyengar, V. T. Krishnamachari and N. Madhava Rao, journalists, academics and writers like B. Shiva Rao, R. R. Diwakar and John Matthai. Contrarians and eccentrics like H. V. Kamath, K. T. Shah, Maulana Hazrat Mohani and Lakshminarayan Sahu were all intelligent people and spoke a lot during the debates. While hardly any of the amendments they proposed found favour with the Assembly they provide points for thought and further discussion right down to the present day. K. T. Shah for example fought for the inclusion of the words 'socialist' and 'secular' in the preamble. This was shot down at the time but we note that the same words came back during the controversial days of the 42nd amendment.

Kamath was the irrepressible argumentative Indian. Speaking about his vain efforts to modify the Preamble and the dominant role played by Nehru and Patel in thwarting his attempts he used an astrological sutra which says that when Guru is in the Kendra position the effects of all other planets vanish: *kim kurvanti grahah sarve yasya kendre Brihaspati!* On another occasion when the items in the Union List were being discussed he moved a resolution that appended interplanetary travel to airways and air navigation. He continued to say, ".... members of the House are welcome to laugh. But fifty years ago if anybody had talked of radios and wireless sets he would have been held up to derision and mocked at, and perhaps stoned. But today radios and wireless sets have become a matter of course, and of everyday occurrence. I am sure Mr. Krishnamachari has got a wireless set of his own in his house. And it is even supposed to be a mark of culture today to have a radio set in every house. Take television. Twenty years ago perhaps television would have been looked upon as an impossibility. But today in America television has become so very common that important meetings and lectures are televised and shown all over the country." Considering what

Elon Musk and Jeff Bezos are doing today and also the fact that interplanetary travel is not a matter of if but when, was Kamath crazy or just too far ahead of his time? I mention these examples to show that the debates were holistic and provided a forum where a wide variety of views were aired and listened to carefully.

Members from religious minorities like Frank Antony, R. K. Sidhwa, H. C. Mookherjee, several Muslim members, and also backward class members notably from Madras and Mysore spoke generally about matters pertaining to their castes or religious groups. These would be called special interest groups in today's jargon. An unusual amount of time in the debates was spent on Assam and the members from this province largely confined themselves to matters pertaining to their state. This emphasis on Assam might appear strange today but the entry of this province into the Union was a matter of touch-and-go till the very end. Assam then included all the seven north-eastern states of today. The proportion of tribals, Christians, Muslims and people of Mongoloid descent was large. There was no land link to the rest of India without passing through 200 km of East Pakistani territory for the road through the Siliguri 'chicken's neck' had not yet been constructed. The other members were particularly sensitive about these matters and the careful wording in some of the pertinent clauses has gone a long way in ensuring that this vital part of the country stayed anchored to India over the decades till the present time when great strides are being made, especially after 2014, for the full integration of Assam, Arunachal Pradesh, Manipur, Meghalaya, Mizoram, Nagaland and Tripura into our country.

The pre-Independence debates of the Constituent Assembly were inevitably of a general nature and clouded by the ambiguity of an impending Partition. The absence of many AIML members was noted. In Britain, the Conservatives led by Churchill were queering the pitch. On 20 January 1947, Churchill said in the House of Commons that "any attempt by the Congress Party to establish Hindu rule on the basis of majority will be fatal to any conception of the unity of India. This unity was a superficial appearance imposed there by the long generations of British rule and it would pass away once the impartial guidance from the outside is withdrawn". He disparagingly said that the INC only represented a single group of people, specifically "whether this meeting of caste Hindus at Delhi can be regarded by the Government as the Constituent Assembly they meant at all". These comments were lambasted in the Assembly. According to Radhakrishnan, "Mr. Churchill's outbursts are bereft of dignity or discretion. Provocative and irrelevant remarks, sneers of derision in regard to our communal divisions, have punctuated his speech on that occasion and on other occasions. I shall only say here that such speeches and such statements cannot prevent the end but can only postpone it and thus prolong the agony. The British connection will end, it must end. Whether it ends in friendship and goodwill or in convulsions and agony, depends upon the way in which the British people treat this great problem."

In truth, Hindus and Muslims were in a state of general equilibrium in Bhāratavarsha till the 18th century and caste (defined as *jati*) was not as pronounced as it became after British mischief came into play. It was the British who stoked the anxieties of the Muslims after 1858 and having done so claimed that there was nothing called 'India' before they entered the picture and that Hindus and Muslims were actually two nations living in one geographical landmass. In the Assembly Shyama Prasad Mookerjee thundered, "....my charge is that the Muslim League has been encouraged by the attitude of the British to imagine that if it does not come it may be able to veto the final decision of the Constitutional Assembly". Support came again from Radhakrishnan who said, "....we wish to tell all those who are abstaining from this Assembly that it is not our desire to establish any sectional government. We are not here asking anything for a particular community or a privileged class. We are here working for the establishment of Swaraj for all the Indian people". Ambedkar added his qualified support by stating that "...today we are divided politically, socially and economically. We are a group of warring camps and let me confess that I am probably one of the leaders of such a camp but Sir, I'm quite convinced that given time and circumstances nothing in the world will prevent this country from becoming one". Members argued that nationalism, not religion, was the basis of modern life. The general sentiment of the assembly which of course did not have many AIML members was that the days of religious states were over and that anyway Hindus and Muslims had lived together in India for over 600 years speaking the same languages and with the same racial ancestry. Muslims in India had not been magically imported from Arabia, Turkey and central Asia. For the very large part they were converted Hindus, especially so in Punjab, which dominates modern Pakistan, where British rule was short and conversions of rather recent origin.

As soon as 12 December 1946, that is immediately after the election of Prasad as President of the Constituent Assembly, Nehru introduced a resolution proclaiming India as an"Independent Sovereign Republic and to draw up for her future governance a Constitution". This resolution was discussed spiritedly and the themes of independence, democracy and republicanism entered the discussions. Jerome D' Souza of Loyola College Madras perhaps summed all this up the best by highlighting a concern of many regarding the absence of God the ultimate authority in the declaration.

> *But the State is not a sort of undesirable excrescence resulting from the surrender of individual liberty. The state is a natural outcome of the nature of man who has to perfect himself in social and community life, with a necessary central authority. That authority comes as Sir S. Radhakrishnan stated from the moral law and that is the basis upon which the rights of individuals and of the State have to be maintained. That ultimate authority, some would prefer to express it as coming from Almighty God as the author of nature and of all moral law. I cannot help expressing a regret that the name of Almighty God finds no place in this momentous declaration. I understand the reasons which moved the hon'ble framer and mover of this resolution in not bringing in anything which may look like a religious profession, but you will permit me to say before concluding my remarks, that if by some way in this momentous preambulatory declaration the name of Almighty God had been brought in, it would have been in conformity with the persuasion, with the convictions, with the spirit of this vast land of ours and its ancient civilisation.*

With such overwhelmingly syncretic sentiments widely prevalent in the Assembly and that too ones like this from a member of a minority community, the attitude of Jinnah and his AIML appear in hindsight as petty and destructive. Unfortunately, theirs were the views which prevailed upon the British in the end. The matter of the Princely States also received attention in the pre-Independence debates. A negotiating committee was formed to talk to the representatives of these states about the nature of their participation in the debates. The British were not helpful even in this matter and left things hanging as to what they intended to do after Independence. There were murmurs is some states like Bhopal, Hyderabad and Travancore about setting themselves up as independent countries. Matters were far from settled. It was felt that the princes could continue to rule their states if they did so within the framework of the Constitution. It was held that just as the British were handing over the responsibility of governance to the people of their Indian provinces so too should the princes of India with their subjects. That the British did not seem to encourage them to follow their example is gleaned by Patel's remarks, reproduced at the end of Chapter 1, as to how independence was finally brokered with the British. It was his strong-arm tactics or shall one say iron-fist-in-the-velvet-glove strategy that quickly turned the tide with all states save Junagadh and Hyderabad and of course the ultimate tragedy, Kashmir where he was not given a free hand by Nehru. With reference to Travancore, it is in hindsight ironical that the Maharaja Chitra Tirunal Balarama Varma, who was by tradition ruling on behalf of the Absolute, brought the Constitution of India into operation in Travancore with the consent of the Deity Padmanabhaswamy after being promised the goal of Rama Rajya for the new country.

In the pre-Independence sessions, a number of issues came up that were subsequently thrashed out in the post-Independence period. These included the rights of citizens, justiciable or otherwise, the fact that these rights could be taken away in a vaguely defined condition called 'emergency', how economic and social rights intersect with fundamental rights, about rights pertaining to freedom of the press, what constitutes a seditious act, the question of the rights of minority communities to establish their own educational institutions, and the abolishment of untouchability. These discussions paved the way for our Fundamental Rights and Directive Principles. A justiciable right is one where a citizen may approach a court of law if he finds that this right has been denied to him, in other words he may seek enforcement of and redressal for their breach. N. G. Ranga termed this "a very important privilege that is being conferred on our citizens." Patel struck the golden mean when he said about Fundamental Rights:

> *There were two schools of thought in the committee and there was a large number of very eminent lawyers who could scrutinise every word of every sentence, even commas and semi-colons, from a very critical point of view. These two schools viewed the matter from two different angles. One school considered it advisable to include as many rights as possible in this report—rights which could straightaway be enforceable in a court of law, rights in regard to which a citizen may without difficulty go straightaway to a court of law and get his rights enforced. The other school of thought considered it advisable to restrict fundamental rights to a few very essential things that may be considered fundamental. Between the two schools there was considerable amount of discussion and finally a mean was drawn which was considered to be a very good mean.*

Also discussed in these early days were the criteria for citizenship, the so-called blood versus birthplace question. This is an interesting point because it impinges on the question of nationhood which is discussed extensively in Chapter 3. Even in the small European nation- states matters like citizenship, nationhood and federalism are subtle issues. Let us note that the concept of a nation-state is itself a rather new beginning, perhaps with the French Revolution. The U.S.A. as a young country largely made up in its first 200 years of European immigrants who had little to lose and much to gain from migrating could opt for a simple birth-cum-naturalisation definition of citizenship which practically defined nationhood. Almost automatically new immigrants were obliged to learn English when they entered, a practice that has been diluted only in recent times with Hispanic immigrants. India is vastly more complicated than Europe: the population is huge, there are many distinct languages each spoken by large numbers of people and originating from two entirely different linguistic streams; the two major religions are sharply differentiated in their fundamental precepts with the smaller one comprising ~15 per cent of the population and around half that community as it existed prior to independence (~25 per cent of the total population) having opted out for a separate country (now two countries, Pakistan and Bangladesh). The culture, diet, habits, customs and traditions of the people of the two main religious groups are both sufficiently similar and yet disarmingly different. Defining nationhood in such an enigmatic land is a daunting task for the lawmaker and indeed for the common citizen. All of us know what it is to be an Indian but most of us seem unable to express it in words on many an occasion. I hope to outline in Chapter 3 that a convenient if somewhat quantitative way of doing so is to compartmentalise identity into religious, political and civilisational segments with varying degrees of overlap among these identities for different categories of people. That post-1947 India has continued to hold together for seventy five years is testimony to the fact that the overlaps between these three identities of a modern Indian are comfortably large, even if they are not exactly congruent. How to move from holding things together to actually leveraging our composite identities so as to strengthen our nation is more properly a task for Bhārat than it is for India because our 5000 year civilisation is the only bedrock cementing factor. This indeed is the theme of this book. There is no question of many nations within one Bhārat. There never was and there never will be.

We revert now to the 'Independent Sovereign Republic' proposed by Nehru for the Preamble of the Constitution. The Preamble was finally settled only in one of the final sessions of the Assembly and all of us know that the country was defined then as a 'Sovereign Democratic Republic'. Words such as 'independent', 'republic', 'democracy', 'federal', and 'federation' were discussed extensively in the sessions prior to and post-independence. Maulana Hazrat Mohani with some irritation said on 17 October 1949 near at the end of the debates:

> *What sort of a republic are we? Some sort of republic that these European countries, these imperialists, who are past masters in this jugglery of words, have coined new phrases; and what are these new phrases? Holland has invented a phrase a republican dominion and France has coined a new word for Vietnam which says that it will be a colonial republic. We admit that Vietnam is a republic and Holland says that they have accepted Indonesia as a republic but it says it is a republican dominion. Instead of the dominion it will be included in an imperial regime and that fraud was brought about by Holland and by France and do you propose that you will also bring about the same fraud to be enacted here?*

The fact that such comments figured, even after three years of debate, shows that certain basic matters were still unresolved in some minds. Let us ignore the fact that 'Sovereign Democratic Republic' was slyly mutated to 'Sovereign, Socialist, Secular, Democratic Republic' in 1975 with the introduction of two new words 'secular' and 'socialistic' both of which are of recent linguistic origin (compared say with 'democracy' and 'republic') and with both having a very specific context. 'Secular' is a word that strictly makes sense only in the context of the Christian Church while 'socialist' is based on an economic model. How can they figure in something as important as the Preamble of a Constitution that is supposed to do justice to the aspirations of 1.4 billion people almost overwhelmingly non-Christian, in a world where the popularity of the socialistic doctrine waxes and wanes? A constitutional preamble that is supposed to be valid over a considerable length of time cannot be something temporal and subjective.

We digress into the history of the terms, 'democracy' and 'republic', the two pillars on which rests the entire edifice of governance in India. These ancient words have a hoary tradition in both India and Europe. Let us consider Europe first and specifically ancient Greece where one might take up the entirely different, indeed totally contradictory, modes of governance in the neighbouring city states of Athens and Sparta. This topic is textbook material in political science and I shall necessarily be brief. In a nutshell, 'democracy' is government by the people, of the people and for the people. The word originated in Athens and is derived from the Greek *demos* meaning village or people and *kratos* meaning rule.

The State exists only for the people. Democracy in Athens went right down to the level of the individual male who could participate in the assembly (*ekklesia*) of citizens who met in a specified place (*agora*, equivalent to our *samsad, sabha*) that was the central institution of their democracy. Decrees of the assembly began with the phrase "It seemed best to the demos," which resembles "We the People" which are the first words of both the US and Indian constitutions. A group of 500 citizens from the assemblies constituted the council (*boule*) a smaller, higher body. The local village (*demos*) was the starting place for legislation and important matters could move up into the council for discussion and adoption as required.

There was a people's court where interestingly there was no presiding judge but rather the appeals were made directly to a jury! The antithesis of democracy is dictatorship and authoritarian rule by an individual or a group, where the individual rights of the people are partly or wholly taken away. According to a 2019 Pew report more than half the countries of the world today are functioning democracies.

The word 'republic' originates from the Latin *res publica* or 'the public thing'. The main feature of a republic is rule by an oligarchy whether or not this smaller group is elected by the free will of the people or whether it is self-organised by those who are strong or ruthless enough to do so. In this sense, the rigorous converse of a republic is a hereditary monarchy where the monarch enjoys full powers. If the oligarchy is freely elected by the people there is a great deal of overlap between a republic and a democracy. It is no wonder that many modern countries like India call themselves democratic republics. It must, however, be emphasised that all republics need not be democracies. China is an example. The former USSR called itself a republic but not a democracy. Almost surrealistically, the former East Germany, and the present day Algeria, North Korea, Somalia and Yemen call themselves democratic republics. Clearly the words 'democratic' and 'republic' are capable of rather subjective interpretations.

The original republic in Europe was the very long-lived Sparta, which continues to this day to fascinate groups as varied as angry anarchists, libertarian admirers, neo-fascist toughs and fitness freaks. Amazingly, it retained its independence for seven long centuries, much longer than any other republic in history. It was indeed a strange place if judged from a modern perspective. One could say that Sparta adhered to Ernest Renan's dictum that unity is always obtained by means of brutality. There was a harsh training regimen forced upon young Spartans which tended to the cruel and violent. The city state eschewed intellectualism, commerce, industry and trade. By making heavy iron bars, which could only be transported in large wheelbarrows, their currency they prevented hoarding and this enabled a certain economic equality. Spartans were reluctant to go to war and were often more merciful to their vanquished enemies than their neighbours, the democratic Athenians. Similarly, the position and status of women was higher in Sparta than in Athens. In an austere republic like

Sparta, devoid of any democratic ideals, the people existed only for the State. In a modern context, these ideas may be seen in a limited sense in the early days of the French Revolution and in an extreme form in Mussolini's Italy and Nazi Germany.

Ancient Rome experimented with several forms of government in its long history. The Roman republic with its senate and consuls lasted for around 500 years before it morphed into an empire: Julius Caesar took full power over Rome as a dictator. After his assassination a triumvirate of Antonius, Lepidus and Octavian, Caesar's nephew ruled. Eventually, Octavian defeated Antonius (Mark Antony) and was crowned Rome's first emperor Augustus. The Roman Empire prospered and survived in some form or another for another millennium. The full about-turn from republic to empire just goes to show that states do experiment with different forms of governance in their history. The 75 years of independent India are statistically insignificant when compared to the 500 years of the Roman Republic and 1000 years of the Roman Empire. Nothing was cast in stone for us in 1950. If a democracy is 'the State for the people' and a republic is 'the people for the State', a liberal democratic republic is the golden mean for the modern age: people and State coexist in comfortable equilibrium with both having rights, duties and responsibilities. No one wants to lurch towards the extremes of wokeness and repression.

We may now turn profitably to ideas of democracy and republicanism in ancient India. There are four issues of note. The first is that the idea of democracy was rooted in the minds of the people through religion as it probably was elsewhere. The second is that republicanism was an important feature of life in some areas possibly because of relatively poor systems of communication between far flung locations and these might have acted as impediments to a centralised monarchy. The third is that the development and progress of democracy, republicanism and monarchy, and at times their *simultaneous* existence, took place throughout the civilised world during amazingly coincident periods over the past 3000 years right down till the present day. For the most part, there was nothing unique about what people were experimenting with in ancient India, Greece or Rome in matters of governance. They had the same aspirations, stirrings and inclinations. The unique feature in ancient India, however, the fourth point, was that democracy, republicanism and monarchy were integrated under the overall canopy of dharma. Each of these points will be discussed briefly.

All religions, ancient and more recent, have upheld the equality of man. Our Puranas affirm that realizing the equality of all men and women (*samatva*) is the same as the worship of God. Democracy gives ultimate power to the individual. The Gita says *yathechchhasitathā kuru* or 'the choice is in your hands'. In ancient India, meeting in the public *sabhas* for free discussion was an important part in the daily life of citizens. Skill in public speaking was a cultivated skill and success in the Sabha was a life ambition for some. Our *neethi shastras*, *dharma shastras* and epics, notably the Mahābhārata, refer to limitations on royal powers, the duties of ministers and the ultimate authority of the people. Monarchs had distinct constraints on their actions and if they were found wanting in terms of the welfare they afforded the people they could be removed, exiled, even killed like Bimbisara. Monarchy was not always hereditary; a king could be chosen as for example Pandu over Dhritirashtra and Yudhishthira over Duryodhana in the Mahābhārata.

The concept that all men and women are morally and spiritually equal is the essence of democracy. St. Paul says in the Bible that there can be neither Jew nor Greek, bonded nor free, male nor female for all are one in Jesus. This is not so far ideologically removed from Sankara's monism based as it is on the *mahāvakyas* of the Upanishads which restate the ultimate reality of *Brahman*. If all of us are purely in the single union of Brahman it follows that we are all the same. Ambedkar reinforces this eloquently when he says that, "if all persons are part of Brahman then all are equal and all must enjoy the same liberty which is what democracy means. Looked at from this point of view, Brahman may be unknowable but there cannot be the slightest doubt *that no doctrine could furnish a stronger foundation for democracy than the doctrine of Brahman*." In Islam, equality is restricted to believers; the brotherhood of Muslims without racial distinctions is the most characteristic tenet of that religion. In ancient China too, the concept of equality was affirmed by constraints on the unrestricted and unbridled authority of kings. The philosopher Mengzi stated that the most important elements in a State were the people next the gods and only lastly the king. When the last Manchu dowager empress Cixi effectively declared the throne vacant in 1908 in her installation of the puppet emperor Pu Yi she had apparently expressed her desire to follow the precepts of the sages of old who taught that political sovereignty rests ultimately with the people. She was practically inviting the republic to step into the shoes of the monarchy. She is reported to have said that by observing the nature of the people's aspirations one learns the will of heaven: *vox populi vox dei*.

The republican tradition was certainly native to the Indian people for at least as long as it was in ancient Greece. It is likely that we had this form of oligarchic rule before the days of the Roman republic. As is said, some of us were ruled by assemblies and others by kings: *kechid deso ganādhīna kechid rājadhīna*. The word '*gana*' means number and the modern name for India is *Bhārat Ganarajya,* the rule by numbers rather than by an individual. Ganesha or Ganaraja is the lord of the ganas, which is the lord of the people. There were many ancient Indian republics, more like town and village corporations, small in size no doubt but fairly well dispersed especially in north-western and eastern India. They were clearly distinguishable from monarchies, their antipodes. In the Shanti Parva of the Mahabharata, Yudhishthira asks Bhishma about the ganarajyas especially about the ways in which they organised their defense. A modified description of the ancient Indian republic is given in the Rig Veda (III, 26) as an assembly of warriors: *vrātam vrātam ganām ganām*. The Aitareya Brahmana, one of the oldest sections of the Rig Veda, says that whole communities were consecrated to kingship and were accordingly termed *vairajya* or devoid of kings. Among the sixteen mahajanapadas or small states that existed between 600 and 400 BCE, mostly in the pre-Buddhist era, three may be definitely identified as oligarchic republics and not kingdoms: Kamboja near the Hindu Kush mountains, Malla in present day eastern U.P. and Vijja (Vrijja) in present day Bihar. Chanakya recognised the nuisance value of the republics to the Maurya empire and that they were so different from kingdoms that the ways of bringing them down were also going to be different—notably he advocated the blood-and-iron methods of Bismarck, the modern day Chanakya, but interestingly Chanakya says that before these methods were attempted one should always try to win the republics over by persuasion (because they could become valuable assets) and if this did not work, one could resort to the time tested methods of bribery and corruption, (sama, dana, bheda, danda: conciliation, gifts, rupture and force).Ganas are also mentioned in the Silappadikaram in the Sangam literature (300 BCE).

The Buddha (BCE 557-477) belonged to the republic of Kapilavastu and was a staunch republican with the will to defend his form of government with force as might be required.

In his time the most important republican clans in the east were the Sakiyas and the Vajjians (residents of Vijja), large groups of around one million people. He is reported to have told his disciple Ananda that as long as the Vajjians gathered together in public clan meetings they might be expected to prosper and flourish. The Buddha had no doubt about republicans using military methods to protect and preserve their State. Even when the powerful king of Magadha was contemplating an attack on the Vajjians, the Buddha asserted that they could not be defeated in armed battle but only through diplomacy or treachery, which are lines of reasoning advocated in the Chankaya-niti a few centuries later. There is no doubt that the ancient Indian republics were resilient and with a great deal of internal strength.

In any larger political state, issues of federalism, that is centralisation versus decentralisation, are bound to crop up. We shall see later in this chapter that the discourse between central and state governments is a continuing one in modern India. Small can often be beautiful. One should appreciate that the establishment of small republics in ancient India, as opposed to large kingdoms, arose from the administrative convenience in managing more compact areas. There are limits to operating a centralised imperial system in a large domain and this was accentuated in former times (before the industrial revolution) when communications systems were poor. The roads in the Roman and Mughal empires had a lot to do with the efficiency of unitary governance. However, practical issues of connections, conveyance and coordination became insurmountable in the end. There is indeed an absolute limit to imperialism that is placed by territorial size, nature and geography. Even the best of arrangements cannot permanently withstand the tendencies of centrifugal disruption. British India was probably too large by the end to hold together. The tendency to disintegrate is not particularly Indian or even Asian. This is perhaps the primary reason why ancient and medieval empires worldwide remained collections of small states, conglomerations of loose almost independent nationalities that paid nominal tribute to a distant suzerain. The Maurya, Gupta, Byzantine, Ming, Mughal and Habsburg dominions were only approximations of empires. A fusion of nationalism as exemplified by democracy and federalism, as exemplified by republicanism has always been the most stable combination in India and will continue to be so.

This smooth synthesis of democratic and republican ideals in ancient India is beautifully brought out in the Atharva Veda (VI, 64) which says, "Do you concur? Be you closely combined and let your minds be concurrent as did the gods of yore sit concurrent about their portion. Be their counsel the same, their gathering the same, their course the same, their intent alike. I offer for you with the same oblation that you do enter together into the same thought. Be your design the same, your hearts the same, your mind the same, that it may be well for you together." The ultimate aims of these assembly deliberations were the people's welfare and the annihilation of the enemy, the principal ends of Vedic life. Such aims and ends ought to be universal for any self-respecting country for all times. The India of 2022 should aspire for nothing less than this.

The point of note in the history of democracy, republicanism and monarchy in India over the ages is that we experimented with these systems around roughly the same time periods as elsewhere in the world. Democracy and republicanism were tried in India roughly between 500 BCE and 100 CE. These yielded to monarchy of various sorts for another 1500 years or so subject to the caveats detailed above. Republics recurred subsequently, for example, in Renaissance Florence or early modern Britain, say Cromwell's Commonwealth. The concept of the republic in modern political life began when Britain's

American colonies split off from the mother country in the revolution of 1776. This period saw the birth of the first modern constitution: the famous US constitution which has already been commented upon several times in this book. In Europe, 1789 was an enormously important year for republicanism and the French Revolution began a whole new political order. Asia followed on a similar parallel track, just a little later because of the colonial interruptions in the 18th and 19th centuries. Still, it cannot be doubted that in the 20th century the inspiration for the Japanese constitutional monarchy, Ataturk's Turkey, the Chinese republic and the freedom struggle in India are inspired by the constitutional achievements in Europe and the US, based as these are on the English Parliament, the US federation, the French Revolution and the socialism of Marx as contrasted with the ideas of John Stuart Mill.

While democracy, republicanism and monarchy are features that one might find anywhere in the civilised world over the ages the unique contribution of Bhāratavarsha to the epistemology of governance is that we were able to bring these aspects together under the canopy of dharma,the eternal element that sustains our world, nay our universe. Dharma is not a subjective interpretation of duty by an individual nor is it a license to do whatsoever one might please in the name of 'way of life'. It is what enables one to distinguish between right and wrong and represents the confluence of ideals, purposes, influences and institutions that shape the character of a human being both as an individual and as a member of society. It is the law of right living. It brings order and stability. It is not seen but experienced and cannot be proved as it is a matter of certainty rather than of deduction. All things sentient or otherwise have their dharma. For sentient beings with an intellect, namely humans, the decision as to what is right and what is wrong is made with a combination of nature, instinct and intellect. The first two factors are intrinsic to one's being. It is with regard to the third that subjectivity creeps in and our ancients prescribed therefore that our shastras as revealed in the Vedas are the points of reckoning. It is because of these shastras that Sanātana Dharma is a religion and not merely a way of life.

Dharma is as fundamental to our existence as is its converse in the physical world, the Second Law of Thermodynamics which governs the progression of things from order to randomness. Like the Second Law there will be many definitions of dharma. In practical terms and with respect to governance, it was said in ancient India that the sovereignty of the people is paramount and rests as such with the moral law, another definition of dharma. People and kings are subordinate to this moral law. Dharma, righteousness, is the king of kings. Kings rule to uphold dharma. It is the ruler of both the people and the rulers themselves, the sovereign of sovereignty: *dharmam kshatrasya kshatram* says the Brihadāranyaka Upanishad. In this sense there was and there is no real contradiction between monarchy and republicanism in Bhārat. If a king did not perform his duty in other words did not behave like a *chakravartin,* the holder of the wheel of dharma, he could be removed and exiled. Monarchy was not strictly hereditary. The sovereignty of the king only flowed from his ability to protect his people and maintain order in society. There was no extra sanctity in the personage of the king. In his efforts he was guided and aided by his ministers who were in effect his touchstones to the minds of the people. The Shukra-neeti, our treatise in statecraft, says that ministers should be powerful, wise and dispassionate. This is what a politician in modern India should be, not like some of the venal, calculating and grasping specimens we see today. We have the advantage of knowing about dharma in our civilisation: we should employ it constructively. And what if anything is higher than dharma? Clearly it can only be the Ultimate Reality. The thousand names of the goddess Lalita Tripurasundari include a description of her as *dharmādhāra-dhanādhyaksha-dhanadhānyavivardhini*, the support of dharma who controls all riches and who increases riches and harvests. This is not an inappropriate description for the aims and goals of any government in the modern world!

These ideas are not as hopelessly outdated and irrelevant in the world of 2022 as they might appear. The Princely States, of which I have spoken about briefly, often acted as custodians of dharma right up to 1947. They may be considered as the continuous thread in our long civilisational history that has upheld *rajadharma*. Especially famous in this regard were Mysore and Travancore known as model states in the pre-independence era. These states did not necessarily need to be guided by the principles of British jurisprudence and could bring in progressive norms that were more characteristic of the dharmic pre-colonial era. Mysore started institutionalising social reforms for backward classes as early as the 1890s. Social change in Travancore took the form, for example, of permitting temple entry of the Scheduled Castes. Neither of the royal houses flaunted worldly wealth and eschewed pomp and show.

B. The Republic as on 26 January 1950

We now proceed to sketch the broad details of the constitutional debates in the plenary sessions between 20 August 1947 and 24 January 1950. The Constitution was not generated in a day; to be precise the formal exercise took exactly 2 years 11 months and 18 days with much of 1948 being taken up by the process of producing a preliminary written draft that was discussed in three readings of the document that stretched out over 100 days mostly in 1949. The members of the drafting committee were the chairman, Ambedkar and ten others: T. T. Krishnamachari, Alladi Krishnaswami Ayyar, K. M. Munshi, N. Gopalaswami Ayyangar, Mohammad Saadulla, Debi Prasad Khaitan, N. Madhava Rao and B. L. Mitter, mostly lawyers. The discussions in the sessions themselves covered a range of topics and the opinions expressed spanned a wide ideological spectrum. This was the case even with so many members from the Congress because in those days the party membership incorporated a wide range of political views that bridged the seemingly impossible gap between *laissez faire* free market capitalism and government directed socialism! All the members were of the same mind in that they felt the social and economic inequities in India, vastly accentuated by colonial rule, had to go. Barring the extreme left or those who believed in overthrowing the system through armed struggle, just about all other views were represented and heard.

The debates on the draft are noteworthy because, with an excuse of clause-by-clause discussions, members had the opportunity to share their general concerns about the new country, its nature, priorities and aspirations. Certain issues cropped up repeatedly which leads one to conclude that they must have been of overarching importance to the Constitution in particular, and in general to the future of the country whose course was in large measure going to be navigated using this Constitution. This book does not attempt to be a comprehensive discussion or detailed analysis of our Constitution. This would need several volumes. For the large part the Constitution has proved to be a reliable and sturdy document and unless there is a radical reworking of it based on a totally different model such as the Gandhian model of 1944 or M. N. Roy's model of the same year, scenarios that now appear improbable, it is likely that it will, warts and all, continue to be our broad template for governance in the foreseeable future. More specifically, I will be concerned in the coming chapters about where and how the Constitution has failed us to lesser or greater extents and what one can do to address and redress these problems. Our country today is poised on a new threshold at its 75th year of independence. It is widely held that India will be one of the most important, impressive and influential countries in the world during the next 75 years. A lot can be achieved by restructuring the economy and increasing innovation and production. These have indeed been identified as priority items by our present government. However, a nagging question remains: are there inherently fundamental flaws concerning the Constitution itself, matters that are so serious that no amount of economic engineering, or more pityingly tinkering, would enable the nation to reach its full potential? To abbreviate, does our Constitution that we hold to be a reliable compass to guide us towards our destinies pose, in itself, a limitation to us realising our full potential?

Accordingly, I revert in this section to backdrop issues that kept recurring in the post-independence debates. I identify seven main concerns:

(1) The absence of a mention of God in any direct or indirect way in the Constitution;

(2) The fact that our 5000 year civilisation and more pointedly Sanātana Dharma is not within the warp-and-woof of the document with only fleeting, even token, acknowledgements, say through the well-known illustrations by Nandalal Bose for the page borders;

(3) That the problems of socially and economically vulnerable sections of society were not being addressed adequately;

(4) That the balance between a strong central government which is essential for the country's unity and territorial integrity and vibrant state governments that allow for an adequate representation of the nation's diversity, was not being struck

properly, or at least not factoring in long term realities, the so called federalism issue;

(5) Whether or not we need a national language in addition to an official language or languages;

(6) Whether we really need an Upper House of the legislature at the central and state levels, the Rajya Sabha and the Legislative Councils respectively and;

(7) Whether our Constitution is a cut-and-paste effort, a hotchpotch of ideas from other constitutions with no intrinsic element inherent to our native genius, and in this sense not really something that belongs to us or is characteristic of us as a people.

These difficult questions have not yet been fully resolved; in some cases they have not even been properly addressed. All of them touch intimately upon our composite identity, the political, the religious and the civilisational and as such are directly within the main theme of this work.

India is a very religious country. Of that, there is no doubt. The recent report (2021) entitled 'Religion in India: Tolerance and Segregation' produced by the US based Pew Research Foundation sampled a population size of 30,000 Indians and concludes that an overwhelming majority of them (Hindus 81 per cent, Muslims 13 per cent , Christians 2.4 per cent Sikhs 1.9 per cent) declared their religious persuasion. For 80 per cent Indians respecting another's religion is a very important part *of their own religious identity* with the respective numbers for the above mentioned four religions being 80 per cent, 79 per cent, 78 per cent and 75 per cent. So much for Indian Muslims being intolerant and bigoted with respect to Hinduism and Hindus! The exact question posed was, "Is respecting other religions a very important, somewhat important, not too important or not at all important part of what being (Hindu/Muslim/etc.) means to you?" Lastly, 85 per cent Hindus and 78 per cent

Muslims viewed respecting another's religious identity as an important part of their being truly 'Indian', which one can take as being one's composite identity. To re-emphasise, we are indeed a religious country and one where the spiritual imbues us with a sense of joy and wonderment. Vivekananda said 120 years ago that, "every improvement in India requires first of all an upheaval in religion. Before flooding the land with socialistic or political ideas, first deluge the land with spiritual ideas. If you attempt to get secular knowledge without religion, I tell you plainly, vain is your attempt in India. It will never have a hold on the people." The Constitution is the most important document that relates us Indians to citizenship, nationhood and a feeling of belonging. It attempts to guide and lead. It is supposed to establish the roadmap. The obvious question, and one that springs to everyone's lips is why does this very long document not mention God, directly or indirectly, even once?

When one looks at constitutions of other countries, their flags, mottos and emblems, with their references to God the above fact appears even more startling. Countries that appear today to be irreligious, materialistic, modern, and 'secular', (whatever this last term may mean) display God prominently in their various national totems. Let us consider the two countries that have influenced us the most in constitution drafting, the U.K. and the U.S.A. The British national anthem begins, 'God save the King'. The motto of the British monarch is, 'Dieu et mon droit' meaning 'God and my right'. It is a country that prides itself on its multi-religious, multi-cultural and multi-ethnic character, one where the State does not interfere one way or another with religious matters, but where a Roman Catholic is not allowed to ascend to the throne and yet the Royal Mint has for the first ever time minted a 20 gram gold bullion bar with a picture of Goddess Lakshmi to commemorate Deepavali 2021. The constitution of the U.S.A.

does not mention God but there is at least one direct reference to God in each of the constitutions of its 50 constituent states. Only Colorado, Iowa, Hawaii and Washington do not use the explicit word God but all four refer to some equivalent like 'Supreme Being', 'Supreme Ruler of the Universe' or 'Divine Guidance.', somewhat similar to the 'Almighty Power' referred to by Prasad on 14 August 1947. The U.S.A. changed its national motto from the secular 'E pluribus unum' to 'In God we trust' as recently as 1955. A total of 40 countries invoke God explicitly in their constitutions and this includes only nine Islamic States. It is in order to mention a few: "Conscious of their responsibility before God and man…" (Germany); "We, the Polish Nation—all citizens of the Republic, both those who believe in God as the source of truth, justice, good and beauty, as well as those not sharing such faith but respecting those universal values as arising from other sources…" (Poland); "May God protect our people…" (South Africa); "In the name of Almighty God! The Swiss People and the Cantons…" (Switzerland); "The Verkhovna Rada of Ukraine, aware of our responsibility before God, our own conscience, past, present and future generations, adopts this Constitution…"; "By the grace of God Almighty…" (Indonesia). France is a very special exception because of the unique origin of its republic and being the home of *laicité* which rigorously excludes any ecclesiastical control. India cannot be compared in any way to France in this regard either in its constitutional origin, its religious history or in the way the two countries have managed the concept of secularism.

For the record, 31 countries incorporate the Christian cross in their national flags and in around ten of them the cross is the only item in the flag (Sweden, U.K., Switzerland for example). Again, 22 Islamic countries have a crescent and star or feature the colour green prominently in their flags. India, however, has a mixed record in this matter. Our Constitution simply does not mention God or any sort of divine presence. The national emblem is indeed of religious origin but of a religion whose adherents number no more than 0.7 per cent of India's population. The flag does contain a religious symbol in the form of a wheel but this again is representative of the same 0.7 per cent religion which contributed the national emblem. The colours of the flag apparently have nothing to do with the Hindu saffron, the Christian white or the Muslim green but as some of our leaders would say these colours denote renunciation, truth and plant life. The official calendar is based on the Saka Era, and while there is some astronomical basis for it, it is not followed in practice by any religious, social or cultural group in the country. Many aspects go back to just Emperor Ashoka and no one else and much is made of the fact that he was a Hindu who converted to Buddhism, the 0.7 per cent religion. What is the purpose of such obfuscation? The only concession to the majority 80 per cent religion is an indirect one in the form of our national motto *Satyameva Jayate* which is drawn from the Mundaka Upanishad. This obviously means 'Truth Alone Triumphs' but this is a universal statement devoid of any religious or spiritual content. The Mundaka, let us also note, is from the Atharva Veda and its content is neither ritualistic nor particularly religious per se. It has to do with the nature of knowledge and is used for teaching and meditation. All in all, this is a thoroughly unsatisfactory situation and one that we as Indians, mostly Hindus, do not deserve. The only rationalisation for all this vagueness, not a justification, is that the Assembly members were so shell-shocked by Partition that they completely avoided any reference to the two majority religions with a combined population of 94 per cent of this huge and highly religious, spiritual country in their anthem, flag, motto, symbols, and above all most dismally in their

Constitution. We have attempted in vain to ignore the Indian elephant in the room.

We next turn to the question as to how and why our ancient civilisation and culture while being extolled continuously and elaborated at length in the debates do not find their rightful positioning and status in the final document. As early as 12 December 1946, Radhakrishnan said, "a nation does not depend on identity of race, or sentiment, or on ancestral memories, but it depends on a persistent and continuous way of life that has come down to us. Such a way of life belongs to the very soil of this land. It is there indigenous to this country as much as the waters of the Ganges or the snows of the Himalayas. From the very roots of our civilisation in the Indus Valley to the present day, the same great culture is represented among Hindus and Muslims we have stood for the ideal of comprehension and charity all these centuries."

What do these words mean to the modern Indian? Their soothing tone might have been appropriate for the time but today they seem curiously dated and stilted, and skirting the main issue. Why were these 'sentiments' not specifically expressed in the Constitution? What is the meaning of 'way of life'? We are told that while Hinduism is a way of life, Islam and Christianity are religions. Is not any religion also a way of life? A few urbanised English-speaking elite today claim that for them Hinduism is a way of life but that they do not believe in ritualistic practices, that one would term *paddhati* and *samskara.* Why call oneself a Hindu if all that one's religion means is a way of life that extends only to secular practices? The problem with the 'way of life' argument is that it opens the door to arbitrary attacks from anyone, Hindu or non-Hindu, because a way of life is just that, variable, subjective and mutable. On the other hand, religion, which is a faith based on that which cannot be proved, is a personal matter and cannot be similarly attacked. In my opinion these three words 'way of life' have been so overused in modern India that they have become practically meaningless. Mercifully, India is not Bhārat and the large majority of us do not hold such strange views. The Pew report confirms that most of us do indeed adhere to paddhati. We do not encourage intermarriage between religions and dietary prohibitions are followed closely.

A big majority (64 per cent) of Hindus (51 per cent of our total population) feel that being Hindu is an important part of feeling Indian while 59 per cent of Hindus feel that knowledge of Hindi is similarly important. This figure, namely 59 per cent Hindus, represents 47 per cent of the total population so that such a sentiment is shared almost wholly by those who claim Hindi as their mother-tongue: as such it is not significant. South Indians in particular do not seem to feel that knowledge of Hindi is an important ingredient of feeling Indian although the language is by now widely understood in the South.

The other word that has been misused and distorted beyond belief within the constitution and without is 'secular' or may one call it the S-word? Originally, it was held that the concept of being secular is innate to Hinduism and that no specific mention of secularism was required in the preamble or elsewhere.

This matter was discussed at length in the context of Article 15, and related articles. Article 15 says that "the State shall not discriminate against any citizen on grounds only of religion, race, caste, sex" while Article 25 guarantees "the freedom of conscience, the freedom to profess, practice and propagate religion to all citizens". We note here that the majority religion in India, the typical one, does not normally resort to proselytisation as do Islam and Christianity, which do so vigorously. Was it necessary to include the word 'propagate' in Article 25?

The word 'secular' originally had a strictly Christian connotation in that it defined a 'secular space' where the State could organise its temporal matters as different from the 'divine space' in which the Church could operate. The main idea behind secularism was a working separation of 'Church and State'. This concept took different forms in two important countries: in France with its concept of *laicité*, secularism was intended to protect the State from the Church. In the U.S.A. it was the reverse: secularism was intended to protect the Church from the State. Reams have been written about two different interpretations of secularism in the Indian Constitution. The original meaning of secularism here was that the State should be disinterested in religion and must be neutral to it, in other words disregard it. This is close to the French interpretation. In a later 1994 Supreme Court interpretation, secularism was held to be a positive concept in that it meant that all religions are entitled to equal treatment by the State. In other words, *panthnirpekshta* was to become *sarvadharmasamabhāva*. In practice, the Indian State has done neither of these things especially so in recent times with its so-called appeasement policies towards minorities, and worse, its mischievous conflation in saying that treating all religions equally is the same as saying that all religions are equal. On 6 December 1948, Lokanath Misra said in the Assembly:

> *Sir, it has been repeated to our ears that ours is a secular State. I accepted this secularism in the sense that our State shall remain unconcerned with religion, and I thought that the secular State of partitioned India was the maximum of generosity of a Hindu dominated territory for its non-Hindu population. I did not of course know what exactly this secularism meant and how far the State intends to cover the life and manners of our people. To my mind life cannot be compartmentalised and yet I reconciled myself to the new cry. The absurdity of this position is now manifest in*

> *articles 19 to 22 of the draft constitution. Do we really believe that religion can be divorced from life, or is it our belief that in the midst of many religions we cannot decide which one to accept? If religion is beyond the ken of our State, let us clearly say so and delete all reference to rights relating to religion. If we find it necessary, let us be brave enough and say what it should be. But this unjust generosity of tabooing religion and yet making propagation of religion a fundamental right is somewhat uncanny and dangerous. Justice demands that the ancient faith and culture of the land should be given a fair deal, if not restored to its legitimate place after a thousand years of suppression. We have no quarrel with Christ or Mohammad or what they saw and said. We have all respect for them. To my mind, Vedic culture excludes nothing. Every philosophy and culture has its place but now the cry of religion is a dangerous cry. It denominates, it divides and encamps people to warring ways... Hinduism is just an integrated vision and a philosophy of life and cosmos, expressed in organised society to live that philosophy in peace and amity. But Hindu generosity has been misused and politics has overrun Hindu culture. Today religion in India serves no higher purpose than collecting ignorance, poverty and ambition under a banner that flies for fanaticism. The aim is political, for in the modern world all is power-politics and the inner man is lost in the dust. Let everybody live as he thinks best but let him not try to swell his number to demand the spoils of political warfare. Let us not raise the question of communal minorities anymore. It is a device to swallow the majority in the long run. This is intolerable and unjust.*

The words of the inimitable H. V. Kamath on the same day also bear repeating:

> *If a State identifies itself with any particular religion, there will be rift within the State. After all, the State represents all the people, who live within its territories, and, therefore, it cannot afford to*

> *identify itself with the religion of any particular section of the population. But let me not be misunderstood. When I say that a State should not identify itself with any particular religion, I do not mean to say that a State should be anti-religious or irreligious. We have certainly declared that India would be a secular State. But to my mind a secular State is neither a godless State nor an irreligious nor an anti-religious State. Coming to the real meaning of this word religion', I assert that dharma in the most comprehensive sense should be interpreted to mean the true values of religion or of the spirit. Dharma, which we have adopted in the crest or the seal of our constituent assembly and .... to my mind, should be inculcated in the citizens of the Indian Union ... that dharma must be our religion. That which is embodied which is incorporated in the great sutras, the mahavakyas of our religions, in Sanskrit, in Hinduism, the mahavakya 'Aham Brahmasmi', then 'Anal Haq' in Sufism and 'I and my Father are one' in the Christian religion, these doctrines if they are inculcated and practised to-day, will lead to the cessation of strife in the world. It is these which India has got to take up and teach, not merely to her own citizens, but to the world. It is the only way out for the spiritual malaise, in which the world is caught today, because the House will agree, I am sure, with what has been said by the mahayogi, Sri Aurobindo, in one of his famous books where he says: "The master idea that has governed the life, the culture, social ideals of the Indian people has been the seeking of man for his true, spiritual self and the use of life as a frame and means for that discovery and for man's ascent from the ignorant natural into the spiritual existence.*

In practice, religion was treated in a guarded manner in the 1950 constitution. In this context we may briefly take up the matter of the Uniform Civil Code (UCC) for all religious denominations. Article 35 as introduced stated that 'The

State shall endeavour to secure for citizens a uniform civil code throughout the territory of India.' The debate triggered conflict. Most of the opposition to it came from Muslim members who moved amendments to keep personal laws out of the scope of the article. On the other side, Hindu members argued that the article was necessary to sustain the country's secular credentials and the constitution did indeed offer the scope to legislate on social reform. Discussion mostly took place on 23 November 1948 with several Muslim members speaking against the UCC quoting intricacies of their rules regarding marriage and religious observances. They said that marriage was a contract in Islam and as such, it was a civil matter. They argued that the right of a group or a community of people to follow and adhere to their own personal law should be among the fundamental rights. Anything that affected personal laws was going to interfere with one's way of life, or so they held.

Alladi and Munshi, members of the drafting committee, mounted a spirited defence of the said article. The former argued that UCC applied to every sphere of civil relations, to the laws of contracts, property, succession, marriage and so on. How then could anyone argue against it? Munshi put forward legal and technical arguments in favour of the proposed Article 35. He said that if Muslim personal law was to be strictly enforced one could not give equal rights to women. However, this was already guaranteed in Article 15 in the fundamental rights and so here was a contradiction. He further said that without this article no religion, including Hinduism, could be reformed with respect to elevating the position of women in society. He argued that without the UCC nothing prevented groups of Hindus from making their own sets of personal laws as was already happening, with the law of Mayukha applying in some parts of India, Mithakshara in others and Dayabagha in yet others. He pleaded with the Muslim leaders to abandon their isolationist view and restrict their religion only to those spheres pertaining to religion while the rest of life must be regulated, unified and modified according to the provisions of the UCC. Both sides argued for and against using examples from other countries that permitted Muslims to follow their personal laws or alternatively to adhere to a uniform law for personal matters.

The contradiction in the position of the Muslims regarding the UCC was pointed out by Alladi who reminded the Assembly that Muslims had no problem in accepting a uniform criminal code during the time of the Raj. Why were they opposing a uniform civil code now? Munshi noted that the attitude of mind that personal law is a part of religion was perpetuated by the British, who had their own reasons for doing so: they wished to steer clear of all social and religious matters pertaining to Indians. In an interesting historical aside, he reminded the Assembly that when Allauddin Khilji introduced some reforms which seemed to go against the Shariat, the Kazi of Delhi objected. Allauddin is reported to have replied "I am an ignorant man and I am ruling this country in its best interests. I am sure, looking at my ignorance and my good intentions the Almighty will forgive me when he finds that I have not acted according to the Shariat."

Ambedkar while summarising the debate emphasised that India had a uniform code of laws covering almost every aspect of human relationship. These included a uniform and complete Criminal Code operating throughout the country, a Law of Transfer of Property and the Negotiable Instruments Acts. In short, the country already had a UCC for all practical purposes. Why were the Muslims objecting to its extension to the areas of marriage and succession/inheritance? In the end, this was the point of disagreement. He concluded that since there was no unanimity on this important topic, it would be preferable to shift Article 35 to the Directive Principles as Article 44. As a directive principle, the State was not obligated to bring it into immediate effect; there was still time and space for the consent of all communities to be obtained.

All of this was unexceptional. A proposed article had been introduced for inclusion as a fundamental right. It was debated. No unanimity was reached. In view of the sensitivity of matter, especially in the immediate aftermath of Partition, it was decided to postpone a decision to a more opportune time and as such in keeping with the intent of the proposed article it was shifted as a directive principle. The reason why the UCC matter is discussed in this section, which covers the unequal treatment of religions by the State, is that when such matters were next considered it led instead to the passage of the Hindu Code Bill (1952) applicable only to Hindus, Sikhs and Jains. A religion neutral UCC as such has not been realised till date. Muslims still follow their own personal laws. The Bharatiya Janata Party (BJP) has repeatedly mentioned its intent to implement the UCC in its manifestos over the years. Even after their eight continuous years in power, this is still to see reality although one begins to see stirrings along these directions now. Nehru claimed when he introduced the Hindu Code Bill early on that he wanted a UCC but felt that the time was "not ripe" in view of the Partition. S. P. Mookerjee was more caustic and as a member of the new political party he had founded in 1951, the Jana Sangh (the forerunner of today's BJP) had said that "I know the weaknesses of promoters of this bill. They dare not touch the Muslim minority. There will be so much opposition coming from throughout India that government will not dare proceed with it. But of course you can proceed with the Hindu community in any way you like and whatever the consequences may be". When the Hindu Code Bill was being passed in 1955, J. B. Kripalani lambasted Nehru and said, "I charge you with communalism because you are bringing forward a law about monogamy only for the Hindu community. Take it from me that the Muslim community is prepared to have it but you are not brave enough to do it". This is a very controversial topic: when asked why he was so strident in attacking Hindu communalism while he soft peddled on Muslim communalism, Nehru replied that it was "because majority communalism was far more dangerous since it could easily pass off as Indian nationalism." Times change—secularism which was considered a good thing in former times has become discredited today. Nationalism, which was scoffed at by Nehru, has become a badge of respectability today, even a qualifier of patriotism. The battle lines for the clash of civilisational values were being drawn as early as the 1950s and the prize was the capture of the 'Idea of India' as interpreted according to one's political preferences.

Similarly, the matter of a national ban on cow slaughter was shunted into the Directive Principles. This was a less sensitive issue compared to the UCC but the discussions were still lively and at times emotional when discussing the issue that "the State shall endeavour to organise agriculture and animal husbandry on modern and scientific lines and shall in particular take steps for preserving and improving the breeds of cattle and prohibit the slaughter of cow and other useful cattle, specially milk and draught cattle and their young stock." Gandhi's preferences with respect to banning cow slaughter were invoked as were Lord Krishna and several Mughal rulers. Several states have banned cow slaughter today but there is no national consensus.

The third area of nearly unanimous concern in the Assembly was the need for the State to ensure adequate representation and protection to socially and economically disadvantaged classes. I have outlined in Chapter 1 that by the early 1940s the Scheduled Castes had convinced lawmakers that their community, as the one that had experienced the worst types of degradation, would have to receive special safeguards in the Constitution. Article 11 states that "untouchability is abolished and its practice in any form is forbidden. The enforcement of any disability arising out of untouchability shall be an offence punishable in accordance with law." To ensure representation for SCs in Parliament, reserved constituencies were set up with universal suffrage. The concept of reserved electorates, that had caused so much damage with respect to Muslims in the pre-independence time, was finally laid to rest. To ensure representation in the education and employment sectors, quotas were laid down, 15 per cent for SCs and 7.5 per cent for the Scheduled Tribes (STs).

Employment in the government service was naturally important in those days when there were so few employment opportunities anyway. The exact wording of Article 16 in the 1950 Constitution is that "nothing in this article shall prevent the State from making any provision for the reservation of appointments or posts in favour of any backward class of citizens which, in the opinion of the State, is not adequately represented in the services under the State." Ambedkar provided a clarification on 30 November 1948. He said that in the matter of reservations there had been two schools of thought: the first wanted to have complete equality of opportunity for all citizens as guaranteed by Article 10. This would imply no reservations for anyone. On the other hand, the other sentiment was that some communities needed heavy reservations in order that they may more quickly come up to the levels of the rest of the population but this would deny the equality of opportunity to all promised in Article 10. So he proposed a third route where there would be reservations but only to a limited degree and further, these would be spaced out in something like ten years by which time it was hoped that some degree of parity would be obtained between communities. Ambedkar cautioned specifically against increasing the number of reservations beyond a limit. He said, "Supposing, for instance, reservations were made for a community or a collection of communities, the total of which came to something like 70 per cent of the total posts under the State and only 30 per cent are retained as the unreserved. Could anybody say that the reservation of 30 per cent as open to general competition would be satisfactory from the point of view of giving effect to the first principle, namely, that there shall be equality of opportunity? It cannot be in my judgment." This is absolutely sound in logic, morality, justice and common sense. Yet, one should note that there is one state in the Union today where the reservations stand exactly at 69 per cent which is just 1 per cent short of the ridiculous figure quoted by Ambedkar to reinforce his very straightforward point. There are *Lakshman rekhas* to everything but this is something that many of us Indians, caught up as we are in emotion, do not seem to realise. I shall return to this and Ambedkar's full quotation later in this chapter.

Even after ensuring reservations for the SC community through a constitutional measure, Ambedkar was realistic about the ultimate future of the disadvantaged communities. He said that legal protection from political exclusion was only a partial indication of the acceptance of SCs into general community life. The ultimate test was their acceptance at a social and economic level. At the end of the assembly sessions he said:

> *Looking back on the work of the Constituent Assembly it will now be two years 11 months and 17 days since it first met on the 9th of December 1946. On the 26th January 1950 India would be a democratic nation in the sense that India from that day would have a government of the people, by the people, and for the people. On the 26th of January 1950, we are going to enter into a life*

> *of contradictions. In politics we will have equality, and in social and economic life we will have inequality. In politics we will be recognizing the principle of one man one vote and one vote one value. In a social and economic life we shall by reason of our social and economic structure continue to deny the principle of one man one value. How long shall we continue to live this life of contradictions? How long shall we continue to deny equality in our social and economic life? If we continue to deny it for long, we will do so only by putting up political democracy in peril. We must remove this contradiction at the earliest moment or else those who suffer from inequality will blow up the structure of this political democracy so laboriously built up by this assembly.*

By 1953, Ambedkar was quite embittered by the experiment with parliamentary democracy in India itself. When asked if democracy was going to work in India, he replied in the negative. For, he maintained that we had a social structure which was totally incompatible with parliamentary democracy, only a top dressing on a soil that was essentially undemocratic. It is a question to ponder today. Have we advanced to the level that would have satisfied Ambedkar? If not, why not?

The presence of the word 'backward' in Article 16 needs comment. The debates reflected ambiguity about this term and there was some feeling that the words 'backward classes' should be substituted by 'depressed class' or 'scheduled class' because the latter have a definite meaning. However, members from the south averred. T. Channiah from Mysore said that in the south the term 'backward classes' had a very distinct meaning. There, the term 'backward' meant either socially or educationally backward. The only classes who did not fit in the context of Article 10 were those who were economically forward. More impolitely put, this meant the Brahmins. He explained that in Mysore, there were two classes A and B in the matter of vacancies for government posts. For the Class A vacancies both Brahmins and the non-Brahmins could apply whereas for the Class B vacancies, only the backward classes could apply. Therefore 'backward' essentially meant 'not a Brahmin'. Channiah emphasised the social and/or educational backwardness of the 'backward classes' as defined by him. In modern parlance what Mysore (and Madras) called 'backward' in 1947 would include SC, ST, OBC, MBC and EBC categories today pan-India. Surprisingly, it would also include so-called higher caste non-Brahmin communities which might appear in the general category today. Mohamed Ismail from Madras confirmed that in his state the term 'backward' had a definite technical meaning and that the Government of Madras had enumerated 150 communities as 'backward' and it is only those communities that counted as 'backward' in the eyes of the government not anyone who was backward in the linguistic sense of the term. Today, the EWS or economically weaker sections have been officially defined by the central government on a purely income basis. Reservations that effectively became punitive with respect to a particular community made them economically weak from a situation where they were practically the only ones who were (at least officially speaking) economically forward.

The fourth area where extensive discussions occurred throughout the debates, whether they were pre- or post-independence, was the structuring of the country in terms of its constituent units. The country prior to 1947 consisted of British India namely provinces administered directly by the Crown through its representative the Viceroy, and the Princely States which enjoyed some degree of autonomy in matters other than critical areas such as defence, external affairs, communications and taxation. At least 30 states issued their own postage stamps, bank notes or coins. This list included big states like Bhopal, Hyderabad, Patiala and Travancore-Cochin. This arrangement where the Princely States were linked through treaties to the British government suited the trading arrangements of the latter and was reasonably stable. It allowed the princes to exert their authority locally and their behaviour ranged from the saintly to the despotic. As we have seen in Chapter 1 many of the pre-independence attempts at drafting a constitution started with the assumption that the British provinces were somehow going to be 'different' from the Princely States in post-independence India.

All this changed abruptly with Independence because it was accompanied by Partition. Suddenly, the matter of the princes did not seem so important and anyway Patel and his secretary in the Ministry of States, V. P. Menon were rapidly sweeping them up into their basket and integrating them into the newly independent India treating them exactly like any other part of the country. The more important matter was Partition. The uppermost feeling in the minds of the Assembly members was that the country which had been brutally sundered with chaotic sectarian violence and a mass exchange of population could not be allowed to further disintegrate. We simply could not afford it. Unity took a front seat. Everything else could wait. The assembly which was ready to frame a federal Constitution began to look at federalism with a suspicious eye. The Assembly did not abandon the idea of federalism altogether—the country was too huge and diverse to be run in a completely unitary manner—but they conferred the central government with extraordinary powers and called India a 'Union of States' rather than a federation. Indeed the words 'federal' and 'federation' do not occur anywhere in our Constitution. The term 'federation' was dropped after lengthy debate. Article 1 begins, "India, that is Bhārat, shall be a Union of States." Kamath said that, "the emphasis should be on the word 'union' rather than on the word 'federal'. The tendency to disintegrate our body politic has been rampant since the dawn of history and if this tendency is to be curbed the word federal should be omitted from this article", a sentiment endorsed by Ambedkar. To avoid an incorrect conflation of terms, it should be clarified that the term 'Union' refers to the Indian State comprising all three organs whereas 'central government' refers only to its executive wing.

This difference between 'Union' and 'Federation' is of utmost importance and more so in the context of the present work. It has been explained in Chapter 1 how a union is different from a federation which is yet different from a confederation. In a true federation, as in the U.S.A. and, to some extent, Germany, the constituent states initially have an identifiable existence as independent or at least largely autonomous entities and come together in a federation because this would give the combined State an additional and synergistic strength that would not have been possible had they remained separate. In the U.S.A. the states are still sovereign in many respects but not in the federal sphere. Such a situation, namely independent states that came together, did not prevail in the India of 15 August 1947. Administrative heterogeneity existed only in the form of the Princely States, but these were homogenised by Patel. The states of modern India (to be clearly distinguished from the Princely States of pre-1947 India despite the repetition of the word 'states' in both terms) are purely creations of the Union. According to the terms of the all-sweeping Article 3 they can be divided, joined, remade or even completely removed from existence by a simple parliamentary majority that does not require anyone else's consent or assent. Even dissent from aggrieved parties does not matter if such is the will of Parliament. Sweeping powers like these are unique in the modern constitutional world.

However, India is more a sub-continent than a country, with an area greater than three million sq. km. and a population of nearly 1.4 billion. It is the most plural society in the world with 22 national languages, 2000 dialects, at least a dozen ethnic groups and seven main religions divided into sects, castes and sub-castes that cut across religions for the caste system is not confined to Hinduism in India. There are nearly 60 socio-cultural groups spread over seven natural geographic regions. Any workable system of governance in such a country must respect and honour diversity. Our Constitution has attempted to do just that and has assigned areas of governance to the centre and to the states even in its strongly centric emphasis. For a start, there are two governments, one at the Centre and the other in the states with a division of powers that are laid out the Seventh Schedule with its Union, State and Concurrent Lists. The Constitution has been made practically indestructible by a judiciary that has been given a very high degree of autonomy and independence. There is a single Constitution for the entire country (now including Jammu, Kashmir and Ladakh too), a single citizenship that does not permit dual citizenship with any other country and a provision for an emergency in any part of the country as declared by the Union. The All India Services are a constitutional authority and play an important part in maintaining the unitary character of government. When it comes to powers, these are weighted heavily in favour of the centre. India may be called a quasi-federation, pseudo-federation, approximate federation, evolving federation, or multi-layered federation depending on one's viewpoint or inclination. What is important is that it is quite different from a federation as is understood in say, Canada, Germany, Switzerland or the U.S.A. India is not a textbook federation. Purists would not call it a federation at all. The evolution of our federalism over the decades has depended on whether there was a single party or a coalition at the centre and will be discussed in Section C of this chapter.

No item saw such intense, impassioned, incisive and at times entertaining and droll exchanges as the lengthy debates on what the Union should choose as its national language. Practically two and a half days were taken up on this single matter which in its present form as Article 343 says:

(1) *The official language of the Union shall be Hindi in Devanagari script.*
The form of numerals to be used for the official purposes of the Union shall be the international form of Indian numerals.

(2) *Notwithstanding anything in clause (1), for a period of fifteen years from the commencement of this Constitution, the English language shall continue to be used for all the official purposes of the Union for which it was being used immediately before such commencement, provided that the President may, during the said period, by order authorise the use of the Hindi language in addition to the English language and of the Devanagari form of numerals in addition to the international form of Indian numerals for any of the official purposes of the Union.*

(3) *Notwithstanding anything in this article, Parliament may by law provide for the use after the said period of fifteen years of (a) the English language, or*

(b) *the Devanagari form of numerals, for such purposes as may be specified in the law.*

For a start, Prasad noted that there were more than 300 amendments that were tabled for discussion and some time was spent on how to handle this large number. Apparently, there was a prior consensus that one language should be chosen as a "common language" and that it should be used for "official" purposes of the Union and that this language should not be English. Gopalaswami Ayyangar, the lead speaker for the drafting committee, said that the Assembly should move towards adoption of Hindi as the official language of the Union. However, he introduced a caveat immediately when he said that the country could not afford to give up English because Hindi had not yet reached a level of development to be used efficiently for all official purposes. He proposed that "English be continued along with Hindi and that for a period of about 15 years English should continue to be used for all the purposes for which it is being used today". Naziruddin Ahmed spoke sensibly and said, "that English should continue for such a period till when an all-India language is evolved" and that one could not make a language suitable for the modern world by a legislative vote, that its suitability required great writers, thinkers, scientists, politicians, philosophers, litterateurs, dramatists and others to have expressed themselves fluently in that language. He concluded that Hindi was a language which was "in a very rudimentary condition" in those respects and lacked maturity of development.

In practical terms all this meant that English would be an official language for an indefinite and unspecified period of time which we now know means at least 72 years from the date of adoption of the Constitution! The discussion on numerals lasted an inordinately and bafflingly long time. It appears in hindsight that some members from the Hindi speaking states were so dissatisfied with Ayyangar's caveat that they filibustered the discussion on numerals beyond reasonable duration. In the end, they did not fully get their way with Devanagari numerals and the international numerals, incorrectly called Arabic numerals formerly, now correctly called Hindu numerals, were to stay. The matter of official state languages was far easier to handle and the decision was taken that "as far as possible, a language spoken in the state should be recognised as the language used for official purposes in that state and that for inter-state communications and for communications between the state and the centre the English language should continue to be used, provided that where between two States there was an agreement that inter-communication should be in the Hindi language, that should be permitted." In courts, however, English would dominate for many years. English effectively became the link language of the Union. Significantly there was no decision on a 'national' language. The discussion was too divisive and at some stages members from non-Hindi speaking states started name-calling the Hindi speakers dubbing them *Hindiwallahs.* T. T. Krishnamachari indeed went as far as saying that "I would sir, convey a warning on behalf of the people of South India because there are already elements there who want separation and it is up to us to firmly try and keep those elements down and my friends in U.P. do not help in any way by repeatedly flogging their idea of Hindi imperialism. Sir, it's up to my friends in U.P. to have an undivided unbroken whole India or it's up to them to have only a Hindi India".

There were many interludes into the merits and demerits of Sanskrit, Urdu, Hindustani and even Bengali and Telugu. Members began squabbling about which language others were using when they addressed the Assembly. One member said that if Hindi was the national language, Sanskrit was the world language. Another was asked to speak in Sanskrit after he advocated its official use. Another said it should be the national language because it was impartially difficult to all! Still another said that Gandhi favoured Hindustani. Yet another said that Urdu was not a language exclusively used by Muslims. One member provided the Kannada equivalents of the chemical elements, hydrogen, carbon, nitrogen and oxygen. Another said that the English language had produced no great men. There was discussion on whether the Roman script should be used for Hindi as had been done in Turkey and Indonesia with their languages. Hindi speakers were disappointed with the continuance of English and said that the wording of the Act was designed to "postpone the replacement of English by Hindi to the remotest possible date." Seth Govind Das spoke vociferously in favour of Hindi. He termed Ayyangar's caveat "retrograde". He rejected the charge that he was communal. It testifies to Prasad's patience that he allowed members to speak as long as they wanted until they literally wore themselves out. Significantly, no one protested that a 'national' language had not been announced; some members seemed to have quietly conflated national and official language (wishful thinking) in their own minds. India still does not have a national language. The idea of nationhood in Bhārat is so complex that it is probably unwise to even try to define a national language.

It is instructive to move fast forward about the language matter and see where we Indians stand in 2022 in this regard. Compared to its position in 1950, English has come to dominate world communication even more. It is the language of computers. It is undoubtedly the language of international science. It is the language of aviation. It has infinite variations and borrows heavily from many languages, the fastest evolving language in the world. It has an incredibly rich and nuanced vocabulary, especially with regard to nouns and adjectives. It is very easy to learn but extremely hard to master. Being heavily dependent on syntax and intonation, it can be forbidding to a beginner. Its light grammar is deceptive and one can easily mis-communicate because of this reason. It is a very subtle language where the position of a comma can completely change the meaning of a sentence. It cannot be replaced in India if the country is to grow into a superpower although some have argued that English alone is no guarantee of this. *For a country like India* which has a great many languages, one could say that English is a necessary though not a sufficient condition to achieve superpower status. Some have said that it was a possibly unintended gift that the British gave us; whatever it may be it has certainly been their most valuable gift to us. We do not have the advantage that China has in that there is only one major language there. However, Hindi which is the mother tongue of 43 per cent of us Indians is more of a link language today than it was in 1950 with the growing influence of television and social media.

Language in India is also important because it is one of the sounding boards of federalism. When one speaks of 'Hindi, Hindu, Hindustan' as some do today, one is harking back to Seth Govind Das, one of the Hindiwallahs of the Assembly, one who offended so many there with his bigoted ideas on a national language. Language is an emotional weapon in political terms and always has been so, and not just in India. It needs tactful handling by the central and even state governments for many states are still not strictly monolingual. Belgium, Canada, Singapore, South Africa and Switzerland are object lessons in how to handle language in a multilingual country. Some Indian politicians claim greatness for a particular language just because it is older than some other language. This is a specious argument: a language evolves because of a need to communicate among individuals in a particular society; if a language continues for a long time without change it could mean that the societal conditions did not change a lot. This might not be such a good thing. Modern English is one of the youngest languages in the world and yet no one can deny its greatness. On the whole, it just may be preferable for Indian politicians to steer clear of the language issue and allow Indian languages, and today English has become one of them too, to develop as society allows them to develop. The language matter should be handled with sensitivity. The new National Education Policy (NEP 2020) has attempted to do something in this regard, at least with increasing the amount of instruction in the mother tongue in the very early years of a child's education. If this is done there will be a real improvement in our productivity, innovation and output in 25 years because it is well known in education circles that creative imagination is best unleashed when a person thinks, feels and works in his or her mother tongue. This is the only way forward but it is a long-haul approach.

The next item of continuing interest in the assembly was the question of the second chamber or Upper House of Parliament, now known as the Rajya Sabha or Council of States. A subsidiary matter was the formation of the analogous Legislative Councils in the states. It was debated on 3 January 1949 and appears in its final form as Article 79 in our Constitution in the form, "There shall be a Parliament for the Union which shall consist of the President and two Houses to be known respectively as the Council of States and the House of the People." In my considered view, the opposition to the formation of an Upper House was more cogently and precisely articulated than the defence put up by the Drafting Committee.

The general drift of the arguments opposed to the second house was that it was an anachronism, peculiar to Britain and a colonial hangover for us. It must be remembered that Britain is a constitutional anomaly. It is the only country in the world with an unwritten Constitution, one that has evolved over ten centuries through tradition, custom and hard, painful experience. It has executed a monarch, forced others into exile and abdication, and even briefly experimented with a republic in over one thousand years of its ancient and bloody history. The Monarch has morphed from an autocratic all-powerful sovereign, like Edward III, Henry V, Henry VIII or his daughter Elizabeth I, to the constitutional figurehead that he is today. Most monarchic power was ceded to Parliament during the rule of the Hanoverian monarchs in the 18th and 19th centuries; many in the House of Hanover including Victoria were more comfortable speaking German rather than English. Indeed even by the time of her accession in 1838, the British monarchs had lost direct touch with their subjects facilitating the decline in their powers. Britain's 'Constitution' if it can even be called that would be a collection of papers, documents, precedents, judicial decisions and parliamentary transcripts. Laws are passed and deemed legal if the Parliament of the time feels them to be so. It is not, in general, a good role model for other countries all of whom have had to write constitutions in time periods limited at most to a few years but still supposed to stand the test of time. As an unwritten constitution, the British Constitution elevates Parliament greatly over other organs of government. Within Parliament the House of Commons is supreme: the power and influence of the House of Lords has gradually been whittled away more so with the abolition of most hereditary peerages in 1999. The House of Lords today is a symbolic body.

The complaint of inferiority complex vis-à-vis the British, raised in our Constituent Assembly, might have had to do with the fact that there were, technically speaking, two chambers in the legislative wing, at least during the last 30 years of the Raj. One should note that the 1919 Government of India Act saw the beginning of the bicameral system in our legislatures with the second chamber being called the 'Council of State'. One needs to consider the meaning of the word 'State' in this expression. It signifies the abstraction of sovereign power and may be contrasted with the 'Central Legislative Assembly' the Lower House which presumably legislated. The Council of State in such a context signifies a wiser advisory body, like the Lords in Britain, which might have a limited and subdued role in legislation. At least, this seems to have been the idea. Our

Constitution makers made a seemingly tiny change, almost certainly in full knowledge as to what they were doing, and changed 'Council of State' in the Montford Act to 'Council of States'. Now, the meaning of 'States' in this designation (written with capital letter S but actually meaning small letter s) is entirely different from 'State' in Montford (capital letter S) and refers to the constituent states of the Union, entities that, and as explained above, can be modified at will of Parliament. It has nothing to do with the State as the seat of sovereign power. The Rajya Sabha therefore became merely a token symbol of federalism. Considering that our Constitution was so centre-dominated, this name change would almost appear to be a sop thrown to the states.

Members were disappointed at this obvious imitation, at least in form, of the House of Lords. Begum Rasool said that although the Britisher had left India his ghost was still stalking around, haunting us. Lokanath Misra said that there was no real need for a second chamber and that they were out of date. Bringing in the civilisational aspect he said:

> *The only argument that is generally advanced in favour of such a chamber is that it will have a sobering effect on the decisions of the Lower House which is more representative of the people and that the people are now restive. I therefore submit that unless the manner of the constitution of this second chamber is changed and we are in a position to accept something which will be purely Indian based on Indian culture of deep, all-pervasive view and on Indian sentiment and temperament based and nurtured on our traditions which alone can have a sobering influence, the creation of an Upper House by itself will have no influence on the House of the People.*

Gandhi had, on an earlier occasion, said that a poor country like India could ill afford a luxury like an Upper House. Mishra too deemed it a "waste of public money and so much waste of time."

Begum Rasool continued thus:

> *When we frame a new constitution, it becomes our duty to make it in such a way as to transform our mentality from that of slavishness to freedom. The old mentality reminiscent of British slavery must be uprooted.... the British have brought India to her present distress and miserable plight. I would like to point out that before framing the constitution of the country, we should scan the history of India during the short period of 1919 to the present day. Sir, from 1919 to 1935 many constitutions were framed but all of them the product of British imperialism. In 1919, local self-government was conceded to India; councils were created, even a council was formed for the centre. It was self-government only in name... the local bodies could not function freely... this system still continues. Similar was the case in the councils; the influence of the elected representatives was weakened by the nominated members; and any programme for the betterment of the country put forth by the elected representatives used to be opposed by the nominated members. That was the state of affairs under the Act of 1919.*

The mode of membership of the Upper House also caused unrest and discomfort in the Constituent Assembly. Election to the Rajya Sabha was complicated and based on an indirect system of proportional representation with an electoral college. The number of members could be no more than half of that of the Lok Sabha. The election was conducted purely in the state legislative assemblies with the members there being the electors. In other words, there was an illogical double representation of a single vote cast by an eligible voter in the popular election to the state assembly, the first time to the assembly itself and the second time, indirectly, to the Rajya Sabha. Imitating the lifetime peerages of the Lords, the Rajya

Sabha membership was a continuous one with a third of the members retiring every two years so that there was a full turnaround of membership only after six years for any given membership on a given date. This raises another anomaly: the longest serving members in any Rajya Sabha on any given day could be representing the political preferences of the general electorate for as long as 11 years prior to that day. This is clearly unsatisfactory if the country is fast-moving as is the case of the India of 2022. Legislation that is clearly important and needs to be implemented quickly can get delayed inordinately and sometimes even indefinitely if the Rajya Sabha is controlled by members of an opposition that was in power in the states a long time back. If these members vote in a partisan manner and according to the directive of a party whip, the main role of the Rajya Sabha as a wiser and more cautious advisory body is completely lost and it merely becomes a roadblock in the progress of the nation. S. L. Saxena called the Upper House "a clog in the wheel of progress". A piece of legislation becomes effective only if it satisfies the dictates of both thermodynamics and kinetics, to use an analogy from chemistry—it must be good and it must be fast.

Gopalaswami Ayyangar who moved the resolution conceded that the Rajya Sabha would slow legislation down. However, he opined that it was a good thing. In his words:

> *...what we really achieve by the existence of this Second Chamber is only an instrument by which we delay action which might be hastily conceived, and we also give an opportunity, perhaps, to seasoned people who may not be in the thickest of the political fray, but who might be willing to participate in the debate with an amount of learning and importance which we do not ordinarily associate with a House of the People.*

Today's Rajya Sabha members, it is true, do not generally

contain those who are "in the thickest of the political fray" but they are an unusual lot. They consist of people who have failed to get elected to the Lok Sabha but still find favour with their political parties for their administrative, legal or parliamentary expertise. Alternatively, they could be outsiders who are inducted into the council of ministers and as such must enter Parliament. Articulate, aggressive and therefore useful lawyers are elected as are 'committed' journalists, highly partisan people who participate in TV debates ostensibly as 'neutral' political commentators, strongly politically polarised ex-bureaucrats, and newspersons, in fact just about anyone who has found favour with a political party that commands the requisite electoral support in a state legislature and is unable or unwilling to seek election to the Lok Sabha. There are still others who are nominated for their 'special' talents—these include Bollywood film stars, cricketers with cult following, Olympics medal winners, classical dancers and musicians, elderly inactive scientists and in general, idle busybodies. The analogy with the Brothers Grimm's 'Musicians of Bremen' is accurate in more ways than one.

All this is a far cry from what Ayyangar intended. All else aside, there is no justification for *any* nominated member in any legislative body in any country. It is a matter of principle. It is true that some countries like Canada and Singapore do have nominated members in their Upper Houses but the legislative responsibilities of such members can be limited. The example of the U.S.A. is not pertinent: the Senate there is a directly elected body and by fixing its membership to exactly two per state, whatever be the population of the state, whether it be California or Montana or anything else, their founding fathers (notably Benjamin Franklin and Roger Sherman) put out a powerful message regarding the federal character of the US polity. No other second house is quite like the US Senate.

The Rajya Sabha membership can sometimes become a pitiable parody of federalism and there are several well-known, even prominent faces who got elected to the Upper House from a state from which they do not hail and have sometimes even barely visited. How can such a legislative body ever represent state interests at the centre?

The final thread of continuing debate in the Assembly was the question as to whether our Constitution is an original document in the sense of expressing the minds and souls of the Indian people, their anxieties and aspirations and providing a uniquely Indian response in terms of the modalities of law making, protection of these laws and their execution. Or is a cut-and-paste effort from other constitutions and put together in haste? One member called it a *kichri* constitution in fact. Another, Ramnarayan Singh termed it, "a fantastic mixture of the various constitutions obtaining in the world". Kuladhar Chaliha said that, "our Constitution is really an amalgam of the American and English Constitutions, with Canada in between." P. S. Deshmukh said it was a rehash of the 1935 Government of India Act although he did add that this might not be such a bad thing. Such a document would hardly have conveyed the hopes and fears of the anxious millions who constituted the new republic. More gravely, Brajeshwar Prasad said:

> *If India is to remain loyal to her ancient traditions she must discard the basic foundations of this constitution. Dharma was the basis of all governments in ancient India. If the will of ignorant and hungry people were ever to become the basis of government in India, it will mean the complete liquidation of all that is good and noble in Indian life. The common man has got no will of his own. He is a bundle of instincts and a creature of environment and heredity. His will can never be the basis of modern governments in any part of the world and especially in India where he suffers from innumerable handicaps. The concept of Dharma incorporates all*

> *that is good and noble in parliamentarianism and rejects the evils that have crept into it. A State based on Dharma will never tolerate economic inequality or social injustice. But it will never accord recognition to popular will as the basis of government. For the will of man is nasty, brutish and short. Dharma is in consonance with the fundamental principles of democracy. The will to will the general will is the core of democracy. The essence of democracy is the representation of the real will of the people as opposed to and distinct from the actual will. The actual will is surcharged with passion and prejudice. The actual will changes from moment to moment, from hour to hour and from day to day. It contains within itself all that is mean, stupid and foolish in human life. It can never be the basis of government. The real will on the other hand is in consonance with the teachings of the great leaders of thought in human history. It is in consonance with morality.*

Looked at from such a wide perspective, our Constitution falls far short of anything this ancient land has stood for. All this and more have remained perennial discussion topics in India for seventy-five years in the mainstream and social media with articles appearing ever so often with lively titles like 'British laws for India', 'Parts of the Indian constitution that were inspired by others', 'Indians do not have a constitution of their own' and 'Sources and borrowed features of the Indian constitution'. Punning on the title of this chapter does our constitution represent India 1.0 or Empire 3.0?

In these contexts, there were two options open to the Assembly at the outset of its sittings. The first was to disregard the various attempts at constitution drafting from the 1895 Swaraj Constitution to the 1947 Indian Independence Act and begin *ab initio* in other words with no memory of these attempts both by Indians and Britishers to frame guidelines for governance and start with an entirely different model, say the

M. N. Roy 1944 Constitution, the Gandhian Constitution of 1946 or one based on a purely Indian concept like *panchayati raj* with the village as the grassroots governing unit. In its practical wisdom the Assembly did not choose such a route possibly because they thought it would be unfeasible and unworkable given the plethora of problems the new country faced. There is no saying whether this might or might not have worked for us. The U.S.S.R. and Communist China chose indigenous paths for governance which were totally different from anything known in the Western world. However, it is most convenient in a liberal democracy, which is what we elected to be, to choose a governance model that parallels the Western democracies with three wings of government, an elected body or bodies that are responsible for legislation and a unitary system of governance with federal elements as appropriate. This is the second option that the Constituent Assembly chose. Given this, it became inevitable that the Assembly would be guided by what other democracies were doing because in the end there are not too many differences in forms of governance in liberal democracies. It is true there may be some country specific differences but the broad outlines will be the same. Accordingly, it is practically impossible not to choose elements from other constitutions in drafting one's own. The topic has been extensively commented upon and I do not find a necessity in reviewing this material. It will suffice to say that there are elements we have taken from the constitutions of the U.K., U.S.A., Canada, Australia, Ireland and Russia among others. In practice, the first two are the most relevant in the Indian context.

Ambedkar was clearly impressed by the US Constitution. It is a visionary document. It is one of the shortest constitutions of the world and possibly the least amended. There have been just 27 amendments in 250 years compared to our 105 in 75 years. It has remained unaffected by time and it shows that it is not necessary to spell out each and every exigency of governance if the system is honest and upright. It is practically 'unwritten' and yet not quite so—the few words that are written are fundamental to human nature itself and not so concerned with specifics of governance. The Preamble reads, "We the People of the United States, in Order to form a more perfect Union, establish Justice, insure domestic Tranquility, provide for the common defence, promote the general Welfare, and secure the Blessings of Liberty to ourselves and our Posterity, do ordain and establish this Constitution for the United States of America." This wording implies that their Constitution will not be perfect: it only speaks of a "more perfect Union". Words like justice, tranquility, defence, welfare, liberty and posterity are more likely to be understood by common people than words like sovereign, socialist, secular, democratic and republic. The US Constitution readily reaches out to its people. Ours, stands aloof and apart. Their declaration of Independence which immediately predated their Constitution speaks about holding certain "truths to be self-evident, that all men are created equal, that they are endowed by their Creator with certain unalienable Rights, that among these are Life, Liberty and the pursuit of Happiness." These sentiments are universal and not particular to America, and herein lies the greatness of their Constitution.

There is a seeming similarity between the US and Indian Constitutions in terms of designations like 'President' and 'Governor' and a bicameral system. However these similarities are superficial. Even our form of a federal structure is quite different from that prevalent in the U.S.A. which is truly federal. As outlined above, our Rajya Sabha and their Senate are utterly different. Above all, as is expanded later in this chapter and also in Chapter 4, the legislative and executive functions are completely separated in the U.S.A. unlike in India where there is overlap. The latter is a feature of countries that follow the so-called Westminster system of governance which is inspired by the U.K. and this is where we may now turn our attention.

The Westminster system is modelled for a parliamentary democracy named after the Palace of Westminster in London and the home of the British Parliament. It is mainly concerned with the operation of the legislature which, and has been explained earlier, is sovereign only if there is an unwritten Constitution, namely only in the U.K. Accordingly, the Westminster model gets modified almost by default elsewhere, almost all former colonies and dominions of Britain, because all of them have written constitutions and legislations passed by Parliament may be reviewed by the judiciary, unlike in the U.K. The key features of the Westminster model are a ceremonial head of State who holds nominal power (British Sovereign, President of India), a cabinet headed by a Prime Minister consisting typically of elected members of the Lower House, a first-past-the-post system of elections in individual parliamentary constituencies as opposed to proportional representation, the presence of opposition parties and a system wherein Parliament can dismiss a government by passing a vote of no-confidence or where a government can be dissolved voluntarily by an elected government in power seeking a fresh mandate from the people at any time during its tenure.

Some commentators have held that there is no one Westminster model and that the concept itself is simplistic and outdated, there being too many significant variations. Generally the Westminster system defines a majoritarian democracy as opposed to a consensual democracy that is characteristic of countries that have opted for proportional representation in their legislative bodies. Yet, differences exist among the Westminster countries themselves. Australia, Guyana, Ireland and New Zealand do not use the first-past-the-post electoral system, Australia, Canada and India have federal systems and only the U.K. has an unwritten constitution. New Zealand moved from bicameralism to unicameralism in 1952 and further to proportional representation in 1993. The most important constitutional difference between India and the other Westminster countries is our federal structure with clearly defined systems of governance in the states which are a diverse and varied lot. Accordingly centre-state relations form an important part of the discourse and dialogue in India as opposed to most of the other countries in this group.

A point of note here is that the Westminster model is a majoritarian democracy and not consensual. This simple fact has been forgotten by our opposition legislators today. As long as there were coalition governments at the centre the democracy was *de facto* consensual but it will not be so in single party rule. Irrational rants that a single party ruling at the centre must necessarily consult with the opposition on all legislative matters resemble King Canute. Asking for every proposed legislation to be sent to a parliamentary committee rather than debating it out on the floor of the House is merely buying time that does not exist. After many decades, India has decisively shifted to single party rule at the Centre, a trend that could continue. If nothing else, this shows that the electorate is finally clear about who it is and therefore what it wants. An opposition that does not respect such an unambiguous and direct mandate from the people is not worthy of participating in a parliamentary democracy.

To conclude this section, one may answer the question as to whether our Constitution is unique to us or merely a hotchpotch cut-and-paste from other constitutions with another question: Does our Constitution capture the spirit and substance of our people so as to address three critical issues that concern Indian nationhood? Does our Constitution:

(1) further national unity and still encourage regional pride, howsoever the latter may be expressed?

(2) facilitate a feeling of common nationhood among Hindus and Muslims, who together make up 94% of our population? and
(3) foster a sense of equality among groups that are widely different in terms of social and economic status?

These issues are unique to us and therefore if the Constitution has been able to address them properly, it follows that it is unique and original to us and not cut-and-paste, whatever be its semantic and linguistic form.

These three issues are the condensate of the seven threads of continuous discussion in the post-independence debates of the assembly and will continue to be highlighted in the rest of the book. These are the test cases, the benchmarks of nationhood and the gauntlets we have to run.

To seek answers to these questions one needs to examine how the Constitution has fared in the 75 years since it was launched.

C. The Republic between 1950 and 2022

The concluding session of the Constituent Assembly took place on 24 January 1950. Jana Gana Mana was adopted as the national anthem. Vande Mataram was adopted as the national song with equal status. The final act of the Assembly was the unanimous election of Prasad, its president, as the first President of the Indian Republic. His nomination by Nehru with Patel seconding was greeted with loud approbation. Prasad was a veteran of the freedom struggle and a long-time associate of Gandhi. His term as president of the Constituent Assembly was marked by dignity, wisdom and humour. While he was being praised at length in the Assembly on his elevation, he remarked that he was going to stop the Assembly discussion for the first time! Not many remember the scholarly fact-filled book he wrote in prison entitled *India Divided* and published in 1946, where he pointed out the contradictions between a State and a nation, noting that the latter is a psychological construct while the former is a technical one. Conflation of these political and civilisational identities has caused much confusion in the seventy-five years of independent India and it is pertinent to note that our first President was well aware of the differences between these two types of identities and made no attempt to hide them.

One must also be aware that Nehru chose to downplay these identity differences and this was the source of tension between him and leaders like Prasad, Munshi and Rajagopalachari, all Constituent Assembly members, during Nehru's stewardship of the country. Prasad exercised his authority in as complete a manner as allowed under the Constitution that was created under his supervision. His differences with Nehru on the matter of the reconstruction of the Somnath temple are often cited. Some matters do not go away and this indicates their relevance to the continuing existence of Bhārat. As recently as September 2021, Anas Haqqani, a Taliban leader praised Mahmud of Ghazni for destroying the shrine. He wrote in the visitor's book, "Today, we visited the shrine of Sultan Mahmud Ghaznavi, a renowned Muslim warrior and Mujahid of the 10th century. Ghaznavi (May the mercy of Allah be upon him) established a strong Muslim rule in the region from Ghazni and smashed the idol of Somnath." The civilisational tensions between Prasad and Nehru continued during the former's 12-year long stint as President of India. It is alleged that when he died a few months after laying down office, Nehru as Prime Minister advised his successor Radhakrishnan to desist from attending his funeral. Radhakrishnan, continuing Prasad's tradition of exercising his presidential authority to as full an extent as the Constitution would allow, disregarded Nehru's advice and went!

It is helpful to formally describe the construct of our Constitution in as brief a manner as is possible. The following section describes the document as it stands today, that is, with all the amendments over the years. There is a preamble, followed by 395 articles listed in 22 parts and 12 accompanying schedules that detail government policy and rules in relation to specific articles. At the time of its adoption in 1950 it ran to 1, 45, 000 words, making it the longest national Constitution ever. Parts 1 and 2 contain 11 articles on the Union, its territories and citizenship. Part 3, with Articles 12 through 35, deals with the all-important Fundamental Rights. Part 4 (Articles 36 through 51) speaks of the Directive Principles. Part 5 (Articles 52 through 151) specifies that there shall be three organs of government, the legislative, executive and judiciary. In the context of this book, Part 11 (Articles 245 through 263) and the accompanying Seventh Schedule, which details Article 246, are important because it deals with the law-making powers of the Union and the States and emphasises the general dominance of the former in this regard. Part 20 contains a single article, the all-important Article 368, which states that, "Notwithstanding anything in this Constitution, Parliament may in exercise of its constituent power amend by way of addition, variation or repeal any provision of this Constitution in accordance with the procedure laid down in this article."

It is interesting to compare our Constitution with others in the world. I refer here to our searches from the Constitute Project, developed at the University of Texas at Austin and the University of Chicago, supported among others by the National Science Foundation of the U.S.A. and University College London. As the longest constitution by far, ours scores in the matter of detail with Brazil and Mexico approaching us; whether or not detail in a constitution is a good thing is another question. We do not rank that high in the level of executive power conferred by the Constitution with France, Poland, Russia, Spain and Thailand figuring very high in this respect. Executive power means the authority of the ministers and the cabinet. We do somewhat better with judicial power and may be compared with Australia, Egypt, Germany and Italy and our judiciary is distinctly more powerful than say, the U.S.A. where it is comparatively weak. France and Poland are among the countries with the most powerful judiciaries. What is indeed impressive is our level of judiciary independence and we rank here with Argentina, Brazil, Italy, Mongolia, South Africa and Turkey. France, Germany and the U.S.A. fare well here but not to the extent that we do. We are about average with regard to legislative power and this is true for most countries in Europe and Asia. The notable exception is in the U.S.A., where the legislative power of their Congress is enormous, possibly because of the strict separation of legislative and executive wings of government. It could further be held that the extent of judicial and legislative power is complementary in any country where judicial review of legislation is possible. Under such see-saw circumstances, both these really cannot be very strong simultaneously and analogously very weak simultaneously. In India, the balance is tilted slightly towards the judiciary. The number of rights we have is about average as also the number of words used to describe them. What is distinctive is the scope of these rights and we score in this department. All in all, the Constitute Project statistical survey conveys the impression that ours is a reasonable constitution all round if it is compared with those of other liberal democracies. The U.K. is not included in the above comparative description. For reasons already outlined, it should be clear to the reader that an unwritten Constitution with parliamentary sovereignty cannot really be compared with other constitutions in quantitative terms.

The Constitution has been tested continuously since 1950 by the courts that are entitled to do so. Certain landmark judgments need to be noted as they interpreted critical provisions and indeed changed the constitutional course of the country. These pertained to important issues like the limits of parliamentary power to alter, amend and add to the Constitution (Kesavananda Bharati vs State of Kerala, 1973; I. R. Coelho vs State of Tamil Nadu, 2007), the powers of the legal executive vis-à-vis Parliament (Indira Gandhi vs Raj Narain, 1975), the limits on individual freedom (A. K. Gopalan vs State of Madras, 1950; Maneka Gandhi vs Union of India, 1978), the right to property (Shankari Prasad Singh Deo vs Union of India and State of Bihar, 1952; I. C. Golak Nath vs State of Punjab, 1967), the constitutionality of the 42nd Amendment (Minerva Mills Case, 1980), as to whether caste is an indication of backwardness (Indra Sawhney & Others vs Union of India, 1992), whether a divorced Muslim woman is entitled to alimony (Mohd. Ahmad Khan vs Shah Bano Begum & Others, 1985), as to whether triple talaq, polygamy and nikah halala are unconstitutional (Shaiyara Bano vs Union of India and Others, 2017) and whether Section 377 of the Indian Penal Code as applied to private consensual sex between consenting same-sex adults was constitutionally legitimate (Navtej Singh Johar vs. Union of India, 2018). Some of these judgements are mentioned in the following sections as they apply to the three trouble spot areas of federalism, religion and social and economic equality.

The Preamble and the discussion of its first sentence in the Constituent Assembly are given in the frontispiece illustration and have been commented upon earlier in this chapter. For the record let us state the full text as it stood in 1950:

> WE, THE PEOPLE OF INDIA, having solemnly resolved to constitute India into a SOVEREIGN DEMOCRATIC

REPUBLIC and to secure to all its citizens:

JUSTICE, social, economic and political; LIBERTY of thought, expression, belief, faith and worship;

EQUALITY of status and of opportunity;

and to promote among them all FRATERNITY assuring the dignity of the individual and the unity of the Nation;

IN OUR CONSTITUENT ASSEMBLY this twenty-sixth day of November, 1949, do HEREBY ADOPT, ENACT AND GIVE TO OURSELVES THIS CONSTITUTION

We note also that the Preamble was changed on 18 December 1976 through the 42nd Amendment and that the first sentence now reads:

WE, THE PEOPLE OF INDIA, having solemnly resolved to constitute India into a SOVEREIGN SOCIALIST SECULAR DEMOCRATIC REPUBLIC and to secure to all its citizens:

We further note that the phrase 'unity of the Nation' was changed to 'unity and integrity of the Nation' in this amendment. This latter change seems to be a tautology and might have been done just for sound bytes in those shrill days of the Emergency. It was the introduction of 'socialist' and 'secular' that caused all the controversy. These changes in the preamble caused many to comment that the 'Constitution of India' had been changed to 'Constitution of Indira' for the 42nd Amendment is most closely associated with the then Prime Minister, Indira Gandhi. There was no constitutional significance in adding these words in the preamble because preambles by definition are non-justiciable. They are like axioms in geometry not theorems. They should contain only self-evident truths.

The 42nd amendment was hugely controversial for the surreptitious way in which it was introduced when most of the opposition leaders were in jail, the speed and chicanery used to ensure that the procedural aspects had been followed but most of all because the words 'socialist' and 'secular' are not universal concepts and certainly not words that reflect any aspect of the Indian spirit. It was a case of unjustified means being employed to secure unjustified ends at a time when legitimate debate in Parliament was severely curtailed. Both words 'socialist' and 'secular' had been discussed threadbare in the Assembly debates and the decision not to include them in the 1950 document was taken after due diligence and deliberation. Lokanath Misra said, "Gradually it seems to me that 'secular state' is a slippery phrase, a device to by-pass the ancient culture of the land." There were three separate attempts to introduce the words 'socialist' and 'secular' into the Constitution by K. T. Shah. Ambedkar was adamant that these words should not be included. He said that Indians should be given the freedom to choose their preferred economic and social framework. It should be noted that this came from the foremost proponent, of his time, of social and economic change in India and testifies to his great objectivity and fairness. He understood well that inserting such terms could only lead to turmoil, discord and mayhem in the political and public discourse. All of this has happened after 1950 and more so after 1976. The connotations and consequences of our excursions into 'socialism' and 'secularism' are tragically obvious today.

There are several reasons why the words 'socialist' and 'secular' ought never to have found a place in our Constitution. Both 'socialist' and 'secular' are states of mind or opinion that may vary quite considerably from one individual to another and for any individual from one time to another. Socialism is certainly not a permanent state of being for a nation and it can degenerate easily into an unacceptable economic policy. It can never be a defining feature, which is what a constitutional preamble should be all about. By introducing these words the promoters of this change were going against India's most basic feature namely its democratic ideal, for in a democracy no one should be able to legislate on a state of mind. Indeed, in a recent writ petition filed against the 42nd amendment, the appellant Vishnu Shankar Jain has said that "in a democratic setup, the citizens cannot be bound to accept a particular ideology and the application of the ideology depends on the will of the people to be reflected through votes from time to time. In this case, the petitioners have said that 'socialist' and 'secular' concepts are political thoughts and seen in the light of the right to practice religion (Article 25), right to free speech [Article 19(1)(a)], these principles are against the principle of democracy.

Socialism is an unnecessary concept in our Bhāratiya society that has traditionally maintained a successful balance between wage providers and wage earners, neither erring towards exploitation nor towards expropriation. The latter sin was committed by our 'secular' government (not by society) through at least eleven constitutional amendments beginning with the 1st and concluding with the 44th when the right to property was finally removed from the Fundamental Rights. India does not have an efficient public social security system, one of the main attributes of a socialist country be it Cuba or Sweden. Margaret Thatcher was at her biting best when she said that "The problem with socialism is that you eventually run out of other people's money." The continuing tragedy of Air India from 1953 to 2021 during which time one of the world's best airlines was converted into a vast bloated inefficient loss-making bureaucracy is the best example as to where Indian type socialism can take one. The airline's reversion to its original owner in 2021 is as direct an admission of failure as one might want from the same authority, the Government of India, which embarked on this foolish expropriation exercise 68 long years ago when it nationalised the airline. Socialism was always a scandal in India. To introduce such a word into a constitutional preamble by Indira Gandhi was nothing short of farcical.

The latter word 'secular' is even more objectionable because, and as mentioned previously, it is particular to the Christian Church and cannot figure in Bhārat that is India where the need for a Church–State divide simply does not arise. The most ardent of secularists cannot opine that Hinduism and Christianity are the same. They are not. Secularism in modern India has come to mean neither the state's disinterest in religion nor equality in its treatment of its religious communities (Articles 14 and 15). Secularism has been degraded by the Congress party to a crude appeasement of the second largest majority community, wrongly called a minority, and goes by the fancy name of religious pluralism. In practical terms, it means the securing of vote banks in critical electoral constituencies where the Muslim vote has been able to swing the result in a particular direction because at least in popular perception, Muslims in India tend to vote as a group whereas Hindus do not. In the Congress years, 'secular' was an acceptable word, even a nice word. Many dynastic regional parties tried to come together under the 'secular' banner to purportedly 'save the country' from 'communal forces'. The bad 'communal' Hindu became the opposite of the good 'secular' Indian. Today, 'secular' has become a bad word, in fact a hated one, because vast sections of the Hindu population link it directly to Muslim appeasement. They have demonstrated their sentiments in the ballot box in

2014 and 2019. What is such a word, that divides more than it unites, doing in the preamble of our Constitution?

Socialism similarly came to signify the potential to exploit a poverty vote bank through slogans like *Garibi Hatao* and *Garibi par vaar, bahattar hazaar'*. Today, socialism in India has come to mean a mass distribution of poverty. It has become a jingoistic slogan of political parties seeking election. It is only in India, courtesy the Congress party and its regional offshoots, that socialism and secularism have been wickedly conflated and this cocktail is in direct antithesis to all that is best in our ancient culture and civilisation. This admixture takes the worst of socialism and secularism, both of which in an absolute sense, *in vacuo*, are admirable concepts. There is nothing wrong with secularism in France or socialism in Norway, both highly advanced and affluent countries. It is their wilful misrepresentation and misinterpretation in India, regrettably also through constitutional amendments, and their electoral convolution at the hustings that has rendered the body politic so perverted, and a distant cry from the idealism and honesty that characterised the members of our constituent assembly.

It was commented as early as the Assembly debates that the word 'secular' had only a vague meaning. There were no definitions and conventions to guide anyone as to what exactly it meant. It was generally felt that this word was being introduced to dilute the idea of a Bhāratiya culture and the history of the Bhāratiya civilisational state. Nowhere in the Constitution is 'secular' defined. Indeed, it occurs just twice, the first as introduced in the preamble in 1976 and the second in the original document in Article 25(2)(a) which states that "nothing in this article shall affect the operation of any existing law or prevent the State from making any law regulating or restricting any economic, financial, political or other secular activity which may be associated with religious practice." Even this article gets into a grey area because it might not be clear if propagation of a religion is such a wide concept that it just might not enter the secular sphere. Again, it is not all clear if deciding the opening and closing hours of a temple is a secular or religious decision. In such an atmosphere it is unbelievable that the 'secularism' word entered the Doctrine of Basic Structure (1973) introduced in the Kesavananda Bharati case. According to this doctrine, which is discussed immediately, the basic structure cannot be abrogated even by a constitutional amendment. Since this predates the 42nd amendment, one may ask whether the introduction of 'secular' in the preamble was even required? The problem with the basic structure is that it is not defined in the Constitution! One is simply supposed to be aware of it.

One finally enters the moral arena, always a tricky matter in a constitutional discussion. Morality, if it is taken to mean widely shared views and value systems as to what constitutes right and wrong, must be implicitly present in a constitution. Morality is one aspect of dharma. In this regard, one may question if there is any moral argument for Bhārat, if not India, being defined as a secular state. Pakistan was carved out of Bhāratavarsha for Muslims alone because of their unwillingness to co-exist with the rest of us. One should not forget that in the run-up to Partition, there were extremist Muslim elements who did not want an undivided Punjab and Bengal because the Muslim populations there would be only in the 55-65 per cent range. They preferred a division of these provinces in such a manner that the new Pakistan would be overwhelmingly Muslim. This bespeaks of a complete intolerance of Hindus living amidst them.

In such a background, the contention of our secular elites in maintaining that because Pakistan is a Muslim state, India defaults into a secular state is patently false. India did not want Partition, Pakistan did. Unlike the Abrahamic religions Sanātana Dharma is *inherently* secular in the finest sense of the term. It is because a full exchange of population was not implemented during Partition (against the advice of several senior Indian leaders), because half the Muslims in undivided India chose not to migrate, and because of the strange terms of the Nehru-Liaquat pact of 1950, we ended up with a denominational composition of roughly 80 per cent and 15 per cent. This happened because of Partition and the way it was implemented and is, if nothing else, mere happenstance. In this scenario, claiming that India is secular because Muslims live here is twisting the truth. Not many in India even knew about the Western notion of secularism before 1947. The concept itself was foisted upon us by the Congress in their great fear of being dubbed a 'Hindu Pakistan' forgetting that the basic dharma of this land is tolerance, forbearance and patience as a sure means of achieving and sustaining the larger good. Bhārat in 2022 cannot be run with artificial props like the Nehruvian idea of India, secularism, socialism, Indira Gandhi's ideas on *garibi hatao,* Rajiv Gandhi's ideas on computers, Manmohan Singh's ideas on prioritising State resources, State protection of minority intolerance, vote bank politics and the state taking control of Hindu temples in the name of self-respect movements. Any Bhāratiya today, *of whatever religion*, should want the country to be run under a canopy where spiritual traditions and geo-cultural strategy are preserved to protect the nation. These are the true ideas of India, its society and its greatness. These are what the Constitution should embody and enshrine, especially in its preamble. Above it all is the basic structure which cannot be defined and should not be defined. In its in-definability should lie its immanence and importance.

For the sake of the record it should be remarked that the Janata Party government (1977-1980) knowingly or unknowingly did not seize the moment to undo the 42nd Amendment. Perhaps their socialistic proclivities were too great. Perhaps they felt that removing just 'secular' and not 'socialist' would draw comments from new quarters. In any event the modified Preamble remains today, a blot and eyesore on the nation. Perhaps another way of looking at the matter at least as it pertains to 'secular' is that with no clear definition as to what secular means, it is open to anyone to regard it in whatever manner he or she might please at any given time, and approach the courts accordingly. Anything that has a large number of contradictory meanings and interpretations has, in the end, no meaning. Still, in the Minerva Mills case the most quixotic portions of the 42nd amendment, namely sections 4 and 55, the latter preventing any constitutional amendment from being called in question in any court on any ground, the former amending Article 31C thereby affording supremacy to the Directive Principles over the Fundamental Rights, were held by the Supreme Court to be unconstitutional. That such irrational and frankly illogical constitutional developments continued in the legislative, executive and judiciary wings of the government right through the history of independent India, but more so in the 1970s and 1980s when the Congress was all-powerful at the centre, is a sad reflection on the calibre and quality of our political leadership. They have simply not lived up to the high standards expected of them by the Constituent Assembly. Ambedkar would not have approved.

The Fundamental Rights in our Constitution define the routes to personality development of an individual and to preserving human dignity. These are covered in Articles 12 through 35 in Part 3. Rights are an essential part of any constitution because they define areas where a citizen may approach the courts if he or she feels that they have been violated. In this respect Ambedkar termed Article 32 as the heart and soul of the Constitution, without which the Constitution itself would become a nullity. This article has been defined as falling within the basic structure. The all-important Article 13 when read with Article 368 defines the power and limits of Parliament to amend the Constitution, and more peculiarly the fundamental rights themselves, for example Article 31, the right to property, which has been seriously crippled through amendments. Several specific cases mentioned in this section have dealt with this issue. Also important are articles 14, 15, and 25 through 30 which may be invoked in issues concerning unequal treatment given to religions, mostly Hinduism, by successive governments. Article 16 is pertinent with respect to reservations for SCs and backward classes. Article 19, concerning freedom of speech has come to the forefront in recent times with the popularity of social media.

According to a realistic Ambedkar:

> *The idea of making a gift of fundamental rights to every individual is no doubt very laudable. The question is how to make them effective. The prevalent view is that once the rights are enacted in law then they are safeguarded. As experience proves rights are protected not by law but by the social and moral conscience of the society.*

What is this social and moral conscience? Are constitutional rights related to duties? Or are they inherent to all humans in civilised societies? Does one need to perform certain duties to enjoy rights? Are inalienable rights restricted to universal concepts such as life, liberty and equality? Are all the rights specified in Part 3 unencumbered and enjoyable by all citizens under all conditions? All constitutions have rights but most do not specify duties. The Constitution of the former U.S.S.R. was one such. It stated among other things that citizens' exercise of their rights was inseparable from performance of their duties.

They were required to work and to observe labour discipline, and evasion of work was criminalised. Citizens also had a duty to protect socialist property and oppose corruption. Military service was also a duty, violation of which was considered "a betrayal of the Motherland and the gravest of crimes". The concept of duties has persisted in the Constitution of the recent Russian federation, but these are confined to items such as the obligation to pay lawful taxes, preservation of cultural and historical heritage, protection of historical monuments, cultural artefacts and the environment. Motherland became Fatherland in the new constitution and the obligatory military service provision remained.

Also interesting is that the 1946 Gandhian Constitution mentioned duties, which it said were inseparable from rights. Article 51A lists duties for Indian citizens but for the large part they are innocuous and non-controversial such as respecting the flag, anthem and the freedom struggle, promoting fraternity transcending religion, and developing a scientific temper. In informal language, Americans would call this upholding flag, mother and apple pie. The connection between rights and duties is a fascinating discussion topic in itself but in the end it should be an instinctive and natural one which any responsible citizen should make and it probably does not need to be specified in a constitution.

In a different vein, the necessity even to justify the concept of rights and then duties (transactional interaction between citizens and government) is a consequence of Western notions of the nation-state and is a feature of constitutions modelled according to that notion. A dharmic state has no need even for such a concept: the role and place of the raja and the praja are intuitive and instinctive. Both act in such a manner to sustain the State to maximum benefit. We need this dharmic element in our constitution. In the words of Aurobindo:

> *Both rights and duties are European ideas. Dharma is the Indian conception in which rights and duties lose the artificial antagonism created by a view of the world which makes selfishness the root of action, and regain their deep and eternal unity.*

Right from the beginning there should have been an even greater emphasis on the Indian people, their culture, their civilisation, their sense of morality and the necessity of their unison with the spirit of the constitution that they had chosen to take for themselves. The judiciary may interpret the laws but it cannot prevent their non-compliance if they are radically against the will of the people. This puts a heavy burden on all three organs of the Union to be in consonance with the sentiments of the people always keeping in mind the separation of powers doctrine. There is now a definite tendency towards judicial overreach and overlap with the legislature. Indira Gandhi was an extreme example of the reverse tendency of legislative overreach into the domain of the judiciary. The following sections attempt to summarise how and why she failed. Attempts by state legislatures today to forcibly legislate towards policies that do not have popular support are similarly bound to fail, whether at the hands of the judiciary or at the hands of the people themselves in elections.

The Directive Principles of State Policy (Part 4, Articles 36 through 51) are, to put it simply, a wish list of our constitution makers of where they would like to see the country go even if they felt that for one reason or another, these matters could not be included in the Fundamental Rights. Ambedkar was clear that the Constitution should be neutral with respect to which political party was in power at the centre and in the states. The Directive Principles provide direction not a mandatory route to governance. He said:

> *The directive principles of State policy principles are like*

instruments of instructions. The inclusion of such instructions in such a Constitution becomes justifiable for another reason. The draft constitution is not a contrivance to install any particular party in power as has been done in some countries. Who should be in power is left to be determined by the people but the group that captures power will have to respect the directive principles. They cannot ignore them. Their breach may not be answerable in a court of law but will certainly be answerable to the electorate at election time.

Some directive principles like Article 43 (living wages) are beyond debate but difficult to detail precisely. Others like Article 44 (uniform civil code) are strongly desirable but remain contentious among certain religious denominations. Articles 39(b) and (c) are, despite their caveats, strongly oriented towards a particular economic model. Article 50, "The State shall take steps to separate the judiciary from the executive in the public services of the State" indicates that this desirable condition may not yet be a reality. Article 51 on promoting international peace and security appears frankly to be trite. All in all, the articles in Part 4 fall in three categories:

(i) those which give sufficient leeway to political parties with different priorities to proceed with their respective agendas;
(ii) those which are clearly in the national interest but cannot enter the Fundamental Rights because of deep-seated fault lines in society;
(iii) those that are so obvious and general to be bland and platitudinous.

If one has to select a single case in the Supreme Court that consolidates ideas on Fundamental Rights, Directive Principles and Basic Structure it would be the matter of His Holiness Kesavananda Bharati Sripadagalvaru and Others vs State of Kerala and Another (1973), referred to informally as the Kesavananda Bharati case. In February 1970, the plaintiff who was head of a Hindu monastery, Edneer Mutt, in Kasaragod District, challenged the Kerala government's attempts, under two land reform acts, to impose restrictions on the management of its property. This quickly led to a consideration of major constitutional matters. According to our Constitution, the power of Parliament and the legislatures to make laws is not absolute but subject to adjudication by the courts. If a law is held to violate any constitutional provision, the Supreme Court may declare such a law to be invalid. The Constitutional Assembly wisely maintained a balance between a proactive legislature and a reckless legislature. In this regard, they further provided the legislature with an amending power through Article 368, in addition to its usual legislative power. However, these amending powers are not absolute. Not only do they need to be passed by special majorities in the Lok Sabha and the Rajya Sabha but they are also within the purview of judicial review. The Kesavananda Bharati case was heard by a Constitutional Bench with a record number of 13 judges and the verdict was given with a narrow majority of 7:6. In brief, the summary statement declared that parliament's amending or constituent power was subject to inherent limitations in that it could not do anything that would 'damage', 'emasculate', 'destroy', 'abrogate', 'change' or 'alter' the 'basic structure or framework of the constitution'. To take a trivial example, Parliament may not pass laws to convert India into a hereditary monarchy or a military dictatorship. Thus came into being this undefined 'Basic Structure Doctrine'. To emphasise, this phrase itself is not found in the Constitution. The Supreme Court 'created' this concept for the first time in the Kesavananda Bharati case and ever since this Court has been the interpreter and the arbiter of constitutional amendments made by Parliament. The fact that the basic structure is not defined contributes both to its flexibility but also to the ambiguity in its implementation. For example, secularism is understood to be a part of the basic structure but with the definition of the term 'secularism' itself being contestable, what is its relevance in the basic structure?

The events leading up to Kesavananda Bharati occurred on the platform of Article 31 of the Fundamental Rights pertaining to property ownership and Articles 39(b) and (c) of the Directive Principles that require "equitable distribution of resources of production among all citizens and prevention of concentration of wealth in the hands of a few". Laws were passed by the Congress government soon after 1950 quoting Article 39 and keeping with its socialist proclivities. These laws aimed at the reform of land ownership and tenancy structures. Cases were filed by property owners and the court ruled in their favour. So, the government brought in the 1st and 4th Amendments removing these laws from the scope of judicial review in the Ninth Schedule. This was in effect a challenge to the judiciary in effect. The social revolution could not wait. The Sajjan Singh case and the Sankari Prasad Singh Deo case were decided against the petitioners diminishing the authority of Article 13(2) that provides for the protection of the Fundamental Rights. However, this raised the question as to whether the Fundamental Rights could be trifled with so easily by a majority party. One notes that all this happened within a few years of our adopting the Constitution. Something as important as Fundamental Rights was being touched. Politics was trumping constitutionality.

The Golak Nath case of 1967, a time of intense political activity and a split in the Congress party, was a curious interlude in that the court said that Article 368 did not confer amending power but merely described the amending procedure and that it was Article 13 that was sacrosanct.

Incidentally the term 'basic structure' was introduced for the first time by the petitioners in this case but only made a full-fledged appearance in Kesavananda Bharati. Simultaneously, in nationalising banks and depriving the princes of their privy purses, the government threw a direct challenge at the judiciary with respect to the relative position of the Fundamental Rights vis-à-vis the Directive Principles, a case of the tail wagging the dog. The entire matter had to do with the Congress claiming to implement its socialist development agenda. Indira Gandhi made a political move and called a snap mid-term poll which she won handsomely. The Constitution itself had become an election issue and the people decided in favour of the government, which then spoke of making radical changes. The communists even spoke about throwing the Constitution out lock, stock and barrel. Through a welter of amendments in the 1971-1972 period, the Congress government of Indira Gandhi restored to Parliament the absolute power to amend any part of the Constitution including Part 3, dealing with Fundamental Rights. Absurdly, even the President was made duty bound to give his assent to any amendment bill passed by both Houses of Parliament. Such was the contentious background of Kesavananda Bharati.

This landmark case was in effect to test the constitutional validity of Indira Gandhi's amendments. The 13 judges provided 11 independent judgements. While it was noted that there were several discrepancies between these judgements, the concept of the basic structure gained recognition, at least, if not universal acceptance. All the judges accepted the 24thAmendment which said that Parliament has amending power. All of them admitted that the Golak Nath verdict was wrong and that Article 368 contained both the power and procedure to amend. However, they made clear that an amendment was not the same as a law as defined in Article 13(2). An amendment is exceptional and needs specific conditions and procedures such as the special majority in parliament. In short, constituent power is superior to ordinary legislative power.

The case also had important ramifications on the separation of powers between the three wings of government, matters of variation between various countries. In an unwritten Constitution like the U.K. Parliament is supreme and there is no difference between legislative power and amending power. The courts are relatively subordinate. In the U.S.A. there is an elected head of the executive called the President and executive functions are strictly separated from legislative functions which are the preserve of a bicameral legislature consisting of two powerful limbs, the Senate and the House of Representatives. A merging of the executive and legislature occurs in the Westminster countries with the Prime Minister and his Cabinet necessarily being Members of Parliament. These aspects will be discussed later in this chapter. From the point of view of the Kesavananda Bharati case, the judiciary claimed its complete independence even predominance over the legislature and all talk of a 'committed judiciary' became a dead letter. Indeed, one of the attributes of the basic structure handed down in this judgment was the separation of powers among the three wings.

We finally turn to the court's attempts at defining the basic structure. Even among the seven majority opinion judges there were differences in this regard. There was certainly no unanimity in what constitutes the basic structure. The Chief Justice of the time mentioned supremacy of the Constitution, democracy and republicanism, secularism, separation of powers in the three wings and federalism. Two others appended the idea of a welfare state and upholding the unity and integrity of the nation. Did they anticipate the change in preamble which came a few years later? Two others came up with a short list that appears more general and as such more acceptable: sovereignty, democracy, unity, individual freedoms and welfare. The shortest and possibly the best list was provided by the judge Jaganmohan Reddy who restricted himself to:

(i) Sovereign, Democratic and Republic in the original preamble (there was no modified preamble in 1973);
(ii) Parliamentary democracy and;
(iii) Three organs of the state. He repeated earlier assertions that the Fundamental Rights and Directive Principles defined the Constitution.

The Judiciary was strengthened by the verdict especially in their assertion that there was a core content in the Constitution that was inviolate. Kesavananda Bharati also led to the decisions of the Indira Gandhi election case a few years later and to her declaring an emergency in 1975. There were murky suspicions related to supersession of certain judges in the Supreme Court by others who were of the minority opinion in the case for she had also criticised the basic structure doctrine in parliament among other things.

Many decades later and with the basic structure remaining undefined, it is open to us citizens to consider these matters from a broader holistic and civilisational perspective rather than remain bound to legalistic interpretations. In the end, it must be laws for men and not men for laws. What is basic structure? As something that remains undefined and is yet overwhelmingly important, nay even vital, and something without which the Constitution itself has no meaning or life, it must stand above the Constitution. What is this that is even above the Preamble? Surely it cannot be anything that is defined by placing tick marks on attributes enumerated by judges and seeing what gets how many tick marks. The people and their government must instinctively grasp the idea of basic structure without requiring a law degree. This basic structure must represent what Bhārat is in a way that is crystal clear to every ordinary person in this vast land. Such a thing can only be our civilisation, our ancient yet utterly modern culture. Bhārat, that is India, has been a unique concept in this world for 5000 years. It is unchanging and yet always changing. It is *nirdvaita* and *bahuroopa.* It is *nirguna* and *saguna.* It is *sthoola* and *sookshma.* It is *svaroopa, svadharma* and *svabhava.* This is what must be reflected in our undefined basic structure. A structure implies order. Dharma provides such order. Dharma tells us about right and wrong which must be the only constant element that maintains order in all civilised life. A musical analogy from our classical tradition could be helpful. The three elements of *shastriya sangeeta* are bhava, raga and tala, the first being the undefinable quality that differentiates a music that lives from something which is dead. The second defines a melodic basis, the agency through which bhava is expressed. The third is the instrument through which raga is communicated. The relationship of bhava to basic structure, of raga to the Preamble and Parts 1 through 4, and of tala to Part 5 and onwards including the schedules is self-evident. The discerning reader will also note that the first syllables of *bhava, raga* and *tala* spell out nothing other than the name of our country.

From metaphysical heights we now descend to a mundane evaluation of the Constitution, its amendments, the laws passed and the performance of single party and coalition governments at the centre and the states after 1950. I have selected three trouble spots of federalism, religion and socio-economic reforms for this exercise. Any sovereign State must have a functioning structure which is based on order. A structure that functions needs three events in sequence: a strategic plan of construction, a methodology to achieve the said plan and the execution of the said methodology. Ideally, there should not be much overlap between these three so that *ad hocism* is avoided. Above all, the execution should be plan neutral. This sequence is fundamental to any man-made functioning structure across subjects, disciplines, endeavours, countries, and even eras and follows from the logical thought processes of which human beings alone are capable. As far as the Government of India and the states are concerned, the Constitution is the plan, the methodology consists of laws, rules and regulations that are introduced from time to time, while the constitutionally protected All India Services handle the delivery of the plan outcomes to the people, the ultimate masters, who have taken this constitution for themselves.

In one of the earliest Constituent Assembly sessions on 13 December 1946, Nehru who was well-aware of all this said:

> *This constituent assembly has not been in session for some days. It has done much formal business, but more is yet to be done. We have been cutting our way and clearing the ground on which we intend to erect the edifice of a constitution. It, however, seems proper that before we proceed further we should clearly understand where we are going and what we intend building. It is apparent that on such occasions details are unnecessary. In building, you will, no doubt, use each brick after mature consideration. Usually, when one desires to construct a building, one must have a plan for the structure that one wishes to erect and then collect the material required. For a long time we have been, having various plans for a free India in our minds , but now, when we are beginning the actual work, I hope, you will be at one with me when I say, that we should present a clear picture of this plan to ourselves, to the people of India and to the world at large. The resolution that I am placing before you defines our aims, describes an outline of the plan and points the way which we are going to tread.*

Since this was a Constituent Assembly, Nehru only

spoke about strategy and methodology. The execution would have to come later and this is why it should be plan neutral. Unfortunately, we have had a situation after 1950 where methodology has sometimes been defined through amendments rather than laws and rules and where undesirable overlap between methodology and execution have been exacerbated by corruption and strongly partisan civil servants, a far cry from Patel's steel frame. We also note that each governance component affects those that follow; bad methodology affects execution while bad strategy affects methodology which in turn affects execution. Strategy is therefore all-important and so the fact that there have been so many amendments ought to raise a natural question as to whether the original document did not capture the spirit and character of the people accurately enough. We may turn first therefore to strategy.

Of the three trouble-spot areas where I have tried to evaluate constitutional performance, namely federalism, religion and socio-economic uplift, the heavy shadow of Partition affected the strategic planning in the first two, right from the beginning. Partition caused the Constituent Assembly to suddenly switch from a federal constitution to a strongly unitary one because the overriding concern was to quench any chance of centrifugal forces which might have caused dissipation and disintegration of the new country. Feared above all was another religion-based Partition. The equivocal position of the Princes was also cause for concern. Kashmir had become a vexing issue by the end of 1947. The founding fathers were indeed well aware of the fact that a political entity called India had not existed till then. They had been all too sensitised by Churchill's comments on the equator in this regard. Indians perhaps hate being proved wrong more than any other people. They possibly refuse to admit to their mistakes with good grace because these are viewed not as mistakes but as loss of face. This could be an

Asian state of mind. Above all, one had to prove to the Britisher that we were capable of managing our affairs. It was all very well for Gandhi to have said that we would prefer our own bad government to a good government of the British, but now that Independence was at hand, rhetoric had to be replaced by hardnosed realism. India simply could not fragment at birth.

We have adequately rationalised the adoption of a union-centric Constitution post-partition in Section B of this chapter. From the viewpoint of examining how well the Constitution has served us in terms of catering to the inherent diversity of India, in other words how it has respected the federal nature of our polity I have analysed this subject from four viewpoints:

(1) that the extent of federalism correlates well with the presence of coalition governments at the centre and conversely diminishes during single party rule;

(2) that independent of who is in power at the centre, the Concurrent List as specified in the Seventh Schedule should be more flexible and capable of modification (add, move subtract subjects) keeping in mind the changing demands of federalism;

(3) that fragmentation of the country is today not the worry it was in 1950 and that the constitution may be comfortably amended so as to enhance its federal character and;

(4) that the reorganisation of states using Article 3 may be effected routinely to better accommodate federal diversity. In the end, unity and diversity are our twin strengths. They should be in obvious synergy. Today all we get dished out on this topic by self-seeking politicians is lip service. The synergy between unity and diversity should be palpable to common citizens. This can only come about if the constitution clearly comprehends *and accepts* our civilisational identity unlike the situation prevailing today.

It is obvious that when there is single party rule at the

Centre and if the same party is also in government in the States, differences between the States and the Centre may be sorted out at the party rather than government level. This was indeed the situation from 1950 till 1967 after which the Congress started losing ground from its pole position. A new situation with weaker central governments (Congress in power at the centre but taking support from the communists, short-lived non-Congress non-BJP coalitions, longer lived coalitions like NDA and UPA based around one of the two main national parties) prevailed for nearly 50 years except for an unusual interregnum between 1984 and 1989 when the Congress had a steamroller majority (sympathy vote in 1984). Coalitions were the rule rather than the exception at the centre. The situation changed dramatically in 2014, further reinforced in 2019, with the BJP obtaining a simple majority in the Lok Sabha and now nearly approaching one in the Rajya Sabha. The BJP has also been in power in several state governments during the period 2014-2022 and even where it is not, it has a sizable number of legislators except in a few outliers like Andhra Pradesh, Kerala, Punjab, Tamil Nadu and Telangana. These distinct political changes post-2014 allow one to easily identify the correlation between increased federalism and coalition governments.

As the hegemony of the Congress was waning, new regional parties mostly hereditary, came to power and demanded more fiscal and administrative autonomy. The Rajamannar committee set up by the DMK shortly after it first came to power and the Sarkaria committee set up by the centre in 1983 to examine Centre-State relations are both well-known and will not be discussed further. The growing dependence of national parties (Congress, BJP, CPM) on support from regional parties (DMK, AIADMK, TDP, TRS, SP, BSP RJD, BJD, JMM, TMC, SAD, NC, PDP) to run their governments at the centre and in the states gave them far more leeway to bargain about and influence important decisions at the centre. These decisions sometimes had a bearing on their specific political platforms. The casualty was the constitution. The obvious effect on the national polity was an inevitable patchwork and highlights a weakness in the first-past-the-post method of elections when a strong two-party system is missing. These issues came to the forefront in the 1990s when both the Congress and the BJP were not so strong.

Article 263 was introduced envisaging an Inter State Council to look into Centre-State relations. The ISC prepared an action plan and examined the Sarkaria committee recommendations. To be frank, the sum of such activities including the formation of other related bodies has been disappointing. The ISC was set up in 1990 when the Congress was out of power and first met in 1992. When the Congress was voted back in, no meetings were held for six years. This underscored the whole matter of federalism in India in a coalition dispensation: it was dependent on immediate political needs of regional parties and no meaningful constitutional reform was going to emerge through legislation performed under such compulsions. Coalitions in the long run do not facilitate healthy federalism. They only promote a perception of federalism that vanishes the moment a new dispensation shows up. In today's highly polarised environment any talk of federalism from the states becomes politically surcharged and after a while bears little relation to diversity which is the real strength of our civilisation. The appearance today of single party rule at the centre and its probable continuance for some time hopefully presages a more stable period constitutionally, one in which there will be genuine progress towards a true rather than gunpoint federalism, a situation where we may aspire to a strong centre and strong states. A numerical balance between states in which the BJP is in power and those where it is not would ensure the required checks and balances against heavy handed actions by the Centre, reminiscent of the 1950-1967 period. Ideally the appearance of a second national party with a clear ideology would greatly strengthen the body politic but it is difficult to see this happening at present. The INC was a mass movement till 1947. After 1950, the Congress became a political party—it seems to have run its natural course in these 72 years when the Constitution has been in operation.

The next point relating to federalism that one needs to consider is whether there are approaches to improving the quality of federalism in India in contexts larger and constitutionally sounder than merely papering out conflicts between the Centre and the States through ad hoc legislation and amendments. Such conflicts become more acute when a regional party enjoys a majority in the state but not in parliament. In these cases it cannot do much more than shout in Parliament and disrupt the procedures during sessions. Are systemic approaches possible? One possibility is to change the system of representation in the legislatures or even more fundamentally the structuring of these legislatures and the mode of separation of powers in the three wings of the Union. These options will be taken up in Chapter 4. In a more incremental approach, one might consider a more systematic evaluation of the subjects in the Union (96th plus the 97th on residual subjects), State (61) and Concurrent (52) Lists in the Seventh Schedule. In this context I refer to a semi-quantitative method of evaluation described in a report entitled 'Cleaning Constitutional Cobwebs. Reforming the Seventh Schedule' by Sohini Chatterjee, Akshat Agarwal, Kevin James and Arghya Sengupta and published in 2019 by the Vidhi Centre for Legal Policy, New Delhi. The approach of Chatterjee et al. is simple. They argue that introduction and transfer of a subject between the three Lists is an essential component of a living Constitution that is constantly keeping its finger on the pulse of Centre-State relations *independent of the political compulsions of regional parties* and their short-term interests. Changes in legislative allocation of subjects should always be permissible provided they are not arbitrary. They should but keep in mind old principles that underlay their allocation in 1950 and also new ones that have become relevant in recent times. The two older principles are 'unity and integrity' and 'balanced economic development'. The new ones are 'cultural diversity' and 'responsive governance'. The reader will note that three of these items correspond to our already identified trouble spots, namely federalism, religion and socio-economic uplift. The fourth, responsive government, is to our mind, not a strategic matter but may be addressed through methodology and more significantly, execution but it is interesting to note that Chatterjee et al. links it with the Seventh Schedule.

The approach taken by these authors is to assign scores to each of the subjects in the three Lists according to the four principles:

(i) unity and integrity;
(ii) balanced economic development;
(iii) cultural diversity and;
(iv) responsive government.

The assignment into one of these Lists or the removal of a subject altogether is on the basis of this weighted score and how an item fares in a decision tree. If a subject satisfies (i) and (ii) but not (iii) and (iv), it goes to the union list. If it satisfies (iii) and (iv) but not (i) and (ii), it normally goes to the State List unless there are some overarching considerations that would necessitate its placement in the Concurrent List. If any or all of (i), (ii), (iii) and (iv) are satisfied it could go into any list but the Concurrent List would need to be considered most seriously.

Illustration with real examples is most effective. Defence

clearly satisfies (i) and (ii) but not (iii) and (iv). It goes to the Union List. Foreign Affairs satisfies (i) and/or (ii) and (iii) and/or (iii) and (iv). Since (i) has a much higher weightage than the three other criteria, this item goes to the Union List. Cruelty to animals satisfies neither (i) nor (ii) but it satisfies (iii) and (iv) because it might touch on local cultural and religious practices. So, it goes to the State List. It is now in the Concurrent List. Transfer of property satisfies (iii) and (iv) but not (i) and (ii). However, it goes to the Concurrent List because there is a need for cross-state uniformity. Education is a most important and significant subject. It was in the State List till 1976 when Indira Gandhi moved it to the Concurrent List under controversial circumstances. Popular perception has it that this move was made in order that the central government could have a more direct say in matters pertaining to the Jawaharlal Nehru University in New Delhi. In any event, education is seen to satisfy both (ii) and (iii) eminently and to a comparable degree, while it is neutral to (i) and passive to (iv). This would make the Concurrent List a clear choice and where (for this subject in particular) the Centre would be greatly strengthened by Article 256 that states that, "the executive power of every state shall be so exercised as to ensure compliance with the laws made by parliament and any existing laws which apply in that state, and the executive power of the Union shall extend to the giving of such directions to a state as may appear to the government of India to be necessary for that purpose."

Using this analysis, the authors identify new subjects that need to be brought into the Lists. These include disaster management, consumer protection and emerging technologies such as artificial intelligence and gene editing. Perhaps Kamath would have been pleased to see interplanetary travel included here in the Union List. Chatterjee et al. finally enumerate subjects that may be safely dropped from the Lists. These include 'Courts of Wards for the estates of Rulers of Indian States', 'Lighthouses, including lightships, beacons and other provision for the safety of shipping and aircraft' and 'Boilers'. Important caveats which do not yield to such analysis are GST (Article 246A) and residuary powers which by their very nature need subjective treatment. The entire exercise is an example of how our Constitution should be handled in 2022, not by instinct, emotion or legalities but by cold, dispassionate analysis, model building and evaluation. It should be a blend of quantitative and qualitative, reason and imagination, substance and shadow. It should move from the analogue to the digital world. In the words of the authors, "such a process will make the Lists reflective of the changing needs of governance and ensure that the Indian Constitution continues to remain resilient in times to come."

We may turn next to the obvious point that the fragmentation of our country is not the worry it was in 1950. We have two natural adversaries who maintain a keen interest in our destabilisation as a single political entity: Pakistan and India started off on a seemingly level playing field in 1947 but due to adroit planning of its foreign policy and by leveraging its great geostrategic location in the Cold War background, Pakistan secured tremendous advantages for itself in the 1950s and for a time it almost seemed that it might even overtake India in certain respects. Today the situation has changed dramatically in both countries. India's slow but steady consolidation of its institutions if not necessarily its economy turned the tide for us. P.V. Narasimha Rao's 1991 liberalisation policy triggered a process that has enabled the present BJP government to take the economy to a critical take off point where one hears about India becoming a $5 trillion economy soon. In contrast, Pakistan has declined: in its obsession with India in general and Kashmir in particular it has compromised its economy and territorial integrity so much that one even hears about a possible break-up of that country into three or four parts. One may say that while the requiem has not yet been written or performed, it is certainly in the realm of the believable.

Our other formidable adversary is China: its weapons against us are more subtle and powerful and are directed against our land and sea boundaries, and our economy. In both cases, however, we seem to have marshalled sufficient defences even if they are not fool proof. I shall not consider the efforts at destabilising our country made by our internal enemies. The latter are for the very large part lackeys of our two external adversaries and certain international syndicates. If our external enemies are unable to destabilise us for a few more years, the internal enemies will most likely fade away. Once our nominal GDP surpasses $5 trillion (some put this critical number closer to $10 trillion), neither of our traditional enemies might be able to marshal the resources and energies to undermine us. Given the psychological and physical security this is imperceptibly giving us already, should we persist with our strongly union-centric Constitution knowing that powers inevitably gravitate towards the Centre? Should the Constitution not be amended as to enhance its federal character and strengthen the states? Again, Ambedkar is worth quoting:

> *However much you may deny powers to the Centre it is difficult to prevent the centre from becoming strong. Conditions in the modern world are such that centralization of powers is inevitable. On the other hand we must resist the tendency to make it stronger. It cannot chew more than it can digest. Its strength must be commensurate with its weight. It would be a folly to make it so strong that it may fall by its own weight.*

In practical terms how does one increase the strength of the states if one stays within the four corners of the present constitution? Here are the main manifestations of the power of the Centre vis-à-vis the States:

(i) the appointment by the centre of governors, its representatives, in whose name the entire state administration runs;
(ii) the power of parliament to legislate for the states in the national interest;
(iii) the ability of the Union. to form and uniform states as per the provisions of Article 3 and;
(iv) the powers given to the Union, during emergencies caused by war or external aggression, and during president's rule following a breakdown of the constitutional machinery in a state.

In principle, these four issues can be softened within limits and the matter is an appropriate subject for public discussion. The appointment of governors could be done with some degree of consultation with the States and could be restricted to completely apolitical persons of high character and morality. They are custodians of the Constitution. A modified definition of what exactly is national interest for the purposes of interventionist parliamentary legislation could be included, as could be a more precise definition as to what constitutes a failure of the constitutional machinery. What probably should not be tampered with is Article 3. It is only this article and the Damocles sword of President's rule that saves the Union from the caprices of state governments run by irresponsible chief ministers.

The fourth and final perspective from which one could analyse the strategic aspects of federalism and diversity increase is the matter of reorganisation of states as allowed by Article 3. It was well understood and accepted in the Constituent Assembly that the States as they would exist on 26 January 1950 were not going to delineate final boundaries simply because there was no single basis for the territorial limits of any single state. Some had been created by the British for administrative convenience, others were truncated bits following partition, and yet others defined the limits of the Princely States.

The first major attempt to encourage diversity was to promote the identity of our languages by the creation of linguistic states. The States Reorganisation Act of 1956 made this possible. Andhra Pradesh, Gujarat, Kerala, Maharashtra and Mysore were early examples. Considering that language in general and imposition of Hindi in particular, were sensitive issues in South India starting with the assembly debates, linguistic states were probably a good idea in the beginning. Today the situation is not quite so clear. Language is not a *sine qua non* of state identity. It could be a criterion for one type of identity but it is not overwhelmingly so. If this were the case East Pakistan would not have come into being. Plural identity has always been a feature in Bhārat. Cultural differences and economic disparities catalysed the bifurcation of Andhra Pradesh into two Telugu speaking states in 2014. A similar sentiment is being expressed in the Vidharbha area of Maharashtra today. Uttarakhand was hived off from Uttar Pradesh in 2000 despite a shared language because of environmental, geographical and cultural concerns. A more intriguing possibility is whether some of the original boundaries of the Princely States could not be restored in a reorganisation exercise towards smaller states. Some of the Princely States (Gwalior, Jaipur, Hyderabad, Mysore, Travancore) were cohesive and efficient administrative units in which there was also a fair degree of diversity. No possibility should be excluded in the early stages of gedanken (thought) experiments on this interesting topic. A far more sinister concern is if the linguistic sentiment is exploited and misused by external enemies to destabilise a State vis-à-vis the Union, moving in the extreme towards secession. In this case, there would be a definite need to divide a bigger State into smaller units even if they share a common language. Language might in such cases unite a State but it would divide the Union. To summarise, the Union could, armed with Article 3, engage itself in a more positive and dynamic approach to States reorgansation without waiting for agitations to build up to a point of no return. The conferring of statehood to Telangana for example, took far too long.

We turn next to religion, our second trouble-spot area and one in which Constitution drafting was seriously affected by Partition. The deliberately low-key strategy for religion laid out in the Constitution had the opposite effect from the intended one: it enhanced religious differences between the two majority religions. The Constitution displays benign neglect of the civilisational aspect of Sanātana Dharma and arguably a simultaneous overindulgence of non-Indic faiths in direct and indirect ways (Articles 29, 30). By the 1980s, the benign neglect developed into an active anti-Hindu stance by governments ostensibly to appease 'secular' vote banks. Whether or not these moves actually appeased these vote banks has never been clear. Such tactics might just have been more effective in rural areas. Appeasement, however, remains a fact till today, at the State if not at the Central government level. Notable examples of anti-Hindu stances by governments are the Ayodhya massacre of 1990, the attacks and killings of Kashmiri Pandits in the early 1990s and the 2018 Sabarimala standoff regarding temple entry by women of certain ages in a shrine where this prohibition has *shastraic* sanction. Sometimes, there may be no anti-Hindu slant intended but there is certainly a perception of one and in the end, this is what matters. One recalls recent interventions by governments in banning crackers during Deepavali, imposing pandemic curfew rules during Onam, playing an evangelical video in a prominent Durga shrine during Navaratri and alleged appointments of non-Hindus to administrative positions in venerated and hoary shrines [permitted by Article 25(2)(a)].

Why such apparently meaningless and needless provocation of the sentiments of a religious denomination that covers 80 per cent of our population by Central and State governments continues unabated is a matter of concern. It cannot be just perverse or cussed thinking. It is probably careless governance that follows from some sort of political calculation. It is worthwhile to recall Brajeshwar Prasad's definitions of 'actual will' and 'real will' of the people (quoted earlier in this chapter). Politicians know that if they can capture the actual will at polling time, it does not matter what the real will is. If anything, political parties in general could lose votes by such activities if a Hindu backlash develops. It is also unlikely that mainstream Muslims and Christians would vote for a party strictly on the basis of provocative actions directed against Hindus.

It has been repeatedly affirmed that Bhārat, that is India, is a deeply religious and spiritual nation and that the predominant and typical religion is Sanātana Dharma, the strength of which is demonstrated by its survival for 5000 years despite onslaughts, philosophical, military and evangelical. Savants like Vivekananda and Radhakrishnan have even taken the concept of neo-Hinduism to a universal stage where the message of the Vedanta goes beyond one's own faith to a universal faith. This is one aspect of Hinduism. The fact that the Vedas are condensed to the Upanishads which are further condensed to the Brahma Sūtras is a challenge to the believer to decipher these most condensed of aphorisms and provides different interpretations for them. It is a reductionist-emergence argument. Neither Sankara, Ramanuja, Madhva nor Vallabha are correct nor incorrect. They are all right. None is wrong. Within the Vedas themselves there are six *darshanas* or ways of looking at the same thing. A different type of condensation of the Vedas leads to a practical prescription for living and is found in the Bhagavad Gita. Such a complex religious structuring which also impinges on social and economic values in its threefold code of *purushārtha*, *varna* and *āshrama*, with each of these having four possibilities each, a 3 × 4 matrix if you will for life itself, cannot be followed in a simplistic yes/no binary fashion. The only binary in Sanātana Dharma is right and wrong, the essence of *Dharma* itself. Even materialistic schools of thought like the heterodox *nāstika* and the hedonistic *cārvāka* are not incompatible with the faith. The core is, however, steadfastly religious in its outward manifestations, ritualistic and *paddhati*-driven as prescribed in the karma *kandas*, the *samhitas* and *brahmanas*. To repeat, Hinduism is a religion and not a way of life. It is indeed unique and cannot be compared with any other religion, especially the more monotheistic varieties. *That such a faith, followed in one way or another by 80 per cent of this country, does not find adequate and fitting representation in our Constitution is the most fundamental flaw in the entire document.* As was mentioned in Chapter 1, a correct technical and legal wording of a document is not of much value if the content is not relevant to the situation at hand. Tyagaraja in one of his compositions sings that if there is no mental strength, doing a *puja* with sweet sounding bells and other paraphernalia is pointless.

The root cause of all this confusion was an ineffectual definition of the word 'secular' in the Constitution and Nehru's attempts to downplay Sanātana Dharma using various arguments and more ominously for India, through a systematic effort in amending critical sections of the Constitution, also through legislation (Ninth Schedule, dilution of Articles 15, 25 through 30 especially the objectionable Article 30). His successors in the Congress overturned the Shah Bano judgement in 1986, and passed the Right to Education bill in 2010 (Article 21A). These matters are so well discussed in the public domain that there is no need for further discussion here. The Hindu Code Bill being passed while simultaneously sidestepping a Uniform Civil Code has already been outlined earlier in this chapter. "When will the Muslims be ready for the UCC?" is a question which many mainstream Hindus may ask. Would it be a case of 'never' just as we would 'never' be ready to remove reservations in the education and employment sectors, and we would 'never' be ready to remove English as a language of primary education? If things that are widely considered as desirable even necessary in a modern and aspiring country can 'never' be done in India, one is tempted to say that they can all be done 'easily' in Bhārat.

The fact of the matter is that politicians, including Nehru, saw an immediate gain electorally in our first-past-the-post system if the Muslim vote bank was firmly consolidated. The aggregate of votes in a majority of the minority and a minority of the majority is often sufficient to win an election in India and this is exactly what was resorted to by the so called 'secular' parties from 1950 right down to 2022. This is what makes the BJP Lok Sabha victories in 2014 and 2019 remarkable which is not the same as saying that the BJP is remarkable. What is remarkable is that such a verdict (simple majority in the Lok Sabha for a single party two times over in five years) carries with it the implication that the people finally identified with a strong common identity that they had not recognised as being intrinsic to them before. This can only be the civilisational identity of Sanātana Dharma. Any attempt by a political party, including the BJP in future elections, to deny this identity can only lead to humiliating defeats in the polls. The BJP was savvy enough in 2014 to identify this need among the people for self-identification, which was castrated out of their beings by secularism, and was able to re-convey this sentiment back to the people at the hustings using denigrating epithets like 'pseudo-secular' and 'appeasement' to describe the Congress. It should be noted that such is the feeling of humiliation among common Hindus of the country as regards being second class citizens in their own country that they might not even mind if the BJP does not act overtly in favour of an agenda that supports Hindutva, the feeling of being Hindu. All that they seem to want at least for now is that someone articulates their sentiments.

It is not that this was unknown as far back as the 1950s. Here is an extract from a letter written by Munshi to Nehru:

> *In the name of secularism, again, politicians in power adopt a strange attitude which, while it condones the susceptibilities, religious and social, of the minority communities, is too ready to brand similar susceptibilities in the majority community as communalistic and reactionary. How secularism sometimes becomes allergic to Hinduism will be apparent from certain episodes relating to the reconstruction of Somnath temple.*

The matter of Hindu temples and their connection with the old princely order is relevant in this regard. All of us know that Hindu temples and shrines are 'managed' by the (State) governments while mosques and churches are not. The dubious interpretation of religious and secular spheres in Hindu temples in the Constitution has already been mentioned earlier in this chapter (Article 25). Through the 1st and 4th Amendments, both pushed through by Nehru, it became much easier for the government to seize temple lands. These lands were not just an income source for the temples. They were crucial to maintaining an entire societal arrangement, what one would call a win-win arrangement between the people, the kings and the religious leaders, noting that in the eyes of the people, the moral authority of religious leaders was as important as the temporal authority of kings.

We are not speaking from the Christian secular viewpoint of insulating Church and State. The nature of Sanātana Dharma is such that it becomes only beneficial, *strategically, economically and socially,* to coalesce the people and their faith under the dharmic umbrella. It is this vital aspect of our life that was discarded by Nehru and the subsequent Congress dispensations in the name of electoral vote-bank politics. Certain Indian secularists opine about having non-Brahmins and SC communities in the priestly fold of Hindu temples. The truth is that only 6% of all Tamil Nadu temples have Brahmin *archakā*s. Any good Hindu would only worry about whether a priest is performing his duties in the prescribed manner, not the *jati* into which he was born. The Nandanār Charitram is still performed in villages all over Tamil Nadu commemorating the incident where Lord Siva asked Nandi to move so that the SC devotee Nandanār could have his darshan. The eminent archakā of the Chilkur Balaji temple, in the outskirts of Hyderabad, C. S. Rangarajan, recently carried an SC person on his shoulders, *muni vahana seva,* re-enacting an episode from the Lord Ranganathaswamy temple in Srirangam 2,700 years ago. All this is in the very nature of the religion.

The nature of the Constitution and the laws of the land make it impossibly difficult for Hindus now to regain even some measure of control on their own temples. Subramanian Swamy undertook extraordinary legal steps for the Nataraja temple in Chidambaram to become free of the government and be fully self-governing. Even BJP governments have joined this bandwagon of temple control, the recent shabby episodes in the greatly venerated Char Dham shrines of Uttarakhand being a case in point. Andhra Pradesh under its current dispensation is another example with no clarity emerging as to whether the management of its richest temple is in the hands of Hindus or non-Hindus (with Christian converts not changing their Hindu names after conversion). To quote Machiavelli, "there is no surer sign of decay in a country than to see the rites of religion held in contempt".

The judiciary has joined the fray with its judgement in the Sabarimala case. The judgement might well have passed legal criteria of the day but the popular will expressed itself clearly enough after the judgement with many women supporting the ban on women entry into *this particular shrine* because only there is Lord Ayyappa a Naishtika Brahmachari (one who undertakes a vow to remain a celibate till his death). In a democracy such events signify that a law needs to be changed. At times like this one wonders if the Constitution should not have had a provision for referendums which would be a higher check on the functioning of the three branches of the state. The crux of the argument was that the deity has no constitutional rights. This may only be expected from a Constitution that does not mention God in a country where the 80% majority religion holds that a *murthi* is endowed with life, but where the penalty for breaking an idol is merely ₹ 200 whereas a possible punishment for murder is a death sentence. If the Constitution says a particular law cannot be changed, then the part of it that says so needs to be changed. If that part of the Constitution that says a particular law cannot be changed cannot be changed then the Constitution is no good. A typical example is the ruling that a status of a religious place is what it was on 15 August 1947 except the Ram Janmabhoomi site (Places of Worship Act, 1991). This is nothing short of rank absurdity and it must be openly called out as such. Anything man-made should be capable of being unmade by man. The Constitution is man-made. It is not a holy book that fell to us from the sky. The only thing in the Constitution that cannot be changed is the basic structure if it is defined without words.

Petty and minor incidents of temple destruction, the loss of property and smuggling of idols out of India, notably from Tamil Nadu temples that have been made to fall into disuse, are so numerous that the matter goes beyond counting. Chief Minister Yogi Adityanath has said in 2017 that he believes that the word 'secular' has been the biggest lie since independence. Harsh Madhusudhan and Rajiv Mantri in their recent fact-filled book *A New Idea of India* provide a long list of real and big grievances that many Hindus feel they have received at the hands of their various governments over the years with respect to their religious practices and observances. Being equidistant from all religions is unacceptable to our secular liberals. They demand religion-based positive discrimination, our version of affirmative action but based on religion rather than on caste or some economic criterion and mostly tilted towards Muslims. All that this will do is to increase the sense of alienation among Muslims and minority communities and push them further into economic backwardness. Regrettably the State constantly comes between people of all faiths and the way they might want to practise their religion. Reform of the Muslim community must come from within the community as many have argued correctly. The State should facilitate this process by staying out of all religions altogether. State-sponsored discrimination against Hindus goes on at subtle levels too. How many of us appreciate that a Parsi, Christian or Muslim may adjudicate in official matters pertaining to how Hindus celebrate Hindu rituals in Hindu temples while no Hindu may similarly adjudicate in any similar religious matter pertaining to any of these other religions? In the end, the specifics do not matter. There are so many cases now that even if a fraction of them are accurate it means that the government is ignoring a vital concern of the people. Nitin Patel, deputy chief minister of Gujarat was unable to restrain expressing his helplessness. In

August 2021 he said:

> *In our country, some people talk about the Constitution, secularism. But I tell you, and if you want to video record this, then do it [...] note down my words. Those talking about the Constitution, secularism, law etc. will do so only till Hindus are in majority in this country [...] The day [...] the number of Hindus decreases, of others increases, there will be no secularism, no Lok Sabha, no Constitution. Everything will be tossed in the air and buried. Nothing will remain.*

That a sitting Chief Minister of one of the larger states of the Union says that secularism is a lie and a sitting Deputy Chief Minister says that there will be no Constitution if Hindus fall to a minority in this country is cause for serious concern by all right thinking people. This is not the fault of mainstream Hindus. It is not the fault of mainstream Muslims. It is the fault of the Constitution and the wilful participation of elected politicians, religious extremists and the non-elected judiciary in its degradation.

Related to the constitutional treatment meted out to Hinduism in general was the matter of how the Union treated its princes. For their own reasons the British did not interfere with cultural and religious affairs in the Princely States. For the most part these states were ruled by Hindu kings and the majority population was Hindu. Dharma was the strong cultural connection that bound these variegated kingdoms. Nehru on the other hand did not hide his contempt for the princes whom he dubbed "gilded and empty-headed maharajas and nawabs who strut about the Indian scene and make a nuisance of themselves". The reason for this animosity is not hard to seek: the princes were a roadblock to establishing Nehru's secular order because it was they who by sustaining the dying embers of dharmic civilisation during the long years of British rule largely prevented its complete disappearance from India.

The constitutional attack on the princes and on our civilisational state was direct and ruthless. The abolishing of the zamindari system and later the privy purses wiped out all sources of income for the Princely States. Without land they became impoverished. In turn, this affected the sustenance of dharma because only kings were its patrons and the temple was the nerve centre of cultural activities. All at once, Hindu science, scholarship, education, fine arts, high artisanship and literature were wiped out. This was a devastating blow for the Hindu civilisational state. The Congress leaders, notably Nehru and his daughter were probably nervous of the mass appeal of the princes long years after Independence. Their treatment meted out to some members of the Jaipur royal house reveals an inferiority complex of some sort and does not behove professional politicians. Even today it is not uncommon in states like Chhattisgarh, Karnataka, Madhya Pradesh and Rajasthan to hear about members of erstwhile royal families being referred to in informal conversation as maharaja, savāri, hukum and so on. This must mean that these royal families produced kings and queens who were very benevolent rulers. The example of the dowager Maharani of Mysore in the context of the formation of the Indian Institute of Science has been mentioned early in Chapter 1. Was this paranoia of royalty another reason for an over centralisation of powers and a diminishing of the federal character of the polity?

In an earlier section I have mentioned that it is difficult for internal adversaries to fracture the political structure of our country. The same cannot be said about their ability to disturb, even destroy our civilisational identity as a nation. Sita Ram Goel in his book 'Hindu Society Under Siege' written in 1994 enumerates four generic adversaries of the Bhāratiya civilisational state: Islamism; Christianism (not to be confused with Islam and Christianity); Macaulayism; Communism. He states also that there is a combination of these four hostile forces making for a complex convolution of external and internal adversaries. Moreover, ideological adversaries are far harder to vanquish than military and economic enemies because their effects on the population are more long lasting.

Goel describes each of them according to the methods they employ. The hard-core Islamist, as differentiated from a mainstream Muslim, has a self-righteous psychology and closed cultural attitude which make it impossible for him to coexist peacefully and with dignity with people of another religion. He feels Islam has the right to use all means, including force, to convert this *Darul-harb* into a *Darul-Islam*. Further, Goel states that Christianity is also an exclusivist religion like Islam and a hard core Christianist, as contrasted with the mainstream Christian, avers that Hindus have never had a saviour, that Jesus whose historicity cannot be questioned is the saviour and has rendered superfluous all previous and subsequent Hindu saints and sages, that Christianity is an ancient Indian religion owing its origin to Thomas, one of Jesus' twelve disciples and that the task of the Christian Church is to complete his mission and ensure that India becomes a Christian country. Undoubtedly, the British period saw a marked rise in the popularity of the Christian Church. Latter day manifestations include the chequered careers of Mother Teresa, Verrier Elwin (a favourite of Nehru), Graham Staines and others.

According to Goel, Macaulayism is characterised by a sceptical attitude towards Hindu spirituality, cultural creations and social institutions, a worshipful, attitude towards everything in Western society and culture as promoting progress, reason and science, noting that ancient Hindu practices must be evaluated by modern Western yardsticks before they become acceptable, and a mental mood to judge and compare India with the West in terms that are unrecognisable in India. Many of these attitudes stem from what scientists would call a frame-of-reference problem. If the Hindus use their own methods of measurement to analyse Western heritage, our Macaulayists would denounce the exercise as unscientific and irrelevant. Bhāratiyas, on the other hand, would find the *gopuram* of the Brihadeswara Temple in Tanjore to be as beautiful as the Duomo in Florence, although each of these ironically represent the high points of two totally opposed viewpoints on life and existence! Perhaps Kipling, arguably the apotheosis of Macaulayism in India, was correct in that East and West could never meet. The Anglophile culture of modern India is a by-product of Macaulayism, and indeed we seem to have developed it into an indigenous art form totally independent of British influence for 75 years. There is even a body of public opinion that holds that India should not aspire to superpower status.

Goel describes Islamism as malevolent, Christianism as mischievous and Macaulayism as mild, but his harshest criticisms are reserved for Communism which he describes as "a foreign imposition of the most malignant character." In India, the Marxist philosophy has been able to gather within its fold Islamism, Christianism and Macaulayism in a grand cabal against the civilisational identity of this nation, the breakdown of which it hopes will lead to a political collapse. While political Marxism is practically dead in India, cultural Marxism thrives substantially because of the cynical pact made by Indira Gandhi with the communists in the early 1970s where they offered her political support is exchange for a free run of our education system. Goel says that Communism is strongest in India today in those areas where Macaulayism had cast its widest spell. The role of leftist historians in distorting the Ram Janmabhoomi affair and delaying its ultimate resolution are only too recent in public memory.

Through this ferocious and determined four-pronged attack on our nationhood from internal adversaries, the Constitution has generally remained a mute spectator, the legislature sometimes a compliant partner and sometimes a passive observer, the executive a willing enough accomplice during certain political dispensations, and the judiciary an impotent bystander. Our outlook is grim at least with the Constitution as it stands at present because in the end the three organs of the Union must operate within the law of the land. As stated earlier, since the dangers to Bhāratavarsha are presently so blatantly obvious, the time seems to have arrived for a relook at the Constitution itself.

The third constitutional trouble-spot, strategy wise, has been the entire question of social and economic uplift of the depressed and disadvantaged classes. Clearly, the stand taken by the Constitution on this matter was not related to Partition but it was regarded as critically important by the Assembly. It is instructive to ask how and why levels of inequality in India reached the depths they did by 1947. Clearly the British played a major role in this for the country was in social and economic equilibrium in 1700 when it was possibly the largest contributor to the world GDP along with China. Restrictions on social and economic ways of life are not typical of Sanātana Dharma with its accent on *purushārtha*. What was the root cause of inequality in India? It was almost certainly a consequence of colonialism, a vestige where land titles (Permanent Settlement, Ryotwari) and educational standards (Macaulay) were reassigned leading to widespread disparity in social status and income especially the latter. Socialism was a corrective mechanism seeking to alleviate poverty while preventing beneficiaries of colonialism to amass further wealth and hence the State took over production and control of resources. The example of the miniscule Parsi community on the western coast is illustrative. For many centuries they remained a poor fishing and trading community but they developed a good working relationship with the British who possibly saw in them a cooperative community not belonging to one of the two major religious groups (and as such innocuous), with the result that during the Raj they rapidly rose in the social and financial ladders through their resourcefulness, entrepreneurial character and cooperative nature, in contrast to their grinding poverty before that time. Article 39 gives it all away when it says that it would like to direct State policy to a condition where, "the operation of the economic system does not result in the concentration of wealth and means of production to the common detriment".

The term 'Backward Classes' was first defined legally in the princely state of Mysore in 1918 where it was sought to induct members of backward communities into various spheres of public service. In 1921, the Bombay government defined 'Backward Classes' as all communities other than Brahmins who were not represented in public service. In Madras, the term continued to construe strata above the untouchables thus including some non-untouchable castes. However, it is noteworthy that the first reference to this term in Madras occurs in the Fort St. George Gazette No. 40 of 5 November 1895 which mentions grants in aid to schools for backward classes, an umbrella term used to denote untouchable and Scheduled Castes (SCs). Subsequently, when this matter came up in the Assembly members from northern India purported that the term 'Backward Classes' was a substitutive term for 'Scheduled Castes'. However, this assertion was challenged by members from Bombay, Madras and Mysore owing to the prior definition of the term there. Chandrika Ram from Bihar (the only state in the north to have a good chunk of backward classes) opined that the term signified those castes that lay in between the supposedly upper castes and SCs.

The Constituent Assembly thoroughly debated the question of who the scheduled castes were, and the issue was settled before Independence without interference from the judiciary. However, the entire matter of who constituted the backward classes was neither addressed by the makers of the Constitution nor the Centre for many years. Given the local vagaries in who and what comprised the backward classes the matter was deferred to the States in 1956 citing that "any all-India list would have no practical utility". The Kalelkar Commission was established in 1953 and was directed to determine the criteria to be adopted in considering whether any section of people should be treated as socially and educationally backward. When it submitted its report it concluded that its four main criteria for social backwardness—degraded status, lack of education, under representation in the civil services and secondary and tertiary sectors—all came down to one common denominator: belonging to a lower caste. The Commission thus drew up a list of 2399 so-called OBC castes, which made up 32% of Indian society on the basis of the 1931 census.

The British were striving to improve representation of backward classes in elected assemblies with ever-increasing powers. The 1919 reform thus brought the government to reserve seven seats of the Bombay Legislative Council for Marathas and 28 of the 65 seats of the Madras Council for non-Brahmins, a category created by grouping the untouchables and the Shudra castes to combat so called Brahminic hegemony. This comfortable quota of reserved seats allowed the Justice Party, a group that claimed to speak for the non-Brahmins, to win the 1920 regional elections and in 1921, the government thereby formed introduced a 48% quota in the administration for non-Brahmins in Tamil Nadu. The term 'Backward Class' was used since the 1920s in Tamil Nadu from the days of the

Justice Party.

When it came to electoral politics post-independence, the Ram Manohar Lohia-Jayaprakash Narayan era of socialist policies in the Hindi heartland provided a fillip to various caste based political factions which went on to rule or establish themselves politically in the demographically large states of Uttar Pradesh and Bihar. In northern India, the proportion of OBC (Other Backward Classes) elected representatives rose from 11% in 1984 to 25% in 1996, whereas that of the upper caste elected officials fell from 47% to 35%. However, OBCs have also been plagued with divisions when competition for power developed between some components of this federation of castes. For example, Yadavs, Kurmis and Lodhis aligned with different political parties but OBC politics remained the order of the day. In many ways, the political moment inspired by Mandal created history: a point of no return had been reached in the assertiveness of the OBCs in the political sphere, so much so that no party could ignore them like before. In fact, irrespective of the party in office, the chief ministers have mostly been OBC leaders in the Hindi belt, the crucible of the ongoing silent revolution over the last ten years, a situation which stands in stark contrast with the one which prevailed before.

Communities which were found to be as disadvantaged as the SCs but could not be declared as SCs, because of the non-existence of the untouchability factor were classified as Most Backward Classes (MBCs). All the schemes available for BCs are commonly applicable for MBCs also. Recognising that the words 'caste' and 'class' were used interchangeably in the colonial period, Justice B. P. Jeevan Reddy held that a caste could also be a class in the Indra Sawhney case. However, abandoning the Bombay-Balaji approach, the court also held that in identifying OBCs, the government did not have to restrict itself only to those communities that were as backward as SCs. In effect, through various rulings and judgements, the courts were saying that *a caste as a whole is socially and educationally backward.*

Accordingly, the courts upheld that caste could be used to indicate backwardness and upheld the central government's decision to provide 27% reservations to 'backward classes'. However, the ruling also stated that reservations could not exceed 50%. This posed a conundrum for Tamil Nadu where reservations were already 69%. To continue with this practice Tamil Nadu was given an exception. The Tamil Nadu government introduced a Bill, called the Tamil Nadu Backward Classes, Scheduled Castes and Scheduled Tribes (Reservation of Seats in Educational Institution and of appointments or posts in the Services under the State) Bill, 1993. The then Chief Minister, J. Jayalalitha, after talks with the Union government 'ensured' that the Tamil Nadu government's Act should be brought under the Ninth Schedule of the Constitution, which meant it could not be challenged in a court of law! The 93rd and 95th Amendments merely affirmed certain aspects that had already been discussed several times and have seemingly put a seal of permanency on the matter.

To highlight the inconsistencies in all of this, one has to only recollect what Ambedkar had said in the assembly on 30 November 1948:

> *Let me give an illustration. Supposing, for instance, reservations were made for a community or a collection of communities, the total of which came to something like 70% of the total posts under the State and only 30% are retained as the unreserved. Could anybody say that the reservation of 30% as open to general competition would be satisfactory from the point of view of giving effect to the first principle, namely, that there shall be equality of opportunity? It cannot be in my judgment. Therefore the seats to be reserved, if the reservation is to be consistent with sub-clause (1) of*

> *Article 10, must be confined to a minority of seats. It is then only that the first principle could find its place in the constitution and be effective in operation. If honourable members understand this position that we have to safeguard two things namely, the principle of equality of opportunity and at the same time satisfy the demand of communities which have not had so far representation in the state, then, I am sure they will agree that unless you use some such qualifying phrase as 'backward' the exception made in favour of reservation will ultimately eat up the rule altogether. Nothing of the rule will remain. That I think, if I may say so, is the justification why the drafting committee undertook on its own shoulders the responsibility of introducing the word 'backward' which, I admit, did not originally find a place in the fundamental right in the way in which it was passed by this Assembly. But I think honourable members will realise that the drafting committee which has been ridiculed on more than one ground for producing sometimes a loose draft, sometimes something which is not appropriate and so on, might have opened itself to further attack that they produced a draft constitution in which the exception was so large, that it left no room for the rule to operate. I think this is sufficient to justify why the word 'backward' has been used.*

According to Ambedkar, the word 'backward' was introduced to ensure that the 'backward classes' as understood in South India would also obtain social equality with the SC/ST communities. If the word 'backward' were not introduced in Article 10(1) of Ambedkar, or Article 16(4) as it is today, the 'backward classes' as defined in Madras, Mysore and elsewhere would not have found preferred representation in the Constitution. This did not mean that the States could later make these reservations supernumerary to the existing SC/ST reservations of 22.5%, but this is what happened in Tamil Nadu and indeed in the rest of the country post-Mandal. The result was that Ambedkar's absurd situation of 30% unreserved positions actually became a reality by the 1990s. The Tamil Nadu Act did not have a basis or rationale for 69%; their only argument was that such reservations for backward classes were well established in Tamil Nadu since the 1920s. The fact that there is a need for reservations for backward classes even after 96 years implies that reservations have either not worked or that they might not yet have uplifted those for whom they were intended. This brings into focus the urgent need to redesign the methodology for affirmative action. Or has forward become backward even as backward become forward?

Proponents of Hindutva see this through rose-tinted spectacles as Hindu modernity primarily to address their critics abroad. The claim made is that Hindu modernity is 'forward looking' unlike its regressive counterparts, the Abrahamic religions of the Indian subcontinent. Nevertheless, this assertion cannot take away the reality that Hindus collectively instituted the Mandal Commission which decided whether a student was admitted to an IIT or AIIMS (campuses of which are located in a cosmopolitan city) based on how far away from the village well members of their caste resided. The imposition of the rural caste order on the entire country affected even those individuals whose ancestors did not even live in the village. As such, it is unclear if this facet of Hindu modernity is regression or progression, an answer that is entirely subject to the person to whom the question is addressed.

We turn next to a methodological evaluation of the Constitution post-1950. Let us consider the subject from four standpoints:

(i) separation of powers among the three wings of the union;
(ii) the Rajya Sabha and its present functioning;
(iii) the effects of the anti-defection law of 1984 and;
(iv) consequences of the first-past-the post system of elections.

All these are matters of method and not really strategy because none is setting forth a plan or design for the nature of the State itself. They are but options for optimal efficiency in obtaining the best results from governance and as variable options they have been switched about in other liberal democracies.

Separation of powers is a device to prevent abuses of power by any one section of the government. It is interesting to note that the varna system envisages a similar system of separation of responsibilities, authority and benefits. The *phalastuti* of the Vishnu Sahasranāmam says that all varnas may chant these names but the accrued benefits are different. While Brahmins obtain knowledge of the Vedanta, Kshatriyas achieve victory. While Vaishyas become wealthy, Shudras gain happiness. The biggest gain by far could be for the Shudras. Knowledge can produce obstacles to *moksha* through competitiveness, hubris and ego.

The gains of victory are temporary and cause harm to others. Besides, victory gained through war needs to be protected in peace resulting in more effort, planning and expenditure. Wealth is ephemeral and is possibly grounded in exploiting others leading to mental anxiety and tension. The Shudra who gains unalloyed happiness is the best-off in such a scheme of things and approximates to the US Constitution in the pursuit of happiness.

The sobering lesson is that no person or group can achieve knowledge, power, wealth and happiness all together. Such was the wisdom of our ancients.

Returning to the question of separation of powers in our Constitution the matter was discussed right through the debates. There are three types of overlap in principle: legislature and executive, legislature and judiciary, judicial and executive. Let us consider the legislature-executive overlap first. This is a feature of the British Constitution and other Westminster countries and means that there is a Union Cabinet headed by a Prime Minister and that all members of this Cabinet must be sitting Members of Parliament. The crux therefore is that many decisions are taken *de facto* by the Prime Minister who is the head of government with his or her cabinet, and ratified *de jure* by the constitutional head of state—who in our case is the President.

The model may not be entirely appropriate in India. In a single party majority condition, too much power is concentrated in the hands of the Cabinet and especially the Prime Minister. Ironically, the power of the Parliament gets diminished in that there is a scramble among legislators to become ministers and ones who do not succeed in their attempts become passive lame duck legislators who are neither able to express their convictions freely on the floor of the House nor vote against a motion proposed by the government. If no single party obtains a majority, a coalition is inevitable and we in India have realised all too regretfully the consequences of coalitions: legislations become captive to local interests, governments become unstable, parties outside the government with even a small number of seats might be able to destabilise the government and above all the possibility of monetary inducements to make legislators change their minds on the floor of the house is a real one. The hybrid model in the French Constitution with powers shared by a directly elected President and the Prime Minster who is the leader of a majority party or majority coalition in Parliament is a delicate exercise that is unique to that country. The US Constitution with its strict separation of the legislature and the executive was discussed at length in our debates but the consensus was to stick with the British model. Separation of the executive from the legislature was suggested in the 1944 M. N. Roy

Constitution. Is it time for a rethink on these lines? Is it time for a change? Can one think of another model?

Separation of the judiciary from the legislature and the executive has been discussed adequately in the context of Kesavananda Bharati case and the imposition of Emergency. Matters were satisfactorily resolved in my view by the mid-1980s and it suffices to say that our judiciary enjoys one of the highest levels of independence in any liberal democracy as revealed in the survey of the Constitute Project referred to earlier in this chapter. This cannot mean that judges should speak out of turn and a recent utterance by a sitting judge of the Supreme Court that "governments will come and go, it is not the government's business to start amending or repealing laws." is definitely not in order. This 'business' is absolutely within the bailiwick of the legislature. In fact it is their only business. All the judiciary may do is to ensure that the actions of the legislature are within the four corners of the Constitution and strike it down if it is not. Overlap between the judiciary and the executive is definitely unacceptable. Ambedkar's words have a ring of finality in them when he said on 10 December 1948 that, "there is no dispute whatsoever that the executive should be separated from the judiciary."

The matter of the Rajya Sabha, Upper House, or second chamber has been repeatedly invoked in the thread of argument developed so far. One should remember that a bicameral legislature was proposed as far back as 1895 in the Swaraj Constitution, our very first attempt at constitution drafting. Various individuals, committees and ultimately our Constitutional Assembly have discussed this matter over the years. There was considerable opposition to the formation of an Upper House in the Assembly. Some felt that it could be there in the centre but not in the States. Yet others felt that an Upper House was a British peculiarity and eccentricity, unsuitable for the new and forward-looking India that had just been born. My view is that after 130 years of discussion, the only fall-back argument for a second chamber is its analogy to the British House of Lords. If one thinks about it dispassionately there is no need for a second chamber unless it is a very special type of body like the empowered US Senate. The follies and foibles that have accompanied the mode of constitution, election and performance of the Rajya Sabha fall far short of what a dynamic progressive liberal democracy should want or need. Other relevant arguments have been put forward earlier in this chapter. In the words of Kamath on 30 July 1949:

> *What after all are the arguments for the creation of second chambers? There are three or four main reasons adduced by the protagonists of second chambers. Firstly, there is the force of tradition in some countries. Happily for our country we have no such tradition. The British, for their own convenience perhaps, introduced this system of second chambers and I hope with the quittal of the British this system also will leave our shores.*

As outlined previously the House of Lords have had a long and chequered history going back to the 11th century. It was a largely hereditary body of noblemen but included members of the clergy as well. Monarchs did or did not consult with them on varying occasions and with varying consequences to themselves. The emergence of the House of Commons in the 14th century was the beginning of a bicameral system. By the early 20th century they, the House of Lords had become unpopular with the people at large, being viewed as representing vested interests only interested in delaying legislation passed by the House of Commons. Their powers have been rapidly whittled down in the past century. Today they are but a symbolic relic of British history. Why such a body should even be a role model for other countries is hard to discern but in any event various countries have adapted the second chamber to suit their particular needs, as has seemingly India.

The Rajya Sabha is supposed to denote the importance of the federal nature of the Indian polity and improve the quality of governance by increasing the positive tension between a strong Centre and self-confident states. Ideally, it should have been the ultimate forum to represent federal and state interests. A state should attempt to leverage its specific local character and advantages to increase its productivity and wealth. In India, under single party rule at the Centre, between 1950 and 1989, and now again after 2014 there seem to be two kinds of states: those where the same majority party is in power in the Centre and the state, and those where it is not. Between 1950 and 1967, the Congress was in power practically everywhere and a particular kind of situation prevailed federalism as such was poorly developed except in the border states, and also in Tamil Nadu. Between 1967 and 1989 the Congress was nearly always in power at the Centre but the states were ruled by a patchwork of regional parties and the Congress. This saw a different kind of situation characterised by a weakening of the Centre. The situation after 2014 has been still different: the Centre has reasserted itself after 50 long years and a number of states are also ruled by the majority party. However, in states where the diversity quotient (different language or religion; sufficiently distinct culture or historical background) is high there has been a tendency for a non-BJP party to gain power. The Rajya Sabha should have been able to capture these various scenarios and make a positive contribution to the activities of the Lok Sabha. However, it has failed profoundly in this respect, all the way from 1950. In practical terms, the Rajya Sabha members have become either unnecessary or disruptionist depending on whether the party in power in the State is the same or different from that in the Centre. In the words of the French politician-philosopher Abbé Sieyes, "if the second chamber agrees with the first chamber it is superfluous and if it disagrees with it, then it is pernicious." It is a no-win situation.

A major weakness, originally perceived as a strength, is the slow turnaround of the Rajya Sabha membership. The idea in the beginning was that an exuberant Lok Sabha might be restrained in its more excessive actions by an older and wiser body which also conveyed the interests of the states as opposed to the Lok Sabha which represents the Union. In such circumstances, a turnaround slower than the Lok Sabha might have been helpful. The implicit assumption here could have been the existence of single party governments at the Centre. This became less likely in a large diverse country with a first-past-the-post electoral system and coalitions became inevitable. The increased importance of regional, hereditary party leaders (the new maharajas) heading small parties ensured that the Rajya Sabha membership became bewilderingly piecemeal. As of early 2022, with the BJP approaching a majority in the Rajya Sabha, a total of 34 parties are represented there with 15 of them having just one member each and just four with 10 or more, BJP (97), Congress (34), TMC (12) and DMK (10). It does not require an expert political scientist to predict the nature of the discourse in such a place. One notes the incidents in August 2021 when the Chairperson of the Rajya Sabha broke down in the House unable to maintain order and conduct proceedings despite the use of marshals. In such an atmosphere the House passed a record number of bills with a record number of amendments with records being broken for the shortest discussion on a bill. What the professional quality of a Rajya Sabha member has been reduced to today is a matter for private consideration by the reader.

Further parodies of the Rajya Sabha are the Legislative

Councils in the states. In truth, the debates in the Constituent Assembly were hazy and inconclusive on this matter. Not all states had second chambers and not all wanted them either. The Assembly did not reach unanimity on the nature of the membership to these Councils and left the matter to be decided by Parliament, a procedure which in itself was contested by some. Today, just six states, Andhra Pradesh, Bihar, Karnataka, Telangana, Maharashtra, and Uttar Pradesh have them and their function or utility is far from clear. In Andhra Pradesh the Council was abolished in 1984 and reinstated in 2005 with the reason for the latter decision being unclear. The Maharashtra Council seems to have had at least one fatuous function to perform in recent memory when an 'appointed' Chief Minister who had not sought election to the Assembly that preceded government formation needed to become a member of the legislature within six months of assuming office. Rather than seeking entry to the Assembly in a by-election he opted for a (safer) back door entry through the Council. As a simple citizen of India, this author feels he would not be exceeding his brief in asking for a review of these legislative assemblies and for their abolishment through special majorities in the Assemblies and further legislation by Parliament, according to Article 169. If the Rajya Sabha has become unnecessary, these Assemblies have become irrelevant.

The third methodological concern to which one may turn one's attention is the The Constitution (52nd Amendment) Act, 1985 under the Tenth Schedule [Articles 102(2) and 191(2)] more popularly known as the anti-defection law. Armed with his steamroller majority in the 1984 election obtained in the sympathy wave following the assassination of his mother, Rajiv Gandhi pushed this legislation, promised in the Congress manifesto, in a record time of eight weeks. His motivation was to usher in a cleaner era in politics and prevent the scourge of floor crossing by MPs and MLAs, the so called *Aaya Ram Gaya Ram* phenomenon, which had reached new lows in parliamentary morality and decency in the 1970s. The Bill was passed unanimously by both Houses of Parliament and the Prime Minster could claim a moral high ground because it was the Congress that traditionally had been the beneficiary of defections. The law disqualified legislators who resigned their party membership voluntarily, if he abstained or voted against a proposed legislation "contrary to any direction" issued by his party, or if he had been expelled from the party under whose banner he had won election. The last condition was the most controversial but there was a caveat in that if a third of the members of any party decided to quit *en masse* they would not attract the provisions of this law. Morality apart, it is possible that there might have been cases of internal dissidence within the Congress that the leadership was trying to curb.

The opposition was quick to pounce on this piece of legislation and L. K. Advani said that it would "muffle dissent forever in a party like the Congress (I) where no internal elections are held and there is no inner-party democracy." Madhu Dandavate said of the Janata Party, "this is the new government's first step towards totalitarianism." N. T. Rama Rao of the TDP who had lost his Chief Ministership through defections in August 1984 was, however, exuberant. In his words, "let us hope that this legislation will mark the beginning of a new political culture." Sadly, it did not and today nearly 40 years later the anti-defection law has become an albatross around the entire institution of disinterested parliamentary debate of the type that was witnessed in the constitutional assembly and in the early years of the republic. The concerns of Advani and Dandavate did indeed come home to roost and the atmosphere of honest debate was stifled. Legislators became playthings of the party bosses who merely issued diktats in the form of whips for every legislation. In the end, the legislator ceased to be a representative of the people who had voted for her and rather she became a rubberstamp of the party. The situation is obviously worse when a single party holds power in the Lok Sabha or Legislative Assembly.

The effects of the anti-defection law have been debilitating because it forces legislators to compulsorily vote according to the wishes of the party on whose ticket, they won their election unless they wish to lose their seats. The question of a conscience vote on broad questions with big policy implications simply does not arise. Already, with the overlap between the executive and legislature and the first-past-the-post system of elections, the prime minster becomes quite powerful. With this law, his or her power along with that of the party president becomes simply enormous. Without such a law seven Republican senators in the U.S.A. voted to impeach Donald Trump while fifty five MPs in Britain from the Prime Minister's party voted against the government's proposal for stricter lockdown restrictions.

In connection with the anti-defection law, Manish Tewari of the Congress posed an even more provocative question recently when he asked whether India even needed a Parliament. All these are disturbing signs for the body politic. When a sitting Deputy Chief Minister says that before long there will not be a Constitution and when a veteran parliamentarian says that we do not need a parliament, our leaders from all political parties need to take note. This state of affairs has gone on for far too long when each individual, small group, caucus or party within the political system have been conducting their affairs in an extremely myopic, self-serving manner with no heed being paid to the welfare of the people who they claim to represent. Tewari called the 1985 law political hara-kiri committed by the Congress, his own party and others for this Bill was passed unanimously everywhere.

Ironically the worst effects of the 1985 law occur when a single party has a powerful majority in the legislature. In a coalition dispensation which is metastable at best the party strengths are all moderate and there is not much any legislator gains in crossing over from one small party to another although it is supposedly easier to find a third of the members to defect with oneself if the overall strength of the party in the legislature is modest. Tewari says that the law did not prevent defection; all it did was to change it from retail to wholesale. However, there is another side to all this—why did the founding fathers not introduce provisions similar to those in the Tenth Schedule in the original document? They would have been horrified if they had learned that an individual legislator would not exercise his political preference according to his conscience and morality after studying seriously any proposed legislation but rather be a puppet to the wishes and whims of his political party. The key word here is morality. In principle, any legislator before or after the 1985 law should have felt morally bound to resign his seat voluntarily if he was at variance with his party on an important piece of legislation and seek re-election from his constituency under a political banner with which he was in greater consonance. Rajiv Gandhi's was a medicine all right but it was a short-term cure. In the long run, the medicine resulted in a new disease.

The reason I have assigned a substantial amount of space in this book to a single law is that its effects have been truly debilitating. It has been the last straw in destroying morality in the Parliament and legislatures leading to a complete lack of motivation on the part of legislators to make better laws for the country. In this atmosphere of immorality and idleness, the attention of parliamentarians and state legislators has turned to physical shows of strengths and calisthenics. It is routine to see legislators rushing to the floor of the well, shouting and screaming, tearing microphones out of their sockets, interrupting other speakers, ceaselessly heckling, making provocative gestures to other members and on occasion even intimidatory gestures towards the chair of the house. There is a crisis of confidence. Since the entire proceedings are televised not much is left to the public to imagine. An unexpressed sentiment could well be, "The way these guys are behaving in Parliament, surely there are others in this vast country who could have done a better job".

Tewari concludes by asserting that India could very easily function with a directly elected executive and a judiciary to exercise oversight. He avers that the legislature has completely failed in its legitimate duties. I tend to agree substantially with his contention that a non-functional legislature is of no use to the country and will revert to these ideas and others in Chapters 4 and 5 where a new model for the constitution and governance are suggested.

Our final methodological concern pertains to the first-past-the-post system of declaring an election result to the Lok Sabha and State Assemblies. At the outset it should be stressed that there is nothing in this method of declaring a winner that makes it an infallible indicator of the will of the people in whose name the elected legislator carries out his business. It is a method that has been used in many countries within or without the Westminster system. There are many variables that can influence whether the winner on such a system truly represents the electorate in her constituency. The alternative system of proportional representation has also worked well in many countries. Let us consider both methods in a comparative manner.

In the first-past-the-post system the winner is the candidate who secures the maximum number of votes in the votes polled. This method is used in around 70 countries. The greater the turnout the more accurately the winner may be said to represent the constituency's will. The lesser the number of political parties in the fray in a particular constituency, the greater is the representative accuracy. In the limit, if there are only two candidates, the one who obtains say 50.1 per cent of the eligible votes cast wins but it should not be forgotten that in such a situation, 49.9 per cent of the electorate prefers someone else. Is this a true representation of the electorate's wishes? As the number of candidates (parties) increases the percentage of required votes keeps falling and in multi-cornered contests in India this has been as low as 30 per cent to secure victory. Small changes in the voting percentages in the 35-45 per cent range in typical multi-party contests can make a big difference in the number of seats obtained by a party such that even a small increase above 45 per cent may result in an overwhelming majority while a small decrease below 35 per cent can sharply reduce the number of seats obtained. The response therefore is highly non-linear in all except two-candidate contests but even here, the elected person does not represent an overwhelming majority of voters if the winning margin is slim. Since we may continue to have many political parties in India for reasons of regionalism and religion it is likely that in many elections to the Lok Sabha the winner may not represent the majority of those who have cast eligible votes. Similarly, a party may have a huge majority in the Lok Sabha and have secured just around 40 per cent or so of the votes cast.

In the simplest form of proportional representation, voters cast their ballots for a party. The number of seats filled in the legislature is proportional to the number of votes obtained by each party. These seats are allotted to names which appear in party lists which might be open (voters may select from names in this list) or closed (decided by the party before the election) and the numbers of legislators are fixed by the parties after the results are declared. Usually, though not invariably, there is a lower cut-off for the percentage of votes that a party needs to get in order to qualify for a place in the legislature. This could be in the range of 3-5 per cent and prevents extremely small parties from entering the legislature. In India, a party would need to obtain just 15 lakh votes all across the country to secure one Lok Sabha seat if there were not cut-off. Around 75 countries follow this type of proportional representation that uses only party lists. These include Brazil, Indonesia, South Africa, Sri Lanka and Switzerland. Some others use modifications of this method and the entire exercise seems to be reasonably successful. It should be noted that this list includes around 20 countries that used to use first-past-the-post and then switched over. No country seems to have made the reverse switch.

In an alternative proportional representation method the electorate may have to cast two votes, one for a candidate and one for a party. This is known as mixed member proportional representation. Candidates may be declared elected if they obtain a majority of votes cast in their names (first vote), in other words using the first-past-the-post methodology. However, the final representation of parties in the legislature reflects the votes cast in the name of a party (second vote). There will be a difference in the proportion of elected candidates, party wise as compared to the proportion of votes secured by the parties in the second vote. This difference is made up using names in a list issued by the party prior to the election. This difference will generally correspond to candidates who have lost narrowly using the first-past-the-post method with the first votes. The idea is to obtain a legislature that representationally fits the mood of the electorate better. The most important country that uses the MMPR method is Germany while others include Bolivia, Italy, New Zealand and Ukraine.

A country with a strong two-party system may use either method and get equivalent results. As the number of parties increases, smaller parties are less favoured in first-past-the-post. Proportional representation is more likely to lead to coalitions but curiously the numbers of elections called over comparable time periods for the two methodologies are largely similar across countries. There is nothing inherently unstable about proportional representation and indeed it is used in a majority of countries today. The question is whether or not first-past-the-post is better than proportional representation for the India of 2022 and beyond. In the Indian context, the only outcome in switching to proportional representation might be an increase in the federal content of the polity but even this is arguable.

In this connection, it is worthwhile to digress briefly into the nature of the opposition to the BJP today. If a strong national opposition party does not emerge soon, the BJP might keep securing simple majorities in the Lok Sabha in the immediate future. The reason is simple: voters in India tend to use a variable combination of factors when casting a Lok Sabha vote. These include party ideology, state of the economy, ability of the party to secure stability, personal integrity of the candidate and a perception about the party's stand on corruption. Federalism and diversity generally play second fiddle in a parliamentary election testifying to the maturity of the electorate. The exceptions may be votes cast for regional parties with sharply distinct, even divisive ideologies (communism, communalism, regional chauvinism). With regard to ideology, the opposition lacks focus and its main intent seems to be restricted to ousting the BJP—not exactly an ideology. Its economic record might be as good or indifferent as the BJP depending on one's subjective viewpoint. It does not exactly emerge as a squeaky-clean outfit, and finally the electorate seems to have sensed that a *gatbandhan* (coalition) would probably lead away from stability.

In summary, whether India stays with first-past-the-post or switches to proportional representation is a subject for discussion in public forums and among legislators considering that so many countries do seem to be doing quite well with proportional representation.

We finally take up very briefly the matter of execution, the last step in delivering the results of legislation and its mode of implementation to the people themselves. This discussion will be necessarily exceedingly brief because I shall consider only some constitutional aspects that affect policy execution. The key body here is the Indian Administrative Service that was created by the constitution in Article 312:

(1) Notwithstanding anything in Chapter VI of Part VI or Part XI, if the Council of States has declared by resolution supported by not less than two-thirds of the members present and voting that it is necessary or expedient in the national interest so to do, Parliament may by law provide for the creation of one or more all India services (including an all-India judicial service) common to the Union and the States, and, subject to the other provisions of this Chapter, regulate the recruitment, and the conditions of service of persons appointed, to any such service.

(2) The services known at the commencement of this Constitution as the Indian Administrative Service and the Indian Police Service shall be deemed to be services created by Parliament under this article.

We note from earlier in this chapter that the formation of the IAS, modelled after the British ICS, was strongly endorsed by Patel, our first Home Minister, who called it the steel frame. In later years, the fact that just 0.01 per cent of the aspirants who write the qualifying exam are finally successful and enter the IAS has led to the community being dubbed 'heaven born'. The ideal IAS officer is supposed to offer disinterested input to the executive who is free to accept or discard such input. Following this, he or she is responsible for administering government policy as decided by the executive. It is because the size of the higher bureaucracy is so small in this large country, their power and discretionary authority appears to be overbearingly large, possibly even oppressive. I do not wish to resort to the popular sport of IAS bashing and just concentrate on matters that have a constitutional bearing. However, two recent quotes about these officers are inimitable and convey the general mood. Sanjay Dixit an ex-IAS officer says, "British invented a missile called civil servant, which does not work and which cannot be fired." Nitin Gadkari, a sitting Cabinet Minister today dismisses them in just three scathing words: *Nalayak, Nikammi, Bhrasht* (worthless, useless, corrupt).

When it was discussing the Constitution, the Assembly was perhaps thinking about the ideal IAS officer in the same way that it was thinking about the ideal parliamentarian, the ideal judge and the ideal minister. All these people might be heaven born in their ideality but sadly enough more earthy than one would wish. Whether it is strategy, methodology or execution, the need of the hour is to find solutions to our Herculean problems. The Constitution cannot reform the IAS *per se.* We might have come to the point where we might ask if we still need our steel frame or has it become a steel cage encircling the people? A different way of choosing our executive might obviate or at least reduce the need for an all-India permanent civil service, For example, each new executive elected through popular vote could bring along with it its own set of higher-level bureaucrats as is the case in the U.S.A. These and other options will be discussed in Chapter 4.

We conclude this chapter recounting what might have been the mood and sentiment that gripped our Constituent Assembly in the euphoria of Independence. The Constitution they adopted was not a perfect document. It was drafted quickly but discussed seriously. It was best suited for the time and it provided adequate scope for the addition of detail and to even break some new ground. Judged from the yardstick of liberal democracies it does not do badly. The Assembly members might be excused for extrapolating to the future and assuming that future generations of politicians, judges and administrators would share their intense patriotism and nationalism—so great was their joy that we had become independent. However, it is only natural that all intense emotions subside and wane, leaving just an afterglow which might even be extinguished with the passage of time. It is here that that both our Constitution and politicians have failed us. The former has missed certain vital aspects of our national identity. The latter have not sustained the faith placed on them by our founding fathers—on the contrary they have even, on occasion, wilfully chosen to renounce that faith.

We have repeatedly highlighted the absence of the religious element in the Constitution of a country where religion is a universal surcharged element. In the words of Vivekananda:

> *Today I stand here and say, with the conviction of truth, that it is so. If there is any land on this earth that can lay claim to be the blessed Punya Bhumi, to be the land to which all souls on this earth must come to account for Karma, the land to which every soul that is wending its way Godward must come to attain his last home, the land where humanity has attained its highest towards gentleness, towards generosity, towards purity, towards calmness, above all the land of introspection and of spirituality—it is India.*

This essential religious element that is the body, mind

and soul of our unique country is not to be found in our Constitution, which in the end should be a pointer and marker of future course of action, a document that should encapsulate the essence of the route that would be best suited for us. In the absence of such a strategic emphasis, any attempt even of the honest type, to take the country forward will be a non-starter. If the Constitution had correctly captured the core of our nation, its kernel, it would have been a source of succour during difficult times. In contemporary times, it is a remote and distant document and the average educated man or woman if asked about it might simply say that it was something that the Supreme Court talks about now and then when they are not talking about the Union Territory of Delhi. I find that many educated people still do not know the difference between the words 'democracy' and 'republic'. In the absence of any guiding beacon light, the stage is set for the entry of bad elements into the legislature, judiciary and the executive.

One does not need to read this book to appreciate the sordid depths to which our politicians, supposedly the ones who are the honest implementers of the Constitution, have sunk. People are bought and sold for filthy lucre, nothing or nobody is above a price, and commission agents abound and thrive. It is even surprising that ordinary people show up every five years to vote for one of them. Is it hopefulness, hopelessness, naiveté or just rank stupidity on our part? As for the judiciary it remains a closed club and appointments to the highest court of the land are the internal preserve of this club. The number of Supreme Court and High Court judges with close family connections to other judges of the same court or high-level politicians of former eras is unbelievable. As for the administrators who take pride in the fact that theirs is a service that has been created by the Constitution and that they serve no other master, it would be appropriate to digest Shakespeare's immortal words, as spoken by Cardinal Wolsey:

> *Had I but served my God with half the zeal I served my king, He would not in mine age have left me naked to mine enemies.*
>
> *Henry VIII, Act 3, Scene 2*

The actions of the executive are neatly summarised by Nani Palkhivala of Kesavananda Bharati fame, as one of :

> *Five-year duration, four-year life, three-year proposal, two-year action plan, one-year action, quarterly review hoping the common man solves his problems on a day-to-day basis.*

Ambedkar was realistic when he said:

> *The three pillars of our democracy are the legislature, the judiciary and the executive. Now to the question of the relationship between the legislature and the judiciary in a federal constitution it is always open to the judiciary to decide whether any particular law passed by the legislature is ultra vires or intra vires. For myself I cannot omit the possibility of a legislature packed by party men making laws which may abrogate and violate the fundamental rights affecting the life and liberty of an individual. At the same time I do not see how five or six gentlemen sitting in the Supreme Court examining laws made by the legislature by dint of their own individual bias and prejudice can be trusted to determine which law is good and which is bad.*

He also pointed out the danger of hero worship in India, in words that haunt and revisit us practically every day:

> *The second thing we must do is to observe the caution which John Stuart Mill has given to all who are interested in the maintenance of democracy, namely, not "to lay their liberties at the feet of even a great man, or to trust him with powers which enable him to subvert their institutions". There is nothing wrong in being grateful to great men who have rendered lifelong services to the*

country. But there are limits to gratefulness. As has been well said by the Irish patriot Daniel O'Connell, no man can be grateful at the cost of his honour, no woman can be grateful at the cost of her chastity and no nation can be grateful at the cost of its liberty. This caution is far more necessary in the case of India than in the case of any other country. For in India, bhakti or what may be called the path of devotion or hero worship, plays a part in its politics unequalled in magnitude by the part it plays in the politics of any other country in the world. Bhakti in religion may be a road to the salvation of the soul. But in politics, bhakti or hero worship is a sure road to degradation and to eventual dictatorship.

Ramnarayan Singh was less polite, if possibly too idealistic for the modern world:

The parliamentary system of government or the party system of government has been provided for in this constitution. I would like to say that it does not suit India. Unfortunately there are already too many parties in our country. There have been parties on the basis of the caste system for a long time. Now if you introduce a new party system what will be the outcome? If under the party system you grant franchise to everyone, the result will be that some scoundrels and capitalists will combine and manage to monopolise all the votes. I know that they would not lack associates. Democracy cannot function in such a way. The way affairs are managed in western countries has something of democracy in it but there too there is no real democracy. I hold that the government based on party system strikes at the very roots of democracy. Under that system only a few persons rule. A few scoundrels and a few capitalists will combine and rule. It is right that in democracy everyone should have a vote and it is also right that an issue should be decided by the vote of the majority. But it should not be necessary that every person should belong to some party or other for arriving at decisions. The party decisions or the directions of a leader should not influence voting. Everyone should be free to vote and should do so honestly. The decision arrived at in this way will be a democratic decision and the country will benefit by it. Otherwise a party leader will give directions and others will vote accordingly. The decision arrived at in this way will not be a democratic decision. It will not be the decision of the panchayat. It is a common saying in our country that Panch is God. He is not a God who has a number of smaller gods under him. It is understood in regard to God that those who sit in His presence are free and dependent to none and that they do not decide any issue and vote on it by looking up to anyone.

It is an open question therefore as to whether the Constitution is both frozen in time and time bound. It is not revealed wisdom from the Divine. It is not a holy book. It had particular and peculiar reference to the times during which it was drafted and discussed. Its further dissection and modification, even to the extent of relooking at its innards might well be a worthwhile exercise noting essentially that its main drawback is the absence of a spiritual presence, the mysterious X-factor, the lack of which is preventing our nation from finding and reaching its full potential. The modern world has become dauntingly competitive. We have the strength of constructive integration and the weakness of destructive differentiation. Centrifugal and centripetal forces are in balance and tension. What one needs is a powerful and instinctive glue or binder that holds this vast nation together.

In conclusion, I maintain that our progress in the seventy two years since we adopted our Constitution has been insufficient given the natural advantages with which we have been endowed. I must emphasise that mine is a politically neutral statement and individual-neutral. The independent Republic of India has seen many governments of different ideological hues both at the Centre and in the States, the time period has been long enough to draw statistical inferences, and both successes and failures have been numerous enough that it should be possible to ascribe this overall insufficiency to an overriding cause which might be so subtle and yet at the same time so obvious that most of us would hardly be aware of it.

Returning to Ambedkar's quotation at the head of this chapter, there are three possibilities regarding good and bad constitutions, and good and bad implementers of the Constitution: (i) the Constitution is bad and the people implementing it are good; (ii) the Constitution is good and the people implementing it are bad; (iii) both the Constitution and the people implementing it are bad. Since I shall maintain that our progress in seventy-two years has been insufficient, I will discard the fourth possibility that both Constitution and implementers have been good. The conclusion is inexorable—with any of the three possibilities above, there is a strong case for reworking our Constitution so as to make it a more reliable guide for the future.

India, or more aptly put Bhārat, is a classic example of a complex phenomenon. It has all the characteristics of complexity, it is multivariate and multifunctional, capable of self-correction and self-healing, it is multi-layered and has different frames of reference within an organic whole. Different levels of self-organisation blend and merge at times but diverge at others. The missing X-factor in our formal documentations of governance is a clear acceptance of our civilisational identity and it to this that I shall turn in the next chapter.

CHAPTER THREE

INTERMEZZO

THE CIVILISATIONAL STATE

Dharma is law in the widest sense—spiritual, moral, ethical, and temporal.

—Arthashastra, Chānakya

WE have detailed in the previous chapter that despite the best-intentioned efforts by its makers, our Constitution failed to weave the motif of dharma into the warp and woof of the country's game plan as an independent nation. India has both gained and lost from history. There was an ancient tradition which was well suited to the geography and culture of the land we call Bhāratavarsha. In times of limited mobility, the land's natural borders were sufficiently formidable to prevent incursions from the outside. This was important in the civilisations of the ancient world. Egypt and Mesopotamia fell because their natural borders were insufficient to prevent attacks from the Greeks and Romans. India was relatively secure geographically and became prosperous. To quote Chanakya again, "If people are prosperous even a leaderless state can be governed." A leaderless state, or in what happened eventually, a state with weak leaders, becomes vulnerable to armed attacks. In our case, these came from the northwest through small geographical chinks during the period following the advent of Islam in Arabia. Repeated attacks also showed up the chinks in our civilisational armoury since there was a clash of cultures and perceptions that could ultimately be traced to the fact that the pluralistic Sanātana Dharma came into strategic conflict with a monotheistic faith determined on attack, pillage and finally conquest. The period after 1600 CE saw a second wave of attack, more subtle this time and possibly more dangerous, from our sea boundaries by a culture that was as divergent from the Bhāratiya mindset and equally determined in its ultimate aims. The rest is too well known to bear repeating. It suffices to say that by 1900, we were at our lowest ebb physically, economically, culturally and psychologically. The only positive albeit tenuous link that history afforded us was dharma which had not been snuffed out completely after twelve centuries of sadness. The 20th century and the two decades that have elapsed in the 21st century have seen a slow awakening of our civilisational impulses, and we have experienced anew the sensations of being in that order, a country, a nation, and more ambitiously in the last decade or so, a civilisation again.

We have adequately detailed in Chapter 1 the incomplete description of our situation by the word 'India'. India may be a sufficient descriptor of us as a country. It is a partial descriptor of us as a nation. *It is completely inadequate as a descriptor of us as a civilisation.* A country is easy enough to explain and its attributes are something known in the form of, say an accepted citizenship which confers on one the ability to hold a passport, a valid requirement to enter another such entity that calls itself a country. In the strictest sense of the term, 'country' is a neutral and somewhat official concept. One may voluntarily give up citizenship of one's country and take up that of another based on rules prevalent in both countries. In some cases one may even hold dual citizenships. Citizenship is only an affiliation to the political boundaries of a country. It is determined by rules and not by principles. It is true that a country has a flag and an anthem and that most citizens feel an unquantifiable emotion whenever they see the flag or hear the anthem. However, every time this happens, the idea of country is being mysteriously conflated in the mind with a higher idea called 'nation'. A nation is a larger concept than a country and if India describes us as a country, Bhārat describes us as a nation. In the words of Ambedkar:

> *Nationality is a subjective psychological feeling. It is a feeling of a corporate sentiment of oneness which makes those who are charged with it feel that they are kith and kin. This national feeling is a double edged feeling. It is at once a feeling of fellowship for one's own kith and kin and an anti-fellowship feeling for those who are not one's own kith. It is a feeling of 'consciousness of kind' which on the one hand binds together those who have it so strongly that it overrides all differences arising out of economic conflicts or social gradations and on the other severs them from those who are not of their kind. It is a longing to belong to one's own group and a longing not to belong to any other group. This is the essence of what is called a nationality and national feeling.*

If one goes by this definition, nationality is more of a journey than a destination in itself. If one can create a feeling of fellowship for one's kith and kin beginning at the most fundamental level with one's community and working one's way up to one's country, given human nature one can also conjure up a feeling of animosity and disunity among one's own essentially dismantling the feeling of kinship. In effect, it would appear that one can both make and unmake nationality! However, the process of constructing a feeling of nationality or nationhood is vastly more time consuming than dismantling it. Let us consider former times. Distance between individuals was a limiting factor to social interaction in the pre-industrial revolution era. Creating a fraternal feeling among individuals separated by distance took years, decades and at times centuries in the medieval era. Additionally the tyranny of distance also worked to vitiate the process thus stretching out the time horizons it might have taken to create such a feeling. To do so, one needs powerful ideas, customs and beliefs in which the entire populace is either invested in or is willing to defend in times of trouble. It is because of this, kingdoms, republics and states in Bhāratavarsha were generally small in size. The Maurya, Gupta, Vijayanagar and later on the Mughal Empire were political entities but only loosely defined in terms of *nationhood*. These were hardly nations in any sense of the term.

However, we get ahead of ourselves. Before one starts to define and redefine nationality in an Indian or in any other context, one should seek to understand what constitutes nationhood and prior to that what constitutes a nation. Tracing the origin of this phenomenon is important for us because we, seventy five years after independence, still need to understand ourselves as a country, nation and civilisation, also in the background of the Partition which continues to be *the* defining moment in any re-evaluation or re-imagining of this land. Accordingly I turn to Europe where the modern concept of 'nation' originated. That continent still remains an active laboratory for conducting experiments on the types of nation-states one might obtain and it is instructive to consider the making and unmaking of political boundaries in the European landmass over the last four centuries. Any excursions further back than that into our ancient past by votaries of the Bhāratiya civilisational state or in finding it inadequate by critics, using Western current liberal benchmarks, are equally theoretical and abstruse and are not grounded in today's realities. In Deng Xiaoping's most often quoted remark, "It doesn't matter if a cat is black or white, so long as it catches mice." Countries are run by pragmatic politicians; nations are spontaneous creations of the people while civilisations are a manifestation of nature's higher laws. None of these are made in academic departments of political science or by newspaper columnists and TV anchors.

The Treaty of Westphalia signed upon the culmination of the Thirty Years' war (1618-1648) laid the foundations of the modern nation-state. This war was pan-European and involved smaller German states allied with Calvinist Sweden, the Protestants, and arrayed against them the Austrian and Spanish Habsburg Empires and France, the upholders of Catholicism. The religious origin of the war lay in the imposition of Catholicism by the Austrian Habsburgs on their Protestant German subjects. The Catholics were, however, unable to overturn Protestantism and the treaty marked the formal end of this conflict. It upheld that the sovereign ruler of a state had sole power over all its internal affairs *including religion* enshrining the principle of *cuius regio, eius religio,* in other words, whose realm, his religion. As a matter of interest on the side, the period coincided with internal fissures within the Vatican and the Papacy as revealed in Galileo's run-ins with them concerning ecclesiastical matters. Apart from all of this, the Peace of Westphalia also resulted in a significant weakening of the Habsburg empires in both Austria and Spain, the strengthening of France as a political entity, thanks to the internal politics within the Catholic ranks played by Cardinal Richelieu, and the assertion of independence of smaller German states from the Holy Roman Empire.

The treaty provisions laid the foundation of the modern nation-state. As religion became an internal matter, these provisions allowed for states to venture into international affairs and diplomacy without fear of being internally destabilised. As a corollary, the powers of the Papacy became curtailed because the Church could not use religion as a pretext to interfere in the internal affairs of a state. With the fighting in Europe eventually subsiding, countries were able to turn their attention towards exploration, commerce and trade. The idea of the modern nation-state, chiefly its sovereignty, was a European one born out of the Westphalian treaty. To be sure, this treaty did not definitively end all warfare in the European continent and the odd war did occur between states. However, successive decades saw rapid advancement in fields that led to modern science and technology ultimately culminating in the Industrial Revolution of the 19th century.

The 1815 Congress of Vienna sought to reorganise Europe by redistributing or carving out new territories. It was also the first international convention that sought to preserve the *balance of power*, a concept by which diplomats and foreign policy doyens abide to this day. This political reconstitution of Europe, the primary agenda item, was chaired by Austrian foreign minister Klemens von Metternich with the proceedings largely dominated by the four so-called 'great' powers of the time, Austria, Britain, Prussia and Russia. The 1815 Congress held that the borders of a state were not sacrosanct but rather could be carved up and redistributed according to the prevailing realpolitik considerations. Scant attention was paid to the cultural and fraternal impulses of the populace when territories were being split up. What was the justification for this cynical stand? Were the members of the opinion that Europe was a unitary civilisation and as such could be subdivided at will into multiple nation- states to suit the times? Did they consider language, ethnicity and religion at all in this exercise? One notes for example that the Christianity–Islam fault line lay fair and square in the heart of the Balkans. Alternatively, was it a means to preserve the larger identity of the European land mass while at the same time de-emphasising national identity that was manifesting itself in the form of revolutionary movements in the nation-states?

The Congress was the successor of the Treaty of Westphalia in terms of the evolution of the nation-state. Westphalia created the nation-state. Vienna breathed a somewhat different type of life into it. Indeed, territories were sliced like salami and stacked together with other states to create unsavoury dishes, and it would only be a matter of time before nationalistic revolutions flared up. The 1815 Congress sought to keep in abeyance nationalistic sentiments and liberalism in Europe. One notes that while 'nationalism' and 'liberalism' were synonymous two centuries ago they seem to be in contradiction at present, almost certainly in India although one could carp about distinctions between Western and Bhāratiya definitions of liberalism, which have to do with differences in the relationship between individuals and society.

Metternich, a key player in the Vienna Congress, merits some discussion for the way his actions influenced political developments in Europe for a century. He was a true conservative eager to preserve the *status quo* during the so-called 'Age of Metternich', the three decades following the Napoleonic Wars. Powerful forces were sweeping across Europe brought about by the seeding of the Industrial Revolution which freed the populace from a primarily agrarian lifestyle. The increased mobility of people led to urbanisation and there was a concomitant delinking of land-associated identity. Rising feelings of nationalism and the attendant political upheaval were inevitable. Yet, using this doctrine Austria suppressed revolutions in Italy, and France in Spain. Russia though had issues with the Metternich system, being greatly upset by the Ottoman Turks' persecution of their fellow Orthodox Christians during the Greek independence movement. Historians see Metternich as a man who, by suppressing revolutionary movements, prevented a natural collapse of monarchies ensuring thereby that they continued artificially for another century before their sudden, perhaps by then, inevitable collapse at the end of World War 1, an event that has been recounted in Chapter 1 as one of the possible nucleators of the 1919 Montford reforms in India.

One of the outcomes of the Metternich system was the *Deutsche Sonderweg* or special path for Germany, which historians suggest might never have occurred in the absence of this system. The Sonderweg was defined quite differently in the mid-1800s from the interpretation it took on during the Nazi era, indeed it was rather more positive in that the German-speaking states sought to distinguish themselves from other Western states by proactively instituting social and political reforms without necessarily having to react to the revolutionary pressures from within. Their thesis lay in the assumption that the German middle class was weak and unable to push for the transition from monarchy to democracy. The unsuccessful revolution of 1848 by the German bourgeoisie necessitated the need to carry out a revolution from the top instead. This was orchestrated by Bismarck on behalf of the Prussian military monarchy. Prussia was the largest of the German speaking states and Bismarck sought to unify these states with blood and iron, *Blut und Eisen*, to create a German-speaking nation-state. The unification was achieved in 1871 with the constitution of the North German Confederation being extended to the entire German empire. The provisions provided for a chancellor to head the executive, appointed and dismissed by the Emperor, but not by the Reichstag, the federal parliament.

The unification of Germany created an extremely federal nation-state in the heart of Europe with the constituent states retaining control over much of their affairs. Prussia yielded substantial powers to pacify Bavaria, the second largest state in the confederation. Bismarck was a gut thinker and in an Indian context one could imagine him as a combination of

Ambedkar and Patel! He changed the concept of a nation-state which till then was being driven towards smaller states, by infusing federalism into the concept. In this respect Bismarck's vision was the antithesis to Metternich's as the latter believed that European states could be subdivided or amalgamated at will. Was Habsburg Austria a federation? In an earlier chapter I have referred to it as an approximation to an empire. Hungary separated for all purposes from it in 1867 and the Austro-Hungarian Empire came into being with twin seats of power in Vienna and Budapest. Bismarck's federation was more tractable as the joining entities gave up their powers and came together in a more cohesive fashion, a true federation. However, the nature of the federation was intriguing in that Germany itself remained a nation-state, later a republic but never calling itself a civilisational state.

Metternich's ideas and the counter to his ideas have therefore led to two opposite interpretations of the term 'nation-state'. His definition of the term remained in currency for a substantial period of time. To reiterate, his nation-state was not the smallest possible indivisible unit held together by ethnic, linguistic or cultural borders but one that could be imagined out of political convenience to further the hegemony of a dominant empire of the time. Accordingly, the Ottoman Empire was dissected after World War 1 by the victorious allies, Britain, France, U.S.A. into political units that hardly overlapped in terms of cultural contiguity. If anything, the artificial borders created in western Asia at that time set apart ethnic groups that had lived together amicably for centuries. The straight lines demarcating the borders of countries in the African continent and, closer home, the creation of Pakistan after World War II as a buffer state between a looming, aggressive U.S.S.R. and an India, still deemed to be within the influence of the Anglosphere, corroborate the same thesis.

Pakistan's creation was facilitated by Britain, following which it became a client state of the U.S.A. soon after by joining the Southeast Asia Treaty Organization (SEATO).

The period after the 1990s has, however, seen the regurgitation towards division into nation-states according to ancient ethnic and cultural fault lines. This second definition of the nation-state implies it is now considered the smallest indivisible unit with natural boundaries that can be held together by the common cultural links among the population. It is with this principle that the erstwhile Yugoslavia was split into Serbia, Croatia, Slovenia, North Macedonia, Bosnia and Herzegovina, the partially recognised Kosovo and Montenegro. This second definition of 'nation-state' seems to be a more stable one than Metternich's and it is difficult to imagine these new countries in south-eastern Europe dividing themselves further into smaller states in the near or remote future.

We turn our attention to other non-European Western countries and the associated makeup of their nation-states. Outside Europe, the relevant geography that merits discussion in our Indian context is the Anglosphere, primarily the U.S.A. and the U.K. Is the U.K. a nation-state? At a fundamental level it is a political creation, an assemblage of four entities, the English, Scottish, Welsh and a part of the Irish nations, held together by the monarchy. Cultural or ethnic commonality does not determine nationhood. Significantly it is the only country where the currency, in this case the gold coin issued by the Royal Mint, is named after the monarch and called a *sovereign*. This unique structuring of the State results in a loose definition of British nationhood. This could also explain Britain's issues regarding integration within the larger European continent through centuries. In present times its unwillingness to adopt the Euro as its operational currency or to join the Schengen zone for customs and immigration purposes are representative.

The most recent example of its general reluctance to integrate more fully with Europe was Brexit. It would seem that the inhabitants of the U.K. do not see themselves as a part of a larger European civilisation, perhaps not even as an extension. The key role of the monarchy in the U.K. as a strong unifying force in a fairly diverse population is unique in the Western world at least at the present time. In our context, I show in Chapter 4 that it is a poor model for us upon which to base a governance structure.

What of the U.S.A. then? The American settlers fought the British to secure their independence but only because they felt that they were not being treated by the home country as it would treat its own people. This is why their Declaration of Independence in 1776 emphasised universal ideas. They thought and emoted like British people who happened to be living in North America. This was the origin of the 'special relationship' between Britain and the U.S.A. strengthened over the years with a powerful glue called the English language which all European immigrants were obliged to learn when they came to the U.S.A. Americans considered *Pax Americana* to be the natural successor to *Pax Britannica* after World War II and their country to be the global power successor to the British Empire. Nationhood in the U.S.A. is an enigma. Ethnicity, culture and traditions seem not to be its important determinants. Is it a civilisational state, albeit defined in simple terms? Can American civilisation be called a civilisation if the country itself is so young? Does Donald Trump represent the civilisational urgings of America? Is this why he provokes such strong likes and dislikes among the American people? Is America going through a churn between defining itself as a civilisational state as opposed to a nation-state?

One of the remarkable features of the U.S.A. is that it is not defined by culture, race, ethnicity or language but the belief in the American dream, a simple trust in principles like liberty and equality. These foundations of the American state draw in, integrate and absorb individuals irrespective of their antecedents. In fact, it is notable that the American society has over generations been able to incorporate successive waves of immigrants into its larger consciousness so easily that children and grandchildren of immigrants are scarcely able to relate to the nations of their ancestors, considering themselves American before anything else. The definition of American nationhood is rooted in fundamental principles. It is not an artefact of political convenience, and is not unlike a civilisational state.

Bhāratavarsha is not just an ancient land but also an ancient civilisation, estimated to be around 5000 years old. Recorded history and archaeological finds of the Sarasvati or Indus Valley communities date back to that era. The exact age of these settlements, or for that matter the Vedas, is not relevant in our context. Ours is an unbroken civilisational thread over millennia which makes Bhāratavarsha unique and distinct from other civilisations of the ancient world including China which considers itself as a civilisation, based on the Han people, rather than a nation. The distinction is that our civilisation is based on Sanātana Dharma which is a supra-religious concept if one were to go by a monotheistic definition of religion. In the words of David Frawley, "To understand Hinduism, we must recognise its primary name as Sanātana Dharma, the Universal or Eternal Dharma, which is not limited to any time, place or culture, but recognises one Self and Consciousness behind the entire universe, in all living beings in all worlds."

Recent linguistic terminologies have caused much unnecessary (political) confusion in modern India. The very word 'Hinduism' is not of Indic origin as pointed out in Chapter 1. Sanātana Dharma is not an 'ism' in the modern linguistic sense. It is a code of conduct that adheres to the higher ideal of dharma and brings the individual and society into an integral, balanced whole made comprehensible to common people through rites, rituals and ceremonies offered originally as oblations to Vedic gods and gradually refined into sophisticated metaphysical concepts culminating around 1000 years ago with Sankara's doctrine of Advaita or non-duality. It is only in India that philosophy, religion and daily life overlap. No other faith combines monism, monotheism, polytheism, agnosticism, atheism and animism without contradiction. The fact that so many 'isms' are required to be put together to describe what a billion Indians understand and instinctively accept is evidence alone that Bhāratiya civilisation is extremely sturdy. It is just that our faith is not comprehensible to the modern liberal Western world used to thinking in binary terms of 'us' versus 'them'. India poses a challenge to the West and curiously also to us Indians as we advance in terms of the power and influence that we will inevitably wield in global politics. India, or should we say Bhārat, is a rara avis but this bird is rather big, and is potentially important and will influence the behaviour of other creatures flying around in the global sky in the future.

A distinctive feature of the civilisational state is that it overlaps with its geographical boundaries to the extent that a political unit may be created out of it. A nation need not correspond to a country but a civilisation almost always does. A civilisational state is based on an idea but is substantially more than that. Geography is crucial. Towards the end of the Lalita Sahasranamam, the goddess is described as *dharā*, the earth and *dharmini*, the essence of dharma in names that follow in quick succession. In Sanskrit, the political state is known as the *rajya* which straddles the underlying civilisation or nation termed the *rashtra.* The boundaries of these two entities may or may not overlap exactly. However, in a civilisational state, the principles of governance of the political state are expected to be derived from the cultural practices of the civilisation. Moreover, the *rashtra* is generally presumed to be more tenacious and immutable than the *rajya* which can change over time due to the temporal nature of governance, *shruti* and *smriti*. These are universal characteristics of any civilisation and are not specific to Sanātana Dharma. In a civilisational state, only *rashtra* influences the administration and bureaucracy in the *rajya* and never *vice versa* irrespective of changes in the actual methodology of governance. The use of state capacity to dilute or degrade the principles of the *rashtra* leads to dissonance between these entities. This was attempted sadly enough in independent India and is the root cause of the contradictions that have bedevilled our country since and sapped the morale and will of the people of this vast land. This is why I have termed the absence of a civilisational presence in our Constitution an error of the first magnitude.

The conception of the Indian state as being civilisational and the communication of this idea to the public at large owes mainly to V. D. Savarkar, who was mentioned early in Chapter 1. Savarkar's contributions were revolutionary and thought provoking because he sought to bring educated Indians out of the soporific and hypnotic effects of Macaulayism that had clouded and confused their understanding of their own nation by the late 19th century. By that time, the effects of systematic mental colonisation had taken root fully and were firmly implanted in the minds of Indians. There was a profound feeling of lack of self-worth. Savarkar's definition of India as the nation of one's birth, one's ancestors and the object of one's love and affection, the *janmabhoomi, pitrubhoomi and punyabhoomi* rolled into one, the land to which one gives one's unquestioning loyalty, and his definition of a Hindu as one who satisfies these criteria is simple and appeals to both heart and mind. Taking a little poetic license and adding *karmabhoomi*, it is not too different from the US concept of nationhood. It should be noted immediately that according to Savarkar, a Hindu is anyone who satisfies the above criteria *whether he subscribes to Sanātana Dharma, Islam or any other religious denomination.* The reader should also note that Savarkar's definition of what being a Hindu is all about is closely adhered to by Ambedkar in his remarks from the 1940s on what being a nationalist is all about. These definitions are exclusivist *as any definition of nationhood must be*, and the reader should be in no doubt about this. The fascinating aspect is that they are enunciated within the rubric of Sanātana Dharma which is inclusivist in character. Radhakrishnan addresses this dichotomy when he says in connection with Hinduism being a faith that is tolerant of other forms of religious worship that, "this does not, however, mean that the Hindu thinkers have no right ideas of God and consider all beliefs to be equally true. They have a sure perception of the highest truth, though they do not insist on a universal acceptance of it. They believe that if the mind is enlightened the truth will be spontaneously perceived" by anyone at all. How far the Indian state has diverged now from this disinterested interpretation of things is seen in its mischievous insistence that the state treating all religions equally is the same as saying that all religions are equal.

Contemporaneous to Savarkar were Vivekananda and Gandhi, both deeply religious souls who satisfy in full measure Savarkar's criteria of a Hindu. Vivekananda spread his message of India as the home of the Upanishads, the universal religion and asked Indians to develop a Vedantic mind within an Islamic body. Gandhi was a strategic complement to Savarkar: a deeply religious Hindu, he took his religion into politics. Savarkar was the quintessential politician who took his politics into Hinduism. Both realised what Vivekananda had preached a generation earlier: the business of India is religion.

Savarkar's main goal was to drive the British out of India *by whatever means it took* and to re-establish the civilisational state of Bhāratavarsha in this ancient land. For him the ends justified the means. For Gandhi, it was the opposite: the means were more important than the ends, which could be suspended or even dispensed if the means were, according to him, unacceptable, for instance the Chauri Chaura violence in 1922. It is because of the primacy that Savarkar gave to the ends that he willingly committed acts which would attract long terms of penal servitude under inhuman conditions. Bhagat Singh paid a higher price for espousing the same line of thought. What Gandhi effectively told the judge during his trial in Ahmedabad in 1922 protesting the Rowlatt Act and Jallianwala Bagh was that if one was dissatisfied with an unjust law and actions by the government, one was free to give the "fullest expression" to such disaffection short of violence. He was not saying anything that was too different in sentiment from what Savarkar was doing. It was, however, the manner and medium of protest that made all the difference. Satyagraha and the Salt March would not have attracted incarceration in the Andamans under most circumstances whereas Savarkar's actions would—in the Britisher's view of things at any rate. A comprehensive account of Savarkar's life and struggles may be found in Vikram Sampath's recent magisterial two-volume biography on this "remarkable son of India", to quote Indira Gandhi.

A century later, Vivekananda, Savarkar, Gandhi and Ambedkar must be taken together by the modern Bhāratiya and viewed as a whole, in composite. Any country should feel proud of having had such a quartet to guide its destinies at such a low point in its history when it lay prostrate at the nadir in its fortunes. It is a matter of great regret and shame that self-professed followers of these titans have reduced their understanding of the teachings of these great men to crude binaries down to the level of street politics and hooliganism. All these patriots were Bhāratiyas in the truest sense. All of them were firmly anchored to the principles of Sanātana Dharma if one excludes Ambedkar's short excursion at the end of his life into Buddhism. All of them were inherently opposed to the evils of the *jati*-based hierarchy with its insistence on birth-based caste as opposed to *varna* which was profession-based and therefore mutable in one's lifetime. In the modern world, the professions themselves are changing. One cannot talk about priests, warriors, merchants and labourers in 2022 without appearing slightly silly. One should look at *varna* in the contemporary context. Today's Brahmin is the thought leader, the one with vision. The Kshatriya is the manager, executive or administrator, anyone who holds physical power. The Vaishya is the wealth creator, anyone who wields economic power and control. The Shudra is the salaried employee. No one can be all four simultaneously. These occupations have nothing to do with 'caste', once again a recent word of Portuguese extraction that does not relate to Indic civilisation. Our heroes above sought to liberate India from the physical, mental and emotional occidental bondage. This was and is the true clash of civilisations and not the simplistic West versus Islam clash of Huntington, which is mostly about control of the planet's energy resources, and not the West versus China war which is mostly about economic control of the planet. These are not civilisational but economic wars. *Bhāratavarsha's war is truly the civilisational war of this world.* This is why my theme for this work is worded the way it is—we are in an ongoing war.

Savarkar's main contribution, namely the politicisation of Sanātana Dharma and relating it thereby to affairs of the State, led to the entry into the public consciousness of the concept of *Hindutva*, a term introduced a few decades earlier. No term has perhaps been more applauded and discarded, lauded and lampooned, in our recent political discourse as this one. No term has suffered more through linguistic distortions and convoluted rationalisations. No term has been more improperly used at the hustings, not even its long suffering cousin secularism. Hindutva is the single Sanskrit word that attempts to capture the instinctive nature of Bhāratiya nationalism that Savarkar tried to define analytically and Ambedkar to articulate emotionally. I do find it surprising that there is so much confusion in understanding its simple meaning. Some say Hindutva is different from Hinduism. Others say Hindutva is identical to Hinduism. Anyone with the most rudimentary knowledge of our *devabhasha* would realise that Hindutva is nothing less or nothing more than feeling like a Hindu. What is important in Hindutva is 'Hindu' not 'tva'. Since 'Hindu' is not an Indic word, it is open to each of us to interpret it as best one can, noting that none of these interpretations may be fully correct. Savarkar's definition is the easiest for the common person to understand. If in today's world this means that a Hindu, best taken as a religion-neutral person, feels that India should demonstrate its civilisational identity to the world as a means of asserting its influence, power and pelf in the comity of nations, then Hindutva is a political concept. So be it. There is absolutely no reason an Indian should feel apologetic about it because success in international forums is more about letting others know that we feel positively about ourselves rather than telling others what we think *they would like to hear* in order that they feel positively about us. The New York Times and the Washington Post are not arbiters of what Hindutva ought to mean to a Hindu. A US university, say Rutgers has no *locus standi* to dismantle anything in this country. Even an Indian university does not. Hindutva is a philosophy that can guide Bhārat in this civilisational battle, a battle which she inherited through the misguided policies of our successive governments. A surgical cure for a botched hara-kiri attempt is bound to be long and arduous. I do not feel there is any quick fix solution out of the morass we find ourselves in today. A vision for India 2.0 needs to be worked out, but this needs time, people and effort.

The word 'Hindutva' was first coined in 1892 by Chandranath Basu in his *Hindutva Hindur Prākrita Itihas*. Basu was a convent-educated civil servant and spent time as a district magistrate in Dhaka before moving on to become a full time author and novelist. Popular imagination has wrongly attributed his word to Savarkar, whose pamphlet *Essentials Of Hindutva* (1923), later retitled *Hindutva: Who Is a Hindu?*, came a full 30 years after Basu. What led Basu to this term? To decipher this, one needs to delve a little deeper into two conflicting thought streams prevalent in India, especially Bengal, in the late 19th century. The more common theme swayed with political trends and tended towards Macaulayism. I have touched on this issue in Chapter 1. Basu's was the antithetical view which held that this so-called Hindu modernity was nothing but an imitation of English ways, in other words mindless Anglophilia. He argued that one should look inwards for a positive change. Gandhi's views on Swaraj took these ideas to a higher plane. As mentioned in Chapter 1, the mood in India by the late 19th century was one of dejection. It led for example to the INC changing its attitudes from being a compliant creature of A. O. Hume to the party of Besant and Tilak. The arrogance of the ruling class which transmuted into an extractive dispensation leading to severe economic deprivation had thoroughly disenchanted the middle class. With their misplaced hopes for meaningful change smothered, there arose a new indigenous discourse in Bengal termed 'Hindu Revivalism'. It is possible that the growing popularity of this type of thinking in Bengal was one of the reasons the British shifted their capital out of that province in late 1911. Revivalist thinking questioned existing *status quo* and emphasised societal reform that was forward-looking and modernist but rooted in the principles of the Sanātana Dharma. It is not to be forgotten that such thoughts, with state support, had just begun to be realised as concrete actions in the distant princely state of Mysore. When the time for an idea comes nothing can stop it. Basu's work should be viewed in this panoply of thought. He evaluated India's indigenous social theories and practices with those of Europe and concluded that the Hindu way of life was superior to the one which the British were professing (and many Indians were indeed adopting blindly). His conception of this theme constituted the vital and defining qualities of 'Hinduness'. To summarise, Hindutva is a natural feeling that any Hindu would have if one accepts that being a Hindu means being dharmic. Political hair-splitting at the altar of Western fads by our so-called secular parties is bound to be washed away in the face of this tsunami of reality that is civilisational Bhārat.

Returning to the world of 2022, the idea of the civilisational state came into the consciousness of the West with the recent rise of China, which prefers to describe itself as a Han civilisation rather than the Western construct, a nation-state. China's rapid economic growth and concomitant increased military clout has compelled the West to think about the idea of the civilisational state, so comfortable were they with the concept of the Metternich nation-state and its successors, the anti-Metternich nation-states of modern Europe. India poses a bigger philosophical challenge than China because our civilisation is pluralistic, and to the liberal West pluralism and nationalism are mutually exclusive. In an extreme view, the latter reduces almost immediately to the Nazis and fascism.

Only under the canopy of dharma is the perfect symbiosis of these two concepts of modern political thought. The difference between the Bhāratiya and Han civilisational states is that because of our syncretic nature, we do not have a concept like 'conquest dynasty' where a non-Han ethnicity (Yuan and Qing dynasties) ruled in parts of the country that would be considered traditional heartlands of the Han people. As there seems to be two types of nation-states, there seems to be at least two types of civilisational states.

There are important lessons for India in all of this. Bruno Maçães in a 2020 article, says that China is treading its own *Sonderweg* and is achieving progress with Chinese characteristics and measured according to the Chinese yardstick, organising its affairs around culture rather than politics and economics confirming Vivekananda's words that, "in Asia religious ideas form national unity". Maçães asserts that the world of the civilisational state is the natural one in the future because if a state develops a successful formula to organise social relations and collective power, it will tend to absorb its neighbours. He maintains that new forms of wealth and an increasingly complex social life will only increase the tendency for such absorption leading to new paradigms being created so that arts and sciences will prosper while complexity would tend to absorb simpler forms of existence. Sanātana Dharma is increasingly relevant to this line of argument because it defines life as a way to see the world and interpret the human condition. Outside the realm, smaller nation-states will continue to offer alternatives, but these would be additional and subordinate because a civilisational state is a higher structural form than a nation-state. Western political societies have had oddly misplaced 'scientific type' ambitions. They wanted their political values to be accepted universally much like they felt a scientific theory enjoys universal validity. In order to achieve this—we shall have occasion to doubt whether it was ever achieved—monumental simplification of their model into binaries was needed. The problem with simplification has always been that one might oversimplify a model to a point where an *essential* feature has been lost. Science never tells us what is true and what is false. It does not tell us what is right and what is wrong. It merely shows what is correct *at the time* using yardsticks of measurement and analysis that are accepted as trustworthy *at that time.*

For Indians entering the world arena as members of a proud Bhārat, the challenge is two-fold. The first is to correctly see themselves in full, in other words to capture their political, religious and civilisational identities. The first is a marker of their country India, the second of their denominational faith, and the last their core identity as a Bhāratiya. Their religious identity is important because India is a very religious country and religion cannot be sidestepped here, not even by an atheist. The civilisational identity is critical because Bhārat, being based in this respect on Sanātana Dharma *and nothing else* incorporates many religions. There is substantial overlap between these three identities. Identifying one's citizenship and one's religion is unproblematic for most of us. It is their overlap with the civilisational identity which varies from person to person *but even here the overlaps are substantial* and a direct proof of this is the 2021 report from the Pew Research Foundation, mentioned in Chapter 2, which shows that people of all religions feel they belong to Bhārat and what is more important, *that everyone around them belongs too.*

India displays a cultural continuum rooted in Sanātana Dharma irrespective of religious affiliation. The Pew Report above on *Religion in India: Tolerance and Segregation* brings out these facets beautifully by carefully surveying a geographically, denominationally and culturally representative sample of

30,000 Indian adults. Numbers and percentages in these sections are taken from the report. Bhāratiya civilisation is unique and confounds both Western and Eastern notions of what constitute a State. The former is more political in nature and centres on the nation-state, in modern times reconstituted as a liberal democracy. The latter is more cultural and civilisational but generally limited by race or ethnicity. Bhārat combines the best of both: it is a liberal democracy *and* a civilisation which has strong linkages with the State (*rashtra* and *rajya*). The report brings out the civilisational aspect of India exceedingly well and the data generated are synchronous with the civilisational nature of our nation. An extremely high 80 per cent of the respondents across religious lines agree that respecting other religions is an important part of their religious identity. I opine that this facet owes its origins to the Sanātana Dharma where each individual is devoted to his or her sect but is also extremely tolerant of other sects and denominations. While this might not have been exceptional in ancient times, this tendency seems to have spilled over into later times when monotheistic faiths came to the subcontinent. These shared values are further accompanied by several Hindu beliefs that cross religious lines. A majority of Hindus (77 per cent) believe in *karma*. However, an identical percentage of Muslims also believe in its philosophy. A startling 32 per cent of Christians and 26 per cent of Muslims believe in the purifying power of the Ganga, which is a central belief in Sanātana Dharma. These beliefs have a distinct local flavour to them and may indeed be peculiar only to the adherents of non-Indic faiths in our country. In fact, it is the glue of the Bhāratiya civilisation that binds together all its residents. An overwhelming number of India's Muslims unanimously say they are very proud to be Indian (95 per cent), expressing great enthusiasm for Indian culture. In fact, when put forth the statement that "Indian people are not perfect, but Indian culture is superior to others", 85 per cent reply in the affirmative.

As the positive aspects of our civilisational identity have been inculcated into the larger population across religious lines, so is also the social class based segregation better known as caste. The caste system (*jati*) is a social hierarchy originating from an older occupation based classification (*varna*). It is now strongly correlated with economic status. This pervasive aspect of our society remains conspicuous even among the adherents of universalist faiths such as Islam and Christianity. About 46 per cent of Muslims identify as General Category and 43 per cent identify as Other Backward Classes. Categories such as *ashraf* and *pasmanda* are surely extant among Muslims in modern India. Similarly, 22 per cent of Christians identify as GC, 33 per cent as SC, 24 per cent as ST and 17 per cent identify as OBC. As stated previously, geography is a central idea for a civilisational state and land is an important marker. The Partition of British India to create the countries of India and Pakistan resulted in a substantial reduction of the geographic catchment of the Bhāratiya civilisation, the Indus River plains. As a result, the subsequent generations have had to dramatically reorient their perspective of their civilisation and associated geography, having now no memory of these lost areas, which have had a strong civilisational and cultural association with us. Despite Pakistan having been carved out as a state for Muslims of the subcontinent, is it not surprising that more Indian Muslims (48 per cent) than Hindus (37 per cent) consider Partition to have been bad for inter-community relations?

Ours has traditionally been a land where various sects, cults and prayer customs have existed simultaneously. Additionally, owing to the polytheistic nature of the Hindu faith, many deities are worshipped. The Pew report highlights this and shows that 61 per cent of Hindus believe in one God with many manifestations. However, what is surprising is that 22 per cent of Muslims and 24 per cent of Christians also believe the same and this is more in line with the traditional civilisational nature of Bhārat rather than the tenets of their respective faiths. Religion and faith remain all-pervasive irrespective of education and income. This runs counter to the principle that as societies become richer their religiosity decreases correspondingly, a phenomenon observed in Western Europe and U.S.A after the World War II. Here, culture and philosophy continue to be fused into an integral whole. For example, 97 per cent of the respondents said they believed in God; this number does not vary across educational levels or the urban/rural divide. Typically, substantial numbers of Christians (31 per cent) and Muslims (20 per cent) reported that they celebrate Deepavali. Especially in the west, 39 per cent Muslims said they participated in the festival, while 33 per cent of them said so in the south. This peculiarity becomes significant when one compares Muslims in India to their counterparts in Pakistan and Bangladesh who barely know about the festival. In their responses to questions about their religious beliefs, Indian Muslims seem to resemble Indian Hindus more than they resemble Muslims in neighbouring countries. For example, almost all Muslims in Pakistan and Bangladesh say they believe in heaven and angels, but Indian Muslims are split on this question. Only 58 per cent say they believe in heaven and 53 per cent in angels; not very different from Indian Hindus, 56 per cent of whom believe in heaven and 49 per cent in angels.

The message of *Sarva Dharma Sama Bhava* or all religions lead to the same destination is embodied in practice in our country. While there seems to be a certain number of individuals (17 per cent) who report feeling discriminated by others across all faiths, this is not a significant number. This is buttressed by answers to the question as to whether we Indians feel whether religious diversity is beneficial for the country. A majority of the respondents (53 per cent) replied in the affirmative with a sizable minority (24 per cent) having no view regarding the situation. In other words only, 23 per cent felt that religious diversity is not good. On the whole, Indians across ages, education levels and regions are proud of their country's diversity. The poignancy of this observation is that diversity is not brought into clear enough focus in our Constitution and system of governance. A possible method of redressal of this issue is our major concern in Chapter 4. As noted earlier, the unique social stratification in India known as caste pervades across all religions including Islam and Christianity where such social layering might not seem to be prevalent. When the question regarding caste based discrimination was put forward to individuals across all religions there were hardly any differences in the responses, and in any case, only 14 per cent of the respondents even said they had faced such discrimination, showing its relative lack of relevance.

Religion and culture are closely tied together in Sanātana Dharma. This is borne out by the fact that a third of the adherents of the two largest faiths affirm that religious identity incorporates culture, ancestry and religion. This similar response irrespective of religion again confirms that culture and ancestry are important markers of Indianness. Also, respecting the integrity of the country and respecting elders are shared values which are shared across all the religious groups. These traits are very typically civilisational and one would say very unique to our domestic culture. Along these lines, the survey reported that 52 per cent of Muslims and 47 per cent of Hindus practiced meditation whereas 14 per cent of Hindus and 11% of Muslims practiced yoga at least once a week. These numbers are lower for Christians but higher for Buddhists, Jains and Sikhs. Vast numbers of Hindu (84 per cent) and Buddhist (78 per cent) women said that they generally wore a *bindi*. Even more surprising is that 18 per cent Muslim and 22 per cent Christian women wear a bindi.

Multiple interpretations of the same faith are uniquely Hindu traits and it is not surprising that 47 per cent of Hindus state that there is more than one true way to interpret the faith. However, the inducing effects of Sanātana Dharma are observed among Muslims where 28 per cent feel there are multiple ways of interpreting their religion. Even 35 per cent Christians concur that there is more than one true way to interpret their faith. Rebirth is a central tenet of the Indic religions namely Hinduism, Sikhism, Buddhism and Jainism. A surprising takeaway is that a fair number of Muslims (27 per cent) and Christians (29 per cent) believe in this concept. That all these reformulations of dharma occurred within a telescoped time scale of 75 years, a time of immense social, economic and religious change testifies to the enormous robustness of Sanātana Dharma in its ability to move with changes and keep adapting itself. Self-healing is an innate feature of a complex system and I shall return to this matter in Chapter 5. The Pew Report shows this self-healing in the most direct manner possible. The system was automatically adjusting itself to the trauma of Partition. This brings us finally to the question of modernity of our traditions, not an oxymoron in the Bhāratiya context.

Hindutva has been placed in the context of modernity by commentators like Abhinav Prakash who observed that the timeless nature of Sanātana Dharma allows for modern scientific principles and liberal values to be compatible with it. According to him, Hindutva envisages a democratic society based on equality and universal rights. I have described in

Chapter 2 that both democracy and republicanism were in complete accord with Sanātana Dharma. Simply because our faith is ancient does not mean it is not modern. This is because the nature of our faith is fundamentally different from most others. The *shruti* component contains universal values true for all time. It is to these that Hindus turn in times of change. The variable *smriti* component is what keeps us modern. In Radhakrishnan's words, "We are today in the midst of a Hindu renaissance, waiting for a new *smriti*, which will emphasise the essentials of the Hindu spirit and effect changes in its forms so as to make them more relevant to the changing conditions of India". The ethical inadequacies of dharma was well-recognised by him as the fact that dharma must be mutable because it needs to be in tune with times that are, socially and otherwise, vastly different from the times when it was cast as a framework for living. In his words, "The rules of dharma are mortal flesh of immortal ideas". The neo-Hindutva movement, if one may term it that, is not unlike Hindu revivalism of the late 19th century. It should be emphasised through all the churning that proponents of Hindutva as a feature of the State have, in the truest modern liberal ethos, never asked for a Hindu *rajya* but have always held that it is Hindu *rashtra* that needs to be established as a philosophical foundation upon which the *rajya* is constructed. The philosophical principles of the Upanishads and Vedas remain timeless as they pertain to human nature, incentives and conduct, and this will never change. As a result, principles that are considered modern in any age will always find themselves in tune with Sanātana Dharma.

It is useful to examine the meaning of the word 'modern'. The dictionary definition is that it "is of the present or recent times, especially the period of history since around 1500". Historians accordingly define their subject in terms of ancient, medieval and modern. The concept of modernity, at least in the eyes of

Western liberals, seems to revolve around the rejection of all that is old and acceptance of everything new. In this context, it is interesting to note the comments of Vāgbhata (625 CE) a seasoned commentator of the *Susruta samhita* and *Chāraka samhita* on old not necessarily being gold. According to him, a thing must be reasonable and not just old to be taken seriously, *Purāna mithye vana sādhu sarvam.* Pankaj Jain compares the primary tenets of a modern society with the theories and philosophies of Hindu thought. He mentions that contemporary discourse considers social equality as being a gift of modern society. However, he points out the existence of equality in the eyes of criminal law in ancient India. Our *nibandhas*, legal digests from the 12th century, do not have any room for unequal punishments while the *Nepala Mahatmya* of the *Skanda Purāna* also highlights equal punishment for all citizens for crimes irrespective of their social stature. Another concept of modern society is the unalienable commitment to democracy and democratic ideals. However, as detailed in Chapter 2, India has had a long history of democracy and republicanism. The *Rājatarangini* depicts instances of the king's decisions being stalled and sometimes even rolled back by his council. While modernity might have ended theocracy in Europe, the separation of the roles of the Brahmins and Kshatriyas ensured that theocracy never really took root in India.

Another sign of a modern society is the rise of scientific and rational thought. While it is true that modernity is responsible for rapid advancements in science and technology, our scientific contributions of yore in astronomy, chemistry, mathematics, medicine and metallurgy cannot be denied. Chemists in ancient India recognised zinc as a metal and learned how to extract it from its ores centuries before anyone in Europe. The iron pillar in Delhi is made of exceedingly high purity metal (difficult to obtain in itself) and has resisted rusting after millennia of open air exposure. Hindu thought is totally in sync with the post-modern concepts of ecology and environmental protection. As a culture, Hindus have revered nature in the form of gods in the Vedic period or, prior to that, in the form of rivers, land trees and the elements. By incorporating environmental sensibilities with popular culture Sanātana Dharma has striven to establish the primacy of nature. In contrast, modern society has seen nature as a resource to be exploited for monetary benefit or so-called progress.

In a slightly different though still scientific vein, Hindu thought is seen to be utterly contemporary with respect to scientific paradigms of today. An example from physics is illustrative. Vivekananda's statement of 1896, a full twenty years before the high noon of quantum mechanics, is noteworthy. He said, "Take anything before you, the most material thing—take one of the most material sciences, as chemistry or physics, astronomy or biology—study it, push the study forward and forward, and the gross forms will begin to melt and become finer and finer, until they come to a point where you are bound to make a tremendous leap from these material things into the immaterial." Serious 20th century physicists of Europe and America recognised in the Vedas, especially the Upanishads, writings that were completely relevant to the frontiers of their subject. Erwin Schrödinger has said, "Vedanta teaches that consciousness is singular, all happenings are played out in one universal consciousness and there is no multiplicity of selves". Robert Oppenheimer spoke of the brilliance of a thousand suns quoting from the Gita as he witnessed the first nuclear explosion in Alamogordo in 1945. George Sudarshan, the well-known particle physicist, speaking about the nature of knowledge has said that any search, academic or otherwise, is bound to lead to God, in other words it becomes spiritual. Aravindan Neelakandan, writing about Sudarshan, has noted that he deplored the fact that "many scientists are very careful to avoid any talk about their personal experiences in their discoveries". Fritjof Capra, Carl Sagan and Ilya Prigogine have all used the dancing Shiva of Ananda Coomaraswamy as a metaphor for reality in their respective realms of science, physics, astronomy and chemistry.

Coming to chemistry, it was traditionally felt using reductionist thinking that one needed to know the structure of something before one could deduce its properties and this was the ruling paradigm of the subject for at least four centuries. As chemistry moved from the regime of the simple to that of the complex in the last 50 years it has been realised that structure need not be a full enough depictor of reality and that a fuller description could be obtained from property which could then be used to induct the structure. Traditional chemistry, from the times of alchemy, held that substances were made up from simpler elements. Our ancients too recognised the five elements in ether, air, fire, water and earth like the Greeks. But they went a step further and said that these elements themselves were composed of more subtle entities called *tanmatras*. These subtle entities have to do with the five sensations. They are based on properties and not upon material composition, which is structure. Unlike the Greeks who went to ether last deeming it the most mysterious, we began with it. Ether is what can be heard. Air can be heard and felt. Fire can be heard, felt and seen. Water can be heard, felt, seen and touched. And finally earth can be heard, felt, seen, touched and smelt. From the immaterial to the material or *vice versa* as Vivekananda observed, Sanātana Dharma sees no contradiction. The epistemology of complexity is now recognised to be of major relevance to modern subjects as widely distinct as monsoon prediction, drug design, systems biology, supramolecular chemistry and neural networks. All of this may be understood within the frame of core principles of thought enunciated by Sanātana Dharma. Indeed to use words like 'ancient' and 'modern' with respect to it is meaningless because it is timeless.

Historically, no time could have been more interesting for us than the present. One should view the State in its modern context, something that began to be defined in two dull Westphalian towns, Münster and Osnabrück, four centuries ago. I feel this is appropriate for an India that is gradually becoming a Bhārat because we need to interact and engage with the rest of the world, notably the U.S.A. and China but also Europe in order that our economy, which is already the world's third largest may be coupled and increasingly synergised with our powerful civilisational structure in order that we synthesise a unique combination. The concept of the nation-state was sharpened in 1815 with a structure but this was an artificial construct imposed from above and it expressed itself more naturally when it became redefined in terms of ethnicity and language in the Europe of the early 20th century. Imposed nation-states like our immediate western neighbour still exist and in this regard we need to take them into account too. What is clear, however, is that we are not a nation-state either of the Metternich type or the anti-Metternich type. We are, were and always will be a civilisational state because this, as Maçães seems to suggest (and might even fear), is our natural state of being. This confluence of economics, culture and religion is, I feel, going to affect all major countries of the world over the next 50 years.

The period since 1947 has been long enough, even in a historical context, for us in this modern world with its ever-telescoping time scales to attempt a re-evaluation of ourselves as a country, a nation and a civilisation. The churning, literally the *manthan*, with *devas and asuras* galore, that we see around us is a natural manifestation of the coherence and the contradictions among us. Any re-evaluation should begin with our Constitution, which is not a holy book but a man-made object, created in slightly under three years. It cannot be a permanent blueprint for a 5000 year entity that now contains 1.4 billion souls. The next chapter outlines the nature of such a possible re-evaluation and also suggests a concrete plan that might be undertaken. The plan begins within the scope of our present Constitution but continues to extend itself outside of it, in other words, a new Constituent Assembly would probably be required. I feel that the inevitable changes this brings about will be accompanied by a positive, constructive and vigorous acceptance of dharmic life so that people's welfare and the vanquishing of enemies, the two precepts that have come down to us from the Vedas, are once again established.

CHAPTER FOUR

INDIA 2.0

BHĀRAT, DHARMA AND FEDERALISM: A NEW MODEL

There is nothing more difficult and dangerous, or more doubtful of success, than an attempt to introduce a new order of things in any State. For the innovator has for enemies, all those who derived advantages from the old order of things: whilst those who expect to be benefited by the new institutions, will be but lukewarm defenders. This indifference arises in part from fear of their adversaries who were favoured by the existing laws, and partly from the incredulity of men who have no faith in anything new that is not the result of well-established experience. Hence it is that, whenever the opponents of the new order of things have the opportunity to attack it, they will do it with the zeal of partisans, whilst the others defend it but feebly, so that it is dangerous to rely upon the latter.

—Niccolo Machiavelli

HISTORY, circumstances and personalities created our 1950 Constitution in its original form while political compulsions and legal interpretations, sometimes straightforward and sometimes convoluted, changed it into its present form. No constitution is the best constitution for a country for all times. Forms of government must be shaped according to past customs and present conditions. In the words of Aristotle, "that constitution is best which at any given moment, in any particular country, most effectively contributes to the end for which all governments exist". I have reiterated in earlier chapters that our Constitution is not a holy book of received wisdom that has come to us from on high. There is a tendency to view it as an immutable document within whose four corners all governance must be conducted forever. A new country begins on a clean slate and the work of a Constituent Assembly is clearly laid out and is not contested. A 75-year-old country is different. There is a certain energy of activation required to acknowledge or admit that all was not well with the basic document itself and a further energy hill to climb were one to attempt radical reform. Machiavelli has put this aptly in a few pithy lines.

A perusal of the preceding chapters has hopefully conveyed to the reader that in sidestepping the matter of India as a civilisational state the Constitution failed to embody the essential spirit of its people. Nationhood may be defined in words and several attempts in such a direction have been listed in Chapter 3 but it is something that is sensed rather than heard, perceived rather than seen and felt rather than touched. It must be so for unless it is a deep, common, unspoken, internal experience of individuals at an *individual* level, a nation will not hold together in the long run. Political arrangements and wars bind not a country together. True nationhood does. In the modern era, a written constitution is the agent that attempts to formalise the feelings of nationhood. It must capture the ineffable and place it in the context of the fathomable. Partition cast a long shadow on Bhāratavarsha and the almost immediate casualty was the Constitution, which missed the civilisational, the dharmic essence of this wonderful land, Bhārat that is India.

Country. Nation. Civilisation. These are words that have been invoked over the years to describe this complex entity we today call India. Another word relevant in this connection is 'State' written with a capital 'S'. When used alone in this book, unqualified with an adjective, 'State' denotes a seat of sovereign power and is most often a formal descriptor of 'country', which is a political state. A State defined this way comes into existence when it is recognised as such by other similar States. A 'nation' may be defined by commonality of ethnicity, language, race, or religion. It does not follow, however, that all such entities qualify to become political states, in other words countries. A nation is different from a country because it might or not be coterminous with it, or alternatively it may well extend beyond it. For example the Jewish nation has existed for millennia while the country, Israel, came into being only in 1948, twenty centuries after the previous Jewish State, Judea, was destroyed and its people dispersed in 70 CE by the Roman emperor Titus. What is the 'Indian Nation'? Is it coterminous with the 'Hindu Nation'? Some may say not, but there is a great deal of overlap between these two nations especially if one uses Savarkar's criterion that all those who were born in this land and love it are Hindus. A. B. Vajpayee remarked in 1988 that for him the terms 'Hindu Nation' and 'Indian Nation' were synonymous. A civilisation, however, goes beyond nations. It is an interpretation of the life condition itself. Accordingly France, Germany and the U.S.A. all nations in themselves as also countries are included in what we call Western civilisation, a corpus of thought that directly or indirectly takes its inspiration from Ancient Greece. The word 'state' may be appended to 'nation' and 'civilisation' and we obtain 'nation-state' and 'civilisational state' the basic differences having been detailed in Chapter 3. In brief, when a political state is coterminous with the nation, the entity is called a nation-state. Since a civilisation goes beyond nations, a civilisational state goes beyond the nation-state.

A key concept in this chapter and one which forms the basis of the new model for India 2.0 is diversity, its acknowledgement, measurement and full-fledged incorporation into a new governance structure. All three areas that I identify as problematic in our Constitution and present-day governance, namely presence of two major religious groups in 80 per cent and 15 per cent proportion, socio-economic disparities, and absence of true federalism may be directly connected with the diversity question. It is well-acknowledged that we Indians are a diverse lot. V. S. Naipaul called us a nation of a million mutinies. In the extreme, we tend to behave like a billion mutinies put together in a chaotic jumble. Each of us seems to have a different opinion on just about everything. We take pride in our diversity even as we are sure about our oneness as Indians. Outsiders often find this diversity to be one of the most baffling features of our country. The reason is not far to seek. In Europe, over the past 150 years, diversity of smaller magnitude has resulted in centrifugal movement into smaller nation-states, the Austro-Hungarian and Ottoman empires, the Balkans several times over, and in recent times Czechoslovakia and the former U.S.S.R. being typical examples.

Diversity is a part of the human condition and flows from ego which is the privilege of sentient thinking beings. It is instructive to consider examples of diversity in some supposedly stable European nation-states, so created to minimise diversity. The German-speaking countries, Germany and Austria have traditionally preferred to remain separate countries over centuries barring the forced *Anschluss* during World War II. Germany itself shows diversity in religion, language and diet between its southern and northern parts. The diversity in the U.K. is considerable and one speaks of the Scottish and Welsh nations. The Irish nation has been divided across the U.K. and the independent Republic of Ireland for a century. The Catalan region in Spain has sought independence sporadically and while Belgium and Holland are bilingual, Switzerland is quadrilingual. English is spoken and widely understood in many parts of the European continent. None of these nation-states, small by our standards, are fully homogeneous in any rigorous sense. Let us consider one of them in more detail.

Italy, unified as a single country in the mid-19th century, was traditionally a mixture of kingdoms, church territories and independent *comuni* or municipalities. In the past a variety of people came and went, Arabs, Greeks and northern tribes. Linguistic and cultural differences are still relevant. For example, in Trentino Alto Adige (the Italian part of Tyrol) in north Italy people speak German and a local language Ladin while in Valle d'Aosta French is used. Trieste in north-eastern Italy belonged to the Austro-Hungarian Empire till 1918. In the southern areas (Calabria, Sicily) local dialects are far from conventional Italian. Sicily, in close proximity to North Africa is different in many ways. This country of just six crores people (between Odisha and Karnataka in population) has twenty regions, first-level constituent entities further subdivided into 106 provinces, next-level entities.

Smaller constituent units have always been recognised as improving administrative efficiency and responsive governance. The provinces, akin to our districts, have the responsibility of policing and a level of autonomy that lets them issue vehicle registration certificates and sanction funds for road repairs. There is no doubt that smaller states improve the ease of living of ordinary citizens. Switzerland has one canton for every 3, 30, 192 people, the U.S.A. one state for every 65, 90, 000 but India a whopping one state for every 4, 92, 85, 714! Switzerland is a small country of just sixty lakh inhabitants but there are twenty-six of these autonomous cantons mentioned in their Constitution's Preamble that are responsible, amazingly, for even passport and residency permit matters! This is a case of true federalism perhaps unrivalled anywhere else and bespeaks a high level of regional confidence.

We have noted that the reorganisation of states in India followed the principles of respecting diversity differences, and have cited the examples of the erstwhile Bombay, Madras, and Central Provinces from the Raj, and the subsequent bifurcation of the monolingual Madhya Pradesh, Uttar Pradesh and Andhra Pradesh in independent India by hiving off Chhattisgarh, Uttarakhand and Telangana. The erstwhile Jammu & Kashmir (J&K) was recently bifurcated with a change of status from a single state to two union territories, respecting cultural and religious differences of the Buddhist region of Ladakh. Language, a powerful determinant of diversity in the past, seems to be less important now with aspirational levels rising and an increased comprehension of the two link languages English and Hindi. The abolishing of untouchability has certainly helped in a big way in reducing diversity at the socio-cultural level. The feeling of being different is an emotional one as Ambedkar recognised and affects individuals in subtle and unpredictable ways. Another person exhibiting his or her identity might increase the same tendency in oneself. On the other hand, an increase in all-round economic prosperity might reduce such feelings. These emotions of feeling different or similar might even be temporal and temporary.

This book is meant for the concerned Indian who wonders about our seemingly hesitant entry into the higher levels of world power and influence. This concern is partly fuelled by a growing conviction that the intelligence, skill, ability and resourcefulness of individuals is not reflected in this slow transition of the country into the club of most influential nations. While there certainly has been some advancement, notably economic, compared to our situation twenty-thirty years ago, the rate of progress still seems to be inadequate. This has been ascribed to our large population, caste and regional proclivities, religious differences, all-pervasive corruption, and the fact that the State must contend with all of this within the framework of a parliamentary democracy with its inherent checks and balances. When there is no more to be said we blame the 'system'. Can a poor country aspire to strength and wealth if it takes a governance route that might be termed a luxury of the rich? Using Occam's razor I hope to show that this plethora of ills possibly arises from a single or small number of ills, the main one being the inherent deficiencies in our Constitution, more specifically its failure to acknowledge and incorporate our civilisational ethos resulting in an imperfect definition of federalism. This chapter is divided into sections which broadly describe the causes of the illness, the symptoms, the nature of the disease, the prescribed medication and finally its administration to the patient to affect a cure in a reasonable period of time, at least before the illness becomes chronic. I outline a fairly comprehensive course of treatment that may be prescribed only by a capable team of doctors, in our case only when single party rule prevails at the centre enjoying a majority in both houses of parliament, a situation that one has not seen in nearly 50 years. One must seize the moment for otherwise all may be lost.

Let us consider the causes first. I have adequately described how the issue of federalism was taken up in the Constituent Assembly, why it switched from a federal Constitution to a unitary one, how it tried to incorporate certain federal features within this strongly Union-centric document, how and why these attempts have led to inevitable frustrations at the State level. Our quasi-federal system has been an uneasy cohabitation between the Centre and the States, a compromise between the conflicting considerations of state autonomy and the need for a strong centre to maintain the unity and integrity of the country. The compromise has come about in the form of the Concurrent List (List III) which has been a bone of contention. Aggressive regionalism has also been a significant challenge to federalism whether it is religion-based or from states geographically distant from Delhi. On occasion this has led to demands for separate statehood. Reasonable demands have been conceded but perhaps the Union has been too sluggish. More serious is when endemic regionalism afflicts a border state because unity and integrity concerns come to the fore. We are surrounded by Afghanistan, Bangladesh, Bhutan, China, Myanmar, Nepal, Pakistan and Sri Lanka, all of whom have independent relationships with one another. In such a situation, any ignition of a regional demand in a border state is accompanied by an added awkwardness.

The absence of any real fiscal federalism is another cause for worry. While the power to levy important taxes must lie with the Centre, the share of the States in the central tax revenues has been a matter of constant dialogue and debate most recently through the GST. In truth, the States have but few options to generate resources independently and they need much wider leeway and autonomy in the matter of interstate commerce, finance, trade and industry. They need to be able to leverage their specific advantages without being under the umbrella of a central regulation which might have been made keeping some other interest in mind, distant from the state's concern. One size may not fit all. All this has resulted in uneven development. Other issues such as the role of state governors, the absence of any real power enjoyed by the States even in the List III topics, and the role of the All India Services and Central Services in the State governments are continuing irritants. Far more serious is the inordinate influence that the more populous states have in the governance of the country vis-à-vis smaller states. We do not have a mechanism to offset this imbalance as the US Senate does in their system. The numbers in their House of Representatives reflect the population of a state (more people, more representatives) while the numbers in their Senate underscore its privileges *as a state in the U.S.A.* whatever its population (each state has exactly two). Both houses have only members elected in the first-past-the-post system and both are *independently* required in the legislative process. The twin nature of the elected representation is a virtually fool proof way of ensuring meaningful federalism. This aspect will be discussed later in this chapter and is the basis for major constitutional reform.

The above are some of the main physical causes for the illness. Let us take up more subtle psychological ones. Independent of the diversity issue in India, a collective malaise that we, especially the urban middle to upper classes, seem to have been afflicted with is our failure to decolonise ourselves and embrace our civilisational identity. In his recent book on this subject, J. Sai Deepak marshals a formidable body of evidence to show that colonisation of the Indian mind was as important a consideration for the British as their commercial interest in India and ultimate desire to seize political power leading to full control of our very sovereignty. Possibly they even felt that a successful attack on the Indian mind would render the subsequent commercial and political conquests easier. Quoting the Peruvian sociologist Aníbal Quijano, he proposes that the concept of coloniality of power, specifically European power, is to be distinguished from mere colonialism and indeed is at the core of the latter. In his words, "colonisation is the process, colonialism is the policy and coloniality is the mindset or the thought that underpins or drives colonialism." It is the "totalising thought behind colonialism, which monopolises time, space and subjectivity, and makes all of them the exclusive preserve of the European coloniser." These are powerful words indeed. According to him, the European colonisers of Asia, America and Africa whether they were from Britain, France,

Holland, Spain or Portugal, all proceeded primarily on this basis. Looking at India between 1603 and 1947, it is not hard to see why the British had easy pickings here. Sanātana Dharma which appears soft if measured with an Anglo-Saxon yardstick was bound to fall prey to this sort of cognitive reworking. It is not that ours is a weak religion, merely that, it is the most vulnerable to this kind of psychological assault because Sanātana Dharma is unique in saying that all have the same rights to belief: the civilisation of the colonisers did not. This war was not fought on a level playing field.

In the words of Dharampal, many years later:

> *It is in such a context that, as time passed, the Indian elite began to look at India through British eyes.*

We are indeed a confused nation. Our academic leaders, technocrats and steel-frame administrators, almost all Hindu, seem to have failed in unshackling themselves from a British mindset. Hindol Sengupta goes as far as to say that we have, in the seventy-five years following Independence, taken Anglophilia to levels that would be laughable in modern day Britain. Sandeep Balakrishna uses the harsh word 'Christianisation'. These so-called elites seem to harbour an instinctive anathema to the value systems enshrined in Sanātana Dharma and crave for Western approval for just about everything. It is only unbridled, emotional pride in one's own civilisation and achievements that can take a country forward and upward. Our elite classes, or should one term them merely entitled, have become intellectual coolies of the West in the same way as our software community have become computer coolies of Silicon Valley. The idea of a Britain long since forgotten, as opposed to the Britain of today, still seems to rule us. I shall discuss Macaulayism later in this chapter. Japan, China and Korea, the other Asian unfortunates of the colonial era, have not only decolonised themselves but are also setting terms for the West in economic and political terms. Instead of emulating these traditional cultures we still seem to be, allegorically speaking of course, in a phantasmagorical world of Kipling, knives and forks, *kedgeree* and *khansamas*. Knowledge of the English language is practically a *sine qua non* of advancement into higher strata. It is one thing to use English as a link language, quite another to treat it as a make-or-break prerequisite for success. Is it English-language apartheid? So much for the socio-culturally privileged. What about the political elite? Have they fallen into this trap too? How Anglicised is our so-called left wing?

In the words of the Vedic scholar R. Krishnaswami Iyer, as early as 1957:

> *It is veritably an evil day when religion and society are at the mercy of politicians who are out to imitate the West at all costs and to make the true Hindu a stranger in his own land.*

It is significant to note that even after turning communist, China never shook off its ancient civilisation. On the contrary, it respects it even more and vows not to repeat its humiliation in former times at the hands of the European. It prides itself in being *Zhong Guo*, the Middle Kingdom between the earth and heaven. This may be compared to the disdain shown by our entitled classes to Bhāratiya civilisation. Japan is an ultra-modern country by any standard. The respect shown by the average citizen there for their age-old culture and civilisation, and the love and care that they have taken in preserving their ancient monuments and buildings is to be seen to be believed. A few years ago we were subjected to some repulsive photographs of hooligans destroying some already desecrated structures in Hampi. Miscreants have vandalised priceless cave paintings in Ajanta by scratching them with crude penknives. How and why did the Yamuna river adjacent to the Taj Mahal, and also in Delhi, become a cesspool of garbage and pollutants? What keeps us silent when local women participate in a religious festival in the same polluted Yamuna in Delhi? Why has the Ganga become polluted practically beyond repair? A dead river is no longer a river in ecological terms. Why have we ignored serious scientific inputs concerning the environmentally fragile upper reaches of the river upstream of Devprayag? This river basin feeds more than 60% of our vast population. Today, it is a disaster area. The Rhine was similarly polluted. An elaborate *but time-bound* programme was initiated and it seems to have been saved. Some speak about the holy Ganga while others pollute it. Why did it take so long to clean the holy Sarayu in Ayodhya? Changing place names may be necessary but is it sufficient? What is it we lack? Why do so many Indians seem not to feel pride in what is undoubtedly our most glorious and unique possession, something that has contributed substantially to world values, culture and civilisation? Perhaps what is needed is a conscious movement to decolonise ourselves. Such mental decolonisation might probably not be automatic just because our economy is growing. On the contrary, one might argue that our economic growth might simply plateau off in the absence of decolonisation. To achieve an exponential growth trajectory, which is what we want and need, we need a positive affirmation of our civilisational identity. In the end, there is nothing intrinsically or inherently wrong or deficient in us as a people. What is missing is the affirmation of dharma. Such a change must come from us as individuals for only then will it express itself as a collective will. In turn our leadership needs to facilitate and enable a condition where affirmation of dharma from each common citizen becomes instinctive. Without such affirmation we may all, starting with the prime minster and ending with the humblest of citizens, be just whistling in the dark.

Even Ruskin Bond, fully British born, seems to have got it better than our elites when he says:

Race did not make me an Indian. Religion did not make me one. But history did. And in the long run, it's history that counts.

Yes, history not only counts, but it just might be the only thing that does. We the citizens of Bhārat need to address it and bootstrap ourselves out of this colonial Anglophile mentality that has gnawed away at our very vitals. Many have of course seen through the game that has been played by some among us. As Machiavelli says in the quote at the head of this chapter, the fiercest resistance to big change always comes from those who were favoured in erstwhile dispensations, the *ancien régime,* as it were. A Bhārat that wears its civilisational identity on its sleeve will not become antediluvian. On the contrary, it will become progressive, modern and above all, rich and powerful. The West recognises this well. Gideon Rachman, writing in 2019 in the Financial Times, identifies India and China as rising civilisational states along with Russia, Turkey and possibly the U.S.A. He terms the civilisational notion as illiberal and condemns it as an exclusivist philosophy without, at least in India's case, attempting to understand the nature of Sanātana Dharma which is inclusivist and synthetic. Rachman reveals a distinct undercurrent of anxiety about China's rise and the thought that India might soon follow suit is latent. He is nervous that in a civilisational state there is "a very different view of the relationship between the individual and society with the latter regarded as much more important". Here too, he is wide off the mark in China, society might indeed be more important than the individual but in Bhārat, individual and society are part of an organic whole, both performing their dharma. Russia is an interesting example. Vladimir Putin has said that it is time Russia embraces the idea that it represents a distinct Eurasian civilisation, distinct from that of Western Europe, and that it was futile of Russia to have struggled to be a part of that civilisation for so many years, specifically since the time of Peter the Great (1672-1725). None of this might have been pleasing to the U.S.A. and yet influential legislators there are asking for India to be upgraded from being a strategic partner to a formal ally, in other words for an alliance agreement. The reason is not hard to seek—India might become a civilisational rival in 50 years but till then it is possibly the best counter that the U.S.A. has vis-à-vis China. The U.S.A. probably realises that India will inevitably become a civilisational state. It recognises further that civilisational power is hard power—not soft power. Our leaders should be able to project forward to a very different world by say, 2075—one in which Bhārat would play a major ideological role.

Let us move next to the symptoms of the disease, the outward manifestations of the internal malaise. These outward signs are palpably obvious to the concerned, apolitical citizen. I can begin with the low quality of discourse in conversations, blogs and discussions by so-called public intellectuals, elites, entitled segments, administrators, politicians and parliamentarians. Exchanges by citizens in social media have become absurdly illogical and irresponsible and the degree of tolerance towards another's viewpoint has touched an all-time low bordering on the abusive. It is more than just an Indian hating to be proved wrong but rather his or her inability to even listen to anyone else. The argumentative Indian (we use this term in its straightforward linguistic sense, not according to the weasel-like interpretation given to it by the person who coined this term) has become the deaf Indian—we seem to have become incapable of listening. Assuming that some fraction of the remarks in social media are made by paid commentators or originate from fake accounts, this cannot be the entire lot.

Basic ethical values seem to have been compromised at an individual level. They must have been because we do not just accept corruption by politicians as a reality or possibly go as far as to condone it, using some specious partisan argument (your politician is more corrupt than my politician). We now *expect* that any politician worth his salt has amassed a large sum of money illegally. Has it become a badge of honour? When a Deputy Chief Minister of a large state was recently arrested and some of his assets attached by the Enforcement Directorate, the fact that the monetary value of these assets was estimated to be 1000 times the entire gross income of the average Indian over a lifetime caused no comment or murmur.

Our media outlets, be they newspapers or television have only added grist to the mill by their highly prejudiced, fabricated, and frankly unbelievable reports from partisan anchors. A film star was found dead in 2020 under what were admittedly mysterious circumstances. One of our prominent TV channels did not stop prime time coverage of this event for weeks. Is this reasonable? The nightly TV debates, especially the ones in English, with most of the participants shouting at the top of their voices do us no credit as individuals, as a nation, and as members of a civilised society. For a start, they are focused on the politics of the day or some sensational snippets concerning Bollywood and cricket, our two national addictions, and no other topic. When they have run out of all topics, Pakistan is the perennial punching bag and a couple of unknown persons from that country are asked to 'participate' but about the only thing that ensues is that these persons get mocked and jeered at by the other participants and the anchor. 'Debates' conducted in this way are unheard of in advanced countries quite apart from the fact that interrupting someone is considered the height of rudeness in almost every society except ours. This is sanctioned demagoguery more reminiscent of Roman mobs howling for blood in the Colosseum. Such debates and rants are not a sign of the independent Indian—they are signs of angry and frustrated Indians, angry because they feel the country has let them down and frustrated because they feel unable to express themselves in ways that are respected in societies that raise the status of an individual.

Agitational responses to real and perceived grievances betray a lack of confidence in the State. The feeling that the law is not the same for everyone is now endemic. In India, one might say "Find me the man and I will find you the rule". The rich and powerful seem to be easily able to obtain easy court hearings in a country where there are 3.9 crore cases pending in the district and subordinate courts, 58.5 lakh cases in the various High Courts, and more than 69,000 cases in the Supreme Court. An important person accused of a misdemeanour and taken into custody seems to be able to secure bail in a matter of days in a country where there were 3, 30, 487 under-trials languishing for years in prison at the end of 2019 awaiting their first appearance in court. Agitations, whether they take the form of squatting on public highways, destroying public property, mindless looting and killing, or general marauding, seem to be for any conceivable cause, real or imaginary. Granting that most of these agitations might be politically motivated and encouraged, this in itself is not healthy. If a political party thinks that it can wrest concessions by promoting *bandhs, dharnas* and *gheraos*, it means that constitutional processes of obtaining redress have failed. Most distressingly and regrettably, any or all of the above methods have been used regularly in institutions of higher learning, again a sad testimony to the utter failure of our education policies all the way from 1950.

In the absence of constructive activity and a work ethic, there seems to be an inordinate obsession with elections and politics, in mindless discussions and arguments. As mentioned above, most of these discussions end in an all-round abuse of the 'System' and a hot cup of tea is enjoyed by all. This is not to say that such informal discussions are not important, but this should not be all of it. Citizens' involvement in politics does not end with casting ballots. Rather it begins there and should involve a continuous monitoring of the activities of the elected people by the 'missing middle' of representation, a vital group of unelected persons who bridge the gap between the general public and the political apex. The problem is exacerbated by the huge size of individual electorates. Social media has helped a little in that it is not possible for a politician of doubtful reputation to stay invisible for long but serious dialogue between an elected legislator and his or her constituents, in say a townhouse setting, is practically unheard of in our country. Such behaviour and apathy is a sure sign of accumulated sense of neglect and alienation.

Discussions about foreign countries, especially our neighbours, seem to focus on emphasising that we are somehow better off than them. Loving one's country is natural and needs no further comment but lack of objectivity on serious matters is something else. When China started publishing a large number of high quality scientific papers around 2000, a widely held opinion in some elite academic circles was that while the Chinese believed only in quantity, we Indians believed in quality and that it really did not matter if we published a smaller number of papers than China. Our 'quality of mind' was apparently better! The 2018 numbers of scientific papers tell their own story: China 5, 28, 263; U.S.A. 4, 22, 808; India 1, 35, 788 and Germany 1, 04, 396. China's annual R&D budget is $400 billion, U.S.A.'s $600 billion and India's $20 billion. The reader may draw his or her conclusions.

Similar sentiments that seem to render India unnecessarily virtuous are expressed in other arenas. After a recent India loss to Pakistan in a cricket match, a Pakistani ex-cricketer gave a clear endorsement of the two-nation theory and another said that a Pakistani player offering *namaz* on the pitch in front of Hindu players had warmed the cockles of his heart. This was unremarkable: Pakistan was formed on the basis of the two-nation theory and at least two of its citizens were sure of their national identity. The Indian response was what was stupefying. We had an Indian ex-cricketer saying that we were all one, the same sentiment that was our undoing in the colonisation experiment by the European conquerors, and a well-known cricket commentator sniffling about how this was not cricket. A TV news anchor and cricket aficionado prattled along the lines of *aman ki asha.* Possibly, everything will be forgotten and forgiven now that an apology has been tendered at least on the *namaz* statement. When Pakistan was eliminated from the above mentioned tournament a few days later playing a third country, there was ecstatic glee from India. Most of this reflects a tragic loss of identity and self-respect on our part coupled with a shrill sense of misplaced injury in our dealings with foreigners. Possibly we try to compensate with a confrontationist and derisive attitude that we adopt towards fellow Indians who we often seem to take for granted. Another TV anchor interrupted, literally mocked a young student he was interviewing on the question as to whether a university should be employing a Muslim in a department where Sanskrit was being taught as an adjunct to dharmic studies and not as a language. Opinions might vary on this sensitive topic but the attitude of the anchor did not seem to inspire much confidence among viewers and rudeness to youngsters is frowned upon in almost all civilised countries. There is little doubt that such behaviour would have been totally unacceptable in countries that are admired and looked up to by these very same individuals who are so ill-mannered at home. It has been remarked more often than not that while we are anxious to say 'please', 'sorry', 'thank you' and 'good morning' to non-Indians, we rarely use these words with Indians.

We come now to the nature of the malady itself and further focussing down from the causes stated above is helpful. These causes have been broadly ascribed to physical and psychological shortcomings in our governance structures and our peoples respectively. The former (pseudo-federalism, religious tensions and socio-economic disparities) have to do with inadequate expression of our diversity in the polity and in governance. The latter (absence of decolonisation) has to do with inadequate expression of our civilisational ethos in ourselves as individuals, in society, government and in the Constitution. It is no surprise that these two broad categories of defects have a common origin in the absence of Sanātana Dharma in our governance structures. Bhārat is a synthesis of myriad individuals, indeed a symphony of sounds and tones that blend into an organic whole. The individual cannot thrive outside of society with all its fault lines while society only exists because of the diversity of the individuals within it. This is the real meaning of 'Unity in Diversity' which implies that unity only flows from diversity. In our emphasis on a Union-centric Constitution we forgot that unity does not come first but rather diversity. Unity in itself can never, by definition, lead to diversity. In Bhārat, diversity and diversity alone can lead to unity. As mentioned in Chapter 1, we seem to be an example of 'Unity and Diversity' and not 'Unity in Diversity'. In India today unity and diversity are invoked separately, practised separately and condemned separately. In Bhārat, there would be no contradiction or confusion. Wherever diversity exists and is allowed to bloom properly unity must and will follow.

A hint of the shortcomings in our Constitution may be gleaned from the Gandhian Constitution of 1946 discussed in Chapter 1, the only one that did not trace its origin to the Anglosphere, barring the HRA Revolutionary Constitution and the M. N. Roy Constitution both of which took extreme viewpoints. To recapitulate, the Gandhian Constitution suggested decentralisation down to the panchayat and village level and took from our older ideas of small *janapadas*. This would be diversity expressed at its fullest. It has been commented in Chapter 2 that our Constituent Assembly faced a fork in the road because its entire roadmap depended on whether or not it took the Anglosphere route or the Gandhian. These routes are mutually exclusive at least in the form in which the Gandhian Constitution was expressed namely the extent to which decentralisation was advocated. I believe that the Assembly made the right choice in going for the Anglosphere route though in all fairness it must be said that Part 9 does mention the panchayats. Their powers as given in Article 243G are, however, restricted to the preparation of plans for economic development and social justice and the implementation of schemes for economic development and social justice "as may be entrusted to them". In 1947, we were just not ready to revert to the Gandhian approach to governance. In 2022, this approach would be downright impracticable given the realities of modern geopolitics and economics. However, the essence of the Gandhian idea is decentralisation. If this were done, not to the extent suggested in the 1946 document but more than what we have at present, there might yet be hope for a breakthrough. The crux of the 1946 Gandhian Constitution is at the core of Sanātana Dharma in that it synergises the collective will of a billion souls into a powerful whole. If one combines this with the best of what the West has to offer, not a copy-paste like the 1950 document but a synthesis of ideas rather than of form, in Vivekananda's words a union of *sattva* and *rajas,* no country would be able to hinder our advance.

There is a modern strategic reason why we should attempt this blend of Bhāratiya and Anglosphere. In a recent tweet, Ruchir Sharma maintains that the political systems of the Anglosphere are "rent-seeking" and designed for rich countries to help them maintain their status quo. This is incontestable. He recommends, however, that we avoid Anglosphere models and look to other Asian countries "with similar challenges and experiences" and improve on their models. This is more debatable. India is not a rich country but it is not poor either. It is more than just aspirational. It is rising, but not as rapidly as what one might want. There is not enough coherence and cohesion. We are unique among Asian democracies in that we are larger, richer and have much greater geostrategic control in our part of the globe, for example the Indian Ocean basin and the Himalayan zone. Finally, we have in our possession a unique weapon, Sanātana Dharma, apart from which our conventional weaponry and the preparedness of our armed forces are enviable. Therefore, our model should ideally be a hybrid of Bhāratiya and Anglosphere, the one which is our foundation and internal strength, the other which will enable us to take on the rest of the world on equal terms. It is this complex conjugate that we should try to seek.

The next hint available to us in identifying a possible governance route towards India 2.0 has been discussed extensively and even practised to a limited extent in the period 1950-2022. I refer to the bifurcation of the larger states and discuss two, Uttar Pradesh (U.P.) and Andhra Pradesh (A.P.), as being representative. The former is a classic case of a state which is so big that it would be the fifth largest country in the world if it were independent, after China, India, U.S.A. and Indonesia. The disproportionate influence that this giant monolingual state has had on politics and governance in India is heightened by the parliamentary democracy we follow with its first-past-the-post system of elections. Political parties aspiring to power at the Centre often concentrate their strategies on U.P. and if they win the seats in this state in the Lok Sabha election convincingly, their route to national power is greatly facilitated. Conversely, small parties hope to fragment the vote here because that would more likely lead to a coalition at the Centre which they prefer. This is the political reality in U.P. In such a situation, a single party in power at the Centre would be naturally disinclined to further divide the state. However, only the Centre can carry out such a division. There is a clear conflict of interest. U.P. was indeed bifurcated in 2000 but the daughter state, Uttarakhand, is tiny by comparison and the reason for its creation was a long-standing demand for statehood from this mountainous region that is culturally, socially and environmentally distinct from the rest of the state. The rest of the state is still huge by any standards.

The States Reorganisation Commission (SRC) of 1955 did indeed recommend smaller states and mentioned U.P. in particular. The chairman of this committee K. M. Panikkar made the obvious point that for a "successful working of a federation, the units should be fairly evenly balanced. Too great a disparity is likely to create not only suspicion and resentment but generate forces likely to undermine the federal structure itself and thereby be a danger to the unity of the country". While the recommendations of the SRC with respect to linguistic states were largely followed, the matter of U.P. was discreetly shelved—it was too important to the electoral fortunes of the Congress and with the state safely in their bag, there was no urgency in following the sensible recommendation of the SRC. Most of what I say about U.P. also follows for Bihar, another giant Hindi-speaking state in the north. There, however, cultural and geographical diversity resulted in the separation of the smaller Jharkhand in 2000 although it is interesting to note that the idea of Jharkhand as a separate state was mooted as far back as 1912! However, in the end, it should not just be culture or geography that should initiate a division into smaller states. It should be plain and simple a matter of administrative convenience. Why are we persisting with states that have such large populations? Around twelve of them have populations well over 5 crore each—only 30 countries in the world are similarly populated. Ambedkar summarised the feelings of the SRC when he said that, "this disparity in the population and power between the states is sure to plague the country." It is a matter of record that in 2011, the sitting chief minister of U.P. Kumari Mayawati had a resolution passed in the U.P. assembly recommending a division into four smaller states, Awadh Pradesh, Bundelkhand, Paschim Pradesh and Purvanchal. This proposal was not well received by other political parties.

Matters in A.P., another monolingual state, which would have had a population of 8.5 crores were it not bifurcated in 2014, resulted in a happier outcome. A.P. was created in 1956 as a Telugu speaking state according to the recommendation of the SRC after the Andhra and Rayalaseema regions were separated from Madras in 1953. The Telangana region was basically the Telugu speaking part of the princely state of Hyderabad but this is not the end of the story. The erstwhile Nizam's dominions in the Deccan were a fascinating blend of languages, religions, culture, diet and traditions, termed pancharangi owing to the presence of the five languages, Telugu, Urdu, Kannada, Marathi and Hindi. However, these linguistic markers were not strictly determinative of religion, culture, diet preferences or tradition within the region. Yet, the Telugu spoken in these areas was distinct from that spoken in the Andhra (coastal) and Rayalaseema (interior) regions. One might have thought that the poorer economic condition in the

Telangana area might have been compensated by the growth of the giant metropolis, Hyderabad, at the centre of that area but the growth of Hyderabad was largely owing to entrepreneurs from the Andhra region. Undivided A.P. is a textbook example of how a rich diversity remained untapped simply because the governance unit was too large. This reveals something quite important about India—it is not just the country that fails to capitalise on its diversity but also the large states. The sub-regions in undivided A.P. could not hold together and demands for a separate Telangana state began as early as the 1960s. When bifurcation finally came in 2014, the two constituent units were in terms of population more evenly balanced than U.P. (twenty-three crores) and Uttarakhand (1 crores). A.P. today has 5 crores and Telangana 3 crores people. I shall argue in the next section that there is a further case for the separation of Rayalaseema from present-day A.P. Here too there are cultural, geographical and (some) linguistic differences. In truth, for all that was said about A.P. being the first linguistic state in the Union, the Telugu spoken in the three regions are different. While they may not be separate languages they are arguably more than dialects. India is indeed a fascinating country, and we Indians should revel in its diversity.

To summarise, the nature of the ailment is that the extent of diversity in the constituent units of the Union, namely the states, is still too large to have been properly captured given their present sizes. The thesis is that once diversity is enabled effectively enough by further *division* into smaller states, civilisational blooming will follow naturally. It is critical to note that in a nation-state the people take their cue from the Constitution whereas in a civilisational state the Constitution flows from the nature of the people. In the latter, the Constitution is an outcome of national identity and not the rationale for it. The simple medicament prescribed and detailed is that the number of states across the country should be increased to that critical extent where diversity is captured *precisely enough* but not to the extent that it becomes *unnecessarily superfluous*. There is a golden mean in between.

We now proceed to illustrate this pictorially using a revolutionary painting technique called pointillism or divisionism: itself an offshoot of the art form known as impressionism that completely changed western art in the late 19th century. This meticulous technique pioneered by Georges Seurat and Paul Signac in Paris in the mid-1880s is a highly scientific approach that attempts to analyse how the eye analyses and synthesises colours. These principles of optics also form the basis for the use of subtractive colours (yellow, magenta, cyan, black) in painting and additive colours (red, green, blue, white) in visual media such as television and computer screens because the technique resembles the way computer screens work, as the pixels on the screen resemble the dots in a Pointillist painting. Interestingly, the original name given to this novel technique by Seurat was *divisionism*, and the reader will note that our governance model itself involves further *division* of already existing states as stated in the paragraph above.

Figure 1 shows a few classical examples of pointillism and public domain pictures meant for educational purposes in elementary schools in the U.S.A. Clearly the technique is easily understood and absorbed by young children. It involves the application of paint in carefully placed dots of pure, unmixed colour. The colours of the individual dots might not bear a close relationship to the larger patches in the final picture as perceived by the human eye.

Pointillism Divisionism

Figure 1. Top: Georges Seurat, *Un Dimanche Après-Midi À L'île De La Grande Jatte* (The Art Institute, Chicago). Middle: Right, Paul Signac, *Saint-Tropez. Fontaine des Lices* (Public domain, via Wikimedia Commons); Left, Georges Seurat, *Portrait of Paul Signac* (Public domain, via Wikimedia Commons). Lower: Left, *Pointillism for Standard 2 children.* Right, *Pointillism for Standard 6 children.* (From http://mistypoe.blogspot.com/)

The visual sensation becomes sharper as the dots become smaller and are more closely spaced. The originators of the technique were undoubtedly influenced by a French chemist of the time Michel Eugène Chevreul who, in his book *Principles of Harmony and Contrast of Colours,* showed that the perception of colour did not depend on the dyes being used but the way different hues were combined. In our context, the feeling of pride in one's diversity in a state of the Indian Union does not depend on the constitutional amendments being used but the way different states are combined to form the Union. To continue, the mode of division of the presently existing larger states into smaller states will be critical to a correct perception of the Union.

The illustration in the top row left is possibly the best known example of the pointillism technique and is in the form of a massive canvas by Seurat that hangs in the Art Institute of Chicago. It shows a number of Parisians enjoying a leisurely summer Sunday afternoon in a small island called La Grande Jatte near the city. The picture immediately below Seurat's is a classic by Signac and shows a Parisian park possibly in the early autumn. The reader should notice that the image is not impaired by the slightly larger dots compared to the ones in Seurat's canvas above. One should also notice that the grey of the gravel pathway in the foreground is enabled by dots of quite different colours and one can discern red, blue, orange and white easily. The black and white is Seurat's portrait of Signac while the two others at the bottom of the figure are drawn for schoolchildren.

It is interesting that musical metaphors were used sometimes to help describe pointillism, most directly that the coloured dots are in a kind of harmony. Signac, who took over the leadership mantle of pointillism after Seurat's untimely death in 1891 at the age of thirty-one, likened the process of choosing his colours to that of a composer considering each instrument while creating a symphony. Now let us examine Radhakrishnan's description of India on 11 December 1946 in the Assembly:

> *India is a symphony where there are, as in an orchestra, different instruments, each with its particular sonority, each with its special sound, all combining to interpret one particular score. It is this kind of combination that this country has stood for. If we are true to that spirit, if that ideal which has dominated our cultural landscape for five or six thousand years and is still operating, I have no doubt that the crisis by which we are faced today will be overcome as many other crises in our previous history have been overcome.*

The analogy to a pointillist painting could hardly be more direct.

We may now profitably consider Figure 2 which is a pointillist depiction of India as a civilisational state. The original photograph at the bottom left is from the Himalayas and shows mountains, sky, clouds, a meadow with flowers and greenery. The diversity of colour in the picture parallels the diversity of our people. The entire beautiful photograph represents our civilisational state of Bhārat. The five dot pictures beginning with the top right show dots of decreasing size, in other words smaller and smaller states as we go along the sequence.

Figure 2. Digital pointillism of an image from the Himalayas. The size of the dots may be controlled. Notice that the image from the first two pictures is indecipherable, that it emerges in the third and that further division in the fourth and fifth frames is unnecessary. The sixth is the actual photograph that was digitised. Pictorial conception of a civilisational state.

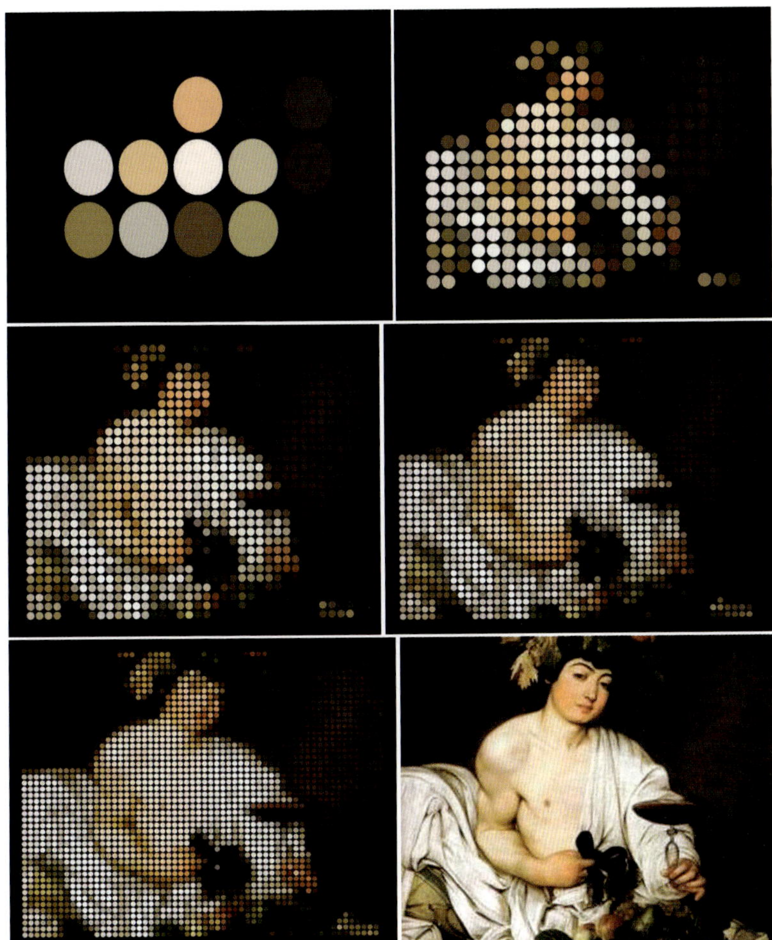

Figure 3. Digital pointillism of *Bacchus* by Caravaggio (Uffizi Gallery, Florence). Notice that the range of colours here is far less than in Figure 2 and that the image emerges earlier roughly in the second frame but quite distinctly in the third. The political analogue would be a contemporary nation-state in Europe.

Such frames are easily generated from public domain software. The picture on the top left could be a representation of India as it is today with twenty-eight states and 8 union territories. The dots do have different colours but it is hard to make out how these colours find a correspondence with the final shades in the original photograph. One may increase the number of dots by the expedient of decreasing the size of each dot, in other words by increasing the number of states from the present twenty-eight to say forty, but one might still get no hint as in the frame on the top right as to what the panoramic view, the true idea of India, is all about. By the third frame (centre row, left) the image suddenly emerges and one can make out mountains, meadow and sky even if the clouds are not clearly apparent. Further decrease of the dot size in the fourth and fifth frames produces no additional clarity that seems worth the effort. In short, there is an optimal value for the number of states that are required for a true representation of our country.

Let us proceed now to Figure 3 which is our pointillist depiction of a small European nation-state based on a common ethnicity, language, culture or an exclusive congruency of two or more of these attributes. Most European countries today conform to such a model. The picture I have selected is the famous *Bacchus* painted by the Italian artist Caravaggio (1571-1610). Compared to the Himalayan landscape in Figure 2, the range of hues is far more limited, in other words the diversity content much lower. As one decreases the number of dots in the frame, one observes a vague human outline in the second frame itself. By the third, all is clear. The fourth and fifth frames are unnecessary. Italy might have more states than it needs!

This brings up the matter of administrative convenience. Diversity arguments apart, a smaller state is easier to administer efficiently. Italy might not need twenty provinces but their one hundred and six regions would surely improve the quality of life for its population of 6 crores simply because they spend less time on routine matters concerning their everyday lives. A second point of relevance is that the pointillist idea works well with dots of equal size. In the context of division of our country into smaller states what this observation tells us is that division into states of equal size is a workable proposition. It is further useful to distinguish between *precision* and *accuracy* here in identifying diversity parameters. These two attributes are independent of each other. The latter determines the correctness of a number used as a parameter in a model, the former the confidence with which one might use it. In our situation, accuracy without precision is of limited value. For division into smaller states, precision comes before accuracy, although in the end both are needed to some degree. Accuracy is unnecessary beyond a point if a measurement is sufficiently precise. Therefore, division into small states need not proceed beyond a certain stage. These arguments above enable one to conclude that what one needs is an optimal number of equally sized small states that show true diverse characteristics.

With this background I present an idea for India 2.0. Figure 4 shows the country as a union of seventy-five states of roughly the same population. A list of new states with state capitals is given in Appendix 1. The states are placed in eight zones, Himalayan, Northern, Central, Western, South-western, North-eastern, Eastern and Southern. A look at Figure 4 will show therefore that states larger in area correspond to more thinly populated regions of the country and vice versa. A few basic observations and clarifications are required almost immediately. When I say seventy-five we mean seventy-five ±5 and when I say states I mean states or union territories. The map in Figure 4 has seventy-seven states. I shall discuss the present union territories separately further in this section. I suggest that except for Delhi they may be conferred separate statehood or be merged with a contiguous state. This is a proposed map for discussion and non-emotional debate by the Indian public at large who are all equal stakeholders in the stability and advancement of our country. I have hopefully demonstrated in previous chapters that the progress and present status and standing of our country could do with improvement.

Bhārat: India 2.0

Figure 4. A model for Bhārat with seventy-five states. Any new state is placed in one of eight zones for easier discussion. In many cases new states have been carved out within existing state boundaries. Goa, Himachal Pradesh, Punjab, Sikkim, Telangana, Uttarakhand and all north-eastern states except Assam retain their present boundaries. Delhi is in a separate zone. There are two union territories. See discussion in the text. Exact boundaries not to scale.

The model with seventy-five states is one of many (which might or not invoke the formation of smaller states) that might be proposed for such improvement and, like reasonable people, I am quite prepared to stand corrected as appropriate. As the great economist J. M. Keynes often said, "When the facts change, I change my mind." The map is based on an earlier one drawn in 2019 by Siby Thomas (see Preface) who himself has taken his from public domain maps showing regions of India where there have been agitations for smaller states within a presently existing larger state. A map published by Supriyo Mukherjee in 2017 is representative. There is no lack of such maps on the subject. Where I go further is when I suggest that seventy-five is an optimal number based on criteria like diversity, federalism and above all, administrative convenience. There is a great advantage in going for states of equal population because governance becomes most responsive in such a situation. With states of equal size, seventy-five states means that each state will have a population of 2 crores. This is an entirely manageable number. The key to progress is the size of the governing unit. The number of people per state in Switzerland, the U.S.A. and India has been mentioned specifically earlier in this chapter.

The scheme of division, which leads to the number seventy-five, borrows from current movements for statehood like Bundelkhand, Gorkhaland, Konkan, Tulunadu, Vidarbha and so on. I have respected existing fault lines. I have also considered historical regions existing since time immemorial, such as Kachch, Kasi, Kongu Nadu, Mallabhum, Mithila and Rayalaseema. Tribal belts such as Gondwana and Kosal have been considered. Significantly, I have restored to a large extent the borders of Princely States which had a good tradition for clean administration and the upholding of dharma. These include Bikaner, Gwalior, Marwar, Mysuru and Travancore. Geography, climate, and agriculture also play a part in the scheme of division, say Karavali, Karunadu, Konkan, Kosal, Marathwada, Rayalaseema and Saurashtra. In most cases, the new states do not fall outside their existing state boundaries. In others like Bundelkhand, Gondwana, Kashi, Mithila and Vidarbha they do. The long felt need for multifurcation of U.P. has been addressed in this new model. The reader will note that the limits of the present states of Himachal Pradesh and the critical border state of Punjab have not been altered. The division of Indian Punjab was carried out by and large efficiently in 1966. It was a far-seeing move of considerable strategic import and one does not tinker with something just for the sake of tinkering. To summarise, it is the principle of seventy-five states that is important and not the exact details which can get sorted out easily. There is no reason to get excessively worried about disputes if a few districts lie on this side of a linguistic or religious divide or that, or whether a state should be divided into three or four or even five smaller states. One should not worry about what we call these new states: whether something is called Bodoland or Bodopur, Gorkhaland or Gorkhapur is not germane to the issue. What is relevant is that a number of new states are being proposed. We tend sometimes to miss the wood for the trees.

A proposed state like Bayaluseeme requires comment. The terminology refers to the plateau region in present day Karnataka. There has been no demand for separate statehood. The term Bayaluseeme is officially used by the state government. It has been shown in Figure 4 with reduced limits from the present government usage of the term. The justification for this new state is that it represents a way to place Bengaluru and Mysuru in different states, leading to the development of the latter as a smart city. Smaller cities like Coimbatore, Kharagpur, Mysore, Nagpur, Pune and Rajkot have lain in the shadows of giant metropolises in the presently-existing states. For all its existing commercial importance Pune has an embarrassingly small, almost primitive airport. This is also true of Nagpur which literally lies at the crossroads of the country, at mile zero. Mysore, a place of some tourist importance, hardly has an airport. Kharagpur remains a nearly backward area for all its educational importance.

The Bengaluru-Mysuru, Mumbai-Ahmedabad, Delhi-Meerut or Chennai-Kovai corridors connecting places in different states will always be important industrially and commercially. Cumbersome protocols need not be employed when one crosses state lines. The new scheme for division recognises and accepts that there will be important interstate business exchanges. These seventy-five states are not watertight compartments. The less one thinks about a state as an ego trip into language or religion the better off we will all be. Language and religion do not help us towards a better economy. Efficient administration does. True federalism is when states interact in a healthy way with the Centre *and also independently with each other*. With many states, proceedings in say, interstate tribunals for the sharing of river waters will become less legal, less emotional, less linguistic in tone and tenor and more realistically attuned to a modern country rather than a point of contention between two individuals near the village well. We share Indus waters with Pakistan unemotionally. Why does the sharing of Kaveri waters always become a melodrama between a Tamilian and a Kannadiga? Are not the waters of this sacred river equally sweet everywhere?

The present bifurcation of Maharaja Hari Singh's 1947 dominions in 2019 was along the right direction. I have taken this forward in the scheme and there are now a total of five states in this vast region, extremely sensitive from the geostrategic viewpoint. I have also not shied away from demarcating regions where different religious denominations might be in a majority. The jugular reaction to this would be that these states might be nuclei for future secessionist movements. I tend not to agree. Smaller states would inevitably reduce such tensions. The Centre already has considerable powers in the maintenance of the integrity of the country's political borders. Certain specific powers would probably need to be enhanced through constitutional changes that must accompany such a division into seventy-five states. These changes will be discussed in the next sections. Without such changes, division into seventy-five states would be meaningless and possibly counterproductive. With appropriate constitutional changes, I feel that fragmentation and disintegration of the Union are quite unlikely. And in the end there must be something called civilisational confidence.

Some states of the Union have continued to raise issues pertaining to federalism and Centre-State relations over the years. It is difficult to sort out these issues in minute detail because some of them have their origins in distant history, from a couple of centuries to many centuries. These issues have also become conflated with current day politics and many of them have regional parties that have participated actively in coalition governments at the Centre. In certain cases the issues are religious, in others linguistic, in some ideological, in still others caste related and there are those where all these factors have been mixed. For a start, a couple of them are rather large and for the reasons justified above for U.P. and Bihar have an inordinate say in national level politics. Unfortunately, or should one say expectedly, almost all of them are border states sharing a land or sea border with countries which range from neutral to downright inimical. Of course countries have only interests and no friends or enemies, but while we are large we might still be perceived as weak enough by our immediate neighbours so that even the neutrals among them will at best play their cards close to their chests. The adversary countries will play with tinderbox states at worst. Every country acts according to its interests and we should do so too.

We maintain that many of the above seemingly intractable issues might get resolved rather smoothly with the new 75-state model of governance. For a start, there would be a great political benefit to the country at large with smaller states because only a large state that is at endemic loggerheads with the Centre can hold governance at the national level to ransom. A small state cannot arm-twist the Union with respect to matters of national security, national educational policy or national financial policy. Home, defence, finance, education and external affairs are truly the big five in the Indian jungle. These areas are of national importance and are critical to developing our sense of belonging to one large country, one large nation and one large civilisation, in other words of being a dominant power that the entire world needs to contend with and take seriously. As elaborated, linguistic pride, religious pride and cultural pride will not diminish in a smaller state. On the contrary these natural outlets for the development of self-worth and regional pride will only be enhanced. The example of the Hindi-speaking states and subsequently A.P. shows for example that language need not be an essential determinant of statehood. We share languages with some of our neighbours. Is it anybody's case that we will start annexing them on linguistic grounds?

We turn briefly to each of the seventy-five proposed new states so that the reader will gain an appreciation for the fact that there is some basis for our choices. The more interested reader will surely find a lot more in a comprehensive search and the following remarks are mere pointers to the fact that no arbitrary out-of-the-box suggestions are being proffered.

Let us start with the Himalayan zone. In Gilgit and

Baltistan five languages are spoken, Shina, Khowar, Balti, Burushaski and Wakhi. There are also speakers of Pashtu, Hindko, Gujri, Punjabi and other languages. All the people are Muslims but belong to different sects, Shias, Sunnis, Ismailis and Nurbakhshis. This sparsely populated region (20 per km) is also anthropologically diverse. Contesting Pakistan's occupation of this area I have included these areas as two states in India 2.0 in the confidence that a powerful civilisational state will have a natural ability to absorb small nations if it provides a sufficiently convincing agenda to them for sharing in a part of a larger agglomeration. It is not to be forgotten that sectarian violence between Shias here and Sunnis who dominate in other parts of Pakistan has been a repeated political feature of this rugged and mountainous region. The bifurcation of the original J&K state in August 2019 has been discussed extensively in many forums. For the purpose of this book, it will suffice to say that the differences between the three regions of Jammu, Kashmir and Ladakh have been trivialised to just the religious. What is not so well-known is that there are major developmental differences owing possibly to factors such as demographics and geography.For example the female: male sex ratio in Ladakh is 946:1000 while it is only 863:1000 in Jammu and 860:1000 in Kashmir. Access to banking and mobile cell phone facilities are also markedly different. The people of the two districts in Ladakh, Leh and Kargil have already demanded separate statehood and have termed their UT status as meaningless. Treating Jammu, Kashmir and Ladakh as one political unit was a part of the ideological agenda of the Congress to showcase to the world that 'secularism' in India was working well and that one could have a state where different religions and ethnicities could live together. This argument failed to convince the residents of those three regions, the rest of the Indian population or, may one add, the international community whose attitudes and reactions to us waxed and waned with larger global currents. Secularism itself was mostly a self-delusionary mirage within that political party. Taking all this into account, I venture to suggest five states from the pre-independence kingdom for India 2.0.

Continuing within the Himalayan region, Himachal Pradesh and Uttarakhand are not the same and they are certainly not the same as Nepal. There are many reasons, geographical and otherwise, for extreme diversity in mountainous regions throughout the world and the Himalayas are no exception. It is a matter of satisfaction that H.P. and Uttarakhand are separate and distinct states and they stay undisturbed in the scheme. The former was a distant outpost of undivided Punjab before 1947 and barring the fact that Shimla, the British summer capital, was located there, there was little to mark this remote area. Today it has an impressively low poverty rate, high literacy and is comparatively advanced in terms of development. Uttarakhand is a wonderful example of non-secessionist regionalism in our country and was created after a seventy-year striving for a separate state by the people of this region. Like Telangana one wishes this demand for statehood had been conceded earlier than it was. Our union-centric mindset and Pavlovian fear of disintegration, post-Partition, coupled with a great concentration of power at the very top of our government has prevented us from carrying out steps related to greater autonomy for states that would have helped them economically, sociologically and psychologically.

Descending into the plains of north India, it has already been mentioned that the division of Indian Punjab in 1966 was well-intentioned strategically, socially and culturally. Punjab with its 1.6 crore Sikhs representing 58 per cent of the state's population is unique in India's post-Partition history. It is quite distinct from Haryana and has been the home of several important social and religious movements and variations within Sikhism. These sects include Nirankaris, Namdharis, Radha Soamis, Gadhars and Akalis. As a border state sharing a nearly five hundred and fifty km border with a hostile Pakistan, what happens in Punjab is of great concern to the Union of India and there is little doubt that it should stay undisturbed within its 1966 limits. Haryana is slightly more problematic. A well-known social activist from that state, D. R. Chaudhry refers to it as a case of "defused identity" and warns that one should not get confused by the malls and high rises of Gurgaon and Panchkula.He warns that "the dark underbelly of the state tells a tale of skewed development and cultural handicaps." He says that Haryana has neither geographical nor linguistic distinctiveness, much less a nationality. The state has an identity crisis and after some thought I divided it into two new states, Haryana and Mewat. The latter was carved out as an independent district after dividing Gurgaon and Faridabad in 2005. It contrasts with north Haryana and from enjoying the dubious tag of being 'India's most backward district' it has become the best performer among the so-called aspirational districts of India. This new state, which also includes small parts of eastern Rajasthan, with Alwar as its capital, could try and develop it as one of the proposed smart cities and its proximity yet slight distance to the national capital could be simultaneously leveraged. Readers are urged to try and obtain more information on this amorphous region in north India and experts could try to ascertain the origins of Haryana's extremely feudal makeup and social fragility considering that certain areas there resemble New York and Shanghai more than any place else. This is certainly a subject where there might be more than one mode of state division. Possibly some might prefer retention.

The division of the present U.P. presented little problem

because there is so much literature and precedent for dissecting it into states. This heavily populated region in the heartland is the crucible of our nation. It would need a whole book or more to describe these lands in detail. They are all ancient and date back to the Puranas and earlier, almost to the Vedas. Modern U.P. is located on what is arguably one of the first populated areas of the planet. Modern history tells of an intertwining of Hindu and Muslim cultures here. Our seventy-five states have not been put forward for politicians to convert them into caste or denominational fiefdoms or to favour any particular political dispensation that prevails today at the Centre or for that matter in any of the 28 current states. The states of Hastinapur, Braj, Panchal and Awadh in the west and centre with state capitals Meerut, Mathura, Bareilly and Lucknow suggest themselves nearly automatically. I have dissected the proposed Harit Pradesh for which there has been an agitation for at least two decades because even the seventeen states covered in that proposal would constitute a state that would still be too large. Smaller states in the region would likely prevent any caste domination, a fissiparous and avoidable tendency. Previous schemes for bifurcation of U.P. have perhaps relied too heavily on caste politics and demography. If administrative convenience is put first, the rest follows easily. To prevent any retrograde movement, deep constitutional reforms and changes are nearly obligatory and are discussed in the last section of this chapter.

Coming downstream, one finds here too densely populated and extremely old regions replete with references from our scriptures. Here, however, one should deviate a little from the previous analysis because one now arrives at new states that are reconstructed and composed with parts of existing states, in other words regions where it might be felt that the presently existing states were not created using logical enough premises such as language. Where a single language is spoken this tendency will be greater such as the Hindi-speaking areas. One proceeds accordingly in this exercise dividing this part of the country keeping the plains area in the northern zones but moving geographically and culturally different areas into the central zone. The eastern zone is multilingual and unproblematic in this respect while north-eastern and southern India do not pose any logistic difficulties in the division exercise. Vidarbha has been separated from Maharashtra and placed in the central zone for reasons which will hopefully be justifiable. According to this scheme of things, Kashi and Doab (Figure 4) belong to the northern zone, essentially the upper Sindhu-Ganga-Jamuna basin.

The identification of Kashi as a new state stems from the long standing demand for a separate Purvanchal state but instead of including the Awadhi, Bhojpuri and Bagelkhand regions in such a state, in what would still be large and account for twenty-three Lok Sabha MPs if the present constituencies continue unaltered, I restricted myself to the Kashi region in the easternmost part of present day U.P. containing the ancient cities of Varanasi and Gorakhpur. The Awadh region of Purvanchal has been identified separately as a new state and the geographically distinct Bundelkhand too which now figures in the central zone (Figure 4). It is notable that the current Chief Minister of U.P., Yogi Adityanath, had as far back as 2008 pleaded for a separate Purvanchal for the "overall development in which the region is lagging far behind in comparison to western and central Uttar Pradesh". That so many prominent national level leaders have been asking for more, smaller states all over the country cannot be described to anti-India sentiments or anti-central government feelings. They are echoing deep seated emotional needs of the people.

The kingdom of Kashi was located in the region around

its capital Varanasi, literally the city between the Varuna and Asi rivers. It was one of the sixteen mahajanapadas (republics) that emerged in north India around CE 600. This kingdom would have covered much of the area centred around today's Varanasi and adjacent south-western part of Bihar namely today's Araria, Bhabua, Bhojpur, Buxar and Rohtas districts. Technically, the territory of Kashi is dominated by people of the Bhojpuri language and culture. At the time of Chanakya, Kashi was still the centre of Vedic and secular education and also known for its military prowess. While Varanasi came under Buddhist influence, Araria remained a dominion of Hindu Shaivite culture, as reported by Chinese pilgrims. The Jataka tales indicate Varanasi was one of the richest cities in India, known for its great opulence and Kashi one of the most powerful states in north India. Varanasi is one of the anvils of Sanātana Dharma and arguably one of the holiest spots in the Indian subcontinent. The Buddha first started preaching in Sarnath which lies in this domain. In latter times there was the entry of Muslims into the area. Varanasi is a living example of amicable coexistence between the communities packed cheek-by-jowl in the congested Madanpura area near the Ganga with the Muslim community being involved in the famous silk weaving business. The internationally known Banaras Hindu University was founded here and was the active centre of resistance to British rule in the early 1940s. History, culture, religion, language, tradition, medicine, science and technology, the finest combination for a modern civilisational state have their microcosm in Kashi.

विश्वेशं माधवं ढुण्ढिंदण्डपाणिंच भैरवम्।
वन्दे काशीं गुहांगंगा भवानींमणिकर्णिकाम्।।

The new Doab state literally traverses the length of the huge undivided U.P. and in our scheme consists of the eight districts of Mainpuri, Kannauj, Etawah, Kanpur Dehat, Kanpur Nagar, Fatehpur, Kaushambi and Prayagraj. As its name suggests it covers the narrow strip of fertile land between the Ganga and the Yamuna. There would be two large cities, Kanpur and Prayāgraj in this state, the latter situated appropriately at the junction of three states, Doab itself, Kashi and Baghelkand. Doab is geographically similar to the new states to its north and is also heavily populated and with substantial land area. The population of such a new district would be 2, 51, 08, 167 (estimated) which is more than the population of one hundred and eighty countries. Its area would be 24, 683 kms which would be more than fifty countries.

One must appreciate the huge scale of our country and the absolute need for more states simply for administrative reasons. The separation of Doab from Avadh is for administrative convenience and also because this region was not part of the original statehood demand for Purvanchal. The existing twenty eight states and eight UTs structure we have is unwieldy and inefficient. An overwhelmingly lopsided union-centric Constitution in such a situation is a sure recipe for disaster.

We continue the mammoth zigzag journey through India and move next to the central zone, a large but culturally, geographically and historically a distinct part of our country. We may begin with the new states Bundelkhand and Bagelkhand, old regions with a rich past and which got irrationally divided between U.P. and M.P. in the early 1950s despite the fact that at the time of independence, thirty six royal kingdoms in Bundelkhand merged with India with a promise of a separate state. After the Telangana demand was conceded and the BJP came into power in the state the demand for a separate Bundelkhand with Jhansi as its capital intensified. The area is hilly and geographically distinct from the river plains and the development is poorer. Seven districts in U.P. and eight in M.P. fall under this region. Bagelkhand to its east has a fascinating history. The rulers of the princely state of Rewa in the middle of this region had sought to retain their autonomy through the later stages of the Raj and during the early years of independence. The formation of a separate Bagelkhand like many of our 75 states needs to be viewed in the perspective of changing from a paradigm where small nations lost their essential character in the cause of national unity to a more mature stage of re-nationalising these regions so that the country now gains from an optimisation of their diversity. In the case of Bagelkhand, regional variations in language, social and cultural organisation, and economic and political structuring were all influenced by the interaction of people with their environment.

All this was lost in the homogenisation following Independence. In the process of building up the Indian nation, the more interesting small nations lost their distinctive identity and flavour the real unique feature of our civilisation. Bagelkhand has been inhabited since the Neolithic and Stone Ages through the metal ages, Mauryas, Guptas, the Delhi sultanates and finally the Mughals. Rewa itself was fully absorbed into M.P. but I have envisaged it as the capital of the new Bagelkhand state. In a modern context, granting statehood to Bundelkhand and Bagelkhand would almost certainly spur a period of constructive political activity and economic growth. The reasons for division are similar in almost all the cases. I have preferred to mention each of our new states at least once by name in this book if only to illustrate the rich tapestry of the Bhāratiya civilisational state.

The central zone is an extensive though sparsely populated hilly land mass in the heart of the country criss-crossed by the Vindhya and Satpura ranges. The region incorporates the former Central Provinces which were under direct British rule and the Central India Agency consisting of a host of big and smaller Princely States including important ones such as Gwalior, Bhopal and Indore. Apart from Bundelkhand and Bagelkhand and the big states mentioned here, there were also smaller ones like Malwa and Bhopawar. The new suggestions Gwalior, Avanti, Nimar, Vindhya Pradesh and Mahakoshal find a ready correspondence with these former states that had real civilisational value addition. I have denoted Vidarbha as a separate state and have placed it in the central zone keeping in mind that it was in the former Central Provinces prior to 1947. Demands for a separate Vidarbha state are sixty years old and the region is quite distant from the state capital Mumbai with many cultural, social and geographical differences.Despite being a Marathi-speaking region, it has always had a distinct identity. It has mineral and forest wealth but it still remains a backward region. Having chief ministers from a region is no guarantee of its development and sustained growth. What is needed is that a state should develop itself as a separate unit, a kind of intrastate *atmanirbhar* that capitalises on its unique distinctiveness. I have left Amravati which is also in eastern Maharashtra in the south-western zone and have designated it as a separate state, separate from Vidarbha as it formed a part of the former Hyderabad state. As far as possible I have respected older cultural fault lines.

The present Chhattisgarh is still too diverse culturally and is divided into a new smaller state with the same name and Gondwana a tribal area that also incorporates a part of present day Odisha and with Raipur as the capital. A justification for division I have employed throughout is to separate coastal and river basin areas from hilly regions and plateaus. This has logistic and economic value and facilitates easy communication and travel within a state. There is also an impetus to create new infrastructure based on geography. A coastal area might allow for easier land transport but an arid plateau area may be more suited to solar energy generation. With increased financial autonomy the new smaller states would be much better placed to optimise their resources and maximise productivity.

We turn next to western India and the division of states in Rajasthan followed a straightforward pattern. Suggested are seven new states with the external borders of today's state remaining mostly untouched as well as the internal borders of the 33 districts. Any district, except parts in the eastern region which go into the new state Mewat which includes portions from Haryana as well, goes into a new state completely intact. Accordingly Bikaner, Churu, Hanumangarh and Ganganagar in the desert region constitute the new Bikaner state. The new Marwar state is formed by including Barmer, Jalor, Jodhpur, Nagaur and Pali districts, all recognised by the government as falling in a region called Marwar, and clubbing this with Jaisalmer district. The interested reader will be easily able to work out how one might arrive at the seven states (Ajmer, Bikaner, Dhundhar, Hadoti, Marwar, Mewar, Shekhawati) in this critical and important region. Bikaner, an ancient kingdom was one of the first to join India on 7 August 1947. If one sidesteps the recent demand for a separate Maru Pradesh with 13 districts of western Rajasthan for the same reason that one discarded the demand for Harit Pradesh and Purvanchal—the resulting state would still be too big and become captive to vested political interests. The principle is the same everywhere —divide the existing state to such an extent that its political control does not fall into the hands of regional satraps and stop at that extent when diversity, be it geographical, cultural, religious, economic (or mere administrative necessity), is fully optimised—that critical point where further pointillist division becomes unnecessary. The reader will see an obvious congruence between the majority of these new states with the former Princely States of Bikaner, Jaipur, Jaisalmer, Jodhpur, Shekhawati and Udaipur. Rajasthan by its very name suggests that it has been the abode of princes. For the most part these ancient kingdoms were staunch upholders of dharma. Regions in the northern part of the state are mentioned in the scriptures. It is not nostalgia for the British Raj that has persuaded us to demarcate the new Rajasthan-derived states according to their old territorial limits. It is an essential component of re-establishing our civilisational nature. This argument need not be trivialised into a rambling discussion on a desirable socialistic pattern of society. Socialism itself needs to be re-imagined as equality of opportunity not as something that results in uniform poverty for all.

Gujarat comes next in the scheme of division into seventy-five states and 3 new states are proposed: Gujarat in the coastal area and Saurashtra and Kachch in the peninsular areas of Kathiawad. The movement for separate Saurashtra state was initiated in 1972, with rumblings as early as 1966 just 6 years after the bifurcation of Bombay into Maharashtra and Gujarat. The original claim apparently was that compared to the Gujarat part of the state, Saurashtra was underdeveloped with lack of good water supply, job opportunities and geographical isolation. It is also linguistically distinct in the manner that undivided A.P. was. The matter was clearly deemed political rather than pertaining to a desire for expression of federalism from the grassroots level. At some level, every state government will resist a demand for statehood by constituent parts of their state because their *status quo* interests would be hurt. With unity of the country having become a reality, indeed overwhelmingly so over the past seventy-five years, Bhārat will be able to afford to think constructively in terms of smaller states, not as a function of improving or upsetting a particular political interest but more as a matter of national interest. All that Vijay Rupani had to say about this, in the days before he became the Chief Minister of the state, was that Gujarat had balanced growth and that Saurashtra and Kachch had given the state two chief ministers previously. People do not want chief ministers from their smaller regions; they want to express their uniqueness and diversity in ways that are possibly not understood by our politicians. Kachch, occupies nearly a quarter of Gujarat's land area and is geologically, climatologically and environmentally extremely different from the rest of the country, quite apart from its value as the westernmost strategic outpost of Bhārat, practically a periscope to look into the territory of our western neighbour. It has great potential for energy resources in the coming decades, both solar and tidal. Its relevance to the salt industry, including the valuable potash minerals, cannot be underestimated and statehood demands from there have persisted since, quite literally, 1947. It was alleged that legislative representation for Kachch was disproportionately small with just one MP and six MLAs. After the Telangana statehood, several of these statehood demands have come to the fore including one for Sindhi speaking people, mostly displaced after Partition.

The coastal region of Gujarat, in other words the Surat-Vadodara-Ahmedabad corridor is by far the most developed economically in the present state and is a natural choice for a key western hub of the entire nation. One notes that the first bullet train in India is undergoing construction in this region. Vadodara, originally Vadapadraka, became an urban centre ten centuries ago being renamed Varavati, Vatpatraka, Baroda, and now Vadodara. Its history has Hindu, Muslim and Maratha periods culminating in the rule of the Gaekwads in the princely state till 1947. With a rich educational and industrial nucleus, it has all the makings of a smart city of the future vying with

Ahmedabad as a twin centre of development. A small state of Vadodara would only help the rapid growth of this corridor. While India is a land centric country, politicians should also look beyond land because land brings with it difficulties in communication and infrastructure. The density of development and the impact of a region to the national economy do not depend on how much land a satrap chief minister feels he or she controls from the state capital. Gujarat is, in many ways, a forerunner of what many other parts of India may become in the future. It is important that it acts as an alternative economic centre to our giant metropolis Mumbai to which I shall turn next along with the state in which it is located, Maharashtra.

Prima in Indis and Gateway of India it always was and will be. Whether it is called Bom Bahia, the pleasant bay, Bombay or Mumbai, the city of Mumba Devi, the *kuladevata* of the local Koli fishing community, the abode of Mahalakshmi the goddess of wealth who rightly resides there, it will always be the same, yet restless and growing, our huge metropolis and business nerve centre that started off just 350 years ago as a small cluster of seven islands with a magnificent natural harbour. The city generates 6.16 per cent of India's $3 trillion GDP and might well survive as an independent city state were it to be located somewhere else in the world. It compares with Tokyo, New York City and Shanghai in its local and international outreach. It is not a Maharashtrian city, not even an Indian city but a world city. It was a real challenge for me to place it in the scheme of seventy-five states. I resisted the temptation to make it a city state since its eventual growth will spill over into the hinterland as it already has into Navi Mumbai and have therefore included it in a new coastal state called Konkan, which itself has a long history of demands for a separate state on linguistic grounds. It is anticipated that Mumbai in a separate Konkan state would trigger significant economic activity in the coastal belt and form a natural link with the other multi-cultural, multi-lingual, multi-religious gem called Goa, which retains its status as a separate state in the scheme. The rest of Maharashtra fell into place naturally and it was unproblematic to designate Pune, Nashik, Marathwada and Amravati as four states each roughly with a population around our national average of 2 crores each. These states were obtained by simple apportioning of the appropriate districts. As mentioned earlier Amravati has a distinct cultural and historical background.

We break the zig-zag course from the Himalayas to the north, centre, west and southwest and move to our eastern extremity, specifically the north-eastern corner, which as mentioned in Chapter 1 nearly did not make it into independent India at the time of independence. There are eight states with six of them untouched from their present boundaries. The name Nagaland has been changed to Nagapur to maintain uniformity with Manipur and also to de-Anglicise place names. The seventh, Assam has been divided into two new states: the new Assam consists largely of the present-day Upper Assam, Central Assam and Barak Valley Divisions while Bodopur consists mostly of present-day Lower Assam and North Assam Divisions. Bodopur is preferred to Bodoland for a reason similar to Nagapur. The constitutional history of the northeast region since 1946 continues to be a research worthy topic. Let us not forget that Manipur adopted a separate constitution before India became independent. Undivided Assam had a rich diversity in religion, culture, language and ethnicity. The region was and is also extremely sensitive from a defence and strategic viewpoint and borders Bangladesh, China and Myanmar. If China is upstream of us with regards to the Brahmaputra and associated tributaries, we are riparian upstream of Bangladesh. The granting of statehood to the seven sisters, namely Assam, Arunachal Pradesh, Manipur, Meghalaya, Mizoram, Nagaland

and Tripura over forty odd years following natural and ethnic boundaries, is one of the success stories of our central governments over the years. It is ironical that while we were able to manage these statehoods in one of the most delicate and fragile regions of the country with respect to centrifugal forces that might have caused considerable damage to the nation, we have been unable to make too much progress in this regard in the rest of the country with at least a half-dozen very large states that are administratively unviable. The northeast division, in many ways, establishes the pattern of division into seventy five states, the archetype that has been proposed for the rest of the country. The diversity differences elsewhere may not necessarily be of the same type as those prevalent in the northeast, and they may not be as acute, but the principle of division is the same. The State should respect reasonable diversity fault lines and proceed with a dissection always bearing in mind that a smaller state is easier to administer and has a greater propensity for per capita economic advancement.

The bifurcation of present day Assam into Assam and Bodopur, with Guwahati and Kokrajhar as capitals, requires comment. The agitations of the Bodo people for a separate state began as far back as 1930. Some momentum was maintained in the 1980s and 1990s and renewed in vigour after Telangana was conferred statehood in 2014; they follow the pattern of similar agitations elsewhere. There are student groups, political groups with differences in opinion (separate statehood versus increased autonomy within the present Assam) and also armed insurgent groups. The matter is thorny and could involve the question of land rights to certain sections. It also touches on the question of migrations across international borders. There is a preponderance of the ST communities here and their welfare is also of concern. There is a definite poly-ethnic character to this region. Doing nothing is not a solution and if a comprehensive exercise to divide the country into seventy-five states is undertaken, Bodopur or for that matter any other state, no longer becomes a special case. It simply becomes a part of an all-India pattern to improve genuine federalism in this essentially diverse nation. In any smaller state, the likelihood of instability is likely to decrease. If the central government clearly demonstrates that its policy with regard to a new state carved out from present-day Assam is not politically motivated but a well-thought out long-term move keeping the larger interests of all stakeholders in mind, there is no reason why one would not move to a reasonable solution.

We move next to the diverse eastern zone that consists of Bengal, Bihar, Jharkhand, Odisha and Sikkim. Much of this region along with Bangladesh was part of the erstwhile Bengal Presidency and gradually secured increasing degrees of autonomy. The fault lines are religious, ethnic, linguistic and also connected with land ownership and tribal issues, notably in the far west of this region. The scheme visualises ten new states here: Mithila and Magadh in the Bihar area, Jharkhand and Odisha with the additional Kosal carved out these two, four new states obtained from present day West Bengal: Mallabhum, Paschim Banga, Kamtapur and Gorkhapur with Kharagpur, Kolkata, Cooch Behar and Darjeeling as state capitals. Sikkim remains unchanged. Mithila, also known as Videha in the Vedic period, is an ancient kingdom and is well known since the times of the Ramayana as the birthplace of Sita. It has a unique cultural identity and a distinct language, Maithili with its Tirhuta script, similar to Assamese and Bengali.

All other considerations aside, there are 9.03 crores people living in West Bengal and the state, like other large ones, will become administratively ungovernable in the context of a modern, forward looking and highly influential nation called Bhārat of the future. Allegorically, one must not live in the past.

Even the present must be planned with an eye to the future. This should not be the India of 2030 but the Bhārat of 2075 that one should plan for. Unfortunately, our long term future is being held captive to the five year cycle of elections with the lottery of a first-past-the-post system in a parliamentary format, with an asynchronous cycle of assembly elections, and the complications of coalition ministries: an unwholesome combination for healthy governance. Geographically and culturally the four states envisaged are distinct and it is not just administrative convenience and large population that justify their creation.

Our state of Paschim Banga includes those portions of the ancient Vanga region that lie within our present borders for most of this region was lost to us at the time of Partition. This region has its distinctive climatic, geographic and cultural character. The larger Banga was also known as Gangaridai by the Romans and Greeks and has references in the Mahābhārata as well. The proposed state retains much of the Sunderbans delta lying in India and corresponds to the Gauda kingdom of seafarers which became a force to reckon with during the Late Classical Period (4th century BCE). This new state would have the compact size and the presence of a huge metropolis in its capital city to become again an important shipping and logistics hub for the rest of the eastern region and to facilitate trade and economic growth with the growing economies of Asia. This small state could well be a Singapore waiting to happen. Its commonality with neighbouring Bangladesh is bound to influence mutually favourable trade and cultural exchanges.

The agitations for a separate state for the Gorkhas, with their ethnic and linguistic diversity, have been long-standing. As in the Bodo demand, this agitation should not be seen as a special case, specific to the current emotions of those agitating and those from whom they want to separate. It is an administrative and strategic matter. Heavily populated states or those with awkward geographies stand to gain economically from further division even in the medium time range. These issues always seem to have a political colouring: in the end, Madhya Pradesh, Maharashtra, Tamil Nadu, Uttar Pradesh or West Bengal are similar with respect to the carving out of smaller states for administrative reasons. None is unique. The principle being stated is simple: Bhārat should move towards seventy five states with roughly equal populations around two crore each for administrative ease and greater federal character in this essentially diverse nation.

We conclude this travelogue with the southern zone. The South is arguably the most interesting region of the country if one considers the question of seventy-five smaller states and a perusal of Chapter 2 might be useful again. This region, consisting of the present day states of Telangana, Andhra Pradesh, Karnataka, Tamil Nadu and Kerala has been continuously confronted with all three of the major issues which are of the maximum concern with respect to the inadequate constitutional provisions made for them in 1950 and subsequently: federalism, religion, and socio-economic factors. Many details have been furnished in Chapter 2. The South is much like the rest of the country and yet it is different. Possibly the fact that the languages spoken here are not of Indo-European origin is one reason for its distinctiveness. However, this cannot be the whole truth: Malayalam is perhaps the Indic language closest to Sanskrit with even Tamil, the most Dravidian of the languages of the south, taking many words from the Indo-European stream at least in some of its variants. Practically everyone from the South would be able to follow basic Hindi if it is Sanskritised rather than Urduised. Commentators have struggled to classify the South. Is it the region where the scripts start curving? Is it the region where people start preferring coffee to tea? These latter criteria are informal and are not intended to be evaluated rigorously but they underlie the fact that diversity in our civilisational state is, teleologically speaking, to be experienced rather than classified. Definitions of phenomena can be enigmatic in complex systems. India is a complex system in itself—Southern India presents a higher level of complexity.

There is diversity within the South and there is diversity within each of the southern states. In these respects, the south is no different from the rest of the country. Telangana, the official prototype of a smaller state within the same linguistic region, inspires many of the choices here. A.P. has been discussed earlier and the case for a separate Rayalaseema is strong with Kurnool being a natural choice for the state capital. Whether or not a new Rayalaseema needs a corridor to the coast in the form of transfer of Sullurupeta and Tada talukas to the new state is a matter for consideration and either option seems reasonable. Karnataka has undergone interesting polymorphism since 1947. Kishen Shastry, in a recent article, provides examples showing the role played by the Mysore royals, referred to several times in the earlier chapters, in stabilising what he terms 'Kannada conservatism' in domains of the present state far beyond the original nine districts of princely Mysore. He says that "Karnataka is a stark exception among the south Indian states, clearly manifesting its expression of religiosity and cultural priorities via electoral politics", and analyses the role of this sentiment in stabilising this desirable decentralised model within the larger Indian cultural ethos. Kannada conservatism emphasises the practice of liberal Hindu values. It should not be forgotten that it was here, as far back as the 19th century, that reservations for socially and economically backward communities were put in place by the *Rajarshi* Krishnaraja Wadiyar IV (whose mother donated the four hundred acres of land for the Indian Institute of Science). It is this unique cultural ethos with its immensely accommodative nature, characteristic of Sanātana Dharma, that has transformed Bangalore, a sleepy hill-station cantonment town of the British, into Bengaluru, the third largest metropolis in the country, the nerve centre of the Indian software industry, a completely multilingual city, where Elon Musk proposes to set up a big manufacturing unit for his electrical cars. Division of present day Karnataka into seven states Bayaluseeme (Bengaluru), Mysuru (Mysuru), Karunadu (Belagavi), Karavali (Karwar), Malenadu (Shivamogga), Kodagu (Madikeri), and Tulunadu (Mangaluru) follows from separatist movements, cultural, historical and linguistic fault lines, and finally administrative convenience.

We have proposed a four-fold division of Tamil Nadu. Kongu Nadu is situated in the western belt of the present state comprising the districts of Coimbatore (Kovai), Tirupur, Erode, Nilgiris, Salem, Namakkal, Krishnagiri and Dharmapuri. The region finds mention in the Sangam era literature. Various political parties have opposed the move for Kongu Nadu but this is almost always the instinctive reaction of stakeholders in an older regime, in Machiavelli's words, "all those who derived advantages from the old order of things" and may be taken as normal, especially if one is extrapolating to a dominant Bhārat 2075. The three other proposed states have been given ancient Tamil names, Pandya Nadu, Chola Nadu and Thondai Mandalam, with the Pallava capital, Kanchipuram designated as the capital of the last one. The latter is a satellite town of Chennai and its choice is inspired by the selection of Gandhinagar as the capital of present day Gujarat, the satellite of the commercially important Ahmedabad, which itself is giving ground to Vadodara as the capital city of a new state. Having a smaller city as a capital in a state that contains a very large metropolis is a standard method of decentralisation. The USA is replete with such pairs, and to mention just a few: Albany and New York City; Springfield and Chicago; Sacramento and Los Angeles; Austin and Dallas-Fort Worth.

We finally turn to Kerala, God's own country. The present population is 3.6 crores and this would be too large if one is aiming for an average of 2 crores per each new state. Trifurcation into Travancore, Cochi and Malabar would give extremely manageable administrative units. The role played by the royals in Travancore has been adequately described in Chapter 2 and is not dissimilar to that of the Wadiyars in Mysore. This has been an ancient *dharmakshetra* while Muslims and Christians came here as merchants and settlers rather than marauders and conquerors. The Orthodox Church is, according to legend, two millennia old. The possibly only surviving Jewish community in India is located here. The unique presence of three major denominations in this narrow coastal strip is a living example of a mini-federation and it is only being formalised by designating three new states of roughly the same area and population with administrative, legislative and judicial autonomy. The division follows *mandal* (region) boundaries as given in www.mapsofindia.com the largest on-line repository of maps on India since 1998. The state is divided in the map in this website into five regions: Southern Travancore, Central Travancore, Northern Travancore, Central Kerala and Malabar.

The first three regions constitute the new Travancore, the fourth Cochi, and the fifth Malabar is largely untouched except that Kasargode district is merged with Dakshina Kannada and Udupi districts in present-day Karnataka to constitute the new Tulunadu state. The suggested capitals are Thiruvananthapuram, Ernakulam and Kozhikode.

We turn finally to our Union Territories (UTs). At the moment there are eight of them. J&K and Ladakh have been discussed already. Chandigarh and Puducherry might be merged with Punjab and Thondai Mandalam respectively, possibly following a referendum. The four enclaves of Dadra, Nagar Haveli, Daman and Diu could simply be merged with Saurashtra or Vadodara depending on geographical convenience. Two of them, Andaman and Nicobar Islands, and Lakshadweep should probably be retained as UTs for geostrategic reasons.

The last one, Delhi, requires comment. As the capital of a huge country that is federal in nature, the exact constitutional position of Delhi is a matter of concern to all of us and needs to be defined both accurately and precisely. The status of capital cities of other Westminster democracies may be considered and examined. The U.K. does not have states and so there is no federation as such. In a parliamentary democracy with an unwritten constitution, London becomes just a very large city in a small country and has the same type of representation at all levels as any other part of the U.K. Canberra and Ottawa are more interesting constitutionally.

Both are small cities sufficiently distant from commercial centres like Sydney and Melbourne in the former case, and Montréal and Toronto in the latter. They are government cities. Canberra is completely surrounded by the state of New South Wales which ceded this small territory to the federal government in 1911. A locally elected legislative assembly has governed it since 1988. However, the federal government maintains authority over the territory and may overturn local laws. Ottawa is even more interesting. With a population slightly more than 10 lakhs, it is a large city by Canadian standards. It has a federal parliament which makes laws in matters of national interest for all of Canada. For other matters it comes completely under the jurisdiction of the English-speaking state of Ontario. However, across the Ottawa River lies the French-speaking province of Québec and this provided a sound enough rationale for its selection as the national capital in 1857.

Delhi when considered as the National Capital Region, NCR is an altogether different matter. When the capital was shifted there in 1911, it was much smaller than the three metropolitan presidency cities of Calcutta, Bombay and Madras, with a population of just 2.4 lakhs and at the provincial extremity of undivided Punjab. Today, it is the second largest urban agglomeration in the country, just a little smaller than Mumbai. The NCR has a population of a little over a crore. As it exists, it is too large to not have proper representation at all levels in the legislative process. Delhi has grown mainly for two reasons: a large influx of migrant population from west Punjab after Partition and the fact that our overwhelmingly union-centric government has created a large workforce there from all over India.

The spillover of this megapolis into Haryana and U.P. and possibly even Rajasthan is considerable. Delhi was given limited legislative authority in 1991 with the setting up of a Legislative Assembly with a government that would "aid and advise the Lt. Governor" who was not necessarily bound by such aid and advice in the matter of subjects like land, police, and public order. A mechanism was provided to refer matters to the President of India in case there was a difference of opinion between the Lt. Governor and the Council of Ministers. The Lt. Governor of Delhi has powers more substantial than governors of our states at present. In practice what this has meant is that when the ruling party in the Centre and Delhi are the same, things are uneventful. When they are different this may not always be the case. The present constitutional situation in Delhi is far from satisfactory and a change is desirable.

In the seventy-five-state scheme, Delhi would continue as

a UT but with drastically reduced territorial limits, say just to the extent that prevailed in 1947 namely the government and ceremonial areas, the diplomatic enclave, the Supreme Court, monuments and memorials of national importance, and old Delhi as also a few suburbs in the immediate hinterland. This UT would be administered *completely* by the central government in the manner that Washington D.C. is in the U.S.A. The latter is situated literally, to use the language of solid state chemistry, in an interstitial site between the states of Maryland and Virginia, both of which are among the 13 original states of the U.S.A. Delhi in this conception would be of modest area, with a considerable floating population and would in my estimate have no more than 20 lakh people. It would have representation in Parliament but not at any other level. The bulk of the population of the present day NCR and most commercial and industrial establishments would find themselves in the surrounding states of Haryana and Hastinapur.

The entirety of Delhi would then revert to being a federal enclave which is what it was always supposed to be. The name 'New Delhi' might also be discreetly dispensed with. If 'naya paisa' went in 1964, 'nayee Dilli' can go in 2022. Similarly the grand-sounding 'National Capital Region' might more simply be changed to 'National Capital Zone'. Delhi belongs to the whole country and symbolises the unity and integrity of the nation. It represents the country, nation and civilisation. Let us not forget Indraprastha from the Mahābhārata or the pre-Mauryan excavations in the area of what is called Purana Qila today, a stone's throw from the Supreme Court. Delhi is a formally envisaged structure and should remain so. It cannot and should not be held captive to local political interests or become a stomping ground for wannabe national leaders. As it has become a mock arena for national level politics whether in the Assembly or in the various students' unions of the colleges and universities located in the NCR it receives inordinate and completely disproportionate attention from the media, many of whom have their headquarters located there. Delhi has also become a symbol of a 'big brother' type central government seeking to enforce its suzerainty over a vast country, a symbol of administrative inefficiency and judicial overreach. Much of this is perceived, a psychological feeling, but common people in distant corners do not identify easily with the 'idea of Delhi' which harks back to an imperial capital of centuries past situated in an extremity of the country.

There are just too many unsavoury connections with the British and the Mughals, some physical but largely psychological. This has not been made any easier by the naming of arterial roads in the heart of the government area after Mughals emperors. Let it not be forgotten that these road names were given when the old British names were discarded. These elusive emotions resist quantification but they play a negative role in the all-important task of balancing healthy federalism with a strong Centre. Many of these problems would vanish automatically if Delhi were drastically pruned down in size. Apart from this, conflicts and contradictions between the central government and that of the UT cannot be solved in an *ad hoc* manner via constitutional tinkering. A remake of our national capital is very much in order.

I have so far described the causes, the symptoms and the nature of the disease. I have then prescribed a medicine. It now remains to outline how it is to be administered to the patient. In this regard, Allopathy seems to be a preferred route because time is of essence, as one would say, *carpe diem* or seize the moment. Another cure might be better but it might also take too long or be too gradual. There is a Russian saying that a deep ditch can only be crossed with a single jump. Incremental action has been the bane of this country since 1947. When Keynes said that in the long run we are all dead he was merely restating a fundamental fact of human existence, one that finds expression in all areas of knowledge. In the context of chemistry what is fastest is not always what is best and the subject generally moves according to what is fastest.

Diamond and graphite are chemically the same and to a chemist, graphite is the best while diamond is one that is obtained the fastest in nature. The gem industry moves ahead because the fastest does not transform to the best even after millennia.

The reader will appreciate that this seventy-five-state model, while it will be legally permitted under Article 3 in the present dispensation of governance, will inevitably entail other substantial constitutional changes. Continuing the analogies from the medical line, the correct medicine administered incorrectly, say a wrong dosage, given at a wrong time interval between doses, whether or not the patient is taking these medicines on an empty stomach, all these things are important and may make a difference between a cure and a worsening of the condition.

In the context of major constitutional changes an almost instinctive concern is how normal governance in the country will go on, even as major changes in its very form are being contemplated. Here, one may safely rely on the sound precedent established by our Constituent Assembly because it was confronted with the same issue. India had become independent in August 1947 and it was a dominion of the crown at that point. It was setting itself up to become a republic completely free of the crown. The Constituent Assembly was the *only* sovereign body in the country between August 1947 and January 1950 when our new Constitution came into effect. How was the governance issue managed in the interim period?

In Ambedkar's words:

With regard to the third question, obviously, the arrangement that we are making now for the purpose of converting the constituent assembly into a legislative body, undoubtedly will be temporary. It would last so long as the function of constitution-making has not been completed. When the function of constitution-making is completed, obviously, one or the other arrangement would vanish and we shall then continue only to function as a legislature.

Prasad added significantly:

The business of the assembly as a constitution-making body should be clearly distinguished from its normal business as the Dominion Legislature, and different days or separate sittings on the same day should be set apart for the two kinds of business.

In the present context, if a seventy-five-state model is to be conceived, two possibilities present themselves:

(1) The existing Lok Sabha becomes a Constituent Assembly and divides itself into constitutional and legislative wings or;
(2) The Constituent Assembly is assembled independently with say half its members from the existing parliament and half drawn from all walks of life.

If one goes by our experience with our 1946 Constituent Assembly, it benefited greatly from the presence of professional politicians including those at the pinnacle of political power, and also from lawyers, authors, journalists and public-spirited individuals. All of them had a strong sense of morality.

The comments of the political people in the Assembly did not reflect biased partisan preferences. Ideas like amelioration of caste inequalities, reduction of income disparities and economic growth were the concerns of all. It is suggested that the second of these above possibilities would be the fairest to the people of India in any future reworking of the republic. Politicians have not covered themselves with glory over the past seventy five years and if the Constituent Assembly is congruent with an existing Lok Sabha, we would only see an affirmation of Machiavelli's cynical words at the head of this chapter. The actions of the judiciary, at least with respect to how common people understand their working do not inspire confidence. The least one may ask for is that any ongoing activity of a future constituent assembly should be free of any kind of judicial interference. As for the executive they should keep far away from anything that is going on in any such a constitutional assembly other than facilitating its day-to-day activities.

The nature of the constitutional and governance changes proposed are specific to the proposal for the formation of seventy-five new states at one go. The reader will realise that these are not piecemeal changes that can be undertaken in our usual incremental way of looking at things. Incremental change is acceptable if the basic model of twenty-eight states and 8 UTs remains unaltered with small increases in the number of states based on political compulsions of the day and our five-year election cycle.

This rationale for seventy-five states arises from constitutional needs, to make the country truly federal, truly secular and truly dharmic. They do not arise from pleasing contemporary political constituencies of various hues. The conclusion is that an optimal number of seventy-five will result in rapid improvements in a short time scale. Therefore the *a priori* assumption is that there will be a unified political and national will for this radical decentralisation.

Given such a situation, the first immediate consequence is that it would be too expensive and cumbersome to have 75 states if one persisted with the present system of governance.

There are three fundamental flaws in the present system:

(1) The inappropriateness to us of the classic Westminster model as practiced in the U.K.
(2) The debilitating effect of having an overlap between the executive and the legislature in the Indian context. This is a special case of inappropriateness as mentioned in point 1 above but it is such a major flaw that it has been mentioned as a separate point.
(3) The unnecessary nature of the second chambers of legislature at the Centre and the States. This too leads from point 1 above and has been adequately detailed in Chapters 1 and 2.

We could, using the parlance of patent law, call these the main flaw and two dependent flaws. Let us take them in turn. It has been emphasised repeatedly that the U.K. system suits only countries that have an unwritten Constitution, essentially only the U.K. It is particularly ill-suited to a country like India with its federal polity. It is also appropriate only if there are two major political parties, which is when the first-past-the-post system of elections produces the most reliable results. It is for this reason that several countries have managed within this system making slight modifications, say Australia, Canada and New Zealand. All of them have two main political parties that are of national character.

The U.K. system is also unsuited to us because of overlap between the legislative and executive wings for reasons outlined in Chapter 2. The Cabinet becomes excessively powerful, and in a country like ours the main aim in the game would then be to secure a minister-ship, which in the worst case scenario leads to an increase in corruption and black money which feeds further elections, which in turn produces legislators who are ever more determined to secure ministerial positions. It is an ever-growing maelstrom and there is no reasonable cure.

Let us not forget that one has also arrived at the conclusion that a combination of Bhāratiya and Anglosphere models is the only one that would preserve and enhance our civilisational clout on the one hand, and on the other enable us to use it in an Anglosphere setting, in other words, following procedures and customs that are well accepted in liberal democracies worldwide. The natural solution is the US model, which as we know was seriously considered in the Assembly and for various reasons, known and unknown, only given symbolic status in our Constitution. Let us turn therefore to this model and switch over with respect to a complete separation of legislative and executive wings, with a President heading the latter and elected by the entire country using the first-past-the-post method (no electoral colleges) for a fixed term of office (five to seven years if only a single term allowed; two four-year terms if two terms allowed; no more than two terms). This president would enjoy veto power over laws passed by the legislature and would select his own cabinet of individuals who are not members of the legislature to hold office at his or her pleasure. In other words, they may be removed or added at any time during the president's tenure. Modes for impeachment of the chief executive would undoubtedly need to be worked out but this is not a major problem even with a unicameral legislature. As an automatic corollary to a directly elected president, the office of President *as it is understood today*, a paste imitation of the British Crown, would cease to exist. Analogously the legislature and executive in each of the seventy-five new states would need to be defined in this way.

The legislature would be unicameral unlike in the U.S.A. and would be elected for any fixed term of office which may or may not bear any relation to the term of office of the President. At the Centre, they would be elected as in the US House of

Representatives and not unlike the present Lok Sabha with constituencies being demarcated by population and possibly occasionally by area. The leader of the Lok Sabha would be a Speaker elected by the members of the house. The legislature would be responsible only for the framing of laws and only it would have this power. Since there is a complete separation of powers it would matter little when legislators are elected, whether they are elected all at once or staggered, and finally and most importantly when elections to the state legislatures are held because a natural corollary of all this is that exactly the same system should be adopted in each of the seventy-five states: one elected Governor who holds executive authority with his or her selected cabinet and a legislature which is elected in a first-past-the-post system from assembly constituencies which are obviously smaller than Lok Sabha constituencies.

The adoption of several important features of the US constitution in India 2.0 is not conceived by us as mere happenstance or casual acceptance of the term 'Anglosphere'. The U.S.A. in 1787 built what had never been built before—a State which recognised the role of its member states, and a union that based its power on the consent of the people. That the founding fathers of that country succeeded in their efforts is proof of their belief in their central dogma, namely that while political differences between member states might be even bitter, their differences *on matters of economic interest* were not acute. They were concerned that the central government should not be weakened unnecessarily in the name of states asserting themselves. Theirs was a constitution based on solid economic grounds and aimed at improving the business climate. They did not confuse themselves with other extraneous matters. These are the very issues that confound us in today's India. Our federal polity needs a real endorsement from our Constitution and not mere lip service in a world that is driven increasingly by economics and not politics. We have the added advantage that our diversity is based not on political differences, which are temporary, but on history and culture, which are permanent. Our unity comes from common interests that are based not only on *artha,* as in the U.S.A. but also *dharma* that is unique to us. If these factors are identified accurately and leveraged swiftly, there is no reason to believe that our growth and rise will not be exponential.

Since the federalism issue would be largely resolved with the seventy-five-state system the irrelevance of the Rajya Sabha and the half dozen Legislative Councils we have now would become fully apparent. The superfluous nature of the second chamber has been discussed since 1895 when the first Swaraj constitution appeared. It had been debated at length in the assembly where prominent national leaders had criticised the notion of an 'upper' house in a country like India. Invoking the House of Lords might have sounded quaint in 1947 but in 2022 it would be downright ridiculous. The incongruities of the Rajya Sabha membership in the decades after 1950 have been adequately described by us. Sarcasm is not the need of the hour nor is excessive prose necessary. With regard to the Rajya Sabha, let us simply quote Leo Amery in the darkest hour of World War II , paraphrasing Oliver Cromwell several centuries before him, when he said in the House of Commons to a sitting Prime Minister:

> *You have sat too long here for any good you have been doing. Depart, I say, and let us have done with you. In the name of God, go.*

It is not incumbent to discuss details of specific changes desirable in a new constitution with respect to federalism, secularism and casteism. These are what one would term as being dependent on a more basic defect in the governance system. Suffice it to say that a new constituent assembly should address the following issues with impartial gravity.

1. To restore the wording of the Preamble to what it was on 26 January 1950.
2. To move as many of the Directive Principles as possible to the Fundamental Rights considering that after 75 years, many of them need stay no longer on a wish-list if the levels of maturity of the polity have increased as they hopefully have. Specifically this would include Article 44 that deals with the UCC, the latter becoming a non-justiciable right of all citizens.
3. To thoroughly rework all those Fundamental Rights that deal with the issue of religious minorities, more particularly certain sections in Articles 15, 16, 21A, 25, 26, 27, 28, 29 and 30.
4. To define a community as having minority status only if it is present to an extent of less than 5% of the overall population and to make the state not the Union the basis of such a definition.
5. To introduce non-renewable sunset clauses for all caste and community based reservations and to make them uniform across the country, in particular to modify Article 16 along with the 93rd and 95th amendments.
6. To reconsider certain aspects of Article 31A.
7. To increase the powers of the central government to impose an emergency and to reduce the extent of judicial review for such provisions.
8. To reconsider all the topics in the Seventh Schedule, especially to prune List III down to the bare minimum of which education, however, must remain one.
9. To review the appointing procedures for all posts to the judiciary.
10. To introduce two benches of the Supreme Court, one for constitutional matters and the other as a court of final appeal.

11. To relate the right of appeal to a higher court to the seriousness and significance of a matter, especially appeal to the Supreme Court.
12. To separate completely the functions of the judiciary from that of the executive.
13. To modify the structure of the IAS such that appointments plateau at a level of joint secretary and with all bureaucratic appointments at higher levels to be made at the pleasure of the President and in the limit, coterminous with his or her term of office. A similar distinction to be drawn in the Foreign Service formalising the difference between career diplomats and appointed diplomats at higher, more sensitive, levels.
14. To separate the authority of the IAS and the state administrative service within a state so that the former is mainly responsible for topics in List I and List III as they apply in the state, and accordingly increase the level of decentralisation.
15. To reconsider and if necessary increase the powers of the IPS and other central level security and crime prevention organisations bearing in mind also that the present office of Governor of a state would be removed, and to decentralise powers of the state police to the district level wherever appropriate.
16. To consider the separation of criminal and security wings of the police services.
17. To ensure that it would enjoy sovereign powers with respect to its recommendations, in other words to remove the power of judiciary review over them, since one is moving from one constitutional system to another.

Many of the suggestions in the above thread may sound radical or utopian, and there are more which would be debated and discussed by legal experts, but constitutional reforms have been regularly undertaken by countries including in our neighbour Sri Lanka, which had a similar colonial administrative legacy and religious diversity. It would be apparent to the reader why these reforms cannot be taken up piecemeal and why and how they are particularly appropriate to the decentralised model with 75 states. To quote Swami Vivekananda, "What we want is muscles of iron and nerves of steel. We have wept long enough".

EPILOGUE
QUO VADIS?

The problems in India are more complicated, more momentous, than the problems in any other country... and the solution of this problem is not so easy, as it is a big and vast one.
—Swami Vivekananda

VIVEKANANDA was completely accurate in his use of the word *complicated* in the context of India's problems, for the country had become complicated enough by his time. Today, a century later, it is only more so. The reader will note that I have described India admiringly as a *complex* system in this book. Our country was practically a perfect example of such a system at till around 800 CE and this complexity was inherent to its dominant faith with its multiple layers of organisation and self-correcting features. This working complex system, however, started to degrade into a debilitatingly complicated system after it came into contact and finally conflict with monotheistic faiths that questioned the very basis of its complexity. By Vivekananda's times it seemed to have all but lost any sense of form or function. What then is the difference between 'complex' and 'complicated'? Many do not realise the significance of this vital distinction. A complicated system is like a high-precision Swiss chronometer or a computer programme and consists of many components each of which may be understood in isolation. The functioning of such a system may also be fully understood as derivable from the functions of the individual components. A feature of complicated systems therefore is that they may be analysed with a reductionist approach. The whole is well-approximated as a sum of the parts.

The fates of history took us from a complex system to a complicated one. A characteristic of a complicated system is that if one of the components stops working the whole system quickly grinds to a halt. Complicated systems therefore need to have built-in redundancies to survive so that when something stops working, an equivalent starts up so that the system resumes. In the context of our Constitution for example, the breakdown came with Partition. Accordingly we set up redundancies—but they were imperfect. A union-centric system of governance subdued our instinctive feelings of diversity and federal character. A set of articles and amendments where minority religious groups were favoured at the expense of the majority only worsened the problem. The majority community began to be actively discriminated against by the State in the name of helping the minorities. By 2014 this led to all communities retreating into behavioural silos. The medicines were worse than the disease. Since the redundancies that were set up between 1950 and 2022 did not address the original breakdown fully, in other words because they were imperfect, the problems became worse and the system in turn became ever more complicated. Far from Émile Zola's cry of "*j'accuse*" to the French state in a matter of discrimination against a member of a miniscule minority, we now have a significant proportion of the population saying "*nous accusons*" (we accuse) to the Indian state for discriminating against them, the majority community.

A complex system is very different. Complexity is well-illustrated by the continuous flow of traffic through an intersection of many roads at multiple levels such as is common in large cities in India and elsewhere, inspired by the autobahns of Germany and the cloverleaf crossings of the U.S.A. There may be many roads approaching the interchange and any vehicle may approach from any road and leave from any road with no vehicle ever stopping. This may be contrasted with the equivalent complicated system where say five roads meet at a circle and the traffic is controlled by lights at each of the points where a road meets the circle. One notes that unlike the modern multi-level interchanges where no traffic is stationary, any vehicle at the signal-controlled traffic intersection is stationary for most of the time (four-fifths) during which time the traffic on one of the four other roads at the intersection is moving. In the former situation a traffic breakdown on one of the roads leaves the traffic in others at the intersection largely unaffected. In the latter situation a simple malfunction of a single master switch would turn off all the traffic lights leading to a chaotic breakdown. If functioning complicated systems need to incorporate redundancies, complex systems are characterised by adaptability. Unlike a complicated system a complex system does not necessarily break down because one of the components is not working. It merely modifies or mutates. This is well illustrated in Sanātana Dharma. Knowing that human nature is inherently diverse, our ancients put in place a system where the sāstras and scriptures could be understood with several interpretations, the six *darshanas* for example or different ways of viewing *Brahman*.

Complicated systems are different from complex ones in that solutions to problems in the former case are size dependent but not so in the latter. The problems of a country with a small number of say, ethnicities, languages or states may be addressed through the device of setting up redundancies. However, even here there are limits. Czechoslovakia did not last all of seventy-five years. Most of the Irish nation sundered itself from Great Britain in the early 1900s. The original Pakistan with two major languages stayed undivided for a mere twenty-four years. The present-day Pakistan with four disparate provinces remains metastable at best. If a huge country such as India becomes complicated, the dimension of the problem quickly becomes intractable. Vivekananda got this right too when he said the solutions to the problem of India were going to be big and vast. Today, a century later, when our country and its governance systems have become more complicated the solutions have become nearly impossible to find. Can they even be found?

A complex system is, however, adaptable and so the solution to its problems does not become more difficult as its size increases. In fact the converse is true. Complex systems work best when they are large because the levels of adaptability become implicit. The problems generate their solutions practically spontaneously. Scientists term this phenomenon self-healing. We have a sad example of this in the medical world: cancer resists solutions because it is a complex disease and the present systems of medicine, because of their inherent limitations, are forced to address it as if it were merely complicated. From the point of view of the disease, it thrives as it spreads more. Type II diabetes is another example of the same phenomenon. The disease becomes progressively worse. If simple systems may be understood with reductionist thinking, complex ones are characterised by their *emergent* nature. Emergence is a situation in which the properties of a system may not be understood so easily as the aggregate of the properties of its constituents. New properties emerge as the complexity of a system increases. The higher order structure is not approximated well as the sum of its lower order entities. In the context of this book, we feel that India is not captured well enough in terms of the attributes of its present states. Whether one calls it a melting pot, goulash, salad bowl, *aviyal, kichdi* or *kootu* it matters not. All these are inadequate simplifications, culinary trivialisations at best, that do not do justice to the problem at hand.

More analytically, I have sought to demonstrate the spatiotemporal nature of a complex system with the pointillist depiction of India in Chapter 4. Let us consider a prototypical large state in India. There will be a certain 'average' character of this state which when combined with other such 'averages' gives an 'average' description of the country. Based on the nature of the problems we have faced for the past seventy-five years and our generally inadequate responses to them, it is reasonable to assume that these 'averages' do justice neither to the Centre and more importantly to the States themselves. This is shown in Figure 2 in Chapter 4 in the frame with the biggest coloured dots. When the dots are made smaller, however, as in the rest of the frames in that figure the final picture emerges clearly. This may be explained according to the principles of complexity and emergence in the following manner: when the states are made smaller, for example let us assume that our one big state is made into four smaller states, the depiction of the former larger state itself becomes not only more precise but also more accurate. To illustrate, suppose the so-called dominant federal feature in a state today is language. The four smaller states would almost always share the same language. However, in the seventy-five-state model, a new feature, say geography, culture, urbanisation, or strategic importance, might well emerge since the former 'unifying' concept is no longer necessary to establish critical identity. It is also more likely that the newer measure of identity is a surer criterion of diversity in a holistic all-India context. In this prototypical case, it may be safely assumed that language was an 'average' common feature of the larger state that served the purpose of demonstrating identity, but once a truer, less political, measure of diversity became uncovered, it was shelved in favour of the new diversity indicator to arrive at a better picture of the entirety of the country. This is what is meant when one says that the whole is more than the sum of the parts. The emergent feature, geography, urbanisation or strategic importance, could not have been predicted from the older measure of diversity, namely language. To summarise, the challenge before us is to remake our non-working complicated system into a working complex system.

This "big and vast" undertaking cannot be the work of an individual or just a group of individuals. It cannot be done piecemeal using incremental steps of which we are so inordinately fond in this country. The making of India 2.0 will take nothing short of a revolution. Revolutions are inspired by passions and a commitment to higher ideals. In the Western world they were necessarily brought about through armed conflict and violent struggle in response to unjust suppression. The American Revolution, the French Revolution and the Russian Revolution subscribed to this pattern. The Bhāratiya Revolution is a silent one and it will be a battle of minds rather than of physical wills. India, at least the India of 1947, did not start this war. Bhārat is capable of winning it efficiently, quietly and methodically if it plans its strategies well. We are a lucky lot of Indians today in that we are witnessing this silent revolution possibly even participating in it. To paraphrase Dean Acheson, a former Secretary of State of the U.S.A in the critical 1940s and early 1950s when Europe was being remade, we are the ones who are "present at the creation" of Bhārat, that is India.

Revolutions, especially the silent and cerebral ones, need the active participation of the Indian State. Only power can bring about on-the-ground changes. An idea without back-up State power is mere theorising and we have had enough of that. Any politician worth his or her salt will not only capture the feelings of the people but also institutionalise them through governance structures.The country has gone beyond fancy slogans and pious nostrums. It is important that the best of new ideas in the coming five years swiftly materialise through concrete actions by our government without ado and ceremony. If a law is passed in Parliament and it takes two or more years to notify the rules for its implementation, it is tantamount to not having passed the law. The present political condition of the country with a single political party in power at the Centre and in many States is perhaps the most favourable one to effect major constitutional and governance changes. One cannot predict how long this situation will last and we should not squander away the gains, electoral or otherwise, that have been made in the past decade through our inaction and lack of wisdom. We have not seen such a situation in half a century and in an open democracy it means that the majority of the people want a complete change. It is preferable to be slightly wrong at the right time rather than to be fully right at the wrong time. What is needed is a synthesis of the best that the minds of the past had to offer us with the vigour, action and urgency of today's generations. The younger an Indian the less he or she would be clouded by the uncertain baggage of former times. It will be the youngest who will have the clearest of minds.

As for the intellectual and cerebral component of this transformation of India 1.0 to India 2.0, many individuals from all walks of life are required whether they be from the law, academia, science, journalism, public service, film world, sports and arts of all types. Private citizens of all colours and hues can and should help through social media which has now established itself as a legitimate means of disseminating ideas. All successful revolutions need the broad based support of the general public and the Bhāratiya revolution will be no exception. We need contrarians too to act as conscience keepers and voices of caution to offer wise counsel. Like the freedom struggle this needs to be a mass movement rather than driven by a political agenda. It is the people who should set the agenda and not politicians. The latter merely sense the idea and carry it through to actuality. A synergy of many individuals channellising their efforts is the only way forward. One could venture to say that this effort did begin in 2014 but the outward manifestations are still too hesitant, too apologetic and too concerned with shibboleths of the past. A revolution is a revolution whether it is violent or silent. There is complete disappearance of the old order. It has been remarked that the American Revolution was more successful than the French because it was carried out more efficiently. The members of the old order in America, the ones who did not wish to fight the British, were not allowed into positions of responsibility and authority after independence. In France, however, the standard bearers of the *ancien régime* were re-inducted after the initial 'Reign of Terror' and this is generally understood to be one of the causes for the further convulsions that France underwent till 1848 and the birth of the Second Republic. The Bhāratiya Revolution therefore needs to be cool-headed: our ideas of inclusiveness should not be falsely interpreted to mean that members of the old order should be given backdoor entries into the new system. Sai Deepak puts this in a different way when he says that the completeness of our preparation for this revolution should reveal itself in the speed with which we effect it and the attitude we take with respect to those who oppose it.

A short digression into the world of social media is, I feel, in order. Media of all types are vital to the functioning of a liberal democracy, the so-called fourth estate. Radio, television and now social media represent increasing levels of advancement in this area. Information is power and once it is provided to citizens, all thinking sentient beings, they will analyse and interpret it individually. In the extreme, all this glut of opinion constitutes informational noise. If something is disseminated that touches the collective awareness of a community a signal is picked up and if it strikes a similar chord in many communities, it grows till it is clearly distinguishable from the noise, the so-called 'signal-to noise' ratio beloved of scientists who seek trends from large masses of data. An early humorous example of the power of the media may be found in the so-called 'The War of the Worlds' incident in the U.S.A. in 1938. Orson Welles, a young radio commentator, aired a program on an imaginary Martian invasion of New Jersey based on the novel by H. G. Wells of the same name. Listeners mistook those bulletins for the real thing leading to widespread hysteria, possibly our first excursion into fake news! More seriously, people believed that one of the underlying causes for the fall of the Berlin Wall in 1989 was the fact that people in East Berlin were always able to watch TV programmes from the West. Social media takes this to a higher level because for the first time citizens are able to see what other citizens are thinking. It resembles an open election where anyone can see how everyone else is voting. It may possibly be likened to an unofficial referendum. The political implications of social media are by now an acknowledged fact and it is employed all over the world as a standard technique to influence opinion. Despite the high noise level from fake news, bot accounts, fake polls and paid comments, the signal asserts itself above the noise in India because we are such a large country. The role of social media in setting the stage for the Bhāratiya revolution is by now well understood by its proponents and opponents, and we shall undoubtedly see increased use of this medium in the immediate future.

This is a war within and a war without. The former is, to start with, the responsibility of Bhāratiyas but the State should follow up in being able to discern true emotions that come from deep within and act on them. The State should also be able to identify the inevitable contrary trends from the *ancien régime* and learn how to sidestep them. Both the people and the State are therefore required in the internal war. However, only the State can fight the external war. Sai Deepak is brutally frank when he says, "A country which cannot get hard-nosed about its civilisational interests and existential priorities shouldn't labour under delusions of becoming a *vishwaguru*. Clarity in vision and a sense of purpose are the first steps to getting a seat at the high table of global powers." We could not agree more. He adds that the most important lesson to be drawn from partition is that it led to the loss of "sacred civilisational space and genocide of Indic communities." This has echoes of Prasad's lament on the eve of independence that we (undivided India) were a country that God and nature intended to be one (Chapter 1). We have stated repeatedly in this book that Partition was the defining moment in this land's civilisational and therefore political history. Our behaviour towards our several Islamic neighbours should therefore show no sign of ambiguity, pusillanimity or vacillation, real or perceived. The days of 'calibrated' and 'nuanced' responses of the Ministry of External Affairs to some of these countries, say Malaysia and Turkey, are over. This has nothing to do with Indian Muslims, who are Indians first and last, but with asserting our civilisational existence rather than being ashamed of it. The Pew report has conclusively demonstrated that today seventy-five long years after independence we are not a nation divided by religion. This alone should give our political leaders enough strength and courage to fight the larger war. Sai Deepak is honest and critical when he says too that, "if Bhārat really wishes to become even a regional power, let alone superpower, it must stop pussyfooting around these issues and understand the value and importance of realpolitik. Smaller countries do better than Bhārat in this regard, and that's seriously unfortunate." Once again we concur.

Sandeep Balakrishna places before us the stark choice between Western intellectualism and *darshanic* timelessness. He is blunt when he says that "the tighter we embrace Western democracy the more Christianised our outlook becomes". Democracy was always known in our civilisation. It is 'Western' democracy that is the problem. He sarcastically points out that the academic high ground in India was captured by those who bracketed "Buddha, Panini, Kautilya, Adi Sankara and Swami Vivekananda with Akbar, Jinnah, Allama Iqbal, E.V. Ramaswami Naicker, V. K. Krishna Menon, Sheikh Abdullah and M. F. Hussain." He adds that a major consequence of the Macaulayisation of Hindus was the creation of this new breed of elite which should normally have become extinct in 1947. They have, however, grown and flourished. He says that what should have remained in museums became India's unofficial political religion—bitter words indeed. Thinkers are what are needed today and it is important that Balakrishna's views and say Neelakandan's, which run counter to that of the Congress ideology, blinkered by communism, are discussed freely. Decolonisation is the most urgent priority of the day if India 2.0 is to become a reality.

Alternative terminologies for the changed political set-up that must accompany the deep-seated civilisational urgings and churnings in this land are already being proposed. Ruchir Sharma has spoken of our Second Republic. Sai Deepak says he would like India to work towards such a second republic. The seventy-five-state model enhances the republican character of our democracy because it increases the federal content in governance. It is noteworthy that other prominent republics in the modern world too have undergone throes as they moved towards forms of governance that were better suited to their inherent indigenous nature. The U.S.A. seems to have been the sole example that got its constitution right at the first shot.

It is instructive to trace the progress of three other republics, France, Germany and China as they moved from an older order to the new. In each of these cases, changes in the form of governance took a period of time in the order of a hundred years and this seems to be usual. It probably takes the collective experiences of a few generations to gel into any firming up of a new form of governance.

France has been mentioned briefly. The chaos of the revolution in 1787 remained unresolved in many ways for a half-century, one of which has been referred to above in their hesitant treatment of the old order. The rise of Napoleon was an attempt at a new form of governance but his ultimate defeat in Waterloo led to a continuation of the so-called First Republic and its floundering existence till 1848. Napoleon's civil administrative systems were however of beauty and simplicity, the Code Napoléon, elements of which continue to be used in France today. In the terminology of complicated systems described above all this activity might be ascribed to the setting-up of imperfect redundancies. The mini-revolution of 1848 saw the installation of a constitutional monarchy of sorts, another experiment shall we say, and this ultimately led to the Third Republic in 1871 which was fully democratic and dispensed with the monarchy altogether, not without resistance from the royalists however. The entire process took a century. The Fifth and Sixth Republics in the post-World War II period, so characterised by the constitutional changes, were more gradual and gentler. Through all this, France stoutly remained a republic, *République Française.*

Germany has been mentioned in the context of the nation-state in Chapter 3. The notoriety of the term 'Third Reich' or *Drittes Reich,* has led to other forms of the German State, not being referred to as Reich (German *Reich,* English *realm,* Latin *rex,* Sanskrit *raj*) at least in the popular imagination. The First

Reich was mostly an illusion originating with Charlemagne and moving on to the Holy Roman Empire and lasting a little over 1000 years. I term this phrase illusory because there was no political entity called Germany during this period or anything that might have been called a German nation. Bismarck has been referred to in Chapter 3 and was responsible for the creation of the Second Reich (1871-1918; 1919-1933), an intriguing combination with a succession of governance forms: federation, semi-constitutional monarchy, qualified democracy and full democracy. Bismarck's greatness lies in the fact that he created a country called Germany where none existed, and that this largely landlocked country led the world in many ways within a short period of time after its creation, certainly in the areas of science and technology where it was dominant by 1900, in the armaments industry and in its military prowess. It did all of this without being a big colonial power at a time when the colonial system was acknowledged as the best route to economic advancement in Europe. Bismarck apparently even encouraged the French to acquire colonial possessions after their defeat by Germany's forces in the Franco-Prussian war of 1870 to distract them. Clearly the concept of a German nation-state was waiting to happen and Bismarck was the catalyst.

The 'Fourth Reich', which we translate loosely as the present German State, began in 1945 and continues as a stable modern entity till the present day. The term *Reich* is not used in Germany today because of the possibly negative connotations of World War II. We view the post-war bifurcation of Germany as an accident which could not resist the deepest stirrings within the German people, a single unit who were divided by an artificial political border for nearly 50 years. What is important to note about modern Germany, *Bundesrepublik Deutschland*, despite the changes in some of its external borders in the 100 or so years after Bismarck, is that his essential idea of a federation where the constituent units surrendered some of their sovereignty for the larger good of the German State continues undisturbed. Germany has veritably witnessed many changes from Bismarck to Weimar, Hitler, the two Germanies, and the present stable dispensation. The lesson for us in India is that if a small country with a limited range of governance variables took 100 years to reach convergence, a subcontinent like ours should not get unduly fretful especially since the signs of impending change are now no longer merely latent but rather, clearly manifest. Indeed, we seem to be a bit quicker than other countries in terms of the people setting the pace for a change of agenda.

China is different from France, Germany and India in that its ruling oligarchy is not freely elected, in other words it is a republic without being a democracy. It is not particularly federal in character and a dominant ethnicity maintains its unitary nature. The transition from Sun Yat-sen, through Chiang Kai-shek, Mao Zedong, Deng Xiaoping, to Xi Jinping shows continuity with change. The former is revealed in that China never denied its civilisational heritage even in its worst periods. Deng Xiaoping, the Bismarck of China, remade the country in such a way that it could change itself economically without a change in its civilisational nature. For a diehard communist, an ideology based on economics, to abandon its economic principles was truly an act of courage and far-sightedness. Like Bismarck he created something good for his country where nothing existed. One might venture as far as to suggest that Deng's policies were accepted with the ease they were because he did not touch China's civilisational fabric. Civilisations as old as China and India do not vanish easily. They might hibernate for years, decades, even centuries but in the timescale of millennia, these are but within the range of what scientists term 'estimated standard deviations'.

Coming finally to India, one need not fear the coming of a second republic, a new India, a Bhārat, a Republic 2.0, an India 2.0 or whatever one might call it. There need be no apprehension, even given our great inherent nervousness regarding change and our tendency to cling irrationally to the past, that a change in governance structure would cause collapse. The weight of history as outlined briefly for France, Germany and China, other republics possibly with different sets of problems but problems nevertheless ought to give us the confidence to overcome the fear of change, namely that it is something to be avoided at all costs. All these countries prospered greatly because they changed and they were unafraid of change. Till the point of fatigue, I have emphasised in this short book that our Constitution is not a God given immutable document. The amendments have arguably made it worse. In 75 years we have experienced democracy, enjoyed autocracy, flirted with monarchy and observed anarchy. What is required are dispassionate intellects, clear-headed politicians, disinterested judges, honest bureaucrats, and objective yet curious citizens who can distinguish between right and wrong. Fear of change might have come about in India during our colonial days. There is no need to be fearful anymore in independent India. As Franklin Roosevelt said during the U.S.A.'s critical days of the Great Depression, the only thing one needs to fear is fear itself.

As in the three other countries described above the condition of the Indian republic has changed over the years that have elapsed since 1950. The initial euphoria evaporated and was replaced by a period of hard post-colonial poverty during which socialism might have been viewed as the only realistic option. Unfortunately this socialism got tied into politics and our long and debilitating engagement with the former U.S.S.R. led to incalculable damage especially in the vital and strategic education sector. Socialism along with our version of secularism got intertwined with the political fortunes of just one family and we were veering towards a quasi-monarchy by the late 1980s with shades of the divine rights of kings. A period of great uncertainty followed by a restoration of the quasi-monarchy in 2004 and its final collapse in 2014 ended the First Republic. The Second Republic has not started as yet but the first is definitely over and we never need fear dynastic rule again. This is especially contextual because the terms republic and monarchy are antipodal. Today we also need not be apprehensive of the two biggest partition-related fears that our constitutional assembly members had: that the country would disintegrate and that religious differences between the two majority faiths would be insurmountable. Both factors are far less important now to being almost unimportant. The strength of the Indian Union and the non-likelihood of its disintegration should allow us to stop making Ambedkar's distinction between union and federation anymore. The states are distinctive enough and it is now only of academic interest that they were not sovereign entities that adhered to the Union in 1947. A state should not become too strong, however. By moving from 28 to 75 states one ensures that no large state can disturb the centre-state balance unduly, mostly politically. Additionally, smaller states will reveal true measures of diversity that will assist in the growth of the civilisational state and increase all-round economic prosperity rather than the present largely false measures such as language and race, and the origin of these two attributes from the distant past. This would constitute modernity not mindless rage at one extreme and maudlin Macaulayism at the other.

Countries are made through circumstances but nations with ideas. An idea is just that, a suggestion, a thought, a hypothesis, or an opinion which needs to stand the test of time before it graduates to anything more. An idea is not an edict or a pronouncement. The word 'idea' has been seriously maligned in the context of our country's identity with the introduction of a term 'The Idea of India' by a member of a group disparagingly called "court poets and philosophers of the dynasty" by Harsh Madhusudan and Rajeev Mantri in their recent book *A New Idea of India*. These authors correctly question the use of the overbearing and presumptuous direct article in the term introduced by the court poets. A far more reasonable approach, since one is talking about an idea, might have been to use the indirect article instead, as indeed Madhusudan and Mantri have done, also with the refreshing adjective that has been thrown in for good measure. The use of the word 'The' in this expression suggests the frustration and anger felt by these poets royal that the State was, in the preceding decades, unable to implement Massimo d'Azeglio's sly advice to his countrymen on the unification of Italy that now that they had made Italy they would have to make Italians. After all, the constitution had been amended so heavily in its first four decades just so that India could be "made" in the manner intended. Why were so many Indians not forcing their feet into these ill-made pairs of tight shoes they had been so generously gifted?

Force feeding of such 'ideas of India' is bound to provoke a counter reaction, especially at a time when the country was already veering away from the artificial socialism and secularism of the older India. It did not take long for Savarkar to be rediscovered and it was pointed out that his ideas, refined by Syama Prasad Mookerjee and others, constituted an alternative idea of India. Ideas became associated with political parties, which is only natural because only those political parties survive in a democracy that have clearly defined ideologies. Madhusudan and Mantri have emphasised with great wealth of detail and concrete examples that a new approach to our administrative structures is an important part of the newness of their idea of the country. However, after all these ideas have been done with and dusted, there remains the oldest idea of India which is also the best!

Idea	Hypothesis	India	Country
Reality	Theory	Bharat	Nation
Certainty	Law	Dharma	Civilisation

A matrix representation of country, nation and civilisation in the context of our land.

If Madhusudan and Mantri have a problem with the word 'The' in the phrase 'The Idea of India,' I have a problem with the word 'India'. There are already two completely contradictory ideas of India. The above authors have now supplied a new idea of India. After a while, a better idea of India will be suggested. India to me is an idea and just that. We do not like to remember Churchill a lot in this country but he was among the first to express the notion of India as an idea. Like all ideas it is open to discussion and debate. It is a hypothesis which needs to be supported with data before it becomes a theory. A theory is something that predicts and in the best case forbids. In this manner it stays on till it is falsified as Karl Popper would have it. The Nehruvian hypothesis (Madhusudan and Mantri are at pains to explain that this may not correspond to the person called Nehru) was sought to be forcibly converted into a theory through the aegis of a constitution that was deformed and distorted well enough by Nehru and his daughter. Falsification occurred easily, as it must for any unsound theory, and unambiguously enough if the 2014 election result is any indication. Countries as we have said can be made and unmade at will because finally they are only ideas given a political form. The history of the 20th century shows this clearly enough. However, a theory is reality as opposed to a mere idea. In our immediate time scale there is no better description of the reality of this land than the nation Bhārat. When a country advances into nationhood it has arrived because it cannot be disturbed so easily.

As we ascend, we find that theories become laws when they become true for all time everywhere. Very few theories, however sturdy and reliable they might be in most ordinary situations, can claim to be in this category. If a theory represents reality, a law is certainty. There can never be an exception to a law. In the context of this book two laws have been invoked, the Second Law of Thermodynamics from the physical world and the Law of Dharma from the metaphysical one. The first takes a system from order to dissipation. The second, its converse, takes a system from disorder to perfect organization. The equilibrium between these two laws literally controls the deconstruction and integration of the entire universe. In *Dharma,* which our faith has codified as a basis of governance of even a modern political state, we have a priceless asset. The revolution that is going on now, and we shall call it the Bhāratiya Revolution, is about the re-establishment of dharma in this ancient land as a means for its exponential rise as a nation in the years to come.

APPENDIX 1

75 STATES OF INDIA 2.0

The proposed new states are given in the order of discussion in Chapter 4, with suggestions for state capitals. New names for certain states and capitals are put up for further consideration.

Himalayan Zone

Gilgit	Gilgit
Baltistan	Skardu
Jammu	Jammu
Kashmir	Srinagar
Ladakh	Leh
Himachal Pradesh	Shimla
Uttarakhand	Dehradun

Northern Zone

Punjab	Ludhiana
Haryana	Jind
Mewat	Alwar
Hastinapur	Meerut
Braj	Mathura
Panchal	Bareilly
Awadh	Lucknow
Kashi	Varanasi

Doab	Kanpur
Central Zone	
Bundelkhand	Jhansi
Baghelkhand	Rewa
Gwalior	Gwalior
Avanti	Ujjain
Nimar	Maheshwar
Vindhya Pradesh	Bhopal
Mahakoshal	Jabalpur
Vidarbha	Nagpur
Chattisgarh	Ambikapur
Gondwana	Raipur
Western Zone	
Bikaner	Bikaner
Marwar	Jodhpur
Ajmer	Ajmer
Dhundhar	Jaipur
Hadoti	Bundi
Shekhawati	Junjhunu
Mewar	Udaipur
Saurashtra	Rajkot
Kachch	Bhuj
Vadodara	Vadodara
Southwestern Zone	
Konkan	Mumbai
Goa	Panaji
Pune	Pune
Nashik	Nashik
Marathwada	Sambhaji Nagar
Amravati	Amravati

Northeastern Zone

Assam	Guwahati
Bodopur	Khokrajhar
Arunachal Pradesh	Itanagar
Manipur	Imphal
Meghalaya	Shillong
Mizoram	Aizawl
Nagapur	Kohima
Tripura	Agartala

Eastern Zone

Mithila	Patna
Magadha	Rajgir
Jharkhand	Ranchi
Odisha	Bhubaneshwar
Kosal	Sambalpur
Mallabhum	Kharagpur
Paschim Banga	Kolkata
Kamtapur	Cooch Behar
Gorkhapur	Darjeeling
Sikkim	Gangtok

Southern Zone

Telangana	Bhagyanagar
Andhra Pradesh	Vijayawada
Rayalaseema	Kurnool
Bayaluseeme	Bengaluru
Mysuru	Mysuru
Karunadu	Belagavi
Karavali	Karwar
Malenadu	Shivamogga
Tulunadu	Mangaluru

Kodagu	Madikeri
Kongu Nadu	Kovai
Pandya Nadu	Madurai
Chola Nadu	Thanjai
Thondai Mandalam	Kanchipuram
Travancore	Thiruvananthapuram
Cochi	Ernakulam
Malabar	Kozhikode

National Capital Zone

Delhi

Union Territories

Andaman and Nicobar Islands	Port Blair
Lakshadweep	Kavaratti

APPENDIX 2

REFERENCES

References are mostly listed in the order they first occur in each chapter. Links from Government of India or state government sources are given without further elaboration

CHAPTER ONE

GENERAL

Constitution of India, 1950
https://www.constitutionofindia.net/constitution_of_india

Constituent Assembly Debates
https://www.constitutionofindia.net/constitution_assembly_debates

The Political Future of India
Lajpat Rai, B. W. Huebsch, New York 1919
https://archive.org/details/politicalfutureo00lajpuoft/page/n15/mode/2up

India in the Years 1917-1918, Report prepared for presentation to Parliament in accordance with the requirements of the 26th Section of the Government of India Act (5 & 6 Geo. V., Chap 61), L. F. Rushbrook Williams

The Federation of India
B. Houghton, Political Science Quarterly, 34 (2), 1919, pp. 226-236 https://www.jstor.org/stable/214143

Swaraj Constitution
S. Srinivasa Iyengar
https://www.abebooks.com/Swaraj-Constitution-Srinivasa-Iyengar-n.d/1131579284/bd

Crucial Decades of Twentieth Century, Volume 3 1930-39
M. K. Kher, Sarup Book Publishers, New Delhi, 2001
https://archive.org/stream/in.ernet.dli.2015.149828/2015.149828.Studies-In-Modern-Indian-History-Crucial-Decades-Of-Twentieth-Century1930-39-Vol-3_djvu.txt

The Extremist Challenge. India between 1890 and 1910
Amales Tripathi, Orient Longman, 1967
http://ndl.iitkgp.ac.in/document
QWdZSk5uckVFeWFrK2grVkNMblhaS1
FjcEFwcW5LWk1GR3dQYytRaGpCbz0

Savarkar: Echoes from a Forgotten Past, 1883–1924
Vikram Sampath, Penguin Viking, New Delhi, 2019

India Divided
Rajendra Prasad, 1946
Bharatiya Janata Party Central Library, 2017
http://library.bjp.org/jspui/handle/123456789/823

States and Minorities. What are their Rights and how to secure them in the Constitution of Free India
Memorandum on the Safeguards for the Scheduled Castes submitted to the Constituent Assembly by B. R. Ambedkar on behalf of the All India Scheduled Castes Federation, 1947

What Congress and Gandhi have done to the Untouchables
B. R. Ambedkar, Thacker, Bombay, 1945
https://indianculture.gov.in/rarebooks/what-congress-and-gandhi-have-done-untouchables

Closing the Ring, The Second World War Volume V
Winston S. Churchill, Rosetta Books, 1951

Gandhi. His Life and Thought
J. B. Kripalani, Publications Division, Ministry of Information and Broadcasting, Government of India, 1970

A look back at the War of Bharat's Independence
Dattatreya Hosabale, Hindustan Times, 14 August 2021
https://www.hindustantimes.com/opinion/a-look-back-at-the-war-of-bharat-s-independence-101628950382177.html

The Case for India
Will Durant, Strand Book Stall, 2007 [First published 1930]
https://www.goodreads.com/en/book/show/4410574-the-case-for-india

India Conquered: Britain's Raj and the Passions of Empire
Jon E. Wilson, Simon & Schuster India, 2016
https://www.amazon.in/India-Conquered-Britains-Passions-Empire/dp/1471101258

Historical Constitutions of India 1895-1946
These following links correspond to the various documents prepared between 1895 and 1945 pertaining to proposed Constitutions for India. The year mentioned in the link is the identifier in the text.

https://www.constitutionofindia.net/historical_constitutions
https://www.constitutionofindia.net/historical_constitutions/the_constitution_of_india_bill__unknown__1895__1st%20January%201895

https://www.constitutionofindia.net/historical_constitutions/indian_councils_act__1909_1st%20January%201909

https://www.constitutionofindia.net/historical_constitutions/the_congress_league_scheme_1916__inc___aiml__1st%20January%20

https://www.constitutionofindia.net/historical_constitutions/government_of_india_act__1919_1st%20January%201919

https://www.constitutionofindia.net/historical_constitutions/the_commonwealth_of_india_bill__national_convention__india__1925__1st%20January%201925

https://www.constitutionofindia.net/historical_constitutions/the_revolutionary__hindustan_socialist_republican_association__1925__1st%20January%201925

https://www.constitutionofindia.net/historical_constitutions/nehru_report__motilal_nehru_1928__1st%20January%201928

https://www.constitutionofindia.net/historical_constitutions/irwin_declaration__lord_irwin__1929__31st%20October%201929

https://www.constitutionofindia.net/historical_constitutions/declaration_of_purna_swaraj__indian_national_congress__1930__26th%20January%201930

https://www.constitutionofindia.net/historical_constitutions/government_of_india_act_1935_2nd%20August%201935

https://www.constitutionofindia.net/historical_constitutions/constitution_of_free_india___a_draft__m_n__roy__1944__1st%20January%201944

https://www.constitutionofindia.net/historical_constitutions/political_demands_of_scheduled_castes__scheduled_castes_federation_1944__23rd%20September%201944

https://www.constitutionofindia.net/historical_constitutions/states_and_minorities__dr__b_r__ambedkar__1945__1st%20January%201945

https://www.constitutionofindia.net/historical_constitutions/gandhian_constitution_for_free_india__shriman_narayan_agarwal__1946__2nd%20April%201945

SOME PRE-INDEPENDENCE EVENTS

Remembering Bhikaji Cama on Independence Day 2021: The First Indian to Unfurl the National Flag on Foreign Soil

Akash Majumder, News 18, 15 August 2021
https://www.news18.com/news/buzz/bhikaji-cama-the-first-indian-to-unfurl-the-national-flag-on-foreign-soil-4083176.html

Establishment of All India Muslim League
History Pak
https://historypak.com/establishment-of-all-india-muslim-league/

Lord Minto and the Indian Nationalist Movement, with Special Reference to the Political Activities of the Indian Muslims, 1905-1910

Thesis submitted by Syed Razi Wasti to SOAS, University of London, 1962 [see p 520 onwards]
https://eprints.soas.ac.uk/33826/1/11010616.pdf

Banglapedia. National Encyclopedia of Bangladesh, 2012
https://en.banglapedia.org/index.php?title=Morley-Minto_Reforms

Montagu Chelmsford Reforms
Slideshare (Scribd)
https://www.slideshare.net/vissu.madasu/1919-act

The Revolutionaries and Congress were Friends not Foes in the Freedom Struggle, speaks of the Hindustan Socialist Republican Association (HSRA).
Bharat Dogra, The Wire, 15 August 2016
https://thewire.in/history/congresss-support-revolutionaries-influenced-indian-freedom-struggle

The Women's Indian Association and Indian Constitutional Thought: Part II
Vineeth Krishna, Centre for Law & Policy Research, 16 March 2020 speaks of Annie Besant and her commitment to gender issues.
https://clpr.org.in/blog/the-womens-indian-association-and-indian-constitutional-thought-part-ii/

Why Ambedkar changed on Separate Electorate. His shift was strategic not voluntary.
Arvind Kumar, The Print, 13 April 2021

https://theprint.in/opinion/ambedkar-changed-on-separate-communal-electorate-his-shift-was-strategic-not-voluntary/638904/

Other constitutions
Constitute. The World's Constitutions to Read, Search, and Compare
https://www.constituteproject.org/

Main Sources of the Indian Constitution
Deepshikha, Legal Bites, 16 January 2021
https://www.legalbites.in/main-sources-of-the-indian-constitution/

USA
https://www.whitehouse.gov/about-the-white-house/our-government/the-constitution/
https://constitutionnet.org/country/constitutional-history-united-states-america

UK
https://www.bl.uk/magna-carta/articles/britains-unwritten-constitution#

Westminster
https://www.cs.mcgill.ca/~rwest/wikispeedia/wpcd/wp/w/Westminster_System.htm
https://constitution-unit.com/2020/08/05/why-there-is-no-such-thing-as-the-wesminster-model/

Sri Lanka
https://constitutionnet.org/country/constitutional-history-sri-lanka
http://www.iconnectblog.com/2015/02/three-key-constitutional-reforms-for-sri-lanka/

https://groundviews.org/2015/01/31/an-eastminster-for-a-new-sri-lanka-the-first-xi-institutional-reforms-for-a-parliamentary-state/

https://www.himalmag.com/sri-lankas-constitutional-ping-pong-2020/

Canada
https://constitutionnet.org/country/canada-latin-america

New Zealand
https://gg.govt.nz/office-governor-general/roles-and-functions-governor-general/constitutional-role/constitution

Australia
https://unimelb.libguides.com/c.php?g=926039&p=6688935

Bhutan
https://www.gov.bt/constitution-of-bhutan/

Partition
Indian Politics and the Elections of 1937
Thesis submitted by David Denis Taylor to University of London, 1971 [see p 45 and p 52 for distribution of seats and method of election respectively]
https://eprints.soas.ac.uk/33670/1/11010433.pdf

The Calcutta Riots of 1946
Claude Markovits, SciencesPo, 5 November 2007
https://www.sciencespo.fr/mass-violence-war-massacre-resistance/fr/document/calcutta-riots-1946.html

Separate Electorates
History Pak
https://historypak.com/separate-electorates/

A Magnificent Gift: Muslim Nationalism and the Election Process in Colonial Punjab.
David Gilmartin, Cambridge University Press, 2004 https://www.cambridge.org/core/journals/comparative-studies-in-society-and-history/article/abs/magnificent-gift-muslim-nationalism-and-the-election-process-in-colonial-punjab/700CF3301CB2681C5F333EF362C645E0

1947 Partition: How Sardar Patel foiled Nawab of Bhopal's plan
Sandeep Bamzai, Daily O, 20 February 2015
https://www.dailyo.in/politics/1947-partition-how-sardar-patel-

foiled-nawab-of-bhopals-ambition-mountbatten-vp-menon-nehru-jinnah/story/1/2155.html

70 years later, survivors recall the horrors of India-Pakistan partition
Vidhi Doshi and Nisar Mehdi, Washington Post, 14 August 2017
https://www.washingtonpost.com/world/asia-pacific/70-years-later-survivors-recall-the-horrors-of-india-pakistan-partition/2017/08/14/3b8c58e4-7de9-11e7-9026-4a0a64977c92_story.html

The Conversation, 10 August 2017
https://theconversation.com/how-the-partition-of-india-happened-and-why-its-effects-are-still-felt-today-81766

Partition of India: They would have slaughtered us,
Steven Brocklehurst, BBC Scotland, 12 August 2017
https://www.bbc.com/news/uk-scotland-40874496

Horrors of Partition
A.G. Noorani, Frontline, 9 March 2012
https://frontline.thehindu.com/other/article30164617.ece

The Great Divide. The Violent Legacy of Indian Partition.
William Dalrymple, New Yorker, 22 June 2015
https://www.newyorker.com/magazine/2015/06/29/the-great-divide-books-dalrymple

Hindu-Muslim Communal Riots In India (1947-1986)
Violette Graff Juliette Galonnier, SciencesPo, 15 July 2013
https://www.sciencespo.fr/mass-violence-war-massacre-resistance/en/document/hindu-muslim-communal-riots-india-i-1947-1986.html

Punjab 1947: Bloodied and Partitioned by Competing Nationalisms
Jaspal Singh Sidhu, The Wire, 19 August 2021
https://thewire.in/communalism/punjab-1947-bloodied-and-partitioned-by-competing-nationalisms

The Big March: Migratory Flows after the Partition of India
Prashant Bharadwaj, Asim Khwaja and Atif Mian

Economic & Political Weekly, 43(35), 2008, pp 39-49
https://www.jstor.org/stable/40278723

Colonialism, Politics of Language and Partition of Bengal
Nurul Kabir, New Age, September/October 2013
https://sites.google.com/fastwebnet.it/bangladeshpaesedacquaedelsorri/home/bangladesh-english/colonialism-politics-of-language-and-partition-of-bengal

Sindh, 1947 and beyond
Priya Kumar and Rita Kothari, South Asia: Journal of South Asian Studies, 39(4), 2016, pp 773-789
https://www.tandfonline.com/doi/full/10.1080/00856401.2016.1244752

Thematic Chronology of Mass Violence in Pakistan, 1947-2007
Lionel Baixas, SciencesPo, 24 June 2008
https://www.sciencespo.fr/mass-violence-war-massacre-resistance/fr/document/thematic-chronology-mass-violence-pakistan-1947-2007.html

A useful descriptive link from the Partition Museum, Amritsar
https://www.partitionmuseum.org/partition-of-india/

A link from the National Army Museum, Chelsea, London
Independence and Partition, 1947
https://www.nam.ac.uk/explore/independence-and-partition-1947

The 1947 Partition Archive
Survivors and their Memories
https://exhibits.stanford.edu/1947-partition/browse/interviews?view=list

CHAPTER TWO

Most of the references in this chapter are from the assembly debates themselves and the speaker and the date are explicitly given in the text. The interested reader is urged to visit the three sites below to find more details and the context in which the statement was made. The debates are arranged date-wise in this meticulous compilation of original data.

Constitution of India, 1950
https://www.constitutionofindia.net/constitution_of_india

Constituent Assembly Debates
https://www.constitutionofindia.net/constitution_of_india
https://prsindia.org/policy/vital-stats/analysis-constituent-assembly-debates

General and Independence
Samvidhaan: The Making of the Constitution of India
Rajya Sabha TV, 20 February 2014
https://www.youtube.com/watch?v=atSSN6ZLzXQ

Article 3. Formation of New States and Alteration of Areas, Boundaries or Names of Existing States.
www.constitutionofindia.net/constitution_of_india/the_union_and_its_territory/articles/Article%203

Indian Constitution at Work, Chapter 9: Constitution as a Living Document https://ncert.nic.in/textbook/pdf/keps209.pdf

The Princely States, the Muslim League, and the Partition of India in 1947
Ian Copland, The International History Review, 13(1), 1991, pp 38-69
https://www.tandfonline.com/doi/abs/10.1080/07075332.1991.9640572?journalCode=rinh20&

The Integration of the Princely State of Hyderabad and the making of the Postcolonial State in India, 1948-56.
Taylor C. Sherman, Indian Economic & Social History Review, 44 (4). pp. 489-516, 2007
10.1177/001946460704400404http://eprints.lse.ac.uk/32805/1/Sherman_Integration_princely_state_2007.pdf

Jaipur's Last Stand
https://www.historytoday.com/miscellanies/jaipurs-last-stand

The Man who Saved India, Sardar Patel and his Idea of India
Hindol Sengupta, Penguin, New Delhi, 2018

Basic Structure Doctrine
https://constitutionnet.org/vl/item/basic-structure-indian-constitution
https://www.clearias.com/basic-structure-doctrine/

Basic Structure Constitutionalism: Revisiting Kesavananda Bharati
Sanjay S. Jain and Sathya Narayan (eds), Eastern Book, Lucknow, 2011

10 Judgements That Changed India
Zia Mody, Penguin, New Delhi, 2013

We the Nation: The Lost Decades
Nani A. Palkhiwala, UBS Publishers, 1994

Indian Constitution was written up, enforced without Explicit Recognition of Individual's Privacy as Fundamental Right.
Venkatesh Nayak, Counterview, 7 August 2015
https://counterview.org/2015/08/07/indian-constitution-was-written-up-enforced-without-explicit-recognition-of-individuals-privacy-as-fundamental-right/

The Indian Machiavelli: Pragmatism Versus Morality, and the Reception of the Arthasastra in India, 1905-2014 Maria Misra, Cambridge Core, 14 May 2015https://www.cambridge.org/core/journals/modern-asian-studies/article/abs/indian-machiavelli-pragmatism-versus-morality-and-the-reception-of-the-arthasastra-in-india-19052014/70B3DDED7317A5F6CA3506EE44E1B680

The Indian Nation and Selective Amnesia: Representing Conflicts and Violence in Indian History Textbooks
Sylvie Guichard, Nations and Nationalism 19(1), January 2013
DOI:10.1111/j.1469-8129.2012.00556.x
Governance and Development https://niti.gov.in/

planningcommission.gov.in/docs/plans/mta/midterm/english-pdf/chapter-17.pdf

Local Self-Government https://cdn.s3waas.gov.in/s301386bd6d8e091c2ab4c7c7de644d37b/uploads/2018/03/2018033064.pdf

Genesis of Local Government Institutions in India. 2. 97-113
Umakanta Nayak, Centurion Journal of Multidisciplinary Research, 2, 2016, pp 97-113
https://www.researchgate.net/publication/342979067_Genesis_of_Local_Government_Institutions_in_India

Cleaning Constitutional Cobwebs. Reforming the Seventh Schedule
Sohini Chatterjee, Akshat Agarwal, Kevin James
Vidhi Centre for Legal Policy, New Delhi, 8 October 2019
https://vidhilegalpolicy.in/research/cleaning-constitutional-cobwebs-reforming-the-seventh-schedule/

HISTORICAL

Rule of Law and Indian Society Colonial Encounters, Post-Colonial Experiments and Beyond.
Ananta Kumar Giri, Jura Gentium, 2005
https://www.juragentium.org/topics/rol/en/giri.htm#75

Democratic Ideals and Republican Institutions in India
Benoy Kumar Sarkar, American Political Science Review, 12(4), 1918, pp 581-606
https://www.jstor.org/stable/1945832
https://www.jstor.org/stable/pdf/1945832.pdf?refreqid=excelsior%3A4dce36750dd572ac6dd9d17fa56c54de

The history of Republicanism started in India not in 1950 but in 600 BC
Mrittunjoy Guha Majumdar, YKA, 27 January 2021
https://www.youthkiawaaz.com/2021/01/republicanism-in-india-

from-ancient-ganas-to-the-contemporary-ganarajya/

Tracing the History of Jury Trials in India
Archisha Chowdhury, Jurisdictio Omnis, 31 July 2021
https://jurisdictioomnis.in/2021/07/31/tracing-the-history-of-jury-trials-in-india/

FEDERALISM

Independence Diary: 'Unity In Diversity' One Of The Most Powerful Thoughts India Gave World
J. Nandkumar, Outlook, 15 August 2021
https://www.outlookindia.com/website/story/opinion-independence-diary-unity-in-diversity-one-of-the-most-powerful-thoughts-india-gave-world/391519

Reflections on the 'quasi-federal' democracy
Aswini K. Ray, Hindu, 9 October 2021
https://www.thehindu.com/opinion/lead/reflections-on-the-quasi-federal-democracy/article36905863.ece

The Mahatma and his Economic Worldview
Jaithirth Rao, Hindustan Times Opinion, 5 October 2021
https://www.hindustantimes.com/opinion/the-mahatma-and-his-economic-worldview-101633419856830.html

Does India Even Need A Parliament?
Manish Tewari, Indian Express Opinion, 7 August 2021
https://indianexpress.com/article/opinion/columns/does-india-even-need-a-parliament-7442286/

SECULARISM AND MINORITIES

Constitutional Provisions for Minorities http://ncm.nic.in/home/pdf/about%20ncm/C_P.pdf

Uniform Civil Code: Sweeping away Communal Segregation
Pratibhaelin, Legal Service India E-journal

https://www.legalserviceindia.com/legal/article-183-uniform-civil-code-sweeping-away-communal-segregation.html

Should India have a Uniform Civil Code?
Raya Hazarika, Legal Service India
http://www.legalservicesindia.com/article/394/Should-India-have-a-Uniform-Civil-Code?.html

The Concept of Secularism in India
Bharatialka, Legal Service India
http://www.legalservicesindia.com/article/1589/The-Concept-of-Secularism-in-India.html

Mughal History Whitewashed in Textbooks, Educationists tell House Panel
Sobhana K. Nair and Priscilla Jebaraj, Hindu, 13 January 2021
https://www.thehindu.com/news/national/mughal-history-whitewashed-in-textbooks-educationists-tell-house-panel/article33570951.ece

Excerpts of NCERT history books
Vikram Sampath
https://twitter.com/vikramsampath/status/1448103395894693889?t=w-hQYGc_wZB2AwbVss_WhQ&s=08

Cultural and Educational Rights: Articles 29-30 under Indian Constitution
MariyaPaliwala, iPleaders, 7 January 2020
https://blog.ipleaders.in/cultural-and-educational-rights/

Secularism: Why Nehru dropped and Indira inserted the S-word in the Constitution
AdrijaRoychowdhury, Indian Express, 17 December 2017
https://indianexpress.com/article/research/anant-kumar-hegde-secularism-constitution-india-bjp-jawaharlal-nehru-indira-gandhi-5001085/

Talks about Constitution, Secularism will last only till Hindus in

Majority in India: Gujarat Dy CM Nitin Patel
Times of India, 28 August 2021
https://timesofindia.indiatimes.com/india/talks-about-constitution-secularism-will-last-only-till-hindus-in-majority-in-india-gujarat-dy-cm-nitin-patel/articleshow/85711056.cms

See also
https://indianexpress.com/article/cities/ahmedabad/dy-cm-talks-about-constitution-law-only-till-hindus-in-majority-7474615/

Scheduled Tribes: Who are they? How to mainstream them?
M. Nageswara Rao, Times of India Opinion, 16 May 2020
https://timesofindia.indiatimes.com/blogs/voices/scheduled-tribes-who-are-they-how-to-mainstream-them/

Are Indian Tribals Hindus?
Why Adivasis Are Demanding Recognition for Their Religions
Santoshi Markam, Wire, 2 April 2019
https://thewire.in/rights/adivasi-religion-recognition-census

AMENDMENTS

42nd Amendment, Was it India's or Indira's Constitution?
Gyan Prakash Kesharwani, Centre for Constitutional Research and Development, 14 July 2019
https://ccrd.vidhiaagaz.com/42nd-amendment-of-indian-constitution/

A critical analysis of the 42nd Amendment Act, 1976
Diganth Raj Sehgal, iPleaders, 7 February 2021
https://blog.ipleaders.in/critical-analysis-42nd-amendment-act-1976/ 'Not The Right People': Why Jury Trials were Abolished in India

James Jaffe, Socio-Legal Review, 1 October 2020
https://www.sociolegalreview.com/post/not-the-right-people-why-jury-trials-were-abolished-in-india

The Constitution (Seventy-third Amendment) Act, 1992

https://www.india.gov.in/my-government/constitution-india/amendments/constitution-india-seventy-third-amendment-act-1992

73rd and 74th Constitutional Amendment Acts
Fourth semester Course-424, Local government and politics in India, Unit-iii
AleyaMousami Sultana, Cooch Behar PanchananBarma University.
https://cbpbu.ac.in/userfiles/file/2020/STUDY_MAT/POL_SC/73rd%20and%2074th-converted.pdf

127th Constitution Amendment Bill: What it is, why it is needed and why the Opposition supports it
Firstpost, 10 August 2021
https://www.firstpost.com/politics/127th-constitution-amendment-bill-what-it-is-why-it-is-needed-and-why-the-opposition-supports-it-9874231.html

CIVILISATIONAL STATE

The Development of Sanātana Dharma in the Twentieth Century: A Rādhāsoamī Guru's Perspective
Diana Dimitrova, International Journal of Hindu Studies, 11(1), 2007, pp 89-98
https://www.jstor.org/stable/25691050

Lalita Sahasranama Stotram
Dharmadhara-Dhanadhyaksa-Dhanadhanyavivardhini
Viprapriya-Viprarupa-Visvabhramanakarini 165

Vishnu Sahasranama Stotram (Phalastuti)
Vedantago-Bramhanas-Syaat-Kshatriyo-Vijayee-Bhavet
Vaishyo-Dhanasamruddhas-Syaat-Shudrah-Sukham-Avapniyat ||3||

China, India and the rise of the 'civilisation state'
Financial Times https://www.ft.com/content/b6bc9ac2-3e5b-11e9-9bee-efab61506f44

A New Idea of India – Individual Rights in a Civilisational State,
Harsh Madhusudan and Rajiv Mantri, Westland, New Delhi, 2020
https://anewideaofindia.com

CHAPTER THREE

HISTORY OF EUROPE

H. A. L. Fisher, Edward Arnold & Co., London, 1936

Bismarck and the Two Germanies, Part II
Harold Kurtz, History Today, 20(8), 1970

The Peculiar Course of German History
Edgar Feuchtwanger, History Review, 43, 2002 https://www.historytoday.com/archive/peculiar-course-german-history

The Peculiarities of German History
Paul Preston, History Today, 35(10), 1985 https://www.historytoday.com/archive/peculiarities-german-history

The Peace Treaty of Westphalia (1648) and its Consequences for International Relations
Vladislav B. Sotirovic, Oriental Review, 9 December 2017
https://orientalreview.org/2017/12/09/peace-treaty-westphalia-1648-consequences-international-relations/

The Silk Roads: A New History of the World
Peter Frankopan, Bloomsbury, London, 2015

My India. The India Eternal
Swami Vivekananda, Ramakrishna Mission Institute of Culture, Kolkata, 1993

Hindu Society under Siege
Sita Ram Goel, Voice of India, New Delhi, 2015

India that is Bharat: Coloniality, Civilisation, Constitution
J. Sai Deepak, Bloomsbury, New Delhi, 2021

Savarkar: Echoes from a Forgotten Past, 1883-1924
Vikram Sampath, Penguin Viking, New Delhi, 2019

Savarkar: A Contested Legacy, 1924-1966
Vikram Sampath, Penguin Viking, New Delhi, 2021

Pew Report (2021) Religion in India: Tolerance and Segregation, Neha Sahgal, Jonathan Evans, Ariana Monique Salazar, Kelsey Jo Starr and Manolo Corich, Pew Research Center
https://www.pewforum.org/2021/06/29/religion-in-india-tolerance-and-segregation/

What does it mean to be Indian?
Ashutosh Varshney, Indian Express, 26 July 2021 pmhttps://indianexpress.com/article/opinion/columns/hindu-nationalism-indian-nationhood-diversity-7421980/

Separatist Movements and the Indian Nation State
Amiya K. Samanta, Presidency Alumni Association Calcutta, Kolkata 700073, Autumn Annual 1998-99, pp 65-71
http://ndl.iitkgp.ac.in/document/enY1MUs2QW1RY1VTdDlkSEFWMHVJU28yLzhHK0NLbmVUMVZ6M0prbGRlbUx1U3Nhb0tSZUVYbHpJcWRodmQ1Wg

Religion and Society
S. Radhakrishnan, George Allen & Unwin, London, 1947

Indian Liberals don't get the difference between Hindu State and Mohan Bhagwat's Hindu Rashtra
Swadesh Singh, Print, 4 October 2019
https://theprint.in/opinion/indian-liberals-difference-hindu-state-rss-mohan-bhagwat-hindu-rashtra/300909/

Hindutva as Modernity
Abhinav Prakash, 1 September 2021
https://www.pressreader.com/india/hindustan-times-lucknow/20210901/281960315853233

We must fight back against this conference of Hinduphobia
Sham Sharma Show, 2 September 2021
https://www.youtube.com/watch?v=x3HHz9CGrIo&ab_

channel=TheShamSharmaShow

What is Sanātana Dharma?
David Frawley
https://twitter.com/davidfrawleyved/status/1450641951787790337?t=JpznsIEcY2WWB_6PUtXrug&s=09

A Hindutva Smokescreen
Avatans Kumar, Times of India Opinion, 1 August 2021
https://timesofindia.indiatimes.com/blogs/indic-positive/a-hindutva-smokescreen/?s=09

Gandhi and Savarkar shared goal of independence, differed on means
Rajiv Tuli, Indian Express Opinion, 19 October 2021
https://indianexpress.com/article/opinion/columns/gandhi-and-savarkar-shared-goal-of-independence-differed-on-means-7576990/

India as a Civilisational State
J. Sai Deepak
https://mobile.twitter.com/jsaideepak/status/1426631396164997121

The Attack of the Civilization-State
Bruno Maçães, 15 June 2020
https://www.noemamag.com/the-attack-of-the-civilization-state/

The Most Intolerant Wins: The Dictatorship of the Small Minority
Nassim Nicholas Taleb, Incerto, 14 August 2016
https://medium.com/incerto/the-most-intolerant-wins-the-dictatorship-of-the-small-minority-3f1f83ce4e15

Hindutva and Hinduphobia
VHP America
https://twitter.com/VHPANews/status/1430438444564688897?s=09

The Devadasi, Dharma and the State
Janaki Nair
Economic & Political Weekly, Vol. 29, No. 50, pp. 3157-3159

and 3161-3167

Whose Authority?
The Separation of Politics and Religion has its Roots in Discourses over whether or not Pontius Pilate could be held guilty of having ordered 'The Death of God'.
Kevin Butcher, History Today, 71(9), September 2021
https://www.historytoday.com/archive/review/whose-authority?utm_source=Weekly+Newsletter&utm_campaign=1db78b64f9-

Are Indians Changing?
Hindol Sengupta
https://twitter.com/HindolSengupta/status/1423130369298079748?s=09

Dismantling Hindutva or Denying Hinduphobia: What Prompted the Largest Grassroots Mobilization of Hindu Americans in History
Suhag Shulka, American Kahani, 7 September 2021
https://americankahani.com/perspectives/dismantling-hindutva-or-denying-hinduphobia-what-prompted-the-largest-grassroots-mobilization-of-hindu-americans-in-history/?s=09

An Enduring System
Ritabrata Chakraborty, Telegraph, 12 October 2021
https://www.telegraphindia.com/opinion/an-enduring-congress-system/cid/1834303

Lalita Sahasranama Stotram
Dharā-Dharasutā-Dhanyā-Dharmini-Dharmavardhini
Lokātitā-Gunātitā-Sarvātitā-Samatmikā 176

Dawn of Dharmatva
Harsh Madhusudan
https://twitter.com/harshmadhusudan/status/1436309392450723847
https://dharmatva.substack.com/p/the-dawn-of-dharmatva

The Reexamination of "Dharma" in Hindu Ethics
Austin B. Creel, Philosophy East and West, 25(2), University of Hawaii Press, 1975, pp 161-173
https://www.jstor.org/stable/1397937

Indic Frameworks For A New Future
Aravindan Neelakandan, Swarajya, 1 September 2018
https://swarajyamag.com/magazine/indic-frameworks-for-a-new-future

Science and Society—What Do They Owe Each Other?
Gautam R. Desiraju, Angewandte Chemie International Edition, Guest Editorial, 14 January 2019
https://onlinelibrary.wiley.com/doi/full/10.1002/anie.201813798

The EU and the Temptation to Become a Civilizational State.
Andrew Glencross, European Foreign Affairs Review 26, no. 2, 331–348, 2021

SOME REFERENCES TO ISLAM AND CHRISTIANITY (GENERAL)

These links are not with reference to any specific item and are meant for general reading.

https://en.wikipedia.org/wiki/Tawhid#Arguments_for_the_oneness_of_God

https://en.wikipedia.org/wiki/As-Saaffat#Summary

https://en.wikipedia.org/wiki/Help:IPA/Arabic

https://en.wikipedia.org/wiki/Shahada

https://en.wikipedia.org/wiki/God_in_Islam

The Quran and the Bible on God's Love
https://luk.staff.ugm.ac.id/kmi/off/XIslam/IslamOnline/LoveofGod.html

The Core of the Qur'an: SūratYāSīn (Q. 36)
M.A.S. Abdel Haleem, Journal of Qur'anic Studies, Vol. 15, No. 2

(2013), pp. 65-82
https://www.jstor.org/stable/24280440

https://theconversation.com/who-is-allah-understanding-god-in-islam-39558

https://www.pewforum.org/2013/04/30/the-worlds-muslims-religion-politics-society-interfaith-relations/

https://www.abc.net.au/religion/religious-freedom-in-islam/10419798

https://yaqeeninstitute.org/read/paper/the-case-for-allahs-existence-in-the-quran-and-sunnah

Recapture of the Iberian peninsula by Christians
https://en.wikipedia.org/wiki/Reconquista

https://www.biblegateway.com/passage/?search=Isaiah+63%3A16&version=ESV

https://bible.knowing-jesus.com/topics/One-God

https://www.openbible.info/topics/other_religions

https://www.biblegateway.com/passage/?search=Exodus+23%3A13&version=ESV

How Did God Get Started?
Colin Wells, Arion: A Journal of Humanities and the Classics at Boston University
https://www.bu.edu/arion/archive/volume-18/colin_wells_how_did_god_get-started/

https://en.wikipedia.org/wiki/God_in_Christianity#Attributes_and_nature

The Fool Says in His Heart, "There is no God": Atheism in the Bible and in Late Antiquity
Craig A. Evans, Houston Baptist University, 2016
https://hbu.edu/news-and-events/2016/04/22/fool-says-heart-no-god-atheism-bible-late-antiquity/

CHAPTER FOUR

BACKGROUND

75 states of India. Map proposed by Siby Thomas (2021)
https://twitter.com/hodlvolk/status/1447449768267960320?s=20

Gandhian Constitution
https://www.constitutionofindia.net/historical_constitutions/gandhian_constitution_for_free_india__shriman_narayan_agarwal__1946__2nd%20April%201945
[This document proposes a large number of governing units]

Where Are Our Mahajanapadas Today?
Geography and You, 7 October 2016
https://geographyandyou.com/where-are-our-mahajanapadas-today/

The Mahatma and his Economic Worldview
Jaithirth Rao, Hindustan Times Opinion, 5 October 2021
https://www.hindustantimes.com/opinion/the-mahatma-and-his-economic-worldview-101633419856830.html

Princely States of India
https://www.worldstatesmen.org/India_princes_A-J https://www.worldstatesmen.org/India_princes_K-W

Five states that refused to join India after Independence
Adrija Roychowdhury, Indian Express, 17 August 2017
https://indianexpress.com/article/research/five-states-that-refused-to-join-india-after-independence/

Revisiting the journey to 29 states
Dhanyata M. Poovaiah, Deccan Herald, 1 November 2018
https://www.deccanherald.com/special-features/revisiting-journey-29-states-701021.html

The Origin Story of India's States
Venkataraghavan Subha Srinivasan, Penguin, New Delhi, 2021

Links to Pointillism

https://www.britannica.com/art/pointillism
https://www.sothebys.com/en/articles/pointillism-7-things-you-need-to-know

https://artincontext.org/pointillism/

https://www.masterclass.com/articles/pointillism-art-guide#what-is-pointillism

Some Links to Smaller States Formation

Our Pasts, Eighteenth-Century Political Formations https://ncert.nic.in/textbook/pdf/gess110.pdf

Separatist Movements and the Indian Nation State
Amiya K. Samanta, Presidency Alumni Association Calcutta, Kolkata 700073, Autumn Annual 1998-99, pp 65-71
http://ndl.iitkgp.ac.in/document/enY1MUs2QW1RY1VTdDlkSEFWMHVJU28yLzhHK0NLbmVUMVZ6M0prbGRlbUx1U3Nhb0tSZUVYbHpJcWRodmQ1Wg

State, Community and Neighbourhood in Princely North India, C. 1900-1950, I. Copland, Palgrave Macmillan, 2005
https://books.google.co.in/books?id=squHDAAAQBAJ&pg=PA18&lpg=PA18&dq=Jaipur+dissimilarities+with+neigbouring+states&source=bl&ots=7Sif9AYhWZ&sig=ACfU3U1apgaH-KXo2fTHQByUD9UWLDnQBA&hl=en&sa=X&ved=2ahUKEwjov8fM__vzAhW8yDgGHcSsDXgQ6AF6BAgiEAM#v=onepage&q=Jaipur%20dissimilarities%20with%20neigbouring%20states&f=false

India may have 50 new states if all demands of new states conceded
Mint, 4 August 2013
https://www.livemint.com/Politics/RoQFPgIGDC76dakAipTpkK/India-may-have-50-states-if-all-demands-of-new-states-conced.html

Is it time to restructure India into smaller states?
Mohan Guruswamy, Quartz India, 1 October 2015
https://qz.com/india/513927/is-it-time-to-restructure-india-into-

smaller-states/

8 Regions In India That Are Trying To Be Independent States Within The Country
Supriyo Mukherjee, ScoopWhoop, 3 March 2017
https://www.scoopwhoop.com/regions-in-india-trying-to-be-independent-states/

STATE BY STATE LINKS TO 75 NEW STATES PROPOSED

HIMALAYAN ZONE

Anthropology of Gilgit-Baltistan, Northern Pakistan
Ethnoscripts, University of Hamburg, 16(1), 2014
https://epub.ub.uni-muenchen.de/69412/1/69412.pdf

History: The Gilgit-Baltistan Conundrum
https://www.dawn.com/news/1587950

Conflict Dynamics in Gilgit-Baltistan
Izhar Hunzai, United States Institute of Peace, Special Report 321, January 2013
https://www.usip.org/sites/default/files/resources/SR321.pdf

Mixed Legacies in Contested Borderlands: Skardu and the Kashmir Dispute
Antia Mato Bouzas, Geopolitics, 17 (4), 2012, pp 867-886
https://www.tandfonline.com/doi/abs/10.1080/14650045.2012.660577

The Kashmir that India Lost: A Historical Analysis of India's Miscalculations on Gilgit Baltistan
Kriti M. Shah, Observer Research Foundation, ORF Occasional Paper No. 334, October 2021
https://www.orfonline.org/research/the-kashmir-that-india-lost/

The History of the Political Ordeal of Ladakh
DawaTondup, Reach Ladakh Bulletin, 6 November 2019 https://

www.reachladakh.com/news/oped-page/the-history-of-the-political-ordeal-of-ladakh

Explained: In Leh and Kargil, different reasons to oppose Ladakh's current status
Nirupama Subramanian, Indian Express, 8 July 2021 https://indianexpress.com/article/explained/in-leh-and-kargil-different-reasons-to-oppose-ladakhs-current-status-7386677/

Jammu, Kashmir and Ladakh have more than religious differences
Prabhat Singh, Mint, 24 December 2014
https://www.livemint.com/Politics/5Zd1AyfLdNyYhU9Jtezy5L/Jammu-Kashmir-and-Ladakh-have-more-than-religious-differenc.html

Kashmir's struggle did not start in 1947 and will not end today
Tamoghna Halder, Aljazeera, 15 August 2019
https://www.aljazeera.com/opinions/2019/8/15/kashmirs-struggle-did-not-start-in-1947-and-will-not-end-today

After two years of disagreement, Ladakh's Kargil and Leh regions now united in demand for statehood
SafwatZargar, Scroll, 7 August 2021
https://scroll.in/article/1002265/after-two-years-of-disagreement-ladakhs-kargil-and-leh-regions-now-united-in-demand-for-statehood

Better to separate Jammu than punish it for our 'crimes,' say Kashmiris
Gowhar Geelani, The Federal, 21 August 2020
https://thefederal.com/states/north/jammu-and-kashmir/better-to-separate-jammu-than-punish-it-for-our-crimes-say-kashmiris/

Jammu-Kashmir and Ladakh: Exploring a new paradigm
Ashok Malik, Observer Research Foundation, ORF Special Report, 7 August 2019
https://www.orfonline.org/research/jammu-kashmir-and-ladakh-exploring-a-new-paradigm-54185/

Book Review in HimalSouthasian (1 January 2000) by Nigel J. R. Allen of "Himalayan Differences" by D. E. U. Baker by Chetan Singh
https://www.himalmag.com/himalayan-differences/

Hill state was carved out after 70 years of struggle
Rajiv Srivastava, Times of India, 17 November 2011
https://timesofindia.indiatimes.com/city/lucknow/hill-state-was-carved-out-after-70-yrs-of-struggle/articleshow/10763132.cms

Himachal Pradesh: A Profile https://niti.gov.in/planningcommission.gov.in/docs/plans/stateplan/sdr_hp/sdr_hpch1.pdf

Non secessionist Regionalism in India: The Uttarakhand Separate State Movement
E. Mawdsley, Environment and Planning A: Economy and Space, 29(12), 1997, pp 2217-2235
https://journals.sagepub.com/doi/10.1068/a292217

NORTHERN ZONE

A Profile Report on Pre-Project Survey of Border Area Development Programmes in Punjab Kesar Singh and U. S. Rangnekarhttps://pbplanning.gov.in/pdf/Annexure-VI.pdf

Sub-nationalism in Indian politics: formation of a Haryanavi identity
Pradeep Kumar,The Indian Journal of Political Science, 52(1), 1991, pp. 109-124
https://www.jstor.org/stable/41855538

A Baseline Survey of Minority Concentration Districts of India, Mewat (Haryana)
Sponsored by Ministry of Minority Affairs and ICSSR
https://www.icssr.org/sites/default/files/districts/Mewat[1].pdf

'Haryana badly needs a cultural renaissance'
D. R. Chaudhry, India Today, 9 October 2006

https://www.indiatoday.in/magazine/guest-column/story/20061009-haryana-badly-needs-cultural-renaissance-784596-2006-10-09

U-turn to Progress: After decades of darkness, Mewat in Haryana's Nuh is moving towards development
Arjun Singh Kadian, daily O, 10 March 2019
https://www.dailyo.in/politics/mewat-haryana-economic-development-transformation-of-aspirational-districts-social-development-niti-aayog/story/1/29837.html

Politics of Harit Pradesh: The Case of Western UP as a Separate State
Jagpal Singh, Economic & Political Weekly, 36(31), 2001, pp. 2961-2967
https://www.jstor.org/stable/4410945

Harit Pradesh: Specifically look at languages, demographics and administrative divisions. https://www.wikiwand.com/en/Harit_Pradesh#/Role_of_specific_rural_communities

Division plan not in tune with demands
Hindustan Times, 16 November 2011
https://www.hindustantimes.com/lucknow/division-plan-not-in-tune-with-demands/story-wFynftF7vtajOJIE2aBEUO.html

Awadh in Revolt, 1857-1858: A Study of Popular Resistance, Rudrangshu Mukherjee, OUP India, 1985
https://www.india-seminar.com/2007/575/575_rudrangshu_mukherjee.htm

The Awadh | Historic Region of Northern India
Shakeel Anwar, Jagran Josh, 24 May 2016
https://www.jagranjosh.com/general-knowledge/the-awadh-historic-region-of-northern-india-1442911783-1

Major Historic Events of Meerut
https://www.meerutonline.in/city-guide/major-historic-events-of-meerut

Harit Pradesh passé, demand for 'Greater Delhi' picks up pace

S. Raju, Hindustan Times, 8 November 2019
https://www.hindustantimes.com/india-news/harit-pradesh-passe-demand-for-greater-delhi-picks-up-pace/story-ySbOcLKZDt8v0iYIMFYJZI.html

Uttar Pradesh is India's broken heartland, break it into 4 or 5 states
Shekhar Gupta, Print, 11 July 2020
https://theprint.in/national-interest/uttar-pradesh-is-indias-broken-heartland-break-it-into-4-or-5-states/458552/

The case against dividing Uttar Pradesh into smaller states
ShivamVij, Print, 13 July 2020
https://theprint.in/opinion/the-case-against-dividing-uttar-pradesh-into-smaller-states/459618/

The Division of Uttar Pradesh Into 4 States: A Forgotten Issue
Yatharth Mishra, Quint, 7 March 2017
https://www.thequint.com/voices/blogs/uttar-pradesh-divide-four-parts-bsp-sp-elections-mayawati-akhilesh-yadav#read-more

Demand for separate 'Braj Pradesh' gains momentum
Hindu, 26 December 2009
https://www.thehindu.com/news/national/Demand-for-separate-Braj-Pradesh-gains-momentum/article16855342.ece

CENTRAL ZONE

Six events that changed history and geography of Madhya Pradesh
Neeraj Santoshi, Hindustan Times, 15 August 2014
https://www.hindustantimes.com/india/six-events-that-changed-history-and-geography-of-madhya-pradesh/story-yUbG8oSZKKtX5EkE6X01PN.html

MP: Movement for Vindhya Pradesh, legislator moves ahead, comes up with flag and logo
Newsbits, 14 April 2021
https://www.newsbits.in/mp-movement-for-vindhya-pradesh-

legislator-moves-ahead-comes-up-with-flag-and-logo-

Vindhyachal state demand stirs row
Rabindra Nath Choudhury, Deccan Chronicle, 10 February 2020 | https://www.deccanchronicle.com/nation/current-affairs/100220/vindhyachal-state-demand-stirs-row.html

BJP MLA demands separate Vindhya state, threatens stir
Rajendra Sharma, Times of India, 10 February 2020
https://timesofindia.indiatimes.com/city/bhopal/bjp-mla-demands-separate-vindhya-state-threatens-stir/articleshow/74051136.cms

'Bundelkhand was separate state in free India, we want it back'
Shailvi Sharada, Times of India, 9 April 2017
http://timesofindia.indiatimes.com/articleshow/58087943.cms?utm_source=contentofinterest&utm_medium=text&utm_campaign=cppsthttps://timesofindia.indiatimes.com/city/lucknow/bkhand-was-separate-state-in-free-india-we-want-it-back/articleshow/58087943.cms

250 people get tonsured to demand separate Bundelkhand state
Economic Times, 13 August 2018
https://economictimes.indiatimes.com/news/politics-and-nation/250-people-get-tonsured-to-demand-separate-bundelkhand-state/articleshow/65386647.cms?from=mdr

Book Review in Economic & Political Weekly [42 (37) 15 September 2007] by Peter Reeves of "Baghelkhand, or The Tigers' Lair: Region and Nation in Indian History" by D. E. U. Baker
https://www.epw.in/journal/2007/37/book-reviews/making-nation.html

Vidarbha state: A Promise Forgotten
Vaibhav Ganjapure, Times of India, 31 March 2019
https://timesofindia.indiatimes.com/city/nagpur/vidarbha-state-a-promise-forgotten/articleshow/68648490.cms

Separate Vidarbha – Pros and Cons and the Vaccination Drive
Nikhil Chandwani, Times of India, 27 May 2021

https://timesofindia.indiatimes.com/blogs/desires-of-a-modern-indian/separate-vidarbha-pros-and-cons-and-the-vaccination-drive/

Decades-old demand for Vidarbha statehood on the wane?
Faisal Malik, Hindustan Times, 16 October 2019
https://www.hindustantimes.com/cities/decades-old-demand-for-vidarbha-statehood-on-the-wane/story-rZpqcgTDLCQq1mdcIxFoDL.html

Separate Vidarbha demand makes sense: ShreehariAney
Mrityunjay Bose, Deccan Herald, 23 September 2019
https://www.deccanherald.com/national/west/separate-vidarbha-demand-makes-sense-shreehari-aney-763357.html

Gondwana and the Politics of Deep Past
Pratik Chakrabarti,Past& Present, 242 (1), 2019, pp 119–153
https://academic.oup.com/past/article/242/1/119/5298761

10 Things you need to know about 'Gondwana State' demand
Akash Poyam, Adivasi Resurgence, 18 December 2015
http://adivasiresurgence.com/2015/12/18/10-things-you-need-to-know-about-gondwana-state-demand/

Why demand for Gondwana state continues to be scuttled
Aparna Pallavi, DownToEarth, 1 October 2014
https://www.downtoearth.org.in/news/why-demand-for-gondwana-state-continues-to-be-scuttled-46694

The Gond kingdoms
Aparna Pallavi, Down to Earth, 1 October 2014
https://www.downtoearth.org.in/news/the-gond-kingdoms-46701

A new sense of purpose for a 'neglected' city [Jabalpur]
A. M. Jigeesh, Hindu Business Line, 27 January 2018
https://www.thehindubusinessline.com/specials/a-new-sense-of-purpose-for-a-neglected-city/article8305066.ece

About Khandwa district https://khandwa.nic.in/en/about-district/
Snapshot: Breathless in Bundi

Beyondlust, 1 April 2015

https://beyondlust.in/tag/hadoti/

Bundi the Indian Princely State (from Flags of the World) https://www.crwflags.com/fotw/flags/in-bundi.html

WESTERN ZONE

Sikar farmer agitation: How the CPI(M) created a 'red island' in Rajasthan
Shoaib Daniyal, Scroll, 21 September 2017
https://scroll.in/article/851229/sikar-farmer-agitation-how-the-cpi-m-created-a-red-island-in-rajasthan

Know the difference between Marwar and Mewar Udaipur Beats, 3 July 2018
https://udaipurbeats.com/difference-between-marwar-and-mewarall-you-need-to-know/

Demand for new desert state gathers steam in Rajasthan
Sudhanshu Mishra, India Today, 13 December 2009
https://www.indiatoday.in/india/story/demand-for-new-desert-state-gathers-steam-in-rajasthan-62887-2009-12-13

Rajasthan: Separate Maru Pradesh demand gains momentum
Times of India, 16 April 2018
https://timesofindia.indiatimes.com/city/jodhpur/separate-maru-pradesh-demand-gains-momentum/articleshow/63776341.cms

History of Shekhawats
https://www.indianrajputs.com/history/shekhawat.php
Discusses various rulers of Hadoti: Bundi https://www.rajras.in/rulers-of-hadoti/

Demand for separate Kutch
Manoj R. Nair, Mumbai Mirror, 16 June 2009
https://mumbaimirror.indiatimes.com/opinion/columnists/manoj-r-nair/demand-for-separate-kutch/articleshow/15932269.cms?utm_source=contentofinterest&utm_medium=text&utm_campaign=cppsthttps://mumbaimirror.indiatimes.com/opinion/columnists/manoj-r-nair/demand-for-separate-kutch/

articleshow/15932269.cms

Statehood demand for Kutch gains momentum
Indian Express, 12 December 2009
http://archive.indianexpress.com/news/statehood-demand-for-kutch-gains-momentum/553204/2

Call to revive movement for separate Saurashtra state
Economic Times, 1 August 2013
https://economictimes.indiatimes.com/news/politics-and-nation/call-to-revive-movement-for-separate-saurashtra-state/articleshow/21536911.cms

Rajasthan State Formation post-Independence
https://www.rajras.in/rajasthan/polity/state-formation-post-independence/

Behind The Saurashtra State Demand
Economic & Political Weekly, 1(2), 27 August 1966
https://www.epw.in/journal/1966/2/letter-gujarat-columns/behind-saurashtra-state-demand.html

Unbordered Memories: Sindhi Stories of Partition, edited and translated by Rita Kothari.
The Wire, 13 August 2017
https://thewire.in/books/sindh-partition-unbordered-memories

Key member of community demands separate state for Sindhis
Economic Times, 12 April 2015
https://economictimes.indiatimes.com/news/politics-and-nation/key-member-of-community-demands-separate-state-for-sindhis/articleshow/46896332.cms

SOUTHWESTERN ZONE

Citizenship, Community and the State in Western India: The Moulding of a Marathi-Speaking Province, 1930s-1950s
O. J. Godsmark, PhD thesis, University of Leeds, 2013
https://etheses.whiterose.ac.uk/4958/1/Godsmark_OJ_History_

PhD_2013.pdf

Dividing Maharashtra: Vidarbha = Serbia; Konkan = Cuba
IndiaSpend, 2 April 2016
https://www.indiaspend.com/dividing-maharashtra-vidarbha-serbia-konkan-cuba-27046

Marathwada sub-regionalism: a factor in Maharashtra politics
Sunil Datye,The Indian Journal of Political Science, 48(4), 1987, pp 512-525
https://www.jstor.org/stable/41855335

Demand for a separate Marathawada https://abhipedia.abhimanu.com/Article/State/NTExNDUEEQQVV/Demand-for-Separate-Marathawada-maharashtra-State

Never mind what Aney said: Here's why separate statehood for Marathwada would be a bad idea
Atul Deolgaonkar, Firstpost, 22 March 2016
https://www.firstpost.com/india/never-mind-what-aney-said-heres-why-separate-statehood-for-marathwada-would-be-a-bad-idea-2689438.html

Pune pioneered Samyukta Maharashtra Movement
Radheshyam Jadhav, Times of India, 30 April 2010
https://timesofindia.indiatimes.com/city/pune/pune-pioneered-samyukta-maharashtra-movement/articleshow/5874479.cms

50 Years of Opinion Poll that gave Goa an Independent Identity
Vikram Doctor, Economic Times, 17 January 2017
https://economictimes.indiatimes.com/news/politics-and-nation/50-years-of-opinion-poll-that-gave-goa-an-independent-identity/articleshow/56632378.cms?from=mdr

Konkani vs Marathi: Language battles in golden Goa
Karthik Venkatesh, Mint, 5 August 2017
https://www.livemint.com/Sundayapp/yO371luBUKFCjhQouRcBCK/Konkani-vs-Marathi-Language-battles-in-golden-Goa.html

How Konkani Won the Battle for 'Languagehood'
Vivek Madhusudan Bhat, Milind Malshe, Sociolinguistics Symposium, Amsterdam, 2008
https://www.meertens.knaw.nl/ss17/contributions/abstract.php?paperID=271

NORTHEASTERN ZONE

Assam-Arunachal Boundary: Steps taken to sink differences
Sentinel, 13 October 2020
https://www.sentinelassam.com/topheadlines/assam-arunachal-boundary-steps-taken-to-sink-differences-506531

Statehood Day for Arunachal Pradesh and Mizoram: Brief history of the two North Eastern states
Firstpost, 20 February 2017
https://www.firstpost.com/india/statehood-day-for-arunachal-pradesh-and-mizoram-brief-history-of-the-two-north-eastern-states-3291898.html

'Need a separate cadre, time zone for Arunachal': CM Pema Khandu
Kumar Uttam, Hindustan Times, 4 November 2019
https://www.hindustantimes.com/india-news/need-a-separate-cadre-time-zone-for-arunachal-cm-pema-khandu/story-WqPKglNXEq0V4zgHbBhs1K.html

After 30 years of Statehood, Arunachal Pradesh Once Again Pushes for Separate Cadre
Karishma Hasnat, News 18, October 9 2019
https://www.news18.com/news/india/after-30-years-of-statehood-arunachal-pradesh-once-again-pushes-for-separate-cadre-2339671.html

Demand for two separate states out of Meghalaya
The Newswire, Outlook, 1 September 2006
https://www.outlookindia.com/newswire/story/demand-for-two-

separate-states-out-of-meghalaya/411593

Demand for 'Garoland' and separate Khasi-Jaintia state echoes again in Meghalaya
https://www.eastmojo.com/meghalaya/2021/07/12/demand-for-garoland-and-separate-khasi-jaintia-state-echoes-again-in-meghalaya/

Hill State People's Democratic Party joins hands with Garo Hills State Movement Committee to revive their demands for separate states
Princess Giri Rashir, EastMojo, 12 July 2021

Assam: Separate statehood demands get strident
News 18, 11 December 2009
https://www.news18.com/news/politics/assam-separate-statehood-demands-get-strident-330323.html

Ethnic Fault-Lines in Assam: A Separate Bodoland?
Leonora Juergens, Institute for Peace and Conflict Studies, 30 April 2014
http://www.ipcs.org/comm_select.php?articleNo=4418

Assam attack: Calls for separate state by Bodo leaders keep region unstable
Rahul Karmakar, Hindustan Times, 6 August 2016
https://www.hindustantimes.com/india-news/demands-for-separate-state-by-bodo-leaders-keep-region-unstable/story-9lEroKknTfhRVgdTcOOlYK.html

Bodo Accord ended demand for a separate state: Assam minister Himanta Biswa Sarma, Sumir Karmakar, Deccan Herald, 28 January 2020
https://www.deccanherald.com/national/east-and-northeast/bodo-accord-ended-demand-for-a-separate-state-assam-minister-himanta-biswa-sarma-799024.html

Nagaland Congress calls for reconsideration of separate state demand

Economic Times, 30 December 2010
https://economictimes.indiatimes.com/news/politics-and-nation/nagaland-congress-calls-for-reconsideration-of-separate-state-demand/articleshow/7189721.cms?from=mdr

In Nagaland, old demand for a new state in the east resurfaces in time for Assembly election
Arunabh Saikia, Scroll, 3 January 2018
https://scroll.in/article/863387/in-nagaland-old-demand-for-a-new-state-in-the-east-resurfaces-in-time-for-assembly-election

Manipur: Govt likely to extend SoO agreement with Kuki militants for another six months
Jimmy Leivon, Indian Express. 21August 2020
https://indianexpress.com/article/north-east-india/manipur/manipur-govt-likely-to-extend-soo-agreement-with-kuki-militants-for-another-six-months-6563383/

Manipur's Kuki rebels demand Bodoland-like territorial council, unhappy about delays in talks
Karishma Hasnat, Print, 29 August 2020
https://theprint.in/india/manipurs-kuki-rebels-demand-bodoland-like-territorial-council-unhappy-about-delays-in-talks/491204/

Mizoram: from UT to State
Sanjeev Chopra, milleniumpost, 5 September 2020
http://www.millenniumpost.in/mapping-the-states-of-india/mizoram-from-ut-to-state-417454

Hmar Struggles for Autonomy in Mizoram, India
LalremlienNeitham, ritimo, Intercultural Resources 1 July 2011
https://www.ritimo.org/Hmar-Struggles-for-Autonomy-in-Mizoram-India

Tripura tribal parties come closer on separate statehood demand, decide to form joint movement committee
Debraj Deb, Indian Express, 17 October 2021
https://indianexpress.com/article/north-east-india/tripura/tripura-tribal-parties-come-closer-on-separate-statehood-demand-decide-

to-form-joint-movement-committee-7576843/

Tribal party from Tripura demands separate state
K. Anupama K, inshorts, 19 Jan 2016
https://inshorts.com/en/news/tribal-party-from-tripura-demands-separate-state-1453179755993

EASTERN ZONE

Mithila and Magadha (700AD - 1100AD)
Laksman Jha, Mithila Sanskrit Research Institute Bihar, 2017
https://www.exoticindiaart.com/book/details/mithila-and-magadha-700ad-1100ad-naw426/

Book review in Frontline by Mohammad Sajjad of "Language Politics and Public Sphere in North India: Making of the Maithili Movement" by Mithilesh Kumar Jha https://frontline.thehindu.com/books/article24200882.ece

Decades Since the Ask, Why Is Mithila Still Struggling for A 'Separate State' Status?
Achyut Anurag, Youth Ki Awaaz, 3 November2020 https://www.youthkiawaaz.com/2020/11/demand-of-a-mithila-state-a-genuine-need-but-unnoticed/

Demonstration planned in Delhi for separate Mithila state
Hindustan Times, 14 December 2009
https://www.hindustantimes.com/india/demonstration-planned-in-delhi-for-separate-mithila-state/story-awHWAfJ7iY0G8yhNegTzJM.html

A Secret R&AW Op, a 'God King' & Sikkim's Merger With India
G. B. S. Sidhu, Quint, 15 May 2019
https://www.thequint.com/lifestyle/books/dawn-of-democracy-truth-behind-sikkims-merger-with-india

Explained: Sikkim, from Chogyal rule to Indian state
Om Marathe, Indian Express, 21 August 2019
https://indianexpress.com/article/explained/explained-sikkim-

chogyal-rule-to-indian-state-sdf-bjp-5921574/

West Bengal Movements: Gorkhaland, Kamtapur, Greater Cooch Behar… The issue of demand for a separate state in Bengal is not new.
PressWire18, 26 June 2021
https://presswire18.com/west-bengal-movements-gorkhaland-kamtapur-greater-cooch-behar-the-issue-of-demand-for-a-separate-state-in-bengal-is-not-new/

Darjeeling is not Kashmir but Gorkhaland demand gets a fresh lease of life
Madhuparna Das, Print, 14 August 2019
https://theprint.in/statedraft/darjeeling-is-not-kashmir-but-gorkhaland-demand-gets-a-fresh-lease-of-life/276501/

Similarities between Gorkhaland and Telangana. 'Demerger' and Statehood
Bivek Tamang and SangmuThendup
Economic & Political Weekly, 50 (38), 19 September 2015
https://www.epw.in/journal/2015/38/notes/demerger-and-statehood.html

Separate state demanded in north Bengal
The Hindu, 29 October 2009
https://www.thehindu.com/news/national/other-states/Separate-state-demanded-in-north-Bengal/article16889177.ece

Cooch Behar raises head for separate state
Sumanta Ray Chaudhuri, DNA, 19 November 2013
https://www.dnaindia.com/india/report-cooch-behar-raises-head-for-separate-state-1323438

Letter W is an Automatic Handicap: Why Mamata Govt Wants to Change West Bengal's Name
Anudev Shah, News 18, 19 November 2018
https://www.news18.com/news/india/letter-w-is-an-automatic-handicap-why-mamata-govt-wants-to-change-west-bengals-name-1943085.html

Explained: The long journey from West Bengal to Bangla
Mehr Gill, Indian Express, 31 July 2019
https://indianexpress.com/article/explained/explained-the-long-journey-from-west-bengal-to-bangla-5858819/

Maps of separate Kosala distributed in Orissa
New Indian Express, 19 December 2009
https://www.newindianexpress.com/states/odisha/2009/dec/19/maps-of-separate-kosala-distributed-in-orissa-114437.html

Cycle rally push to separate state demand in western Odisha
Ajit Nayak, Times of India, 24 August 2014
https://timesofindia.indiatimes.com/city/bhubaneswar/cycle-rally-push-to-separate-state-demand-in-western-odisha/articleshow/40857600.cms

Activists demand Western Odisha as separate state with 'Kosli' as official language
Business Standard, 26 September 2019
https://www.business-standard.com/article/news-ani/activists-demand-western-odisha-as-separate-state-with-kosli-as-official-language-119092601639_1.html

JPP demands 'Greater Jharkhand'
Economic Times, 1 August 2013
https://economictimes.indiatimes.com/news/politics-and-nation/jpp-demands-greater-jharkhand/articleshow/21530820.cms?from=mdr

SOUTHERN ZONE

Andhra and Telangana: A vast and bitter cultural divide
Firstpost, 20 July 2011
https://www.firstpost.com/politics/andhra-and-telengana-a-vast-and-bitter-cultural-divide-41427.html

Telangana issue: Linguistic affinity fails to keep Telanganities

together with Seemandhra
India Today, 30 July 2013
https://www.indiatoday.in/india/telangana/story/telangana-issue-linguistic-affinity-fails-to-keep-telanganities-together-with-seemandhra-153048-2013-02-01

Andhra Pradesh - end of an era
India Today, 30 July 2013
https://www.indiatoday.in/india/south/story/andhra-pradesh-end-of-an-era-172182-2013-07-30

India's state divisions evolve past language
Umika Pidaparthy, Aljazeera, 4 Aug 2013
https://www.aljazeera.com/features/2013/8/4/indias-state-divisions-evolve-past-language

The story of India's 29th State — Telangana
Hindu, 1 June 2016 (updated 16 September 2016)
https://www.thehindu.com/news/national/telangana/The-story-of-Indias-29th-State----Telangana/article14384461.ece

Within five years, Andhra Pradesh capital Amaravati has gone from a promised utopia to 'ghost town'
Mayank Aggarwal, Scroll, 17 August 2019
https://scroll.in/article/934122/within-five-years-andhra-pradesh-capital-amaravati-has-gone-from-a-promised-utopia-to-ghost-town

Silence on Amaravati from Right, Left and Centre shows everyone has a vested interest
Abhishek Kadiyala, Print, 2 June 2021
https://theprint.in/campus-voice/silence-on-amaravati-from-right-left-and-centre-shows-everyone-has-a-vested-interest/670142/

JAC plans to scale up Amaravati protest into a mass movement
Hindu, 10 December 2020
https://www.thehindu.com/news/national/andhra-pradesh/jac-plans-to-scale-up-amaravati-protest-into-a-mass-movement/article33302564.ece

Carve out greater Rayalaseem"
S. Murali, Hindu, 27 July 2016 https://www.thehindu.com/news/national/andhra-pradesh/%E2%80%9CCarve-out-greater-Rayalaseema%E2%80%9D/article14511155.ece

Administrative divisions in Karnataka 1872-2001
https://www.censusindia.gov.in/2011census/maps/atlas/29part2.pdf

North Karnataka: Will it be a separate state?
K. Mohan Das, Deccan Herald, 2 August 2018
https://www.deccanherald.com/opinion/perspective/north-karnataka-separate-state-684638.html

Explained: The Demand for a Separate North Karnataka State
Arun Dev, Quint, 28 Jul 2018
https://www.thequint.com/explainers/north-karnataka-bandh-for-separate-state

Demand for separate north Karnataka will rise if no monsoon legislature session in Belagavi: JDS leader
New Indian Express, 17 July 2021
https://www.newindianexpress.com/states/karnataka/2021/jul/17/demand-for-separate-north-karnataka-will-rise-if-no-monsoon-legislature-session-in-belagavi-jds-leader-2331486.html

Tulu Nadu activists observe Rajyotsava as Black Day, demand statehood
Coastal Digest, 1 November 2016
http://www.coastaldigest.com/tulu-nadu-activists-observe-rajyotsava-black-day-demand-statehood?page=2

If Goa is a state, why not Tulu Nadu? Demand for new state becomes stronger
Sarayu Srinivasan, News Minute, 3 November 2015
https://www.thenewsminute.com/article/if-goa-state-why-not-tulu-nadu-demand-new-state-becomes-stronger-35653

Coorg and the reorganisation of States

C. M. Ramachandra, Hindu, 20 October 2013
https://www.thehindu.com/news/national/karnataka/coorg-and-the-reorganisation-of-states/article5253820.ece

The Way Forward for Kodagu: A political road map http://www.coorgnews.in/way-forward-kodagu-political-road-map/
[Source: 'Rise and Fall of the Coorg State' by P.T. Bopanna. Rolling Stone Publications, 2009.]

Karnataka Speaker demands separate statehood for Kodagu
M. Anil Kumar, Times of India, 18 July 2012
http://timesofindia.indiatimes.com/articleshow/15034018.cms?utm_source=contentofinterest&utm_medium=text&utm_campaign=cppsthttps://timesofindia.indiatimes.com/city/bengaluru/karnataka-speaker-demands-separate-statehood-for-kodagu/articleshow/15034018.cms

A bridge between languages. Karwar Konkani
Karthik Malli, Deccan Herald, 24 October 2020
https://www.deccanherald.com/spectrum/a-bridge-between-languages-906284.html

The Malnad check-Met
Niranjan Kaggere, Bangalore Mirror, 23 May 23, 2017
https://bangaloremirror.indiatimes.com/bangalore/cover-story/the-malnad-check-met/articleshow/58795891.cms Government of Tamil Nadu. Chennai District
https://chennai.nic.in/history/

For Mysore, it was a prolonged fight for freedom
R. Krishna Kumar, Hindu, 16 August 2021
https://www.thehindu.com/news/national/karnataka/for-mysore-it-was-a-prolonged-fight-for-freedom/article35933306.ece

South India: Cheras, Cholas and Pandyas
PriyanshiJajoo, Glimpses of History, 18 August 2020
https://glimpsesofhistory.com/south-india-cheras-cholas-and-pandyas/

Kongu Nadu: A region not formally defined, yet the subject of a 'bifurcation' debate in Tamil Nadu
Arun Janardhanan, Indian Express, 15 July 2021
https://indianexpress.com/article/explained/kongu-nadu-a-region-not-formally-defined-yet-the-subject-of-a-bifurcation-debate-in-tamil-nadu-7401673/

A case for shifting the state capital from Chennai
V. Sriram, Citizen Matters, 12 October 2020
https://chennai.citizenmatters.in/chennai-tamil-nadu-second-capital-madurai-trichy-20510

Support For Madurai As Second Tamil Nadu Capital Grows
G. C. Shekhar, Outlook, 18 August 2020
https://www.outlookindia.com/website/story/india-news-support-for-madurai-as-second-tamil-nadu-capital-grows/358890

In Tamil Nadu, murmurs of state bifurcation provoke a backlash
Divya Chandrababu, Hindustan Times,19 July 2021
https://www.hindustantimes.com/analysis/in-tamil-nadu-murmurs-of-state-bifurcation-provoke-a-backlash-101626668302705.html

Dravida Nadu to Tamil Nadu: Evolution of the state's identity
New Indian Express, 17th March 2018
https://www.newindianexpress.com/states/tamil-nadu/2018/jan/20/dravida-nadu-to-tamil-nadu-evolution-of-the-states-identity-1759188.html

District Wise Population of Kerala by Religious Community - 2011
http://www.kscminorities.org/pdf/District-Wise-Population.pdf

Samithi to protest demanding separate Neyyattinkara district
Times of India, 29 November 2019
https://timesofindia.indiatimes.com/city/thiruvananthapuram/samithi-to-protest-demanding-separate-neyyattinkara-district/articleshow/66872064.cms

The demand to bifurcate Malappuram district and the political tussle around it
K. C. Arun, News Minute, 28 August 2019
https://www.thenewsminute.com/article/demand-bifurcate-malappuram-district-and-political-tussle-around-it-107975

CHAPTER FIVE

Vivekananda Reader, M. Sivaramkrishna, Swami Narasimhananda (ed), Advaita Ashrama, Kolkata, 2012, p 258

Chemistry – The Middle Kingdom
Gautam R. Desiraju, Current Science, 88(3), 2005, pp 374-380
https://www.jstor.org/stable/24110202
[Complex and Complicated – Emergence]

The Choice Between Western Intellectualism and Darshanic Timelessness
Sandeep Balakrishna, Dharma Dispatch
https://www.dharmadispatch.in/commentary/the-choice-between-western-intellectualism-and-darshanic-timelessness

The First Republic is dead. Do we want the Second Republic to be created by choice or compulsion?
Ruchir Sharma
https://twitter.com/ruchirsharma_1/status/1461635865369890819?s=20

J. Sai Deepak on the Second Republic https://www.youtube.com/watch?v=49-QEvcsqN8

A New Idea of India – Individual Rights in a Civilisational State
Harsh Madhusudan and Rajiv Mantri, Westland, New Delhi, 2020
https://anewideaofindia.com

INDEX

R

S

U

V

W

ABOUT THE AUTHOR

Gautam Radhakrishna Desiraju was born on 21 August 1952, in Chennai and is presently an honorary professor at Indian Institute of Science, Bangalore. He is a recipient of several prestigious international awards such as the Alexander von Humboldt Forschungspreis, the TWAS Award in Chemistry and the ISA Medal for Science of the University of Bologna. He was President of the International Union of Crystallography between 2011–2014. As IUCr President, he proposed to the United Nations that 2014 be celebrated as the International Year of Crystallography. He spearheaded this resolution and inaugurated the Year in UNESCO, Paris in January 2014 sharing the podium with Irena Bokova, the then Director General of UNESCO.

Prof. Desiraju's scientific contributions are significant. His work has led to the development of a new chemical concept, Crystal Engineering, wherein he is acknowledged to be a world leader. At the same time, his original work on weak hydrogen bonding has been held by some to be one of the influential ideas in the last half century of chemical thought. With the importance of the generic component of the pharmaceutical industry in recent years, the work of Prof. Desiraju is of direct importance to the Indian pharmaceutical industry and to the general public in the context of bringing cheaper drugs to the masses.

Citations are the true measure of the impact of a scientist's work. Prof. Desiraju is the second most highly cited Indian scientist today, with three authored books, two edited books, 450 research papers, 65,162 citations and an h-index of 100. He has received a Ph.D honoris causa from Universidad Nacional de Córdoba, Argentina, Rayalaseema University and Gulbarga University. He was awarded the Acharya P. C. Ray Medal of the University of Calcutta for innovation in science and technology. He is presently chairman of the Governing Council of Bose Institute, Kolkata. He has constantly campaigned for making our scientists look towards swadeshi ideas rather than being copycats of the Western world.

He has authored several commentaries on science, the evolution of chemistry as a subject, emergence and complexity, and research habits and practices in various cultures. He has also written articles about the state of science education and research in India, and about the status of chemistry research in India, where he has identified problems and suggested solutions in situations that are, in part, expected in a country that is rooted in the traditional but aspires for the contemporary.

He strongly believes that if a sense of "Indian-ness" is inculcated, a modern competitive spirit and adherence to professionalism will enter automatically. He feels that this is now largely lacking and has led to our present sluggishness. This book is an attempt to highlight this issue with reference to what he believes is the core issue in India: an unsuitable system of governance that does not optimally dovetail the economic realities of the modern world with our essential civilisational nature. Our present system of governance is, of course, laid out in its most basic form in the Indian Constitution and this therefore is the subject of **Bhārat: India 2.0**